e on or before the latest date stamped

WITHDRAWN

DESIRING ROME

DESIRING ROME

Male Subjectivity and Reading Ovid's *Fasti*

RICHARD J. KING

THE OHIO STATE UNIVERSITY PRESS

Columbus

Copyright © 2006 by The Ohio State University.
All rights reserved.

King, Richard Jackson, 1960–
Desiring Rome : male subjectivity and reading Ovid's Fasti / Richard J. King.
    p. cm.   Includes bibliographical references and index.
ISBN 0–8142–1020–1 (cloth : alk. paper)
ISBN 0–8142–9097–3 (cd-rom)
1. Ovid, 43 B.C.–17 or 18 A.D. Fasti.   2. Desire in literature.
3. Calendar in literature. I. Title.
    PA6519.F9K56 2006
871'.01—dc22
                        2005031877

Cover design by Janna Thompson Chordas.
Text design and typesetting by Jennifer Shoffey Forsythe.
Text in Adobe Apollo.
Printed by Thomson-Shore, Inc.

The paper used in this publication meets the minimum requirements of the
American National Standard for Information Sciences—Permanence of Paper
for Printed Library Materials. ANSI Z39.48-1992.

9 8 7 6 5 4 3 2 1

CONTENTS

LIST OF ABBREVIATIONS

A&A	*Antike und Abendland: Beiträge zum Verständnis der Griechen und Römer und ihres Nachlebens*
Acta Arv.	*Acta Fratrum Arvalium quae supersunt.* Ed. W. Henzen. Berlin: G. Reimeri, 1874
Agrim.	The ancient writers on surveying: Blume, Lachman and Rudorff 1842, Blume, F., K. Lachmann, and A. Rudorff, 1848, 1852
AJA	*American Journal of Archaeology*
AJAH	*American Journal of Ancient History*
AJPh	*American Journal of Philology*
ANRW	*Aufstieg und Niedergang der römischen Welt*
BA	*Bollettino d'arte*
BMusImp	*Bollettino del Museo dell'Impero Romano*
BMCR	*Bryn Mawr Classical Review.* http://ccat.sas.upenn.edu/bmcr/
BullCom	*Bollettino della Commissione archeologica Comunale di Roma*
CAH	*Cambridge Ancient History.* Vol. X *(The Augustan Empire, 43 B.C.–A.D. 69)*, eds. Alan K. Bowman, Edward Champlin and A. W. Lintott. 2nd ed. Cambridge: Cambridge University Press, 1996
CIL	*Corpus Inscriptionum Latinarum.* Berlin: G. Reimer, 1862–
ClAnt	*Classical Antiquity*
CJ	*Classical Journal*
CPh	*Classical Philology*
CQ	*Classical Quarterly*
CR	*Classical Review*
CSCA	*California Studies in Classical Antiquity*

CW	*Classical World*
Dar.-Sag.	Daremberg-Saglio: Daremberg, Charles and Edmond Saglio, et al. eds. 1877–1919. *Dictionnaire des antiquités grecques et romains d'après les textes et les monuments.* Paris: Hachette
DArch	*Dialoghi di archeologia*
GIF	*Giornale italiano di filologia*
Gramm. Lat.	Keil, H. 1961. *Grammatici Latini.* vol. 7. Hildesheim: G. Olms Verlagsbuchhandlung
HSCPh	*Harvard Studies in Classical Philology*
ILS	*Inscriptiones Latinae Selectae.* Ed. Hermann Dessau. Chicago: Ares, 1979; originally published, Berlin: Weidmann, 1892–1916
Inscr. Ital.	*Inscriptiones Italiae Academiae italicae consociatae ediderunt.* Unione accademica nazionale. Rome: La Libreria dello Stato, 1931–
JRS	*Journal of Roman Studies*
LIMC	*Lexicon Iconographicum Mythologiae Classicae.* Zürich: Artemis, 1981–
L-S	*Harper's Latin Dictionary.* Ed. E. A. Andrews. Rev. Eds. Charlton T. Lewis and Charles Short. New York: American Book Co., 1879
LSJ	Henry George Liddell and Robert Scott. *Greek-English Lexicon.* Rev. Oxford: Clarendon Press, 1940; with supplement, 1968
MD	*Materiali e discussioni per l'analisi dei testi classici*
MEFRA	*Mélanges de l'École française de Rome. Antiquité*
MemPontAcc	*Memorie della pontificia accademia di archeologia*
Der neue Pauly	*Der neue Pauly: Enzyklopädie der Antike.* Eds. Hubert Cancik and Helmuth Schneider. Stuttgart : J. B. Metzler, 1996–
OCD	*Oxford Classical Dictionary.* Eds. Simon Hornblower and Antony Spawforth. 3rd ed. New York: Oxford University Press, 1996
OLD	*Oxford Latin Dictionary.* Ed. P. G. W. Glare. Oxford: Clarendon, 1985
PBSR	*Papers of the British School at Rome*
PCPhS	*Proceedings of the Cambridge Philological Society*
PL	*Patrologiae Latinae,* ed. J-P Migne. Paris
Platner	Platner, Samuel. 1929. *Topographical Dictionary of Ancient Rome.* Rev. T. Ashby. London: Oxford University Press

PVS	*Proceedings of the Virgil Society*
RA (or RevArch)	*Revue archéologique*
RE	*Paulys Real-encyclopädie der classischen Altertumswissenschaft.* Ed. G. Wissowa. Stuttgart: J. B. Metzler, 1894–. *Supplement,* 1913–1978
REA	*Revue des études anciennes*
REG	*Revue des études grecques*
RhM	*Rheinisches Museum für Philologie*
RIC	*Roman Imperial Coinage.* Edited by Harold Mattingly and Edward A. Sydenham. London: Spink, 1923–94
TAPA	*Transactions of the American Philological Association*
TGL	*Thesaurus Graecae Linguae.* Henri Etienne, Charles Benoît Hase, Wilhelm Dindorf, and Ludwig August Dindorf. Paris: A. F. Didot, 1831–1865
TLL	*Thesaurus Linguae Latinae.* Leipzig: Teubner, 19–
ZPE	*Zeitschrift für Papyrologie und Epigraphik*

ACKNOWLEDGMENTS

t his book results from over a decade of interest in Ovid's *Fasti*. Initial interest arose during a seminar at Indiana University on Ovid's *Heroides* and *Fasti*, conducted by Professor Betty Rose Nagle. Especially perplexing to me were perceptions of the poem's incoherence and fragmentation in mid-twentieth century scholarship and even assessments of the poem as literary failure. Were there responses to the *Fasti* that did not dismiss it? My dissertation, "Spatial Form and the Representation of Time in Ovid's *Fasti*," directed by Professor Eleanor Winsor Leach, provided an opportunity to investigate its thematic fragmentation and lack of unity by exploring how representation of global, imaginative space (such as that of Augustan world-mapping, astronomy-astrology, and Roman augury) might support a "spatialized" view of time.

The present book approaches the poem's fragmentation quite differently. Where the dissertation attempted to overcome, even escape, the insurmountable qualities of fragmentation and incompletion in the *Fasti*, this book explores how these qualities call for recognition and dialectical encounter with the exiled author of the broken form.

Many individuals have encouraged me and supported my efforts. I thank Betty Rose Nagle for introducing me to the *Fasti* and Eleanor W. Leach for providing me crucial guidance in my earliest efforts. I also thank Micaela Janan for her instructive comments aiding revision and Thomas Habinek for his encouragement in response to a paper I delivered at the Lambda Classical Caucus of the American Philological Association addressing the role of Germanicus as addressee.

Desire and Ovid's Fasti

O vid's *Fasti* is an anomaly in Greek and Roman literature, because no other poetic calendar survives from classical antiquity. Other poems contain features of Ovid's *Fasti*, but lack its calendar structure. Its periodic epigrams on celestial phenomena are comparable to lists of seasonal labors and astronomical events in Hesiod's *Works and Days* and recall thematically Aratus' *Phaenomena* and Manilius' *Astronomica*. Moreover, Callimachus' *Aetia* and Propertius' fourth book had presented verse etiologies of cults and shrines, and influenced the *Fasti* in literary technique, such as Callimachus' report of interviews with the Muses as divine sources of knowledge. But no other extant poem assumes the *Fasti's* outward structure, Rome's civic calendar. Introduced by prefaces explaining the origin of each month, the books of the *Fasti* each represent constellations and festivals according to the chronology of days within separate months of the Roman year.[1]

Yet another anomaly is that only the first six of the planned twelve books exist—"January" through "June." Ovid probably never composed the last six, or else he drafted them only in outline. As Ovid declares at *Tristia* 2.549–52 (9 CE), exile imposed by the emperor Augustus in 8 CE "broke" (*rupit*) the *Fasti*. However, references to events in Rome during his exile at Tomis (modern Romania) show that Ovid revised portions of the *Fasti*, especially in 15–17 CE after the death of Augustus (14 CE); revisions include rededication of the poem to Germanicus Caesar (1.1–26), who was Augustus' adopted grandson and adopted son of Tiberius, the new emperor.[2]

How are readers to interpret long-term incompletion of a poem begun after 2 BCE, but still incomplete in 17 CE? Recently, scholars have explained this incompleteness as reflecting Ovid's exilic exhaustion at managing the politics that kept him in exile. Rededication to Germanicus after the accession of Tiberius indicates resumed hope of return, but continued incompletion suggests failure of these hopes.[3] Earlier explanations aligned lack of completeness with artistic frustration over the calendar's discontinuity: the poem's elegiac couplets (alternating hexameter and pentameter) did not produce enough narrative continuity to hold together the calendar's disparate references. Consequently, the poem failed to provide a unifying "narrative" decorously representing Augustan Rome's festival calendar. Under this (problematic) aesthetic interpretation, the discontinuous *Fasti* falls short in comparison with the continuous hexameters of Ovid's epic *Metamorphoses*, which successfully joins disparate tales into a larger ideological narrative, moving from Chaos to universal cosmos under Augustus.[4]

This book accounts for the incompletion and discontinuity of the *Fasti* differently; it embraces lack of completion and discontinuity as troubling "blots" (of Ovid's unmanageable "real" life), obscuring direct views of the poem and provoking the reader's desire of wholeness and (narrative) continuity. Due to these interruptions, a "direct view" of a unifying whole is impossible. To look into and interpret the blot of incompletion and discontinuity, readers might have to assume an angular or "skewed" vantage point upon the whole. These angular views enable readers to observe new objects of interpretation previously unnoticed—centered on antagonisms in Roman culture, but related to Ovid's own exile from the Roman symbolic order, represented by the calendar.

Genre and Elegiac Subjectivity

Such angular views toward Ovid's broken poem are conditioned by several features of the text. Among these are the poem's elegiac genre and Ovid's autobiographical role within it. Poetic genres entail wider assumptions than mere aesthetic form; they are embedded in the hierarchical construction of Roman culture around binary concepts, particularly that of gender. Of special interest is the tension between epic

and elegy (e.g., Hinds 1987, 1992; cf. Heinze 1919).[5] In Rome's hierarchy of genres, epic depictions of active heroes earning manly honor
(*virtus*) in battle and in civic office hold a higher station than the love-
elegist's political withdrawal and sexual indulgence in the domain of
women. Elegy had typically suggested the love-poet's weakness as a
man (*vitium*), his deviance from the ideology of manly honor or his
lack of self-control. Composing the *Fasti* in elegiac couplets places
Rome's religious calendar in relation to what had been an erotic verse
form. Ovid is reconstructing elegy in its surface themes, but doing so,
I argue, to enable the expansion of desire as an object of view in the
realm of the state.[6]

In the *Fasti* Ovid grounds his handling of these generic tensions in
his role as first-person speaker ("I"), an autobiographical voice derived
from prior erotic elegy. In that role, Ovid exposes in the monthly prefaces complex antagonisms and uncertainties that he experiences while
composing his elegiac calendar. Such a projection of Ovid's own subjectivity becomes legible in his comments in the monthly prefaces
about his own "literary" life-course. These comments track a thematic
shift in his elegies from love to religion, a shift paralleling conventional male maturation, but applied to Ovid's authorial persona.[7] Here the
poet's maturation is figured in his attempted age-appropriate change in
objects of literary desire, from erotic play to religion and the state
marked in the calendar. Through this "maturation" of literary objects,
Ovid appears to ascend a Roman hierarchy of genres, from the lower,
less mature, less manly erotic elegy (the domain of frivolous boyhood,
sometimes femininity) to the higher, more manly objects of the calendar—objects more nearly approximating the epic domain of male civic
virtue.

Ovid was over fifty years old when revising the *Fasti,* and in his
prefaces he shows himself still unsure and equivocating along his
belated path of moral-literary maturation. Various divine-symbolic
challenges test Ovid's author progress in successive monthly prefaces, where Ovid confesses to uncertainty and variously (mis)handles
these challenges. Why? Such authorial confessions split the image of
order that inscribed calendars tend to present. Ovid's own fractured,
equivocating "I" reveals behind the calendar's surface many lost,
potential, or or alternative meanings occluded by a public calendar's
show of symbolic, ideological order. Ovid's equivocation, the poem's
incompletion, and other anomalies of language in the poem invite the
reader to take up angular positions toward the poet and his poems,
but also toward the civic calendar. The author's equivocation models

for readers uncertain, angular, or excluded modes of viewing Rome and its calendar.

Calendar as Screen

Another feature of the *Fasti*—evocation of Julio-Claudian ritual calendars—frames how the *Fasti* appears to readers. Scholars such as Elaine Fantham, Carole Newlands, Geraldine Herbert-Brown, and Alessandro Barchiesi have demonstrated that, as a calendar poem during the late Augustan and early Tiberian periods, the *Fasti* was positioned with respect to the emperor's revival of Roman purity and simplicity in renewed rituals and moral laws as remedies for prior deviance, thus "saving" Rome's original cultural identity within a complex multi-cultural empire.[8] Marble incised calendars visibly materialized this ideology of Roman ritual wholeness by presenting in solid form a master sign of Roman national rites and festivals. This ideological use of calendars explains their great rise in frequency during the Augustan and Julio-Claudian periods.[9]

But Roman inscribed calendars do something quite different from what Ovid does in his *Fasti*. Though fragmentary now, calendar inscriptions once were "complete"; Ovid's *Fasti* was probably never complete. The inscriptions set the calendar in stone; by contrast, Ovid's *Fasti* is still in progress and produces long poetic digressions upon variant meanings of rituals and mythological tales about the constellations. Deriving from Rome's legendary origins (Romulus), Julio-Claudian calendars had a design of 365 days shaped by Julius Caesar and then regulated by Augustus in their state capacity as *pontifex maximus;* Ovid poses as a seer-poet (*vates*), but was a popular love-elegist, exiled in part for writing about sex (*Ars amatoria; carmen et error, Tr.* 2.207). While stone calendars display a public form founded by and received from others, Ovid innovatively transposes the calendar into the miniature register of an erotic verse form, elegiac couplets (6.21–24).[10]

How might readers interpret these and other differences between Ovid's *Fasti* and inscribed marble calendars (or the men who displayed them)? Both seem to negotiate, in their different ways, the psychosocial function described by Jacques Lacan as the "screen." "Screen" labels the process by which the subject assumes an identity, a representation, by which he negotiates his place within a surrounding milieu. The subject's "screen" mimics elements of that milieu, thereby masking or shielding itself from view or hostility, or presents the subject to that milieu in a form appropriate to it. Lacan describes the "screen" function, by way of animal mimicry, as that appearance by which the animal presents itself to the gaze of others, a kind of "mask, a double, an envelope, a thrown-off skin, thrown off in order to cover the frame of a shield."[11] The subject uses that "skin" or "shield" to contend over desired objects (food or sexual partners), or serve as an erotic lure or invitation to sex with a partner. Like the animal, the human subject assumes images of the culture's repertoire—here in Rome—to situate himself within a Roman cultural milieu. However, Lacan continues,

> Only the subject—the human subject . . . is not, unlike the animal, entirely caught up in this imaginary capture. He maps himself in it. How? In so far as he isolates the function of the screen and plays with it. Man, in effect, knows how to play with the mask as that beyond which there is the gaze. The screen is here as the locus of mediation.[12]

A subject, aware of this cultural screen, can enjoy its manipulation. In the *Fasti* Ovid "plays" with the calendar as screen to present, yet conceal himself, as a wavering "I"-speaker. Thus, a major difference between Ovid's poetic calendar and most inscrbied marble calendars is the degree, not the presence/absence, of play with such a screen.[13] The course of this book describes particular ways in which Ovid plays with the calendar as psychosocial screen of his own identity in relation to a Roman national identity figured by the calendar.

Gaze

If, as Lacan suggested, animals and humans produce screens for the gaze of others, what is this gaze? It is the general, persistent sense that one is being watched, to which the subject adapts itself (the subject being the object of the gaze). This gaze approximates spectacle in its effect[14]: the subject produces the screen or mask for the Other, the source of whose gaze cannot be easily determined, but is figured in "powers" that seem ominous (perhaps in nature), or else the gods or ghosts. These forces are presumed to insist on the symbolic order of things (the proper way of things) and to make demands or express other wants through anomalies in that order. One might think of Roman divination, the reading of signs to discern what the Other wants. So gaze opposes eye or view, which is the subject's looking at an object. In the prefaces of the *Fasti* Ovid portrays his encounter with signs of the gaze of the Other. He reports seeing and receiving information about symbolism from gods. But there are inconsistencies or conflicts in the Other(s), and an uncanny sense that Ovid's report of these signs to his audience-reader is being watched—seen from many complex quarters.

A question to ask is, for whom—for which gaze—does Ovid produce his *Fasti*.[15] While this cannot be answered with certainty, there are signals inside the poem—e.g., dedications to Germanicus (1.1–25), Augustus (2.9–18), and a sequence of monthly prefaces telling readers about Ovid's encounters with gods who claim honor for a respective month. Ovid's representations of members of the imperial family and the gods seem to figure as tokens of the Other. However Ovid's approach to them suggests their failure as stable hinges or powers upon which to order the world. Nonetheless, in these prefaces, Ovid submits to the desire or guidance of Others, even to that of his general readership: at 6.1–2 Ovid presents readers with alternative desires of the Other—rival divine wishes—and asks readers to choose the one they desire. Such an interchange of choices shows the *Fasti* as a screen of desire, in the Lacanian sense, as a "locus of mediation," where the poet plays with screening his own desire of knowing what the complex Other would want. But difficulties arise along the way. These anomalies generate the reader's desire to know what Ovid wants or means by presenting particular gods and their desires, while playing with the calendar as a screen of the Roman symbolic order.

Fantasy

The subject's relation to screening of desire depends upon fantasy. As a way of coping with the lack of knowing what the Other wants, fantasy stages the coordinates of desire as a "scenario" or narrative setting into which the subject may enter by identifying with one or a shifting set of positions within it. Fantasy is the mechanism by which the subject's desire (lack) is constituted, articulated, and "played out" with the screen of culture. In his monthly prefaces, Ovid stages successive fantasies of how his desire is articulated with the screen of the Other, here figured as the calendar.

The chief mechanism by which fantasy structures desire is repetition of key configurations, existing prior to the subject, known as "primal" or "original" fantasies, since they stage the origin of the subject itself. The main function of the primal fantasy is to stage the subject's view of his own origin—where he comes from as a subject. The classic primal fantasy is the "primal scene," which stages the subject's impossible view of his own conception or birth (at parental coitus). But there are other primal fantasies, namely, the seduction fantasy staging the origin of sexuality and the castration fantasy staging the origin of sexual difference.[16]

"Constructed and generated culturally," these fantasy scenes preexist the subject and are transmitted "through the cultural discourse of history," which includes legends, myths, and rituals forming part of the received family, communal, national traditions. It is within this pre-existing screen of cultural images that "the subject must find his way." But most important for discussion of the *Fasti* is that those primal fantasies in the culture's symbolic repertoire "are themselves dependent on and shaped by the variable contexts of those 'instances'"—of the individual subject's entry into the cultural fantasy of his historical milieu.[17]

Repetition can structure a subject's fantasy in relation to the cultural screen through "retroactivity": a subsequent ("secondary") scene recalls to view a prior (primal) scene. Retroactive recognition either revises that earlier scene or initiates its meaning for the first time. In retroactivity, primal scenes do not have a predetermined meaning or point of identification for the subject within them, but have culturally conditioned potentialities, so that, as Farmer observes, "fantasy is the product neither simply of the subject's 'internal' imagination nor of the culture's 'external' imposition but the negotiational coarticulation, or 'setting,' of both."[18] The subject enters this cultural fantasy retroactively at one or more shifting positions in his particular relation to the cultural repertoire.

Crucial to Ovid's *Fasti* as a fantasy-screen of Roman culture is the inconsistency and even conflict Ovid finds among the gods over what they want from Ovid. The sequence of prefaces portray Ovid "maturing" by shifting through a conventional hierarchy of objects of desire, from youthful sexual dalliance to objects of religion and state figured in the calendar. But they also expose within the ideological fantasy (the

cultural screen) the inconsistency of the (Roman) Big Other supposedly ordering that life course. The double-faced, back-watching god
Janus initializes in "January" (1.63–288) a sequence of prefatory fanta-
sy-scenes in which Ovid will encounter this split Other. As a manifestation of this Other, Janus, who was once Chaos, now become Cosmos,
stages for Ovid (and the reader) an impossible view of his own origin,
his primal scene. That scene engages the reader in fantasy views of the
origins of Roman social order, Roman identity, and the New Year.
Other gods whom Ovid subsequently meets also articulate views of
what seem in stone (calendars) to be stable temporal structures, but in
Ovid's poem frame complex dynamic moments of fantasy screening—
revealing, yet concealing—fundamental conflict in the symbolic order.
The gods communicate a threat, a specter, of disorder that lies beyond
the screen.

This threat is always imminent because the very presentation of a
coherent fantasy-screen of total order necessarily excludes or represses
the inconsistent anomaly, and the represented always threatens to
return. According to Slavoj Zizek, antagonism is the kernel of the Real
within cultural ideology—what is unrepresentable and excluded from
the symbolic order and its ideology. The fantasy-screen tries to conceal
that kernel of antagonism, which returns in the form of a specter
threatening ideological stability. Thus, while Ovid aims to present a
"complete felicitous year" (*felix totus annus*, 1.26), gods entering Ovid's
poetic calendar threaten any stable order, as the shadow—the sup-
pressed antagonism (other half)—of the fantasy of order.[19]

Male Homosocial Desire:
The Author-Reader Relation

Other psychoanalytic tools will address how the poem mediates the
relation between Ovid and his reader and will be introduced in subsequent chapters. But one dynamic broadly affects how this book
approaches the *Fasti*, the male homosociality of its author-reader relation. If the *Fasti* is a screen, a "locus of negotiation," with whom does
Ovid negotiate? For whose gaze does Ovid present his relation to the
calendar-screen? For the rites and festivals? The gods (the Other)? A
provisional answer might be Germanicus Caesar, to whom Ovid
rededicates the work after Augustus' death. By dedicating the *Fasti* to

Germanicus, who cut a figure of heroic manhood (1.1–26), Ovid enlists the prince as ideal male reader, signaling a wider elite male readership (ch. 2).

According to Eve Sedgwick's model of "male homsocial desire," same-sex relationships in English literature portrayed a range of dynamics, from rivalry, to cooperative bonding, to sex between men.[20] Her analysis of such variable relations adapts René Girard's observation of "triangular desire" which, as Sedgwick observed, usually involved two males vying for esteem from each other through the medium of a female character or feminine traits attributed to one or other of the male parties involved. Direct male homosexual relations, in varying degrees depending upon the culture, inspire "homosexual panic" at the specter of the loss of gendered esteem. Among Sedgwick's examples are narratives in which male characters compete for greater manly honor by manipulating female characters as tokens of esteem or ascribing the shame of femininity to the other man. The "love triangle" thus repeats a fundamental cultural model, "male traffic in women" as observed by Lévi-Strauss, but appropriated by Gayle Rubin in reading patriarchy, from a feminist perspective, as built upon physical and metaphorical exchange of women as tokens of honor between men.[21]

Occasionally this book will use Sedgwick's model to elucidate particular narratives in which male characters broker esteem between each other by manipulating ("trafficking in") female characters. But an equal interest is in the status of the "weakened," fragmentary, incomplete text as a reflection of its exiled (symbolically castrated) poet. The primary homosocial relation of interest is that between Ovid as author and a critical male readership, negotiated through the token—the screen—of the broken text. This book posits the *Fasti* as screening relations between the male author and his male readership much as "woman" is trafficked between men in literature and culture generally. To some degree this positioning of the *Fasti* as text trafficked between men mimics the function of displays and pronouncements of calendars in civic space: they too were a "screen" by which Roman males brokered with other men competitive desires of greater civic status through display of a largely cooperative ideological symbol. In this sense, as manipulable tokens of rivalry, calendars were stationed, as are women in Sedgwick's model. Ovid's *Fasti* can be read as an ironic elaboration of this field of male homosocial, civic desire in elegiac couplets.

But Ovid's elegiac screen, the *Fasti*, remained incomplete and unstable. Moreover, Ovid invites his ideal male reader (and others implicitly) to evaluate and guide his compositional process (1.1–26; ch.

2). His submission of his text to critical control of another man adumbrates a fantasy scene of critical re-viewing of Ovid's poem. But critique of the text's failure and Ovid's delayed authorial maturation (ch. 4) was far from certain, because male readership was far from unitary, even within the individual.[22] Ovid's invitation to the prince's critical, disciplinary re-view of the poem frames a fantasy scene around anxious author-reader desire of correction and textual consummation.

Exile shapes this scene of correction, because the fractured incompletion of the *Fasti* (*Tr.* 2.549–52) reflects the exile that separated Ovid from the social rituals—recitation and critical dialogue—sustaining literary composition in Rome.[23] In exile, Ovid lacks (desires) his cultural supports against the savage violence of his place of exile. This detachment causes "error" and flaws in his poetry (e.g., *Tr.* 3.14.21–52, 4.10.111–14, 5.1, 5.7).

This literary homosociality informs the author-reader relation, because exile separated Ovid from direct involvement with his group of mostly elite male literary friends in Rome—a male homosocial network. When Ovid names members of his literary circle in Rome, they are all males (*Tr.* 4.10; *Ex P.* 4.16). It is not that women did not read Ovid's poetry (far from it). Rather, what caused Ovid's exile (the poetic cause, at least) was male moralizing over this very specter—Ovid's erotic poetry addressing or being (mis)read by women (*Tr.* 2). Exile marks a hostile triangulation of male homosocial desire (rivalry) between the elite male poet and his elite male critics. This thought lurks in Ovid's *Fasti,* where (im)proper handling of the cultural screen—the *sacra* and the ritual calendar—has the potential to mediate how Ovid relates to the Roman (male) symbolic order.

Ovid's "elegiac" play with the screen of religion and state in the Roman calendar, his invitation to Germanicus' critical guidance, his periodic vacillation over meaning, and the poem's very incompletion frame the *Fasti* as offering readers a fantasy scene of composition and critique in which they can police the text for blemishes, ostensibly seeking to guide composition of a *felix totus annus,* a "complete felicitous year" (1.26). But, as the following discussion will show, Ovid exploits wordplays and anomalies of divine conflict as trouble "spots" to encourage readers to take up an angular view in order to track the troubling pun or the repetition of conflicts among the gods. This slanted view, upon the whole image or text, is what Lacan called *anamorphosis.* His example, Hans Holbein's *The Ambassadors,* provides the image of two men with books and other signs of learning, but in the foreground is a slanted blot or anomaly. Only if the subject moves to an angular viewpoint and looks back at it, does the anomaly present a meaningful image, a skull as diacritical mark upon the work.[24] Likewise, in Ovid's *Fasti*, Ovid's language invites the reader to take up slanted retroactive slanted views of Rome's calendar. We shall see (ch. 5) how "slanted" emphases or viewpoints activate auditory versions of anamorphosis ("voice" and *llangue*) that influence how the text communicates subjectively.

An Outline of This Book

To interpret Ovid's *Fasti* in terms of male homosocial rivalry, we first should observe how Roman civic calendars projected elite male self-image. Chapter 1 interprets the history of Roman "calendar presentations" as "screening" the tension in male homosocial desire between cooperation and antagonism. Broadcasting Roman mastery of time, the unified visual structure of marble calendars offered a symbol of governance. Elite and upwardly mobile Roman males publicly displayed copies of this calendar not just as practical instruments, but as symbols linking the donors' names to participation in the field of governance, screening cooperation with a network of elite male governance. Yet the display of inscribed Roman calendars (remaining mostly from the Augustan period) also signaled the competitive desires of upwardly mobile males who wanted to symbolize their rising position within the field of male social positions. By offering elite male readers an incomplete elegiac version of the calendar, Ovid, former love elegist, enters this competitive civic field, but in a broken style, disassociated from the competitive dynamics of male homosociality. Positioning Ovid's symbolic breakage (exile) against the Roman calendar screen, the *Fasti* implicitly comments upon the dynamics of his exclusion from Rome.[25]

Chapter 2, "Ovid, Germanicus, and Homosocial Desire," describes how Ovid's rededication of the *Fasti* to Germanicus Caesar stations his calendar poem as a medium of male homosociality negotiated between the male author and his male readership, as adumbrated by his princely addressee. Two factors impact this author-reader relation: the popular identity of "Ovid" as an erotically errant, now exiled, elegist, desiring return to Rome, and Germanicus' popular identity as an ideal male military leader—a heroic prince, adopted grandson of

Augustus and son of Tiberius, and potential heir to imperial rule.[26] Gender difference impacts the male author-reader relation in the tension between the manly excellence (*virtus*) of Germanicus and the convention of elegiac poetry (and elegists) as unorthodox elite males swayed by their soft "feminine" desires. These gendered differences frame the coordinates of the author-reader relation, mediated through the prolonged process of composition and critical guidance of the incomplete text. When interpreted retrospectively from subsequent scenes of poetic inspiration, Ovid's dedication stations this text and its male author in a passive, "feminized," or receptive position with respect to his ideal male reader, who is to exert an active masterful role, correcting a vacillating, incomplete, elegiac treatment of Rome's calendar. Ovid's *Fasti* would then assume a conventionally weak or "feminine" elegiac position of "woman" in the classic "male traffic in women."

The subsequent monthly prefaces are unusual, because in them Ovid projects an image of himself as an authorial subject experiencing divine apparitions, which act as an interface—or cultural screen— between Ovid and his elite male readers, who can observe and judge Ovid's negotiation of his own elite male identity through his handling of these symbolic threats to (specters of) Roman male identity. Chapters 3 and 4 will examine how these monthly prefaces engage the anxieties of Ovid's elite male readership.

Chapter 3, "*Fasti*, Fantasy and Janus: An Anatomy of Libidinal Exchange," examines Ovid's encounter with the god Janus as a programmatic treatment of the first month, January (Book One). Janus was the Roman god of doorways and beginnings who possessed two faces, one looking before him, the other looking "behind." I examine Janus' double gaze and the vacillation of his discourse (his double orality) as a sign of elite male anxiety or wariness before the critical gaze of other men—a double-face wards off fear of being taken "from behind" (*a tergo*, *F.* 1.91–92), the "behind" being a well-known site of Roman elite male anxiety and feared lack or loss of control. [27] It is the metaphorical locus of penetrative vulnerability "from behind" (trauma). Janus' double orality—his second "rear" mouth and his ambiguous discourse—covers (ironically) for what would be "behind," and allows for negotiation of peaceful "exchange" with the poet.[28]

Chapter 4, "Monthly Prefaces and the Symbolic Screen," examines the temporal construction of Ovid's male authorial subjectivity— Ovid's temporizing self-presentation in the remaining sequence of monthly prefaces (February, March, April, May, and June; Books Two to Six). I argue that Ovid temporizes or delays specifying his own position or stance toward the conflicts in ways that turn this very equivocation into an ideological object of critique in the calendar screen. Specifically, Ovid casts himself as *maturing* into manhood, as his elegies are doing (February preface), moving generically from elegiac (erotic) play toward epic (civic) duty, but never really arriving. The cultural expectation that elite males will outgrow play to take up social-political responsibilities (burdens) provides a conventional narrative trajectory designed to contain ([fore]close) suppressed alternative male subjectivity—a narrative containment or "closure" from which Ovid seems to digress and which he appears to avoid, if not disrupt.[29] Why keep returning to the same scene of "choice" or maturation? Ovid returns to the fantasy origin of manhood—where he would seek to fit into the Roman symbolic order. His trajectory is specifically modeled on the scene of Hercules' initiation into manhood at his famous "Choice" at the crossroad between Virtue and Vice (Prodicus the Sophist, in Xen. *Mem.* 2,1,31–34; Cic. *Off.* 1.118; Ov. *Amores* 3.1). Chapter 4 suggests that "Hercules' Choice" provides a mythical-fantasy scene underlying the monthly prefaces. By returning repeatedly to the primal scene of the imposition of manhood—to the act of compulsory choice, where one must renounce other potentialities for the sake of virtuous duty—Ovid seems in fantasy repeatedly to renounce manly duty. This renunciation of male citizen identity reveals typical Ovidian cultural attitudes, as did refusals (*recusationes*) of epic themes of war in earlier Roman elegy. But in the *Fasti* Ovid's refusal to become a "complete" male citizen subject is staged against the civic background of late Augustan ritual tradition and is interrupted by exile, a literary-political response that one might call "symbolic castration." This "symbolic castration" is not the traditional psychoanalytic fear of losing a penis, but a lack or loss of total mastery: Ovid loses control over both his poem and his literary-political circumstances. Insofar as the broken *Fasti*, a work in progress, still seeks to broker its exiled author's wholeness or full relation with idealized male citizens, the *Fasti* symbolizes the author's loss or lack (symbolic castration) by its very form.

Following an examination of Ovid's self-staging in the prefaces in chapters 3 and 4, chapters 5 and 6 demonstrate how the instability of elite masculinity informed the themes and interpretation of the first two books of the *Fasti*, Ovid's "January" and "February." Chapter 5, "Under the Imperial Name: *Augustus* and Ovid's "January" (*Fasti*,

Book One)," illustrates an interpretive strategy in which anomalous
sound-play and social indecorum provide critical positions from
which one may observe the emergence of untoward meanings at vari-
ance with a totalizing "Augustan" view of January, meanings centered
on conflict over the meaning of "Augustus" (1.587–616) as a heritable
title or legacy (inheritance) of dynastic manhood within the Roman
symbolic order. The specter of untoward "sound effects" (and meaning) around the "phallic" *nomen Augusti* radiates out to affect surrounding text and to indicate implied insecurities of male identity
during the transmission of power from Augustus to Tiberius.

Chapter 6, "Patrimony and Transvestism in February (*Fasti*, Book
Two)," examines paternity or "fatherhood," a key theme of Book 2, as
a split, an anxiety-provoking signifier in Rome's Julio-Claudian
milieu. "Father" is figured dramatically, in Augustus as "Father of the
Fatherland" or *pater patriae* (2.119–44, Feb. 5) but also in Tarquinius
Superbus, as split between savior and destroyer. In "February," Ovid
problematizes "fatherhood" as a Roman cultural value that screens
(both expresses and conceals) anxiety around a split in Roman paternity. Transvestite images screen a strategy of managing anxiety before a
father of undetermined attitude (cf. Ovid's exile). The transvestism of
Hercules in the "Hercules and Omphale" tale (2.303–58) heralds a
symbolic strategy for preserving elite male autonomy under tyranny.

This scheme first situates Ovid's poem against the background of
Roman public calendars, examining both as instruments of elite male
self-image. Then, in this context, the book examines Ovid's engagement with an ideal, yet potentially critical, late Augustan, early Tiberian male readership through rededication of his poem to Germanicus,
the Julio-Claudian prince. The next two chapters articulate Ovid's
identity as a poet at work by examining his fashioning of self-image in
the prefaces of successive month-books. First, because of its programmatic illustration of anxiety and conflict, Ovid's prefatory dialogue
with Janus receives special attention in a separate chapter. But the next
chapter turns to the prefaces of February through June; here interest
lies in Ovid's staging of his own potentially deviant male identity as an
object of critique, in order to illustrate anxious cultural conflicts in late
Augustan, early Tiberian Rome. The last two chapters form a pair providing close analysis of the month-books January and February. These
analyses illustrate how Ovid's handling of ritual and mythological
themes within month-books communicates with readers' anxieties
about two fundamental supports of citizen male identity in the context
of imperial power: authority and paternity symbolized by archetypal

titles of the emperor, *Augustus* and *pater patriae*. As a whole, the book makes an argument that the very brokenness of the *Fasti* communicates as a symptom of an anxious lack of and desire for completion and mastery peculiar not only to Ovid in exile, but also to citizen male identity in imperial Rome.

CHAPTER ONE

Elite Males, the Roman Calendar, and Desire of Mastery

T he typical Roman calendar projects an image of more or less stable governance by organizing references to public activities into a synopsis of the composite year. In that scheme, symbols coordinate the timing of religious, juridical, political, and commercial activities in Rome according to the months and days. Calendars contemporary with Ovid's *Fasti* unsurprisingly demonstrate a similar attempt to integrate conflicting events and persons into a regularized unity. Perhaps more surprising is the archeological record that implies a vast increase in production of incised marble calendars in the Augustan and Julio-Claudian period.[1] This increase marks an intensification of the calendar's traditional function as a symbol and instrument of stable governance.

Elite desire to master conflict and turn it into a unified image of governance implies how, from another vantage point, the calendar image conceals or manages unresolved tensions between conflicting desires. Ovid's treatment of the calendar engages this dynamic of conflicting desire and assimilates it to the erotic desire conventional to elegiac verse. Struggling and failing to represent the Julio-Claudian calendar in a complete, unified poem, Ovid invites Germanicus and other (male) readers into a critique and consultation over the *Fasti* (1.1–26). Such an invitation has the potential to direct attention to conflicting elements or problematic "lapses" inherent either in the Roman calendar or in its treatment by Ovid, a notoriously lapsed exiled poet. Alternatively, readers might combine these responses. In any case, the Roman civic calendar and its projected image of governance provide a cultural "screen" projecting elite male identity, while simultaneously concealing ambivalence and conflict behind it.

This chapter examines how male competitive desires in the civic arena underwrote the function of the calendar as a medium of elite male identification, a kind of "screen" of identity. Fundamental to Ovid's elegiac rendition of the calendar is his very failure as exiled erotic elegist to project total mastery of calendar form, while also revealing conflicts over meanings that the symbolic order of the calendar was supposed to conceal. I begin this chapter with a synchronic analysis of the typical Augustan calendar, which will show how calendar structures articulated an image of civic mastery and governance. I then present a history of men publicly presenting the calendar (both orally and visually) in order to track the calendar diachronically as a medium of male homosocial rivalry (a form of politics). I end with a discussion of how, with its conflictive history, the calendar provided a pre-existing repertoire of representations, a "screen," through which Ovid ostensibly tries, but fails, to project a "proper" elite male authorial identity before an elite male audience. Ovid's invitation to readers to correct the poem lures them into an anxious fantasy scene (a staging of rival desires and positions) surrounding conflicts, failures, and the problem of their "location" in Ovid, in readers, or in the Roman calendar and culture.

Extant Calendars and Their Design

Dating from 84 to 55 BCE, the earliest extant calendar fragments, the *Fasti Antiates Maiores*, represent on painted plaster our only example of a pre-Julian calendar.[2] But all the remaining fragments, typically of incised marble, represent the Roman calendar year after its reform by Julius Caesar in 46 BCE (Macrob. *Sat.* 1.14.13; Plut. *Caes.* 59.5). The vast majority of these are Augustan or Julio-Claudian. Moreover, they were erected for the most part in the public spaces of Italian communities. The discussion here turns to calendars contemporary with Ovid's *Fasti*. What were these calendars like? How were they organized?

Calendar Symbols and Their Distribution

Dating from after 20 CE in the reign of Tiberius, the *Fasti Amiterni* is an example of a contemporary Julio-Claudian calendar.[3] The basic design is that of a list. Tabular columns representing separate months organize symbolic letters to represent days and various civic activities inside the months. Using spatial distribution of these letter-symbols in parallel monthly lists, calendars posted a synopsis of coordinated civic and commercial activities unifying several months or a whole year.

Roman calendars (*fasti anni* or *fasti annales*) always show the months as vertical columns with the month name inscribed above. Abbreviated month names appear at the first "entry" (day) of each column along with other letter symbols (July through December). But a repeating cycle of letters, A through H, the so-called nine-day "nundinal cycle" vertically listed at the left side, defines the tabular column of each month by supplying entries for each day. These letters originally aided determination of the market days or *nundinae* (every eighth day), which in the early Republic were also days for assemblies and courts. Their link to the market system had faded by Ovid's day, but F. 1.54 refers to this "nundinal cycle" indirectly (*est quoque qui nono semper ab orbe redit;* "there is also a day that always returns after a ninth day"). The nundinal letters remained, probably because they also aided calculation of periods associated with Roman law and were basic to calculation in banking (interest and due dates).[4]

Yet, the nundinal letters (articulating all the month columns) also provide a "place" for other symbolic letters and commentary at appropriate days. These additional large capital letters refer to the "qualities" and rhythms of the Roman judicial and electoral systems. For example, F, N, and NP indicated whether or not on particular days the praetor could hold his court in the forum and rule on judicial procedures.[5] The letter C (for *comitialis*) marked days permissible for elections, *comitia*. However, a few certain rituals temporarily interrupted conduct of the praetor's court. The abbreviations EN, QRCF, QS[T]DF referred to these rites.[6] Additional large capitals abbreviate the names for festivals. The public games for the gods (and the people), the *ludi*, are so labeled in smaller capitals, for example in July and September. Thus, Roman calendars coordinated rhythms of commerce, law, government, religion, and entertainment.

Fasti Amiterni (plate LXII in Degrassi 1963). Courtesy of the Istituto Poligrafico e Zecca dello Stato, Rome.

The simultaneous, parallel display of multiple month-columns enables visual parallelism between repeated internal structures. The large capital letters K (on the 1st day), NON (5th or 7th) and EID (13th or 15th), distributed down each month column, refer to a set of "dividing days" in each month, the Kalends (*Kalendae*), Nones (*Nonae*), and Ides (*Eidus* or *Idus*).[7] Romans used these terms when formally stating dates for events, citing the number of days (counting inclusively) *before* the *next* dividing day. For example, Ovid was born on March 20 (43 BCE), or "the 13th day before the Kalends of April," *ante diem XIII (tredecimum) Kalendas Apriles.* To aid calculation of dates, Julian calendars often list Roman numerals vertically between each dividing day to the right of the nundinal letters (PR or *pridie* designates the "day before" each "dividing day"). Finally, as if the whole monthly list were an accounting ledger (perhaps an apt comparison), the total count of days in the month often appears in large (Roman) numerals below each column.

Most important for the presentation of temporal order is the fact that abbreviations for the month names, the dividing days, and the total days repeat horizontally across the vertical month-columns. Parallel positioning organizes a visual impression of stable monthly repetition. This ordered visual space supports interpretation of the Roman epigraphic calendar as a synoptic display of temporal governance.

But ironically, despite visual parallelism, the time between the Kalends and Nones and between the Ides and the next Kalends varies. While the Kalends is always the first day, the Nones is either the fifth or the seventh day. And while the Nones is always (counting inclusively) the ninth day before the Ides, the length of the months in the Julian year varies from 27 (or 28) days in February to 30 days in some months, to 31 days in others. This means that the number of days after the Ides varies. However, despite this variable timing between the monthly divisions, inscribers often positioned the Nones, the Ides, and the number of total days in parallel visual position and distributed the nundinal letters to evenly occupy the tabular space. In using parallel synoptic spaces, Roman calendars represent as *conceptually analogous* units of time that are *variable in practice.*

Visual Hierarchy and Register of Communication

By now readers will recognize in the Roman calendar a hierarchy of lettering. In addition to the large capitals articulating the temporal skeleton, there is other, commentative information in small capitals. Among the large capitals are also abbreviated names for the chief festivals, whose titles are generally neuter plural adjectives, perhaps modifying *festa* or *sacra,* referring to gods, rituals, or celebrants (Saturnalia, Feralia, Lupercalia).[8] These names belong to the temporal skeleton because they were prominent and provided Romans an informal way of referring to dates, as we might say April Fools or Christmas instead of April 1 or December 25.[9] By contrast, the small capitals designate ritual and political information that is "minor," commentative, or at least less central to the basic temporal structure.

This contrast between large and small capitals provides more than simply a visual hierarchy; it also differentiates two registers of communication. The large capitals communicate quite differently from ordinary language. They articulate time by spatial distribution, in a mode of communication that Suzanne Langer has called "presentational" (versus "discursive"). Such a mode here depends as much on iconic array as on discourse to display articulated ideas (time itself).[10] In contrast, as A. K. Michels observed, the small-capital notations possess a rudimentary syntax. This corresponds to Langer's "discursive" mode of communication (cf. performative and constative discourse[11]).

The syntax of the small letter, Michels notes, "consists of the name of the divinity in the dative (sometimes in the genitive) occasionally followed by a reference to a place, for example, *Minervae in Aventino*" ("For Minerva on the Aventine"). Julian calendars often place the word *Feriae* ("festival") before the god's name; sometimes they are simply "understood" (so elided).[12] Commonly the verb is elided. Thus, for example, a simple entry would read: "[There is, or will be celebrated] a festival for Minerva on the Aventine Hill."

Thus, "syntactic" (cf. syntagmatic) notes in small capitals comment on "times" arrayed visually within the paradigmatic large-capital frame.[13] While the large capitals concern temporal structure, small-capital notices indicate specific places in Rome for rituals of specific gods. Such information lies *outside* the temporal scheme itself.[14] This split between a large and small capital, synoptic paradigm and discursive comment, may have derived from a prior regime of public calendar communication (for "oral ceremony," see below), but it had an intermediate visual form in late Republican calendars (i.e., *Fasti Antiates Maiores*, ca. 84–55 BCE).[15]

The Roman Calendar: A Brief History

This hierarchy of registers in communication might suggest a difference between what is assumed (time itself) as self-evident, "presentational," knowledge of time, and what cannot be assumed, or is uncertain (therefore needing discursive explanation). At any rate, it is in its fragmentary "discursive" register where the largest Augustan calendar, the *Fasti Praenestini*, erected about the time of Ovid's exile in 8 CE (more below), offers commentary upon the origin of the Kalends, Nones, and Ides,[16] and reveals an archaic world of oral "calendar ritual":

> hae et | [ceter]ae calendae appellantur, | quia [pri]mus is dies est, quos pont[i]fex minor quo | [libet] mense ad nonas sin[gulas calat] | in Capitolio in curia Cala[bra]. (suppl. Degrassi[17])

> These and the other days are called "Calends" because it is the first of the days that on the Capitoline Hill in the Curia Calabra the *pontifex minor* proclaims each month in anticipation of the individual Nones.

This notation refers to cultural practices available, as Varro says (*L.L.* 6.28), only in ritual *vestigia*, "traces" or symptoms of Roman origins in ceremonial practice. Other texts tell us that the rites of the Kalends and Nones depended on observation of lunar phases to inaugurate each lunar month.

The Moon and Oral Ceremony

Varro, Macrobius, and Servius[18] attest that the early Romans partitioned each month into the same three sequential phases that later inscribed calendars do in visually parallel, analogous spaces, using Kalends, Nones, and Ides as "dividing days." But they did not post the calendar on a tablet. Instead, priests ceremonially inaugurated each month and orally proclaimed its days and festivals. Oral proclamation "published" the early calendar month by month. A priestly attendant (*pontifex minor*) had the task of sighting from the Capitoline *arx* (citadel) the new crescent moon. When it appeared, he was to announce it to the "king" (*rex*). This "king" would originally have been Rome's first king, the legendary Romulus, who instituted Rome's ten-month calendar of 304 days, probably based on the lunar month, not the solar year.[19] The king and the pontiff would then sacrifice to Juno Covella (of the hollow of the moon) and announce whether five or seven days would lapse until the Nones. This announcement made the day the "Kalends" (from *calo*, to call out or declare). The Nones would be the first market day of the month, when the people would go to market and also hear from the *rex* the rituals of the month. This Nones declaration (*sacra Nonalia*) would correspond to the "presentational" register of the large capitals in the epigraphic calendars. The *rex* probably also announced for what gods the rites were to be performed, where and how to perform them, perhaps the reasons for them.[20] This would correspond to the "discursive" register of the small capital notices.

Presumably, the ruling king performed these rites until the founding of the Republic (traditionally, 509 BCE). However, fearing divine wrath because there was no "king" to perform certain rituals, the people insisted on the creation of a "ritual king," *rex sacrorum* (in the Republic and perhaps the Empire). He continued "calendar" rites on the Kalends and Nones, inaugurating each month, while the *flamen dialis*, a priest of Jupiter, continued to sacrifice the "Ides sheep" (*ovis idulis*[21]) on the Ides (*Eidus*), the next market day when people would return from their farms. The rites of the *rex* (*sacrorum*) and his pontifical attendant inaugurated the lunar month and announced its days and chief rituals. Under this system, the priests (chiefly the *pontifices*, headed by the Pontifex Maximus) would have observed the lunar phases to anticipate when the next crescent might appear and to estimate whether five or seven days should lapse between the next Kalends and Nones. Consequently, this calendar of lunar months had an extemporaneity to a degree, sanctioned by sacrifice and oral declaration of the list of days and festivals at public ceremonies.

Furthermore, this calendar also required substantial intercalation, the insertion of more days to cause the reckoning of lunar months to coincide with the turn of the seasons and the agricultural labors, so important to the availability of sacrificial offerings to the gods at their festivals (Cic. *De leg.* 2.19–20, 29). Our solar calendar more nearly represents the seasonal and solar phenomena, so it requires less intercalation than did the old Roman lunar calendar. Moreover, our calendar system has regularized intercalation, so that only one day is added to February every four years. The early Roman calendar did not "mechanize" intercalation; it was left to the discretion of priests, which made intercalation of Rome's unusual 22- or 23-day intercalary month subject to negotiation.[22]

From the Regal Period to Flavius

Romans associated their earliest calendar with Romulus, the first king (Ovid, *F.* 1.27–42), but they assigned to Numa, the second king, the first calendar reform. Numa is said to have added two months to expand Romulus' original ten-month (implicitly lunar) calendar to accommodate it to the solar year (*F.* 1.43–44, 3.151–4; Liv. 1.19.7). But, as Michels has argued, Numa's alleged shift of the calendar from a lunar to a solar basis is probably a retrojection by later Romans (starting perhaps with M. Fulvius Nobilior, cos. 189 BCE; see below), who wanted to ascribe Pythagorean mathematics and knowledge of solar movements to Rome's legendary wise king, who was supposed to have founded many other ritual institutions.[23]

However, Livy's narrative of Numa's calendar reform identifies mastery of male rivalry as the central motive. Numa's ritual reform shifted the citizenry from a condition of war to that of peace, following the death (or assassination) of Romulus and Numa's inauguration as king. This political change created a decline in discipline among the adult male citizens, which Numa sought to restore by other means (Liv. 1.19.1–2). Where Romulus had used armed training, military organization, and martial authority to organize the people, Numa developed other disciplinary practices—public and private rituals—by which in peace he could master antagonisms within the citizenry. Fear remained central to governance, as it had been under Romulus (Liv. 1.9). But in place of Romulus' fear of hostile neighbors fended off by military practices, Numa substituted fear of divine hostility mediated, within the citizen body, by scrupulously observed rituals (1.9.4). Thus, by constructing an alternate ideological system, Numa's reforms channeled the fearful minds of the fierce populace within a regulated scheme of civic and ritual ceremonies figured in his calendar.[24] Numa's calendar reform was central to his imposition of new ideological practices.

But according to Livy, before presenting his new "lunisolar" calendar of rituals, Numa drew the attention of his male citizens with a sex story—a fantasy of their king's sexual "congress" with the goddess Egeria (one of the *camenae*, Latin Muses akin to nymphs) and with claims that Egeria had advised him to institute new rites and a new calendar (Livy 1.19.4–7). Livy describes the reasoning for Numa's tale:

> Since he was unable to penetrate [*descendere*] their minds without some miraculous fiction, he pretended that he had nightly congress with the goddess Egeria and that it was upon her counsel that he instituted the rituals that were most acceptable to the gods and appointed priests to serve each god.[25]

Egeria first instructs Numa in his calendar reform, including a supposed shift from a purely lunar to a mixed lunisolar calendar (ascribed to Numa; Liv. 1.19.7). This means that Numa, or rather his calendar, "descended into" his male citizen's spirits by way of a fantasy female, the goddess Egeria, and a tale of Numa's consorting with her. The tale of Numa' sexual congress with a female deity provides the means by which Numa brokered entry in the spirits of his male citizens and leveraged in his own esteem among them (in Livy and Ovid, *F.* 3.151–54, 261–62).[26] But, whatever we make of Egeria, Livy's account attests desire (political, cognitive, and sexual) at the very "conception" of a new calendar, a desire for political mastery or hegemony over the male citizen body—a male homosocial relation—that is brokered through a tale of Numa's sexual, yet intellectual, congress.[27]

Livy reports that Numa appointed a *pontifex*, Numa Marcius, to write down the all "the rituals, with what victims, on what days and at what temples sacrifices would be made" (1.20: *eique sacra omnia exscripta exsignataque attribuit, quibus hostiis, quibus diebus, ad quae templa sacra fierent*). While this record probably aided the *rex sacrorum* in announcing the month's festivals, it was probably a list of the festivals with their approximate dates in particular months, not the complete synopsis of the late Republican or Augustan *fasti anni*. Nor does Livy say Numa posted this list.

It is impossible to know for certain when a "calendar" was first displayed publicly in a written visual form, but Livy records that Ancus Marcius, Numa's grandson and fourth king of Rome, ordered the *pontifex* (*maximus?*) to transcribe onto a whitened board (*album*) the records of the *sacra publica* found in the "king's commentaries" and to display this board in public (Liv. 1.32.2). If it actually occurred, this posting may have included a list of festivals for each month. Although Numa is said to have included in his religious reforms and so within his *commentarii regii* a list of *dies fasti et nefasti* (Liv. 1.19), it seems unlikely that Ancus posted a full list of daily "qualities" per month, because a shift to a fixed list of days would be necessary for such a display, and a true lunar calendar and oral announcement, adjusted to lunar phases, would obviate against such a list.[28]

However, Livy also describes Ancus Marcius' calendar as a competitive instrument of governance, whereby he legitimated his succession as king. Posting Numa's calendar was Ancus' first regal act, strategically aimed at recalling his grandfather's forsaken rituals of peace, in stark contrast with the warlike rule of his immediate predecessor, the third king, Tullus Hostilius (Liv. 1.32.1–2). Posting the *sacra* echoed his grandfather Numa's policies and provided the visual symbol for Ancus' own peaceful hegemony over the populace. Posting the calendar acted, then, in a field of competitive governance expressing Ancus Marcius' desire to secure succession by imitating his royal grandfather (Numa).

Yet, as already suggested, there are problems with these historical accounts. Varro (*De L. L.* 6.28) and Macrobius (*Sat.* 1.13.8; 1.15.5) attest, but do not historically situate, Rome's lunar calendar: as Michels remarks, accounts of Numa's solar calendar erase any period when Romans had a true lunar calendar. The Republican pre-Julian calendar blended lunar and solar attributes. While it had a year of 355 days, a length related to the standard 354-day lunar year, it had four months of 31 days, an impossible length in a true lunar calendar. The pre-Julian calendar also intercalated a distinctly Roman 22 days, to attempt to match a solar year (they cut February from 28 to 23 or 24 days, variably, and added an intercalary month of 27 days).[29] For Michels the invention of this Roman method of intercalation provided crucial evidence. She reasoned that, by the end of the fifth century BCE, Roman months' beginnings were no longer determined by arrival of the lunar crescent.[30] This required a shift during that century from a lunar calendar (and its intercalation) to the Republican lunisolar calendar with its specialized 22-day intercalation.

Michels further surmised that this shift to a lunisolar calendar is more likely to have occurred during the period of the decemvirs (451–450 BCE) than during the legendary reign of Numa.[31] Cicero understands that the decemvirs posted a calendar as part of the Twelve Tables (*Att.* 6.1.8). Moreover, Macrobius, citing Sempronius Tuditanus (cos. 129 BCE) and Cassius Hemina (mid-second cent. BCE), observes that the decemvirs brought a bill *de intercalando* before the people (*Sat.* 1.13.21). While there is a record of an earlier law on intercalation (472 BCE; Varro at Macrob. *Sat.* 1.13.21), Michels argues that that law referred to lunar intercalation.[32]

But what prompted the shift to a cyclic lunisolar year? Michels's answer again recalls the dynamics of elite male political competition: expulsion of the kings and the creation of a new pair of annually elected chief officers, the consuls. These two magistracies, objects of keen competition among the ruling elite (patricians at first), would require precise determination of magistrates' terms. A more regularized calendar would reduce opportunity for quarreling among elite contenders over the predecessor's departure from office. At this time, Rome would also have shifted the beginning of its calendar year from March (still marked in Ovid's day by initiatory rites on March 1) to January 1.[33] Priestly officers could then more accurately calibrate Rome's calendar to the solar cycle, using observations at the winter solstice on December 21 as a checkpoint to adjust intercalation.[34] The central point here is that elite male competition for public office required greater attention to the calendar as a measure of terms of office.

But Cicero surmised that letters on the decemvirs' public calendar (in the Twelve Tables, ca. 450 BCE) must have been eroded or the tablet had been hidden from view, because otherwise there would be little point to Gnaeus Flavius' posting of *fasti* around 300 BCE.[35] Multiple other sources of the first centuries BCE and CE attest that Flavius (curule aedile in 304 BCE) displayed a calendar in the Roman Forum containing the list of days for legal action (*dies fasti* and *nefasti*) along with *dies comitiales*.³⁶ Cicero's hypothesis of erosion or concealment assumes that, before Flavius, the calendar of the Twelve Tables had already presented legal qualities of the days. Probably, some scheme of *dies fasti, nefasti* and *comitiales* had existed for centuries, but had been kept hidden (otherwise what would Flavius' have consulted?).³⁷ However, as Michels argues, this list of legal qualities was separate from the list of festivals (*feriale*) and had probably remained within the purview of priests. They were not posted. In the very early Republic, the *rex sacrorum* orally announced the legal qualities at the *sacra Nonalia*. If absent, one had to request information from prominent men in the City. The calendar in the Twelve Tables probably posted only a monthly list of the named days (especially major festivals).³⁸

But what happened to the oral ceremonial announcement of festivals on the Nones? Macrobius implies that the rites of the Kalends and Nones ceased with Flavius' posting of the days (Macrob. *Sat.* 1.15.9). But this seems misguided. As John Sheid has argued, performance of these monthly calendar rites probably continued down into the Augustan age, because they still served a socio-religious function by affirming the temporal order, a ritual supplement inaugurating the month. In addition, Varro, writing perhaps as late as the early Augustan period, refers to the rites of the Kalends and the *sacra Nonalia* in the present tense; the late Augustan *Fasti Praenestini* seems to do this as well,³⁹ although lacunae prevent confirmation.

But once again, historical narrative situates Flavius' posting of *dies fasti* as an invidious act among ambitious citizen males (rich plebeians, equestrians, and patricians). It was perhaps as scribe of Appius Claudius (Sex. Pomponius, *Dig.* 1.2.2.7) that Flavius, the mere son of a freedman, wrote up the *dies fasti, nefasti* and fixed the *dies comitiales* for elections (see Introduction). The legal and social import of Flavius' calendar is shown by the fact that, at the same time, Flavius also "published" the formulas that one had to utter precisely even to bring legal actions (*legis actiones*). By publishing both the calendar of legal days and the legal formulae, Flavius breached elite male class privilege, because he divulged "religious" secrets kept by elite priests.⁴⁰ Prior to Flavius' postings in the Forum, noble patrons controlled such knowledge; after Flavius' public revelation, it extended to non-elite males, who could then bring legal actions without depending on an elite patron.

Reaction by nobles—patricians, but especially equestrians—was vigorous, we are told. Important in these events is the fact that plebeian and noble were competing over the same emblems of power and privilege, among which was, I am claiming, the calendar itself. Desire for the same symbol of power and knowledge reproduced social privilege and status—i.e., identity—through replication of (literally copying) the object itself (the calendar).[41] Control of the calendar was not the legacy of the freedman Flavius; knowledge of and access to the calendar was the patrimony of noblemen.[42]

Other tokens of status were at stake. One issue concerned even Flavius' right to stand for curule aedile; another, his right to deference while in high office—ceremonial deference even from nobles would signal acceptance of Flavius as one of the elite. For example, when Flavius as newly elected curule aedile visited the home of his ill colleague, young nobles (equestrian and patrician), packed the seating in the bedroom. They showed disdain toward Flavius by refusing to rise in deference to his high rank and give him a seat, as would be customary for a high official (the seated position holding higher honor). In response, Flavius commanded that his formal seat of office, the curule chair, be placed to block the front entryway of the house, so that no one could leave without first standing before him, thereby acknowledging his seated position in public office. Thus, Flavius' publication of the calendar complemented his ascent in social scale.[43]

Another issue was Flavius' right as tribune[44] to use ritual language to found temples. As tribune of the people, Flavius had vowed to construct a temple to the goddess Concordia to "harmonize" the conflicting social orders—plebeians and nobles (equestrians and patricians). The senate refused to allocate funds, so he used fines collected from convicted usurers to create a smaller bronze shrine to Concord overlooking the assembly ground in front of the Senate house. But then, to dedicate the shrine, religious law required that the dedicator utter the precise oral formula, orally dictated by the Pontifex Maximus. On this occasion, because Flavius was merely a plebeian tribune of the people, the *pontifex* (Cornelius Barbatus, cos. 298 BCE[45]) refused and so had to be compelled by vote of the people to dictate the formula for Flavius.[46] The orality of dedicatory rites allowed the patrician priest to withhold the precise formula, much as nobles had concealed the judicial calendar and legal formulas.

Flavius' publication of a juridical-electoral calendar of days and the legal formulae in the public Forum was a gesture of political competition among men and belongs within a larger context of competitive elite male identity suggested by another incident from Flavius' life. Upon his election as aedile, the majority of the nobles are said to have discarded their gold rings and the *phalerae* or ornaments decorating their horses, both badges of their class distinction—as if these tokens had lost symbolic value by being widely disseminated.[47]

The Late Republic: From Fulvius Nobilior to Julius Caesar

Flavius' career situates his revelation of *dies fasti* and *nefasti* (and legal *formulae*) within a competitive field, in which production of calendars afforded ambitious men a means of self-display in a wider field of competition. The play of this political ambition is eventually expressed in both practical improvement and in ideological aggrandizement of the calendar form. This is most visible in monuments posted by prominent Roman males in the Late Republic.

In 179 BCE, Marcus Fulvius Nobilior set up what some scholars think was a monumental *fasti* (a calendar) with a commentary in a temple that he built honoring *Hercules Musarum*, "Hercules of the Muses." We know this calendar through citations of its commentary in various authors. Macrobius reports (*Sat.* 1.12.16) that *in fastis, quos in aede Herculis Musarum posuit,* Fulvius claimed that Romulus named the months of May and June after Romulus' two divisions of the male citizen body into "elders" (*maiores*) and "juniors" (*iuniores*). If this was a posted calendar, and it contained interpretations of month names[48] and comments on intercalation (Macrob. *Sat.* 1.13.21), its size was probably large.

The temple was vowed during Fulvius Nobilior's conquest of Ambracia (189 BCE),[49] for which he held a triumphal procession for this victory over the Aetolians (187 BCE). Consequently, Fulvius' calendar in the temple was part of a larger triumphal display, in which he placed not only his calendar, but also terracotta images of the nine Muses taken from conquered Ambracia (in Greece) and a marble statue of Hercules playing a lyre as *Musagetes* or "leader of the Muses."[50] Fulvius also transferred into his temple a bronze shrine of the Latin Muses or Camenae attributed to Numa. This shrine had originally stood at the fountain in the Grove of the Camenae, where Numa was said to have had his "congress" with his divine wife and "muse" Egeria (Liv. 1.21.3). But M. Claudius Marcellus had transferred it to his temple of Honos et Virtus, placed there along with booty from his siege of Syracuse (212 BCE). There it stayed, until Nobilior's temple was built and dedicated in the 180s.[51] The placement of Nobilior's calendar and statues of the Muses within his new temple symbolically contains and surpasses Numa's calendar and shrine of the Camenae.

Ramifications spread from Fulvius' relationship with another associate of the Muses, the Roman epic poet Ennius, who had gone on a military campaign to Aetolia (Ambracia) with Nobilior (cos. 189) to record in verse Nobilior's heroic exploits. Ennius included praise of Nobilior in a play called *Ambracia* and in Book 15 of his eighteen-book *Annales,* an epic poem celebrating the history of Rome to his own day. In it, Ennius depicts Roman history "as the sum total of heroic exploits proceeding from the *virtus* of the individuals—of the outstanding individuals, the great nobles and magistrates who had led disciplined armies to victory."[52] Ennius famously began his *Annales* with an invocation to the refined Greek *Musae* rather than the rustic Latin *Camenae* in Book One, and extended this preference in a proem heading Book Seven.

Moreover, Ennius' *Annales* complemented his patron's calendar, because its chronographic title and linear narrative recall the old chronicles or records kept by the Pontifex Maximus, the *Annales Maximi,* a source and inspiration for prose *annales* in Roman historiography. These records originally took the form of an annual whitened board (*album*) with notations of significant events in the year, perhaps tracking days in the civic calendar, the *fasti anni.* [53] As Servius noted (*ad Aen.* 1.373), the Pontifex Maximus wrote the names of the consuls and other officials of the year at the top of the whitened board (*tabulam dealbatam*); below he noted events conducted *per singulos dies.* Cicero says that the chief pontiff recorded "all the events of each year" (*res omnis singulorum annorum*) on a *tabula.* References by Cato and Cicero to particular *prodigia* in the *annales* imply that they recorded specific dates.[54] Consequently, it is not unreasonable to see Ennius' composition of his *Annales* as a form of epic-historical narrative poetry complementing Fulvius' *fasti* posted within his temple of Hercules Musarum. [55] As a whole, the temple complex signaled both Fulvius' military (Hercules) and intellectual (Muses) mastery, and Fulvius' *fasti* contributed to this gesture. Ennius' *Annales* and Fulvius' triumphal military procession further complemented this display of governance.

But Fulvius' self-display was not without competitive countermoves. While Fulvius vowed his temple as early as 189 BCE, he did not dedicate it until 179 BCE, when he held his censorship with Marcus Aemilius Lepidus. [56] Why the delayed construction? These two men, Fulvius and Aemilius, had been involved in a long spat over their respective positions. Competition was only put aside in 179 during their co-tenure as censors overseeing Roman morals, but only upon the insistence of other prominent men, such as Quintus Caecilius Metellus, who delivered a speech urging them to put aside their differences. The peaceful agreement between Titus Tatius the Sabine and Romulus the first king were the legendary models that Metellus cited. Cato the Elder also spoke harshly against Fulvius, protesting that Fulvius had led poets into the province (Aetolia).[57] Cato objected to prominent military conquerors using poets to propagate his fame in poetry. But this is the very relationship signaled in the temple of Hercules Musarum by the juncture of Hercules, arch symbol of the conquering (male) general returning in triumph, and the Muses: the Muses offer suitable epic means to glorify the manly feats (*virtus*) of a "Hercules," while the Herculean male offers patronage and protection to his Muses (or poets).[58]

Such a conflictive context suggests that Nobilior's calendar was not simply a practical tool, but also served the symbolic function of indicating Nobilior's possession of the cultured ability to manage the state (he was consul during his conquests).[59] In its composite form, this display expressed Nobilior's identity as a cultured Hercules and his desire for prominence, perhaps even predominance, in various fields of knowledge and power.[60]

Elite male identity may partially explain why Ovid recalls Nobilior's temple of Hercules Musarum at the end of his own *Fasti* (6.797–812). But Ovid notes the refurbishment of this temple (in 29 BCE) by L. Marcius Philippus, the step-father of Augustus. Ovid's placement and treatment of this reference have suggested to some a sense of closure for the poem, an uncertain issue addressed later.[61] Most immediately relevant is that Nobilior's calendar symbolized the mastery of a kind of knowledge important in governance. Philippus' refurbishment, including construction of a *porticus Philippi* surrounding the temple of *Hercules Musarum,* may have conveyed a sense that Nobilior's calendar within it was his family legacy or patrimony. Through the name Marcius Ovid recalls a relationship between Marcius Philippus and Ancus Marcius, the fourth king of Rome mentioned earlier.[62] As already noted, Livy's narrative identifies Ancus Marcius as the first leader to display a list of festivals on an *album*. This act signaled Ancus' own political program by recalling his grandfather Numa's ritual calendar (Livy 1.32.2). Moreover, Livy states that Numa, perhaps related to the Marcii, appointed one Numa Marcius as the first pontifex to keep a written list of the *sacra,* a feature of later calendars.[63] The "family" patrimony of L. Marcius Philippus included care of Nobilior's calendar and of Numa's shrine of the Camenae, housed famously with the calendar in Nobilior's temple of Hercules Musarum. Nobilior had displayed knowledge of solar time by referencing in his calendar commentary the *lex Acilia,* which had compelled priests to intercalate (191 BCE).[64] Later, Q. Marcius Philippus, while censor with L. Paullus (159 BCE), set up the first properly functioning sundial in the Roman Forum. The history of Roman sundials complements that of the calendar in portraying the struggle for symbolic mastery through more accurate representations of solar time.[65]

But from the early second century, pontiffs had controlled the right of intercalation at will. In a less pejorative sense, this control of intercalation enabled negotiation because, as is noted by Censorinus (*De die nat.* 20), Ammianus Marcellinus (26.1.12), and Solinus (1.43), priests could decide to intercalate or not and could thereby lengthen or shorten occupancy of political office or the profiteering or losses in state contracts (such as tax farming). While governor in Cicilia (51–50 BCE), Cicero wrote a letter requesting that his friend Atticus persuade the *pontifices* to avoid intercalation so that he might return to Rome more quickly (*Att.* 5.9.2; 5.13.3, 5.21.14).[66]

Caesar's alteration of the 355-day year to a 365¼-day solar year eliminated such priestly decision making.[67] A simple "mechanical" rule was to be applied: intercalation in February at the end of every fourth year. The application of Greco-Egyptian mathematics, geometry, and astronomy aided this solution.[68] As Pontifex Maximus (and dictator), Caesar made known his new solar calendar and method of intercalation by edict, helped by another *scriba* named Flavius (cf. Appius and Cn. Flavius), who drew up a table of days (Macr. *Sat.* 1.13.2). This solar adaptation had a major impact on the dissemination of the Julian calendar, so that it remains the basis of the modern calendar in the West.

However, for some elites, Caesar's calendar reform was just another contestable move in a competitive game, signaling Caesar's desire of domination (dictatorship).[69] As Plutarch reports, even Caesar's calendar reform

. . . furnished occasion for blame to those who envied Caesar and disliked his power. At any rate, Cicero the orator, we are told, when some one remarked that Lyra [a constellation] would rise on the morrow, said: "Yes, by decree," implying that men were compelled to accept even this dispensation.[70]

By deviating from the seasonal cycle, the pre-Julian calendar had allowed elite males enough flexibility to manipulate (participate in) civic timing. The old calendar's erroneous element had a consequent "need" of intervention, which enabled negotiation of power (temporal strategy) among the elite. Julian calendar reform and systematic presentation of a "correct" year portended the reduction of elite participation in governance and the end of the Republican oligarchy. In this political context, the astronomy serving the Julian calendar exemplifies tyrannical, quasi-divine authority even over heaven itself.

Augustus, the Calendar, and the Field of Social Relations

But, despite Caesar's reform, there was still an *error*, or deviation, in intercalation. Priests failed to interpret properly the new instructions for intercalation (intercalating one "leap day" every three, rather than four, years). In 8 BCE, Augustus as Pontifex Maximus remedied this *error* by instituting a new calendar adjustment, omitting intercalation for twelve years, until the year 4 CE, the date when he adopted Tiberius as his son.[71] This correction coincided with two interventions into the Roman landscape. First, in the years 12–8 BCE, Augustus constructed a massive, piazza-like, calendar-sundial in the northern Campus Martius, the *Horologium Augusti*. Crucial to its form and function were grid lines of bronze laid into pavement and an obelisk imported in 10 BCE from Heliopolis in Egypt to serve as its *gnomon* or pointer.[72] Bronze lettering labeled the grid-lines with the names of the months, the zodiac, and the winds in both Greek and Latin.

Construction of this sundial probably aided recognition of the error in Julian intercalation.[73] But it also symbolized the imperial dominance of Augustus. The inscribed base of the obelisk recalled the emperor's pivotal role in historical time. Booty from Egypt, the obelisk recalled Augustus' re-conquest of Egypt in 31 BCE, when he had defeated Marcus Antonius and Cleopatra. The return of Egypt recalled the restoration of Rome's worldwide empire under the leadership of Augustus. Yet, the dial also symbolized mastery (appropriation) of Greco-Egyptian knowledge—astronomy of time and space—under the figure of the gnomon's science (*gnomonike*), also used in Augustus' mapping of the empire, indicating mastery of both space and time.[74] The inscribed base of the obelisk-gnomon stationed the emperor at the center of cosmic order and figured his orderly governance as the divine goal or "object" of history.[75]

Secondly, about 7 BCE, Augustus intervened in the Roman cityscape by creating 265 precincts (*vici*) within 14 urban regions (*regiones*). He also revived local clubs or colleges (*collegia*) of male freedmen. Similar colleges of local officials had been abolished at the end of the Republic because they had formed riot gangs around prominent political patrons, such as Clodius.[76] Revising these local groups as administrators of new precincts, Augustus harnessed their competitive drive around his own patronage. The new posts opened up avenues for local rivalry for prestige among freedmen, expanding the field of male social connections to the emperor.[77]

Augustus differentiated the "field" of officers in geographic space and social rank. While equestrians administered larger regions, freedmen *magistri* with slave *ministri* (servants or helpers) formed a *collegium* that maintained a shrine at the crossroad (*compitum*) of a *vicus*. Here these local officials acted as priests, who on ceremonial occasions could wear the citizen's *toga* and who performed ceremonies in public view before statues of various gods and their altars. Among these deities were the Lares and Genius of Augustus, the patron or sponsor of the district, bearing the likeness of Augustus as the spirit of the emperor, protective father figure of the people.[78]

Reciprocal exchanges characterized relations between the local colleges and the emperor.[79] The emperor bestowed on the local cult group statues of his personal Lares and Genius and expensive statues of other gods. But the emperor purchased some of these statues using coin offerings (*stipes*) that the populace gave annually on New Year's Day "for the health" of the emperor (the *strenae*).[80] Not only did this exchange of economic and symbolic capital attest a link between Augustus' health (*salus*), local patronage, civic identity, and the felicitous inauguration of the calendar year (ch. 3); it also "bonded" citizen males of vastly different ranks to a field of governance, centered on the emperor. The local shrines and offices provided a medium for pictorial and ritual display of this relationship.[81] These religious and administrative reforms channeled the competitive ambitions of potentially marginal males into a more comprehensive and localized field of governance focused around the fatherly or "patronizing" guidance of the emperor. Indeed, it was in his role as Pontifex Maximus (elected 12 BCE), protector of state religion, that Augustus both reformed Julian intercalation and fashioned himself as "father" of all citizens (by transferring the city's hearth cult of Vesta into his own home and distributing statues of his Genius as head of the "family" into the City's *vici*.[82] This "household" imagery suggested, as a political metaphor, that individual households of individual *patres* were now unified into one *domus* governed by Augustus as *pater* of all, *pater patriae*, "father of the fatherland," a title voted on Feb. 5, 2 BCE (Ovid, *Fasti* 2.127–28).[83]

How do the marble calendars belong to this local political context? Extant calendars can often be linked, with varying likelihood, to local *collegia* or municipal governments. At least the names of each year's local officials could be inscribed in the annual listing of magistrates (*fasti magistratuum*), often physically attached to the incised calendar.[84] Such altars and calendars represented Augustus, the dominant symbol of governance, or imperial males as patron(s) of these local religious-administrative groups that mediated connections between local administration (the *vici*) and central authority. Local ceremonies at the site would enhance associations between performers (handling the statues of Augustus and Lares) and the emperor or his household.[85]

The display of calendars in the local setting thus became a means of local esteem. Incised marble calendars at the neighborhood shrines indicated, as much as did statues and altars themselves, the competing desires of local officials to position themselves within the field of imperial governance.[86] "Augustan" calendars provided men of various stations a means of "projecting" a public identity by mimicking Augustus' public mastery of cultural knowledge, exemplified by his massive calendar-sundial.

The *Fasti Praenestini* and the Example of Verrius Flaccus

But how could local presenters enhance their individual self-images by repeating the basic calendar form? They could make their calendars larger and enhance the calendars' visibility. Using marble, a presenter could highlight the stable monumentality of the Augustan calendar as a socio-political gesture of ritual revival; yet at the same time, marble would call attention to the presenters' investments (political and financial) in the calendar and its ritual symbolism. As a corollary of enhanced size, presenters could add decisively more detail to diurnal entries (cf. Verrius Flaccus' calendar below), as discussed earlier, or make explicit their own role as local official and dedicatee in inscriptional prefaces or accompanying lists of magistrates.[87]

Another technique would be style. Reproducing the calendar in an unusual manner would draw attention to its presenter. In addition to enlarging a calendar, one could stylize its formal structure or resituate it contextually. Calendar presenters did not greatly innovate in design.[88] Breaking with conventional form risked viewer misrecognition of a calendar, or perhaps hostile judgment of the calendar or its presenter. Augustus' *Horologium*, a sundial-calendar, was so enormous that it merged sundial and calendar (other portable sundials designate lines for months, so imply calendar use) with features of a memorial (the obelisk commemorating the Battle of Actium and its central role in empire) and a public space (piazza).[89] That was indeed innovative, but then Augustus already held a preeminent position in social relations.

An example of a freedman using enlargement and innovation in calendar presentation to augment his public identity is Verrius Flaccus, the famous scholar and teacher of the Augustan period. Verrius probably designed and sponsored the monumental *Fasti Praenestini* at roughly the same time as Ovid was exiled while composing his *Fasti* (8 CE).[90] Erected off the forum of his home town, Praeneste (modern Palestrina), Verrius' calendar was also a memorial to Verrius' own scholarly ambitions. It mimicked, yet rivaled (through enhanced size), those of prior elite males (cf. Fulvius Nobilior's). As Suetonius informs us:

> Verrius died at a ripe old age under Tiberius. He has a statue in Praeneste in the upper portion of the town Forum, within a hemicycle, in which he had published the calendar that he had set in order and had incised upon its marble walling.[91]

The statue of Verrius within his hemicycle (calendar panels 1.95 meters high lining a space 8 to 5.44 meters in diameter[92]) may have been innovative, although it is difficult to know due to our fragmentary knowledge of the sites of calendars. The hemicycle also contained marble decorative fountains with concave marble panels depicting in relief a suckling wild sow and a lioness with her young—images evoking those on the Ara Pacis Augustae, part of the Sundial complex in Rome. Verrius seems to have had access to craftsmen in prominent shops in the City.[93] Thus, notations in Verrius' calendar recognizing ritual milestones in the life of Augustus and the imperial family complemented the reliefs; they symbolized the wider field of governance (beyond Praeneste) in which the local freedman Verrius had moved. This freedman, who had served as tutor to Augustus' own grandsons and heirs Gaius and Lucius, had risen above other freedmen and rivaled freeborn elites in prominence.

Fasti and Identity: the Imaginary, Symbolic and Real

The difference between Ovid's *Fasti* and Verrius' calendar display illustrates the three registers or "orders" of psychosocial subjectivity, as described by Jacques Lacan.[94] On the one hand, the statue of Verrius in his hemicycle provides an image "mirroring" the look of Verrius—his face and body. The mirroring recalls what Lacan termed the imaginary, where identification of a unified, coherent self proceeds from observing sameness or likeness between the subject and various objects, reflecting back those traits. These "objects" may be things, such as an actual mirror (Lacan's metaphor for the imaginary process, the "mirror stage") or people, with which the subject identifies as reflecting and bolstering a unified self. Observing sameness produces identity but requires constant discovery of new "mirrors" that can bolster a coherent self-image.

But the placement of Verrius' statue inside the calendar hemicycle poses a double view. One might still interpret Verrius' calendar, the fruit of his own labor, internally as another imaginary reflection of Verrius: his statue and the inscriptions provide narcissistic views of each other through an academic screen—Verrius the antiquarian. Yet, simultaneously, the calendar group also displays an inter-subjective social function, what Lacan might call the symbolic order. The location of the calendar within the forum of Verrius' hometown, Praeneste, illustrates the re-inscription of Verrius within a social domain in marked contrast with his humble origins. A life-narrative tracking Verrius' passage from status as a slave to that of freedman (*libertinus*, Suet. *Gramm.* 17), from Praeneste to acquaintance with the emperor at the center of Rome's symbolic order, is shown by his public display of the Augustan calendar, his object of scholarly care. The calendar exemplifies this symbolic function, because it is a "signifying chain" of codes (*iura*, F. 1.38, 45) organized, as Ovid says, into a *seriem rerum*, a "chain of events" (1.61–62). Placement of Verrius' statue "inside" the symbolic order of the calendar-hemicycle illustrates the operation of the Lacanian symbolic, in which the subject expresses a demand for love—recognition in the social-symbolic arena (cf. the forum location) as an autonomous subject rather than object.[95] This demand for recognition and love is relevant to Verrius' status as a former object, a slave, now an elevated position within the symbolic order before his fellow townsmen.

But the projection of symbolic identity (identification with Augustus, with the calendar) is also troubled. The Roman calendar of rites and festivals configures what Pierre Bourdieu called a "synoptic illusion" that shields from view inconsistency and conflict behind a coherent image.[96] That image enables the subject to revive a sense of unity or wholeness by placing something unified over real gaps in knowledge of self and the social-symbolic order. What cannot be symbolized and recognized within the symbolic order is then repressed. From this repressed unknown, the Real can return. Here the Lacanian Real refers not so much to everyday reality as to what cannot be signified, but will intrude, as disturbances or specters, upon the symbolic and imaginary orders—such as in apparitions, ominous signs in "abnormal" nature, or the uncanny. The calendar, as synoptic illusion, provides a rationalized scenario of ritual repetition—an ideological fantasy—that persons can use to screen the Real of conflicting forces that otherwise threaten to split the subject's imaginary and symbolic identifications. Spectral return of the Real adumbrates the dark, repressed underside of ideologies (fantasies) bolstering the symbolic order.[97]

Verrius and Ovid respond differently to the Real. Verrius' monument uses the calendar as a point of unity in the symbolic, what Lacan called a *point de capiton,* a quilting point, that stabilizes a reading of the symbolic order.[98] Verrius seems to identify himself with the orderliness of his calendar; his portrait statue was literally stationed before the massive calendar inscription. Identification with the calendar's synoptic illusion retroactively stabilizes Verrius' symbolic and imaginary identities, pinning down him and his life-narrative by inscribing him into an ideological order of things, fashioned from the point of calendar creation.

Ovid's unfinished *Fasti* approaches the calendar and the Real in at least two radically different ways. First, although Ovid inscribes an autobiographical image of himself within the calendar's symbolic order (as does Verrius' calendar-monument), he also claims to meet the Real: in addition to uncanny sound-effects and wordplays at the level of poetic texture suggesting the irruption of untoward meaning (chs. 5–6), Ovid reports meeting gods while composing his calendar. As reported in the monthly prefaces (chs. 3–4), Ovid's search for the origin of month names reveals these names, potential points of unity (quilting points in the calendar's symbolic code), as objects of conflict luring apparitions of antagonistic deities. Ovid leaves divine conflicts unresolved in the prefaces of May and June, which exposes him and his text to the judgment of his readers.

This judgment might threaten Ovid's place within the calendar's symbolic order, but by 8 CE that threat had been realized, at least in part, by exile, which, Ovid says, fractured the *Fasti* (*Tr.* 2.552). In one sense, exile intruded, like the Real, upon Ovid's place or identity in the symbolic order, rending Ovid's identification along with it. In another sense, the exilic trauma, excision of Ovid from Rome, marks his poetic voice as symbolically dead, outside the symbolic order, though his body is still alive. This positioning of Ovid between symbolic and physical death might recast his post-exilic *Fasti* as itself a quasi-spectral return of the Real.[99]

CHAPTER TWO

Ovid, Germanicus, and Homosocial Desire

esire may seem irrelevant to Ovid's dedication of the *Fasti* to Germanicus Caesar (15 BCE–19 CE; *F.* 1.1–26).[1] After all, the *Fasti* represents the rites and festivals of the Roman calendar along with the rising and setting constellations. It does not express desire for a mistress. Yet, Ovid explains constellations with stories of erotic desire comparable to Catullus 66 (translating Callimachus' *Coma Berenices*). While inclusion of such tales in the *Fasti* exploits the fact that Germanicus, perhaps as an adolescent, had composed a Latin version of Aratus' Greek *Phaenomena*,[2] those tales are but one aspect of libido in the poem. Another is "literary desire" transacted between the author and reader.

On one level, this literary desire mirrors what Roman calendars express as civic gestures. We have seen in chapter 1 how displaying a public calendar signaled a sponsor's desire for position within a competitive network of male social relations. In the *Fasti*, Ovid "publishes" a Roman calendar, signaling his desire for civic inclusion within this network, through imaginary identification with the act of "presenting a calendar." In this sense, Ovid's address to Germanicus (1.3, *Caesar Germanice*) echoes calendar *praescriptiones* that name imperial patrons.[3] The name *Caesar* thus stations the presenter (Ovid) within a field of elite male social positions.

Yet Ovid's poetic dedication exceeds this convention. Stone calendars presented an unbroken form, concealing the moral or cognitive errors of their sponsors. By contrast, Ovid's *Fasti* remains unfinished,

41

and he thematizes his error and need of Germanicus' guidance (1.4, 25). While poetic dedications typically seek inspiration from deities, and Germanicus is partly Ovid's surrogate Muse or Apollo,[4] exile intensified Ovid's desire for help from an imperial prince who could extend aid or destroy Ovid's hopes of return. Exile "broke" Ovid's *Fasti* (*Tr.* 2.549–52); it interrupted its composition, and separated Ovid from the cult(ural) milieu that would support its completion.[5] Incompletion, therefore, betokens poetic lack and Ovid's desire. By inviting Germanicus to guide his *Fasti,* Ovid expresses desire for the prince's disciplinary support, which is threatened by the poet's exilic deviance, but which is bridgeable in a shared cult and culture of both the Muses and *sacra.*[6] Requesting guidance in literary-religious *sacra,* Ovid brokers a kind of dialectical interaction between men of culture, between an exile and his Roman (male) readership, symbolized by Germanicus.

Ovid wrote the dedication to Germanicus late in his exile (15–17 CE),[7] when other exilic works represent poetic composition as largely an elite male enterprise. It is this male homosocial literary context that this chapter identifies in Ovid's dedication to Germanicus as screening (concealing yet revealing) the uncertain trajectories of desire between men, enacted through the literary process. First, I will analyze this relation between the male poet and male addressee through Eve Sedgwick's model of male "homosocial desire" and posit that the unfinished, "erroneous" text acts somewhat like a "feminine" object trafficked between men to mediate their relation. Secondly, I will show that the dedication frames the poem not merely as a votive to a god-like patron, but as abject "devotion," *devotio,* of the poet to Germanicus. This *devotio* to Germanicus threatens (perhaps ironically) to debase Ovid's authorial autonomy and manifest general uncertainties of elite masculinity under imperial dominance.[8]

Finally, I will explain how Ovid represents, yet displaces, his literary subjection to Germanicus' judgment in the form of his personified "Page" (*Pagina,* 1.19). While the unfinished *Pagina* may be differentiated from the "written" woman of erotic elegy, "Sheet" or "Page"[9] realizes the "fantasy" (*mise en scène*) of Ovid's encounter with heroic Germanicus. Page is a grammatically feminine "screen [or support] for the projection of [rival male] desire"—here a desire for textual completion, still unfulfilled.[10] This "feminine" textual object trafficked between Ovid and the imperial prince displaces gender anxieties arising from Ovid's passive authorial submission to his masterful addressee. In the last major section of this chapter, a comparison between the dedication of the *Fasti,* the introductions of "March" and

"June" (Books 3 and 6), and earlier Ovidian love elegy will illustrate Ovid's reworking of erotic inspiration into an unstably gendered relation between his own passive literary position and the prince's heroic, even divine, mastery as guide and inspiration.[11]

Homosocial Desire in Author-Reader Relations

Exile and Desire of Friendship and Patronage

From exile Ovid portrays his poetry as composed within a male social network, including both relatively equals or "friends" (*sodales, amici*) and superiors. For example, his last letter from exile (*ex Ponto* 4.16) identifies himself among thirty-one fellow poets; all are male. His autobiographical poem, *Tristia* 4.10, locates his first fame as starting within a *sodalicium*, comradeship, of leading male poets (39–60). Poetic "comradeship" involved recitation and critique.[12] But Ovid's exilic memory of friendship ranges beyond literary composition into intimate bonds of mutual advice. He recalls saying upon departure for exile (65–68): "My companions [*sodales*], whom I have cherished with a brother's love—O hearts joined to me with Theseus' loyalty!—while I may, let me embrace you."

Intimate bonds with male friends enabled mutual support (cf. Cicero and Atticus).[13] As Ovid tells a friend (*Tr.* 3.6.9–14; cf. Graecinus, *Ex P.* 2.6.5–6):

> You were concealing nothing in such a way that I was unaware of it, and you used to tell me many things to be buried in my heart. You were the only one to whom I told any secret I had, except the one that destroyed [exiled] me. If you had known that secret too, you would now have the benefit of your companion's safety [*salvo fruerere sodali*], and I would be safe due to your advice.

Ovid's exilic poetry often conjures memory or contemporary fantasy of these bonds (*Ex P.* 1.8, 2.4, *Tr.* 4.10.117–22).

The rededication of the *Fasti* to Germanicus complements Ovid's exilic construction of male bonding.[14] However, Germanicus was not Ovid's *sodalis*, a close friend of roughly equal status.[15] Instead, Germanicus was a *comes*, comrade, of other men (Salanus, *Ex P.* 2.5) whom Ovid addresses on more intimate terms, in order to broker access (cf. *Ex*

P. 1.2 to Paullus Fabius Maximus; 2.2 to Messalinus), an effort paralleled by Ovid's asking his wife to approach Augustus' wife, Livia (*Ex P.* 3.1.113–166).[16] Ovid's formal request for Germanicus' corrective scrutiny and guidance contrasts (cf. *officio . . . tibi devoto, F.* 1.5–6) with relaxed addresses to closer companions (Atticus, Brutus, Carus, Celsus, Cotta Maximus).[17] This evidence differentiates Ovid's readership between addressees exercising imperial scrutiny (Germanicus, Tiberius, Drusus) and readers who would align themselves with Germanicus, who are yet Ovid's intimate *sodales* (a male external audience within a known interpretive community). There were also hostile readers who sought to expose deviance in Ovid's poetry (e.g., *Rem. Am.* 357–98; *Ex P.* 4.16). Thus, in exile, Ovid's literary composition occurred within a network of male social relations ranging from intimate bonds of friendship, to hierarchical relations of patronage, to hostile competition.[18]

Sacra, Literary Cult(ure), and Male Homosocial Relations

Religion provides a juncture, a mode of bonding, between men despite perceived inequalities. For example, in the dedication Ovid characterizes himself and Germanicus as poet-priests (*vates rege vates habenas,* 1.26) sharing, despite inequality, literary and religious "rituals" (*sacra*) important to completing the calendar poem. These social-literary "rituals" included dinner parties (*convivia*) and after-dinner drinking bouts (*comissationes*) where men exchanged recitation and criticism of literature, at least of works in progress like the *Fasti* (but also finished works).[19] Ovid ascribes cultic qualities to such literary gatherings when he calls his a *sodalicium,* assimilating it to an all-male religious society (*sodalitas* or *collegium*) centered on worship of deities, e.g., Bacchus (*Tr.* 5.3) or the Muses (*Tr.* 4.10.19–20, 37–42, 113–22; cf. Prop. 3.1.1–4). In exile, Ovid portrays literary recitation and critique as *communia sacra,* social rituals shared among men to form a bond in literary community.[20] Sacralizing these practices enables a literary cult(ural) bond between Ovid and Germanicus by providing a "respectable" cult(ural) screen that both articulates and conceals differences in autonomy and dependence.

Germanicus receives Ovid's dedication for good reason. After Augustus' death, Germanicus became *Flamen Augustalis,* special priest of Divus Augustus at Rome and model for provincial priesthoods of the imperial cult, a ritual expert for Ovid's ritual calendar-poem honoring Augustus and the *domus Augusta* (e.g., *F.* 1.9–14, 527–36, 719–22; *Tr.*

2.549–52). Moreover, Germanicus was among the first members of the new "Augustan brothers," *sodales Augustales* (Tac. *Ann.* 1.54), the very men Ovid mentions at *F.* 1.3–12: Germanicus, Tiberius, and Tiberius' son Drusus, although Tacitus adds Claudius. These men inherit *festa domestica vobis*, "the festivals of your household," and *praemia* (rewards) recorded in calendars (*F.* 1.7–12). As *Flamen* and *Sodalis Augustalis*, Germanicus had a role relevant to guiding imperial ritual. [21]

But Ovid also invokes Germanicus as a deity, a *numen* (1.5–6), which suits imperial cult. References to public imperial worship appear in the *Fasti* (e.g., 1.527–36, 587–616, 721–22; 2.631–38; 3.415–28, 3.697–710; 4.19–22; 5.545–98), but in exile Ovid describes personal devotion, as when he prays to silver statuettes received from Cotta Maximus, representing Augustus, Tiberius, and Livia (*Ex P.* 2.8), or he prays for Germanicus' succession to imperial rule (*Ex P.* 2.5). In *Ex P.* 4.9.105–18 (15 CE), the poet reports worshiping images of Divus Augustus, Tiberius, Livia, Germanicus, and Drusus inside his house at Tomi, at an altar (*ara*) within a domestic shrine (*sacrum*).[22] This shrine inside Ovid's exilic home shows one way imperial cults "infiltrated" frontiers within private homes: Ovid is transmitting a modified Roman culture, both literary and ritual, to the (imagined) edge of Rome's empire. As a draft protocol for worship, Ovid's *Fasti* might lure the attention of Germanicus, the *Flamen Augustalis*.[23]

As *cultor*, Ovid composes poetry praising "Caesar" and the imperial house (*Ex P.* 4.13.19–38). Such poetry, itself an object of cult and cultivation—shared between Ovid, Roman literati (cf. Salanus, *Ex P.* 2.5.66), and even Cotys, king of the Getae (*Ex P.* 2.9.64)—intersects with Ovid's exilic use of *cultus* and *sacra* as metaphors for civilization and literary composition.[24] Ovid's *cultus* connects varied symbolic "fields." Rituals of patronage "cultivate" relations between Ovid and well-placed men, including Germanicus (via Salanus, *Ex P.* 2.5.71–6, and Suillius, husband of Ovid's stepdaughter, *Ex P.* 4.8).[25] Ovid also longs for *cultus* of land (agriculture), a future benefit of Augustus' civilizing *Pax*. But agriculture also symbolizes Ovid's desire to cultivate literary "crops."[26] Thus, the history of Ovid's elegiac *cultus* screens shifting objects: where formerly *cultus* had meant male or female urbane skills of erotic seduction, exilic *cultus* is adoration of the emperor, his house, and perhaps other elite patrons. By rededicating the *Fasti* to Germanicus as priest-poet (*vates*) and demigod (*numen*), Ovid invites the prince to mediate various registers of "ritual" and cultivating in the poem. But most immediately, Ovid uses the concept of ritual to broker literary-social relations with his reader.

Literature, Male Homosocial Desire, and the "Feminine"

Building upon René Girard's observation of archetypal love triangles in narrative, Eve Sedgwick developed her notion of male homosocial desire "to demonstrate the immanence of men's same-sex bonds"[27] in Western social structures represented in the literature. To oversimplify, male homosocial relations include a scale of *rivalry* and *cooperative bonding* between men over shared objects of desire (desired to accrue esteem from other men), such as wealth, sexual objects, and social position, and, this chapter suggests, panegyric poetry and ritual devotion. According to Sedgwick, male homosocial desire (from competition to cooperation) becomes comprehensible through the theory of "male traffic in women"—the channeling of ambition and esteem through women, valued tokens of male esteem among men: trafficking women broadcasts male esteem in the eyes of other men, so that circulation of women binds men together in rivalry or cooperation.[28]

However, the range of male homosocial desires also includes culturally variable expressions of same-sex eroticism, toward which men in Western societies have often been acculturated to respond with varying degrees and kinds of anxiety, including "homosexual panic" (homophobia).[29] Yet, Sedgwick observes, male homosexual/homosocial relations often borrow from this gender economy by manipulating a "feminized," passive, position ("butch"/"femme" binary and sexual penetration) in relation to a more dominant, sexually penetrating, therefore masculinized male position. In this male homosocial economy, the "feminine" (trafficked) position is represented as an abject, dominated role to be feared. Moreover, this phobia of the feminine position in relation to other men governs male homosociality at large because the individuals and institutions controlling the range of male relationships do so, crucially, by determining the objects of "homosexual panic" or gender anxiety that threaten to invert maleness into its opposite, femininity, subjecting "failed" manhood of an individual or group to the control of other men. In patriarchal societies (because they are male dominated), this gender economy controls society at large, including both patronage-friendship and, this chapter suggests, literary composition. As noted above, ritual is another of these institutions.

How might the dynamics of male homosocial desire apply to the Roman context in which Ovid devoted his *Fasti* to Germanicus? Discussion below elaborates the view that literature of praise, augmenting imperial male esteem, was one of the objects of imperial male desire. In this sense, such literature and potentially its author are assimilated with a feminized position in the gendered economy between men. From exile, Ovid fashioned a male homosocial context from which such anxieties might emerge. In submitting his unfinished, potentially erroneous *Fasti* to the critical guidance of Germanicus, Ovid offered readers an image of himself as an errant poet in an apparently passive authorial position, subject to another man's guidance and vulnerable to criticism (moral, religious, literary) from male readers in a homosocial compositional process. Literary composition, a kind of social ritual (*sacra*), brokers the "trafficking" of text (the *Fasti*) with Germanicus. As the next section suggests, imperial cult was a potential medium for this homosocial "trafficking" of literature. Other male authors had trafficked in this type of authorial position in relation with powerful patrons, such as Maecenas and Augustus. This indicates that the unequal relations between them can involve gender anxiety expressed both directly and indirectly. In the *Fasti*, however, Ovid screens such anxiety by way of a particular mode of religious devotion applied to Gemanicus, the imperial heir.[30]

Devotio and the Poet

One negotiates the favor of gods by offering sacrifices and services. Ovid specifically offers the *Fasti* as a "service" to Germanicus (*officium*, 5), addressing him as a god (*numen*, 6), in the language of patronage (1.1–6):

> tempora cum causis Latium digesta per annum
>   lapsaque sub terras ortaque signa canam.
> excipe pacato, Caesar Germanice, voltu
>   hoc opus et timidae derige navis iter,
> *officio*que, levem non aversatus honorem,
>   *en tibi devoto*, numine dexter ades.

> I shall celebrate in song the times with their causes distributed according to the Latin year and according to the constellations rising and setting at the edge of the world. Receive this work with peaceful countenance, Caesar Germanicus, and direct the course of my anxious ship, and be favorably disposed in your divine presence toward my service—don't be averse to a small honor—*a service, see, so devoted to you!*

Franz Bömer identified this use of *devotus* (6) as the first in all of Latin literature meaning *deditus*, "devoted, absorbed, addicted." Previously, it had meant *exsecrabilis*, "cursed" or "vowed for destruction."[31]

This "signal" use of *tibi devoto* marked by *en* indicates a particular mode of relation between Ovid and Germanicus colored by historical military contexts, particularly the famed deaths of P. Decius Mus, his son, and grandson (of the same name) in the middle of combat (340, 295, 279 BCE respectively). By utterance of prayers, these men "cursed," together with themselves, all the enemy's forces to a mutual death at the hands of the gods, in order to save Rome and the Roman army. The prayer of *devotio* turned the devotee into a willing scapegoat for the army and the country.[32] In our context, the term *devotus* might signify Ovid's willing self-sacrifice or "service" for the country or for someone highly valued, like Germanicus (*officio . . . en tibi devoto*).

Subsequent military uses of *devotio* or *devotus* designate a soldier's strong loyalty to his general; such a bond between a military leader and his men could lead one to endure pain and even death for the other.[33] According to Valerius Maximus (2.6.11), devotion to the chief in Celtic military bands was so strong that they "considered it immoral to survive a battle, when he had died for whose security [*pro salute*] they had devoted their life's breath." Valerius praises the Celts for defending both the security of the nation (*patriae incolumitatem*) and their loyal bond (*fidem amicitiae*) with bravery and constancy.[34] Describing bands of military *devoti* (*soldurii*, hence "soldiers") among Celts in Gaul, Julius Caesar emphasizes both their surrender of life for the chief and their living and sharing "all of life's conditions together with those *to whose bond* [*amicitiae*] *they dedicated themselves*" (*quorum se amicitiae dediderint*) (*BG* 3.22). Caesar's *dediderint* is the synonym Bömer supplied (*deditus*) for Ovid's *devotus* in his commentary on the *Fasti*.[35] *Devotio* passes beyond the usual modern American "friendship." *Amicitia* in these passages concerns an "adhesion" to manly honor (*virtus*), to which Cicero could apply the word *amor* in terms familiar from Plato's *Phaedrus* and *Apology*.[36] Catullus had applied this language of loyal bonds to his love and commitment to Lesbia. In military contexts, this is perhaps the "unit cohesion" of heroic men that Valerius Maximus and Caesar saw among the Celts, but that Cicero sought in loyal political friendship. Hellenic myth and philosophy idealized this cohesion as a basis for well-ordered governance, while acknowledging problems in its attainment (flattery, greed, conflicting values).[37]

In this context, calling his *Fasti* an *officium tibi devotum* signaled Ovid's self-sacrificing devotion to Germanicus, an attitude reflected in

popular demonstrations before and after Germanicus' death. Germanicus would have known of these bands of *devoti* operating not only
among the Gauls, but also the Germans, where in military campaigns
"Germanicus" upheld his title, inherited from his father, and Tiberius'
brother, Drusus (38 BCE–9 BCE). He also served as governor of the
"Three Gauls," where vows and oaths of loyalty were offered to Rome
and Augustus at the altar (*ara*) of the Three Gauls, first erected by
Drusus. There was the *ara Ubiorum* in Germany.[38] In 14 CE, upon the
death of Augustus, troops in Germany expressed desire to swear alle-
giance to Germanicus, not Tiberius. Germanicus effectively swore an
oath of loyalty to the security of Rome and Tiberius, providing a model
for his troops.[39] However, by expressing desire of Germanicus, the
troops positioned him as an object of devotion potentially rivaling the
emperor. Ovid treats Germanicus, therefore, as an alternative avenue of
patronage.[40]

   Devotio had entered the "civilian" imagination long before Germanicus was born (15 CE). Dio Cassius narrates its dramatic "debut" in 27
BCE, just after Octavian received the title "Augustus" (53.20.2–4):

> And while various persons were trying to compete with one another in
> different kinds of flattery of him [Augustus], one Sextus Pacuvius, or, as
> others say, Apudius, surpassed them all. For in the Senate he dedicated
> himself [ἑαυτον . . . καθωσίωσε] to him in the manner of the Iberi-
> ans and advised the others [senators, presumably] to do the same. And,
> when Augustus blocked him [from access to an altar, where he could
> swear his oath], he ran out to the crowd standing in front [of the Senate
> House] and, since he was tribune of the people, he went up and down the
> avenues and streets, and compelled first those men [in front of the
> Curia] and, then also others, to dedicate themselves to Augustus. From
> this incident, even now, when supplicating the ruler we are accustomed
> to say, "We have dedicated ourselves to you" [σοὶ καθωσιώμεθα].

Dio characterizes *devotio* as a fanatical mode of male self-surrender to
the emperor and his family through self-promoting performances of
loyalty (vows and oaths).[41]

Gladiatorial Devotion

Practices of *devotio* so intensified in the early empire, that occasionally freeborn males displayed it by swearing to fight as gladiators in

class-abasing self-sacrifice for the emperor's life and health (*pro salute*). Such *devotio* was popular at Caligula's accession,[42] but already in the early part of Tiberius' rule gladiatorial and theatrical performances by elite males (and females) had so offended class-gender dignity that in 19 CE the Senate passed a decree (*Tabula Larinas*) banning young people of senatorial and equestrian families from swearing oaths or contracts (*auctoramenta*) to perform as pantomimes and gladiators. The Senate had earlier (11 CE) restrained gladiatorial displays (Dio 56.25.7–8), although Augustus had allowed some "devotions" as showing elite military prowess and loyalty to him.[43] In 15 CE equestrians performed as gladiators at games that, according to Dio and Tacitus, Drusus sponsored in his own name and that of his brother Germanicus (Dio 57.14.3, Tac. *Ann.* 1.76.5–7). Conservative elite anxiety over abject self-display characterizes the period in which Ovid offered his *Fasti* to Germancius as an *officio . . . tibi devoto.* Indeed, in poems from exile Ovid compares himself to a gladiator undergoing deadly literary "combat" (hostile critique).[44]

In the preface of February (*F.* 2.9–18), Ovid characterizes his literary devotion as a "martial" display (*militia,* 9) using poetic *arma* (9). With literary (not literal) pikes, horse, helmet and sword (11–14), Ovid performs a *munus* (10, 17) imaginatively for the view (*respice,* 18) of godlike Caesar. Ovid "performs" for Caesar a sacral "diversion" from Caesar's worrisome warfare (*pacando si quid ab hoste vacat,* 18), a *munus* (2.17) or metaphorical "show of loyalty" (*studioso pectore,* 15).[45] The word *titulos* (16) might anticipate the plaques carried by Caligula's *devoti* displaying their promise to fight as gladiators for the emperor.[46]

But if, as often thought, Ovid fashioned the current February preface after Augustus' death and funeral (14 CE),[47] Ovid's "military" *munus* may reflect cults of the dead, *Parentatio,* February 13–22, heralded at *F.* 2.33–34. *Munus* (2.10, 17) might then suggest "last service, office to the dead."[48] But gladiatorial displays were conventional among elite funeral rites. Elites participated in Augustus' funeral: senators carried the body of Augustus out of the *Porta Carmentalis,* mentioned at *F.* 2.200–201, to the area of the Mausoleum of Augustus, where knights, armed on horseback, performed a *decursio* honoring the deceased emperor (soon *Divus* or deified).[49] This honor is intimated by Ovid's placement of his own *munera* (literary *militia; cf. equi,* 2.12) as preface to his "February," a month involving extensive funerary rites. For example, he tells of Romulus' divinization into Quirinus (*Quirinalia,* Feb.17, 2.475–512) and two other funerary rites during *Parentatio* (offerings to ancestors), the *Feralia* (2.533–616, Feb. 21) and *Karistia* (2.617–638, Feb.

22). These rites provide allusive heroic models for honoring Augustus (at 2.119–44 Ovid compares Romulus Quirinus to Augustus). For example, Ovid traces the *Feralia* to Aeneas' games for Anchises (*F.* 2.543–46) and associates the *Karistia* with worship of Caesar (2.631–38).[50]

Only one other use of *militia* appears in "February," at 2.508: the ghost of deceased Romulus asks the people not to weep but to bring incense to placate him as "new Quirinus" and "cultivate ancestral practices of soldiery" (*et patrias artes militiamque colant*). The *Quirinalia* occurred during the *Parentatio*. But, as chapter 4 shows, Ovid also characterizes his *militia* with ambiguity to anticipate other *sacra* in the month (e.g., the *Lupercalia*). But implicitly, if after the death of Augustus Ovid introduces this month of funerary rites with metaphorical poetic soldiery called *munera* (2.10 and 17), we might reasonably construe the gesture as signaling, however ironically, a range of *devotio* to deceased Caesar that included popular gladiatorial-type displays.

Germanicus and Ovid's Devotion

In the context of imperial cult, gladiatorial *devotio* suggests passion unto death, perhaps even erotically charged, like that of the Sacred Band of Thebes or the devotion of Hadrian's lover Antinous for the sake of Hadrian's health.[51] Greek and Roman writers sometimes attributed sexual (bodily) submission to Celtic military devotion to the chief. Depending on whether the audience was Greek (Aristotle, Athenaeus) or Roman (Diodorus citing Posidonius), eroticism drew interpretation as an idealized loving bond or a fearful sexual specter.[52] For Romans, connotations of sexual passivity among citizen warriors threatened symbolic loss of male esteem in *devotio*.[53]

Characterizing his *Fasti* as a "service devoted to" the prince (*officio tibi devoto*), Ovid implies surrender to, absorption in, or love of Germanicus as inspiring leader at a time when (14–18 CE) devotion to Germanicus possessed social currency, built upon military successes and celebrated fertility with his wife Agrippina the Elder and also shown by public demonstrations of despair at the death of Germanicus (19 CE).[54] Ovid shared this popular devotion. In the last couplet of *Ex Ponto* 2.5 (75–76) Ovid expresses to Salanus, Germanicus' partner in oratorical rehearsals, the wish that,

> succedatque *suis* orbis moderator *habenis:*
> quod mecum populi vota precantur idem.

May [Germanicus] as governor of the world succeed *to reins that are his own*—the people pray the same prayer along with me.

Ovid's dedication of the *Fasti* also concludes with a vow expressing devotion from Ovid (and the people) to the prince (*F.* 1.25–26):

> si licet et fas est, vates *rege* vatis *habenas,*
>   auspice te felix totus ut annus eat.

> If it is permitted and divinely sanctioned, as a poet-priest *guide the reins* of a poet-priest, so that, with you as guiding seer, the whole may proceed happily.

What repeats from *ex Ponto* 2.5 is the image of the ruler as "charioteer." What differs is Ovid's use of the image to represent his personal submission to Germanicus' mastery or "rule" (*vates rege vatis habenas, F.* 1.25). As discussed in chapter 1, civic calendars were traditional instruments of governance, offering a kind of "rei(g)n" upon society. Ovid devotes himself and his calendar-poetry to a prince who then can discipline him and his poetic calendar according to a desired (still lacking) form (1.26). Shared composition of the *Fasti* expresses the potentially shared, but perhaps conflicting, desires of these two *vates* (1.25).

Language of Prayer

Scholars have observed that Ovid's prayer language constructs the prince as a deity whose guidance and inspiration the poet requests (*numine dexter ades,* 1.6).[55] It has not been noticed that this language indirectly recalls imperial cults of loyalty, specifically prayers offered *pro salute,* "for the security," of the state and for the emperor and his family, typically at the beginning of the year (January 1 and 3, respectively).[56] Ovid supplicates Germanicus (1.17–26):

> *da mihi te* placidum, *dederis* in carmina vires:
>   ingenium voltu statque caditque tuo.
> pagina iudicium docti subitura movetur
>   principis, ut *Clario* missa legenda *deo.*
> quae sit enim culti facundia *sensimus* oris,
>   civica pro trepidis cum tulit arma reis.

scimus et, ad nostras cum se tulit impetus artes,
   ingenii currant flumina quanta tui.
si licet et fas est, vates rege vatis habenas,
   auspice te felix totus ut annus eat.

Give yourself to me gently, and *you'll have given* your powers over to poetry: my talent succeeds and fails at your glance. About to undergo the judgment of a learned prince, my Page reacts, as if sent to *the god at Claros* [Apollo] for reading. For *we sensed* what the eloquence of your cultivated mouth is, when it waged judicial warfare on behalf of anxious defendants. *We know* as well how greatly rushed the flood of your talent, when your impulse toward our arts took action. If *it is permissible,* and if it is divinely sanctioned, visionary poet, guide the reins of a visionary poet, *so that, under your auspices, the whole year may* go *felicitously.*

Si licet et fas est is a widespread prayer formula, but the verbs *dederis* (17), *sensimus* (21), and *scimus* (23) appear in conditional clauses framing the suppliant's intent in vows, including *devotio.*[57] Such formulas appear in annual vows of the Arval Brethren for the health of the emperor and his house (*vota pro salute rei publicae, principis*) to Jupiter, Juno, and Minerva at the beginning of each year: e.g., "If you *will have given* a good outcome as we *perceive* that we are stating it . . . [we will offer sacrifices]" (*si . . . eventumque bonum ita, uti nos sentimus dicere, dederis*).[58]

As a "good outcome" (*bonum eventum*), the Arval Brothers sought that "the emperor . . . and . . . [certain family members] *will live and their household will be safe*" (*si imp[erator] . . . et . . . quos me sentio dicere, vivent domusque eorum incolumis erit*).[59] Ovid distributes such prayers several times in "January" (book 1): he begins the year (*F.* 1.63–86) by praying for increased years for Tiberius and the imperial house (upon Tiberius' accession to rule, 1.613–16) and again praying for long years for the imperial house at the Ara Pacis (1.719–22).[60]

But most salient for the dedication is that here Ovid's wish differs from conventional *vota pro salute*, because he petitions not the health (*salus*) of Germanicus, but *his own* security, now disturbed by exile and represented by his still broken calendar poem. Like the annual *vota pro salute*, Ovid's wish for felicity is still connected with the Roman year (25–26: *si licet et fas est, vates rege vatis habenas,/ auspice te felix totus ut annus eat*), but his redirection of devotional prayer for the sake of his own life and death, bound up with (in)completion of the *Fasti*, is symptomatic of the anxious uncertainty of literary dominance and submission in the dedicatory "picture" of Ovid. Here, a didactic poet (ordinarily authoritative) openly submits his work to another man, an imperial prince, for guidance, correction, and completion of the text, although the prince was not Ovid's *poetic* superior. A figurative language contributes to this anxiety. First, in mixed equestrian-nautical metaphors, Ovid invites the prince to "guide" the course of his literary "ship" (*derige navis iter*, 4) and, as priestly poet (*vates*), to "steer" the reins of a seer-poet (*vates rege vatis habenas*, 25). A second figure is more "literary": Ovid displaces his submission onto his personified "Page," *Pagina*, quaking (*movetur*) when "about to undergo the judgment of the learned prince" (*pagina iudicium docti subitura movetur/principis*, 19–20).

Page between Poets: Screen of Literary Desire

The submission of Ovid's personified Page[61] to Germanicus' judgment performs a rhetorical-compositional "fantasy" recommended by "Longinus" in the first century CE, a technique reflecting previous traditions of rhetorical practice (*On the Sublime* 14.1–3). [62] To compose "sublime" discourse, one should vividly imagine how ideal writers (Homer, Demosthenes) would express one's ideas. Even better, the speaker should imagine how "heroes" would judge the discourse (14.2) as if delivered in a "judicial court and theater of his own words" (τοῦτον ὑποτίθεσθαι τῶν ἰδίων λόγων δικαστήριον καὶ θέατ–ρον). Here one should pretend "to undergo "straightening" (correction) of one's own writing before such great heroes, judges and witnesses" (ἐν τηλικούτοις ἥρωσι κριταῖς τε καὶ μάρτυσιν ὑπέχειν τῶν γραφομένων εὐθύνας πεπαῖχθαι). "Longinus" here counsels authorial visualization of his composition in a "fantasy," φαντασία, which "Longinus" subsequently applies to compositional content (15).

Ovid applies this advice by taking Germanicus, a *doctus princeps* (19–20), as his ideal "Longinian" reader (*numine*, 6; cf. ἥρωσι), exercising judgment as would Apollo (*iudicium docti . . . principis*, 19–20; δικαστήριον and κριταῖς), "correcting" Ovid's course (cf. *derige*, 4; *rege*, 25; εὐθύνας, "straightening"). But due to exile, Ovid's personified *Pagina* performs as Ovid's surrogate, "screening" his late exilic, unfulfilled, literary desire (fantasy) of compositional encounter. It is the *Pagina* who is "about to undergo" the *iudicium* of a *doctus princeps* (cf. ὑποτίθεσθαι and ὑπέχειν; *subitura*); yet, in this "fantasized" submission to judgment, it is Ovid's creative talent (*ingenium*) that rises and falls in response to Germanicus' *facial expressions* (*voltu*, 18), as if the poet (or Page) sees and reacts to the judge-critic's non-verbal cues.

Moreover, through fantasized surrender of Text, Ovid invites the prince into a position of inspecting (*recognosces*, 7), guiding (*derige*, 4; *rege* 25), even inspiring Ovid's art: "we know too what great rivers of your talent flow when it acts upon our [poetic] practices" (*nostras artes*, 23). Of course, by comparing Germanicus with Apollo at Claros (20), a god of both poetry and divination, Ovid lures the prince into applying oracular insight to interpretation, to "get behind" or penetrate Ovid's linguistic surface, his "Page." This implies potential observation of literary symptoms of failure or conflict between elements of surface text implying (projected) latent meaning (intentional or unintentional).

However, even as Ovid's dedication poses Germanicus as an object of devotion and his text/self as a passive object of Germanicus' literary attention, Ovid also asks that Germanicus "receive the work" (*F.* 1.3–4). This request implies potential inversion of the trajectory of activity and passivity between the male author and ideal male reader. Anxiety colors this uncertainty through the traditional association of receptive passivity with femininity. The personified Page, feminine in grammatical gender, "screens" this gender anxiety, both projecting "Ovid's" surrender, quaking like a leaf (*Pagina*) in the hand of Germanicus (*movetur*, 19; cf. *timidae navis*, 4; *pavidos metus*, 16), luring Germanicus into both reception and critical (re)action, and yet shielding the exiled author from direct presence in the scene of judgment. Meanwhile, *Pagina* remains the medium supporting the fantasized literary desire exchanged between Germanicus and Ovid. This mediating function places the new elegiac, ritual *Pagina* (the *Fasti* itself), trafficked (*missa*, 20) between Ovid and the prince, in a position somewhat similar to that once held by the elegiac "written woman," the erotic textual representation of the beloved that the poet trafficked with readers. Ovid's *Fasti*, devoted to Germanicus, retains "feminine" elements of earlier erotic elegy (relative to men of public careers) under the image of its author's submission of self and Page to princely scrutiny.[63]

As we will see (chs. 3–4), Ovid's personified "Text" ("Page") also "screens" uncertain interpretive control in his depiction of variable, multiple meanings of the cults in the Roman calendar. Authorial uncertainty about meanings exploits the traditionally open symbolism of Roman Republican religion, but Ovid's uncertainty invites the prince to wield "imperial" governance (1.4, 25), such that princely surveillance of *Pagina* "restages" a literary fantasy of textual submission to

imperial authority on an ideological, civic "stage." As an interface of
literary desires between poet and prince, Ovid's "Page" screens (intimates, yet hides) this anxiety.[64]

Ovid's personifed *Pagina* presents rites, yet stands receptive to the
disciplinary literary vigor of Germanicus as hero, evident when Ovid
asks Germanicus to receive the work in peace (*excipe pacato voltu . . . hoc
opus*, 3–4), seeks to receive the prince himself placidly (*da mihi te
placidum*, 17), and requests that Germanicus put his *vires*—effort,
vigor—into the songs of the *Fasti* (*dederis in carmina vires*, 17). Germanicus' virility in discourse appears both as "armed" civic oratory at
21–22 ("[your eloquence] bore *civil weapons* [*civica arma*] to protect
trembling defendants") and as poetry ("We know as well in what
quantities the rivers of your talent run when your *attack* [*impetus*]
advanced upon our art [i.e., poetry]," 23–24). These invitations reorient
the trajectory of Germanicus' assaults (*impetus*) from war to peaceful
activities—toward poetic and rhetorical production of a calendar
poem (cf. singing of *aras*, not *arma*, 13). The word *vires* (17) makes
patent what the surrounding language of martial prowess implies—
Ovid needs Germanicus' vigor as general, orator, and poet.

Poetic Inspiration, Gender Instability, and Homoerotic Specter

While in one sense Ovid's dedication projects a "politically correct"
submission of self and text to Germanicus' guidance, his language
implies a less correct Ovidian eroticism. Scholarship has overlooked its
signs, eclipsed by Germanicus' role as Ovid's "Apollo" or "surrogate
muse," traditional sources of poetic inspiration. But in subsequent
monthly prefaces, Ovid receives inspiration from divine external
sources, both masculine and feminine. Their penetration of the poet's
mind-body displaces the male citizen's traditional self-control with
quasi-sexualized religious and poetic visions. This external inspiration
reported in subsequent prefaces can retroactively alert readers to
potential "gender trouble" in Ovid's devotion to Germanicus.[65] While
the "devotion" is textual rather than sexual, its "homo-textual" literary
encounter contains a hazy specter of eroticism that looms only in hindsight, retroactively, from later prefaces.

Patrons, Poets, and Erotic Exchange

Transposition of eroticism onto poetic friendship or patronage was not new.[66] Catullus had eroticized an evening of poetic (re)production with Calvus (Cat. 50), and, as Ellen Oliensis remarks, Horace responded to his patron Maecenas' desires for poetry (*Epod.* 14, *Odes* 2.12, *Epist.* 1.1; Maecenas in Suet. *Vita Hor.*), loyal reassurances (*Odes* 2.17), or companionship (*Epist.* 1.7). Horace often triangulated these desires through "shared" erotic-sympotic pleasures (the charming courtesan Licymnia in *Odes* 2.12). In sharing pleasure, courtesan, or poetry, the two form a bond. *Odes* 2.17 demonstrates Horace's (perhaps ironically) loyal love of his patron by celebrating their shared condition of life and death, a state resembling *devotio*. Citing his bond with Maecenas, sealed by *sacramentum*, the soldier's loyalty oath to his leader, Horace reassures Maecenas that they share one soul (*anima*, 5–9) and will perish on the same day (cf. suicidal *devotio*).[67]

Ovid himself had manipulated male gender and sexual anxiety in "dedicating" his *Amores* not to a real patron, but to Desire (*Cupido, Am.* 1.1–2).[68] Ovid is penetrated by the arrow of Desire (*Cupido*), a male personification of a psychic force, sexual libido (*Am.* 1.1). The arrow's wound transmits to Ovid "eroticism" as a theme for composition. The next poem portrays Desire, his thematic incubus (or incubating "theme"), creeping upon the poet in bed (1.2). Initially Ovid panics, but then surrenders to the god and is "taken" as slave in an imagined triumphal procession (cf. *Am.* 1.2). The poet's divine inspiration and master, *Cupido* takes Ovid by force rather than seduction. Amor-Cupido's shaft provides Ovid both a divine object-cause of devotion and material for poetic treatment (*Am.* 1.1.19–20).[69]

In the *Fasti*, Germanicus displaces *Cupido-Amor* as the "commanding" influence on Ovidian elegy. Germanicus, heir to Caesar, was descendant of Venus, the mother of Amor-Cupid, and perhaps concerned with Venus' image in the *Fasti* (*F.* 4.17–22, cf. 79–84). Both Germanicus and Cupid have militant roles. Both celebrate triumphs. Ovid not only celebrates Cupid's triumph (*Am.* 1.2), but also compares *Amor-Cupido* to his relative Caesar Augustus in triumph (*Am.* 1.2.49–52).[70] In exile, Ovid had addressed a poem to Germanicus that celebrated Tiberius' triumph in 12 CE (*Ex P.* 2.1) and promised Germanicus a poem when he, too, celebrated a triumph (cf. *praemia . . . feres, F.* 1.12). In January, 15 CE, the Senate granted Germanicus that triumph (Tac. *Ann.* 1.55.1), but he did not celebrate it until 17 CE (May 26;

Tac. *Ann.* 2.41, 2.26). Ovid's revised *Fasti* begins with Germanicus' tri-umphalism: he alludes either to this triumph or to its decree at the end and, perhaps, beginning of his inaugural prayers to Janus for the year (15 or 17 CE; *F.* 1.281–84; perhaps *F.* 1.63–70).[71] As Ovid had once yield-ed to triumphant *Amor* as a horse yields to reins and harness (*Am.* 1.2.15–16), so now Ovid yields his reins (*habenas*) to Germanicus' tri-umphant control (*F.* 1.4, 25).

Eroticization of divine inspiration occurred in earlier poetry and had been theorized in Platonic philosophy;[72] however, it remains restrained before the prince in the formal traits of Ovid's devotion. But its presence in the dedication becomes discernible to wary Ovidian readers in retrospect from subsequent prefaces.[73] Chapters 3 and 4 address how the deities in these prefaces convey content impacting male homosocial, author-reader dynamics. The following discussion examines how Ovid's eroticized divine inspiration in the prefaces of March and June retroactively impacts interpretation of Ovid's textual devotion to Germanicus.

Mars and Ovid: The Preface of "March"

The preface of "March" (Book 3) opens with Ovid pacifying the aggression of Mars, god of war and dedicatee of the month-book. Ovid will eventually ask Mars to contribute to the *Fasti* by explaining why matrons worship him on the Kalends of his month (3.167–72). But the opening address to Mars dramatically recalls Ovid's placation of Germanicus (3.1–12):[74]

> bellice, depositis clipeo paulisper et hasta,
>   Mars, ades et nitidas casside solve comas.
> forsitan ipse roges quid sit cum Marte poetae:
>   a te qui canitur nomina mensis habet.
> ipse vides manibus peragi fera bella Minervae:
>   num minus ingenuis artibus illa vacat?
> Palladis exemplo ponendae tempora sume
>   cuspidis: invenies et quod inermis agas.
> tum quoque inermis eras, cum te Romana sacerdos
>   cepit, ut huic urbi semina magna dares.
> Silvia Vestalis (quid enim vetat inde moveri?)
>   sacra lavaturas mane petebat aquas.

Warrior, with shield and spear put aside for a while, come and loosen your luxuriant hair from your helmet. Perhaps you'll ask "What's a poet got to do with Mars?" The month being hymned got its name from you. You yourself see that fierce wars were conducted to completion by the hands of Minerva: does she have less time for refined skills? On the example of Pallas [Minerva], take time to plant the head of your spear: you'll find something to do while unarmed. You were also unarmed that time when the Roman priestess captivated you, so that you might give great seed to this city. Silvia the Vestal (what forbids my starting with her?) was going for water to wash the sacred implements in the morning.

Ovid then recounts Mars' rape of Silvia the Vestal Virgin. As Stephen Hinds has observed, Ovid's address to Mars aims to pacify the war-god, asking him to lay aside his spear and take off his helmet.[75] But Ovid attends to Mars' "radiant hair" (*nitidas comas*), a beautiful physical attribute visible beneath the god's helmet. The word *inermis*, "unarmed," in lines 8 and 9 suggest that Ovid is disarming Mars, a role famously belonging to Venus herself (or her son Amor) who seduces Mars with erotic charms.[76]

Lucretius had asked Venus, "mother of Romans" (Lucr. 1.1), to lure Mars erotically and make him and Memmius, his warlike patron-addressee, receptive to Lucretius' poetic explanation of Epicurean peace.[77] Venus' mouth and tongue (kisses) had eroticized verbal exchange, passing Lucretian poetry through the inspiring, seductive "flows" (kisses) of her mouth into Mars'.[78] Here, Ovid also lures Mars into a less warlike posture. But there are differences. Ovid directly persuades Mars by recounting Mars' rape of Silvia; Lucretius approaches Mars indirectly through Venus. Moreover, Venus and Silvia are not equivalent in power or agency: the former is a willing divine seductress; the latter, a mortal, unwillingly raped. But for both authors, telling erotic incidents invites a male readership (Lucretius' Mars, Memmius; Ovid's Mars, Germanicus, then others).

Ovid's tale has pragmatic functions. First, it sets in ironic tension Mars' rape of a Vestal Virgin (ordinarily a criminal act) with its result, reproduction, rewarded by Augustan moral legislation and its depiction in contemporary art (Silvia's twin sons Romulus and Remus and the Lupercal). But secondly, Ovid elaborates Silvia's dream-text (echoing her dream in Ennius' *Annales*) as the more immediate result that seems to anticipate Mars' insemination of the twins Romulus and Remus in her womb (F. 3.27–38).[79]

Ovid's Silvia story provides Mars a model of (re)productive fantasy. Silvia's visionary trees recall Minerva, whom Ovid also cited as a model for "putting the point of his [Mars'] spear" somewhere (*Palladis exemplo ponendae tempora sume / cuspidis, invenies et quod inermis agas*, 3.7–8). Minerva famously "planted" her spear in the soil of Athens, from which sprang the sacred olive tree, Athens' commodity and emblem.[80] Together, Minerva's *exemplum* and Silvia's rape imply a euphemistic meaning of "spearhead" (*cuspis*), phallicizing the weapon and weaponizing the phallus as instrument of fertility. In the Silvia tale, Mars "plants" his "phallus-spear" (cf. his ancient agricultural function), and Silvia dreams of two palm trees, comparable to Athena's olive trees.[81] Ovid thereby shifts Mars in the scene (fantasy) of male prowess between violent war and sexual peace, an oscillation suiting elegy's *militia amoris*.

But Minerva was also patroness of scribes, poets, and actors among others (*F*. 3.809–48, esp. 833–34; *F*. 6.649–710, *Quinquatrus Minores*). She had a four-day festival in March during which Ovid was born (*Quinquatrus*, March 20, 43 BCE; *Tr*. 4.10.11–14). Implicitly, then, Minerva models poetic inspiration; her very name signified artistic ingenuity.[82]

Implicitly, Ovid cites Minerva and Silvia as *exempla* showing what the war god can do *with the poet* (3.3) using his "spearhead."[83] Minerva's *cuspis* articulates an insertive role for Mars, while Silvia's reproductive vision implies Ovid's own receptive desire for poetic inspiration and (re)production. Their stories align: both Ovid and Silvia are "priests" who "receive" Mars' inspiration (Ovid, a *vates*, 1.25, 101; 6.8, 21; Silvia, a *Romana sacerdos*, 3.9; *ministra*, 3.47) and produce Mars-inspired discourses (3.167–74, below). The alignment of Ovid and Silvia suggests that, within elegy's *militia amoris* (the warfare of lovemaking), the implication of Mars' desire and rape of Silvia extends beyond the bounds of Silvia's pregnancy as (partial) metaphor for Ovid's relationship to Mars' poetic inspiration. Ovid seeks from Mars something similar to what Silvia received, Mars' spiritual, if not sexual, *semina* (3.10).

Readers might then suspect flirtation beneath Ovid's initial address, "Perhaps you may ask, 'What's a poet got to do with Mars?'" (3.3). As the priestly poet (*vates*) of a calendar poem, Ovid wants to "conceive" from Mars a vision of "causes" (explanations) for rites in Mars' month. An erotic model of inspiration, *militia amoris*, underlies Ovid's final request from the god (3.167–74):

"si licet *occultos monitus* audire deorum
    vatibus, ut certe fama licere putat,

cum sis *officiis*, Gradive, *virilibus* aptus,
   dic mihi matronae cur tua festa colant."
sic ego. Sic posita dixit mihi casside Mavors
   (*sed tamen in dextra missilis hasta fuit*):
"nunc primum studiis pacis deus utilis armis
   advocor, et gressus *in nova castra* fero."

"If it is permitted for priestly poets to hear the secret promptings of
gods, as certainly reputation thinks it is, Marcher, although you are fit
for manly duty, tell me why mothers worship at your festival." Thus I
asked. With his helmet laid aside, Mars replied in this way (*but his dis-
chargeable spear was still in his right hand*): "Now, for the first time, I, a god
handy in arms, am called up for pursuits of peace, and I'm making
advances upon an unusual camp."

Complimenting Mars as "fit for manly services" (*officiis, Gradive,
virilibus aptus*, 169), Ovid exploits the innuendo for Mars' manhood,
his penis/spear (a man's services). What has Ovid to do with Mars
while mothers worship him? Ovid also wants Mars' manly "service" in
order to conceive "hidden promptings" (*occultos monitus*, 167), analogous to Silvia's visionary discourse. But Ovid has persuaded the god to
remove his helmet (*posita . . . casside*, 3.171) to release his radiant hair,
just as requested at 3.2 (*ades et nitidas casside solve comas*). Removal signals Mars' openness toward Ovid's poetic "proposition."[84]
   So Stephen Hinds properly observed that Ovid "disarms" Mars,[85]
but overlooked sexuality's role within this homosocial exchange. Sex
with women (the Silvia rape story) is the open signal that Ovid traffics
with Mars, a desire that most Roman men shared. But Ovid traffics in
the Silvia tale in order to lure Mars into a relation with himself as poet
(3.3). In the "traffic-in-woman" model, Ovid here bears a similarity to
the woman and is vulnerable to assimilation to her role; yet he can
manipulate this dynamic to his advantage. In the March scenario,
Ovid positions Silvia to lure Mars into a kind of "textual encounter"
with himself, screening a "textual relation" between himself and the
guiding inspiration of Germanicus, his ideal (male) reader.
   The spear presents the "point" of anxiety. Mars still wields it, but
seems taken with "pursuits of peace," poetry (*studiis pacis deus utilis/
advocor*, 3.173–74). Faced with Ovid's request for "secret promptings,"
Mars finds a new, "inspired" use for his spear, as he explains the
matrons' festival (173–252); the spear becomes an instrument of inspiration. Indeed, Ovid earlier characterized pikes (*pila*) as Roman

instruments of "eloquence" (3.103–4). But the Roman erotic lexicon used weapons as euphemisms for the penis,[86] and "pregnancy" is the narrative end of the rape of Silvia, Ovid's tale, and the rape of the Sabines that Mars recounts. Mars himself signals an erotic subtext in his phrasing *pacis deus* (F. 3.173), which echoes Propertius 3.5.1 (*Pacis Amor deus*) and betrays elegy's *militia amoris* as his interpretive register.[87] Still grasping his spear, Mars continues: "Now, for the first time, I, a god handy in arms, am called up for the pursuits of peace, and I'm making advances upon an unusual camp [*gressus in nova castra fero*]" (3.173–74). The "camp of love" is a typical *militia amoris*.[88]

Mars then continues eroticizing the didactic encounter[89] between him and Ovid: Mars' *nunc primum* and *nova castra* (3.173–74) is marked by homoerotic innuendo. The lines do offer an official surface meaning of heterosexual fertility (" . . . when matrons give me offerings, I am called up for 'manly service' of them [cf. *officiis virilibus*, 169; making them "mothers"]."). *Nunc*, however, points to *Ovid's* own immediate, pragmatic need of Mars' service. Another meaning answers this need: "Now for the first time I [Mars] am being solicited to serve peaceful pursuits and am making advances upon a camp I have not experienced before (*nova castra*)."[90] Then Mars sustains the sexual innuendo, perhaps baiting hypercritical readers searching for deviance in Ovid's poetry (cf. *Rem. Am.* 357–96). Armed with his "spear," Mars says, "It is no bother to try. I enjoy *getting pleasure with this part* [or *way*] too, . . ." (*nec piget incepti: iuvat hac quoque parte morari*). Here Mars deploys a common innuendo for sexualized body "parts" (*parte*); *quoque* ("also"), with the demonstrative *hac* stressing the innuendo. *Morari* is another euphemism for "sleep with" or "get delight from." [91] To what "part" or "way" does *hac parte* refer? No answer is stated. But the pregnancy model surrounding the scene suggests Mars' penetration of Ovid. Elegy's *castra* of love had usually been a heterosexual fantasy, but here the "engagement" to which Ovid invites the god is "strange" or "unusual" (*nova*) for Mars, because it refers to both poetic and homosexual inspiration (thus "homo-textual"), and it is Mars' "first time" (*nunc primum . . . advocor*, 3.173)[92] in "homo-textual intercourse," a playful metaphor for poetic inspiration from a divine external source. A perceptive reader might venture that Mars' phallus-spear "pricks" Ovid, so that Mars now assumes Amor's position over Ovid, substituting a spear for Love's arrow (cf. *Am.* 1.1–2).[93]

The "June" Preface and Sexualized Inspiration

The preface of June begins with Ovid's retroactive anxieties about prior scenes of divine inspiration, anticipating one thing that prospective readers will criticize—Ovid's very claim to have seen gods (6.3–4). But as the poet explains (6.5–8):

> *est deus in nobis,* agitante *calescimus* illo;
>   *impetus* hic sacrae *semina* mentis habet;
> fas mihi praecipue *voltus* vidisse deorum,
>   vel quia sum vates, vel quia sacra cano.

> There is a god inside me; I get hot when it prods me; this impulse holds the seeds of sacred mind: it is permissible for me to have seen the faces of gods, either because I am a seer or because I am singing of sacred matters.

This passage repeats themes from Ovid's dedication to Germanicus. *Impetus* (6.6) and "god in Ovid" (*deus,* 5) recall Germanicus' divinity (*numen,* 1.4; *Clario deo,* 1.20) and *impetus,* his "assault" flooding up to (according to) Ovid's "arts," *ad nostras . . . artes* (1.23–24). Interpreting the dedication of the *Fasti* retroactively, a reader might align the activity of Germanicus' *numen* and *impetus* with the action of the *deus* "inside" Ovid and its *impetus*—an instinctive drive putting passion (*impetus*) into (Ovid's elegiac) poetry (1.21–22). But "our arts" (*nostras artes*) at *F.* 1.23 might still allude to Ovid's notorious arts, his arts of erotic seduction (cf. *Ars amatoria*), now transferred to (sublimated in) devotion to and inspiration from gods, including heroic Germanicus.

A perceptive readership can observe this sexualization of devotion retroactively from subsequent depictions of inspiration, such as that in the preface of June. When Ovid says in Book 6 that a god *in nobis,* "inside me," causes visionary *impetus* or passion, when it prods, and he "becomes inflamed" or "warm" (*calescimus,* 6.5), the poet sexualizes external divine inspiration guiding his poetic production. Elsewhere in Ovid *calesco* describes sexual arousal. Here, Ovid gets hot when the god agitates or prods, *agitante . . . illo,* which again has a potential sexual meaning.[94]

Moreover, Ovid suggests a Platonic[95] sexual-agricultural metaphor, in which the god "Love" (in the *Symposium*) releases divine *semina* inside the poet. These seeds emerge as visionary, vatic discourses (*impetus hic sacrae semina mentis habet,* 6.6), not unlike the divine double (contradictory) pregnancies (antagonistic twins) and dream vision that Silvia experiences from Mars' *semina* (3.9–10).[96] So, divine *impetus* not only sexualizes Ovid and his poetry, but also fertilizes him, rendering him pregnant with literary-religious vision. In the case of Mars' inspiration of Ovid, the language appropriates rape and reproduction as metaphors for poetic (re)production between men. Mars "seeds" Ovid's mind with the *semina* or "reasons" for ("origins" of) raping and impregnating women (i.e., Romulus' desire of a successor; Mars' tale of the "rape of the Sabine women," their motherhood, *F.* 3.179, 252).[97] Similarly, at 1.17, Ovid asks Germanicus to give himself to Ovid, and put his *vires* into poetry (*da mihi te placidum, dederis in carmina vires*); Germanicus' *vires* stand in place of the *magna semina* that Mars gave Rome, via sex with Silvia (3.10, *ut huic urbi semina magna dares*). Thus, Ovid restages the anxious uncertainty of his textual incompletion—his desire for textual fulfillment—by professing devotion to Germanicus and surrendering to divine inspirational "filling" of his lack of, or separation from, not only divine knowledge, but also Rome (in exile) and supportive homosocial bonds.

Ovid "Full of Her God"

This model of divine inspiration metaphorically assimilates the poet-text to "woman" filled with *semina* and "pregnant." Ovid knew very well the humor, even "camp," of this gender slippage as Seneca the Elder demonstrates in his anecdote about Aurelius Fuscus (Sen. *Suas.* 3.5–7), the teacher or *auditor* of Ovid's declamations (Sen. *Contr.* 2.2.8). Fuscus once tried to impress Maecenas (literary patron and Augustus' trusted adviser) by producing discourse that reflected, Fuscus claimed, Vergil's *plena deo*, "she full of the god," perhaps referencing the Sibyl in ecstasy in *Aeneid* 6.

Junius Gallio, a friend of both Seneca and Ovid (*P.* 4.11), once went with Seneca to the home of M. Valerius Messalla (Corvinus, Ovid's patron), where they heard the Greek orator Nicetes speak *suo impetu* (cf. Germanicus' *impetus*, *F.* 1.23; a god's in Ovid, 6.6). When asked his impression by Messalla, Gallio replied, *plena deo*, "she's full of her god," or "she's pregnant with her god." Then, whenever Gallio had heard a new "hot" declaimer (*caldos*; cf. Ovid's *calescimus*, 6.5), Messalla always asked him, "Was she full of her god?" The phrase became habitual for Gallio, who was caught off guard once at the home of Augustus where, after hearing the declaimer Haterius speak, Augustus asked for Gallio's opinion. This time he said, "He too was full of her god" (*Suas.* 3.7, *et ille erat plena deo*). The off-putting gender mixing (*ille* and *plena*) prompted Augustus to ask what he meant by the remark. Gallio explained the origin.

Ovid knew and used this conceptual mannerism. No Vergilian manuscript records *plena deo* as Seneca claims (*Suas.* 3.5), but Ovid thrice uses it, once in his tragedy, the *Medea:* "I'm carried here, there, alas, full of the god" (*feror huc illuc, vae, plena deo*). He uses it twice in the *Fasti*, both times describing Carmentis, model for Ovid's own vatic inspiration. At *F.* 1.474 Carmentis' *carmina* are *plena dei*, "full of god." At *F.* 6.538, Carmentis herself "becomes full of her god" (*fitque sui toto pectore plena dei*). Finally, Fuscus, who started the expression, was Ovid's own rhetorical trainer (*auditor*). Gallio reported (*Suas.* 3.7) that "his friend Ovid" (*suus Ovidius*) liked the phrase very much (*valde placuisse*).[98]

This gender deviance in male poetic inspiration, mildly mocked by some in a male homosocial context, may have at least two effects when looking back upon interpretation of Ovid's dedication to Germanicus. First, Ovid compares Germanicus to Apollo at Claros (1.20). Claros is significant: in narrating Germanicus' consultation of Clarian Apollo, Tacitus is astonished that a male priest (*sacredos*), not a woman (*femina*), spoke in Apollo's voice (*Ann.* 2.54).[99] Claros models Ovid's passionate *devotio* and vatic relation to Germanicus-Apollo's *numen* (1.4), who causes Ovid to become *plena deo*. But secondly, as argued above, a personified Page (*Pagina*, 1.19–20) screens Ovid's relation to a semi-divine, heroic prince who is to guide, judge, and inspire the *vates* Ovid as he resumes composition of his half-finished poem. The Page thus functions as a screen of this homosocial desire; "she" reveals, yet conceals, the act of submission, because it is "she," the Page, not Ovid, who expressly is to "go beneath" (*subitura*, 19) Germanicus' inspiring rule. Thus, at least one important task of the Page is to screen a male homosocial, author-reader desire.[100]

CHAPTER THREE

Fasti, Fantasy, and Janus: An Anatomy of Libidinal Exchange

a fter "devoting" himself and his text to Germanicus (1.1–26; ch. 2), Ovid soon heralds the presence of Rome's two-headed god Janus, who announces a "prosperous year" for the prince (*faustum annum*, 1.63–64). He then describes the inauguration of the consuls and their annual vows typical of New Year's (65–88), and ponders the function of Janus' two-headedness at the inauguration (89–92). These musings lead to Ovid's report of how Janus had once "appeared" to him in response to similar reflections (93–144). Having recounted Janus' explanation of his dicephaly, Ovid relates their extended dialogue about other symbols associated with the god (145–298). This reported dialogue with Janus is unique in ancient literature, and its length draws attention to a distinctive authorial event in the first and longest episode of the *Fasti*. One might ask what Ovid intends by explaining so extensively what Janus means.[1] As noted (ch. 2), Ovid invited Germanicus himself into a role as inspiring deity. Might Ovid's two-headed Janus, a god granting access to other gods, present an inter-face screening (implying yet concealing) relations between Ovid and the Roman (male) reader generally, but also between Ovid and Germanicus particularly?

As already observed, Ovid expected some readers to doubt that he actually saw gods (6.3–4); those readers may view Ovid's report of Janus' apparition as mere "fantasy," in the sense of "not real" or "fictional." But Janus concerns "fantasy" in another sense, as a psychosocial screen of desire. In this sense, Janus' epiphany tells the "truth." It articulates around Janus the field of Roman ritual that bolsters Rome's symbolic order. But, at the same time, the epiphany intimates, yet veils from full view, anxious antagonism between men (or between mortals and gods). Thus, Janus projects an image of a universal (Roman) order, or cosmos, here in its late Augustan, early Tiberian, "reality." Yet Janus' inconsistencies also imply a fundamental antagonism, a looming lack or failure, the Real, ready to return to that social order (chaos). Two-headed Janus emerges as an ideological fantasy-specter "screening" this uncertainty within Rome's sustaining structure (cf. ritual, calendar, and ideology). In this context, Janus also embodies the specter of Roman male wariness, as a psychic stance mediating this uncertainty. Rome's social order was patriarchal, founded upon relations between men (homosociality), and could be threatened, and perhaps thereby defined negatively, by what lay outside "proper" Roman manhood (women or "feminine" acts and identities of men). As we will see, Janus' odd physique symptomizes male wariness at the loss of face (esteem) due to disavowed flaws or deviances within the network of male homosocial relations. On this level, Janus' dicephaly is both a male psychosocial defense against hostile critique and itself a "bodily" deviance from the norm manifesting the ailment of paranoia.

The psychoanalytic (Lacanian-Zizekian) concept of ideological "fantasy" will aid interpretation of Janus' "body" as a spectral return of the repressed Real in response to Ovid's fundamental question (89), "What god shall I say that you are, two-formed Janus?" This question expresses Ovid's desire to understand how such an anomaly as Janus' two-headedness participates in the inauguration of Rome's new consuls and a felicitous New Year. In effect, Ovid produces on the inaugural day a fantasy-scene in which Janus' two-headedness and other symbols provide "coordinates" for expression of various wants, desires, and intentions through symbolic tokens exchanged between men not just for New Year's Day or for the whole Roman year in the abstract, but also for Ovid's *Fasti* as a representation of such a year and such a transaction of desire between the author and his readers.

I will begin by observing how in 1.63–92 Ovid prepares his readers to view Janus as a bizarre object of visual desire or curiosity by manipulating levels of kinesthetic vividness (*enargeia*) to draw attention to Roman "national" feeling at the state inaugural ritual-ceremonial representation of complete satisfaction (wholeness) in the unity of Roman empire. My analysis will next turn to depictions of Janus that share Ovid's emphasis upon back(side)-watching, namely, Persius (*Satire* 1) and Varro (*Antiquitates rerum humanarum et divinarum*), especially as censured by Augustine (*City of God*). These two texts illustrate how Janus' dicephaly signals wariness, particularly about the elite male "backside" (*terga*). I will then show how Janus' "appearance," both his apparition and his dicephaly, offers a spectral figure responding to Ovid's basic curiosity—what does Janus' two-headedness really mean?—a fundamental quest for meaning beyond mere form. This approach will suggest that both the consular inauguration and Janus' revelation of his two-headedness manifest "primal fantasies," i.e., scenes in which the subject assumes a view of his or her own conception. Ovid's festival description alludes to a psychosocial, if not a historical, origin for Roman male subjectivity, annually renewed within Roman cultural practices. Like Janus himself, New Year's practices screen (cover, yet reveal) the fundamental antagonism within homosociality itself and the type of retroactive (male) subjectivity that results.

Finally, the ensuing dialogue between Ovid and Janus offers Janus' interpretation of the prayers and New Year's gifts exchanged between men. Analysis will show that Janus outlines an exchange of tokens of "value" in an economy of desire symbolically brokered between men, resulting in a cooperative, yet antagonistic (perhaps paranoid) relation. Ultimately, Ovid's exchange of words with Janus brokers access to a Peace that both Ovid and Germanicus share ultimately in a creative bond founded upon composition of the *Fasti*. Consquently, the state of the *Fasti*—whether complete or half—betokens a relation between poet and reader, complete or partial, mirroring the symbolic function of Janus on New Year's Day.

Inauguration, National Feeling, and Conformity

Ovid does not immediately present Janus' theophany. Instead, he leads his readers to it, by stages, through graded levels of immediacy.[2] First, as we have seen (1.1–26; ch. 2), he used an "I" first-person address to Germanicus (second person) to present his own subjection to criticism and guidance, an introduction performing the function of personal *devotio*. The next section (27–62; see ch. 1) surveys the "flat" Roman calendar, its "code" of months (27–44; *annua iura*, 38) and named days (45–60; *variorum iura dierum*, 45), "applying to the whole calendar" (*totis haerentia fastis*) and forming its *seriem rerum*, its "sequence" or "enchainment of events" (61–62). While the calendar survey began vividly with a second-person address to Romulus as founder (1.29) and to "Caesar" as Ovid's own addressee (31), and with an allusion to Romulus' calendar ceremony (1.37–38; see ch 4), Ovid still ends the survey by constraining these dramatic elements into the "enchainment" (*seriem*) of the calendar code (*iura*), i.e., its symbolic sequence.

But as soon as Ovid has surveyed this sequence, he shifts back again to the "dramatic" (1.63–88),[3] announcing (63–64): "Look, Germanicus, Janus is heralding an auspicious year for you, and he is present first in my poem" (*ecce tibi faustum, Germanice, nuntiat annum / inque meo primo carmine Janus adest*). Ovid then addresses Janus in prayer (65–70) with three epithets in an ascending tricolon: first, as *biceps*, "two-headed" (65); secondly as "the origin of the silently slipping year" (*anni tacite labentis origo*, 65); and, thirdly, as "you who alone of gods above see your own back(side)" (*solus de superis qui tua terga vides*, 66). This final two-headedness is the climactic, most important one discussed below. Ovid then prays for Janus' favor upon three levels of government, arranged in a "descending" tricolon: first upon "the leaders, by whose labor the land and sea keep secure their peace"(*ducibus, quorum secura labore / otia terra ferax, otia Pontus habet*, 67–68)—i.e., the emperor and the imperial princes; secondly, upon "your senators" (*dexter ades patribusque tuis*, 69); and, finally, upon "the people of Quirinus" (*populoque Quirini*). Ovid concludes by requesting: "with your nod [Janus] unbolt [your?] fair temples" (70). This gradation of leaders in Ovid's prayer echoes New Year's vows offered for the security of the state (*nuncupatio votorum pro salute rei publicae*).[4] During the Republic, such vows sought *salus* (security) for the senate and the Roman people (cf. Ovid's *dexter ades patribusque tuis populoque Quirini*, 69), but during the empire, prayers for the emperor and his family were added (cf. Ovid's *dexter ades ducibus* . . . , 67–68). That Janus announces an auspicious year for Germanicus (*nuntiat* 63) informally recalls *nuncupationes* of the *vota publica*.[5]

Vivid ecphrasis then intensifies national feeling in the ensuing ceremonies. Ovid's figurative language collapses different senses into each other to produce a kinesthetic merger luring the external audience into the "national scene." Crucial is Ovid's issuance of ritual directions, as if he were a priest or master of ceremonies (*vates*)[6] commanding the people to hush their antagonistic speech and attend (71–74):

> prospera lux oritur: linguis animisque favete;
> nunc dicenda bona sunt bona verba die.
> lite vacent aures, insanaque protinus absint
> iurgia: differ opus, livida turba, tuum.

A prosperous day is rising: show favor in speech and attitude; now blessings must be spoken on a blessed day. Let ears be free of dispute, let insane quarrels cease at once: postpone your work, envious crowd.

Ovid commands lawyers and litigants in the Forum Romanum, the location of the ceremony, to be quiet for the event. These authorial-vatic directives usher the perceptual attention of both his internal (Forum) and external (reading) audiences toward the following ecphrasis (75–86):

> cernis odoratis ut luceat ignibus aether,
>> et sonet accensis spica Cilissa focis?
> flamma nitore suo templorum verberat aurum,
>> et tremulum summa spargit in aede iubar.
> vestibus intactis Tarpeias itur in arces,
>> et populus festo concolor ipse suo est,
> iamque novi praeeunt fasces, nova purpura fulget,
>> et nova conspicuum pondera sentit ebur.
> colla rudes operum praebent ferienda iuvenci,
>> quos aluit campis herba Falisca suis.
> Iuppiter arce sua totum cum spectet in orbem,
>> nil nisi Romanum quod tueatur habet.

Do you see how the air glows with fragrant fires, and spikes of incense crackle on lit burners? The flame repeatedly strikes the gold of the temples with its glistening and the quivering ray scatters upon the top of the temple. There is a procession in spotless [white] garments onto the Tarpeian citadel, and the populace itself wears the same color on the festive day. And now new fasces [consuls] proceed, new purple gleams, and the conspicuous ivory chair feels its new weights [consuls]. Young bulls unused to work, whom the grass of Falerii has fed in its meadows, offer necks to be axed. When Jupiter gazes upon the whole world from his citadel, he has nothing except Rome to survey.

The inversion of activity and passivity (the chair "feels" the consuls, 82) and the conversion of flickering light and crackling sound into quasi-speech (*flamma verberat*, 77) induce in readers' imagination the sensual effects of ceremonial "sublime," perhaps comparable to Sappho's erotic sublime (Longinus, *On the Sublime* 10.1–3). But here ritual sublimity draws the imagination of the Roman subject aloft (*sublimis*) to the Capitoline (heavenly) citadel and into an experience of "national feeling" and divine felicity at an annual festival inaugurating both the new year and the new consuls. This "national feeling" involves participation by various parts of this audience (community) in a communal enjoyment framed by inauguration, which seeks secure renewal (cf. *salve,* "good health," 87) of this enjoyment (cf. *faustum annum,* 63; *otia,* 68; and *laeta dies,* "joyful day," 87).

But this national ceremony, however unified, betrays fear of the theft of enjoyment, fear that some person or group (internal or external) may either threaten or have a perverse relation to a supposed "original" Roman enjoyment.[7] In other words, the inaugural scene (63–88) constructs a festival ethos of communal sharing among men precisely while articulating envied distinctions between them, (re)producing a fundamental tension between an outward show of what Victor Turner called *communitas* (inclusive community, festival sharing, brotherhood, and social non-differentiation) and indirectly endorsed rivalry, hierarchical structure, and social exclusivity—a kind of authorized "theft" of enjoyment.[8] While the ceremony celebrates collegiality among Roman officials (Janus' two heads perhaps symbolize dialectical power sharing between two consuls or peaceful transmission of power from one year to the next), that ceremonial collegiality masks everyday antagonism evident in the Forum.[9] While the inaugural festival temporarily stages "communion" or shared enjoyment within the whole community, it also reiterates the structural hierarchy by installing consuls at the traditional pinnacle of aristocratic (male) public authority.[10] The emperor and his household now challenge this pinnacle. Ovid's poetic version of traditional vows for the security of public life (63–70) mirrors the ranked hierarchy of male power structures articulated in the public prayer (see above).[11]

Finally, we have seen that as "priest" Ovid orders repression of antagonism (*lis*) between men on New Year's (71–74). It seems that a show of conformity takes precedence over antagonism; the envious crowd (*livida turba,* 74) in the forum was not typically so complacent. New Year's Day requires a ceremonial display of goodwill. Harmonization of senses in Ovid's ceremonial ecphrasis includes the crowd's sartorial "uniformity": white unblemished togas of the processing elite (*vestibus intactis*) are reflected by the same color (*concolor*) among the standing *populus* (79–80). Homogeneity climaxes in a communal vision of Roman universal empire, when the entire world appears "uniform" to Jupiter, looking down from his lofty citadel: the world appears uniformly "Roman" (85–86).[12]

This ritualized conformity ratifies, yet disguises, submission to the law of hierarchical distinction, which as object of envy constitutes "theft of enjoyment" for the disenfranchised (slaves, freedmen, poor plebeians). These "thefts" occur not only in litigious legal wrangling, but also in the almost constant war—termed "labor" at 67—on Rome's frontiers, waged by imperial leaders like Germanicus to preserve the "Peace" (67–68, 285–88, 713–18), despite multiple Augustan closures of Janus' double-gated shrine in the Forum Romanum signifying peace (Aug. *RG* 13; *F.* 1.257–82).[13] An irony of sorts, this "labor" recalls contemporary wars far from the City (cf. Varus), but also past civil war. Inconsistently, Janus screens "prospect" and "retrospect" of both Peace and War.[14]

Janus' De-Formity

But Ovid does not linger on conformity. He next asks Janus about his "dicephaly" (89–92), shifting focus from ritual uniformity to divine deformity (89–92).

> quem tamen esse deum te dicam, Iane biformis?
>   nam tibi par nullum Graecia numen habet.
> ede simul causam, cur de caelestibus unus
>   sitque quod *a tergo* sitque quod ante vides.

> Yet, biform Janus, what god should I say you are? For Greece has no deity matching you. Tell at once the reason why you alone of the celestial beings see what is both fore and aft.

Ovid focuses on Janus' bodily "otherness" or difference, and will ultimately use Janus as a figure of difference (deviance) in community. But Ovid starts from Janus' physical anomaly, his two faces or mouths (*bina . . . ora*, 96) or two heads (*ancipiti . . . imagine*, 95). Ovid observed this deformity in his initial prayer, perhaps imagined to be performed before the statue of Janus Geminus in his two-doored shrine in the Forum Romanum: "you, two-headed Janus, . . . who alone among the gods see your back(side)" (*solus de superis qui tua terga vides*," 66).[15] Thus, lines 89–92 perform a "double take" or deferred reaction to the deviance of Janus' statue from physical norms.

Ovid's emphasis on Janus' *tergum* is unusual (1.65–66, 89–92, 114). Non-literary prayers to Janus use flattering epithets; they do not refer to his two heads; they *never* note that Janus watches his *tergum* or "back(side)," which is precisely what attracts Ovid's curiosity (*terga*, 1.66; *a tergo*, 92). Janus himself refers to his "behind" at 114, "what is before and behind *on* me seems the same" (*ante quod est in me postque videtur idem*). An inscriptional parallel is *Geminus* ("twin," "double" or "two-fold"), but it is a far more respectful epithet. So, while other literary sources call Janus two-headed, Ovid isolates Janus as a divine oddity, as *the only god* to see his behind (*solus*, 66; *unus*, 91–92).[16] Why? What is Ovid getting at? Satiric uses of Janus in other works evoke the anxieties at stake.

Persius' Janus: Satire 1

For example, the Neronian satirist Persius uses Janus to represent the paranoia of elite Roman males about flattery, envy, and literary-social critique (*Sat.* 1.58–62):

> *o Iane, a tergo* quem nulla *ciconia* pinsit,
> nec manus auriculas imitari mobilis albas,
> nec linguae quantum sitiat canis Apula tantum!
> *vos, o patricius sanguis, quos vivere fas est*
> *occipiti caeco, posticae occurrite sannae.*

> O you Janus, whom no stork nor hand moving to imitate white ears, nor tongue as long as a thirsty Apulian dog's has poked from behind. You, O noble-blooded, who may live with no eyes in the back of your head, encounter the mocking at your rear.

Persius' Janus (*Sat.* 1.58) embodies male wariness contrasted with an elite male who lacks "eyes in the back of his head" (62). A "Janus" would be ready to thwart jibes of a "stork" or other mocking hand gestures by inferiors made from the rear after he has recited poetry at a banquet (58–60). Guests offer praise to his face, mockery *a tergo* (behind his back).

While J. C. Bramble clarified the meaning of the gestures, no one has noted how Persius' language sexualizes elite male paranoia of social critique among other men. The backside (*tergo*, 58) is the fantasized locus of anxiety, while Persius' adjective *postica* (62) connotes the anus, reinforcing this earlier reference to the *tergum* (*a tergo*, Pers. 1.58).[17] Gestures—a stork, the ass-ears, and the dog-tongue addressing the elite back(side)—indicate a possible (anal) wariness of ridicule.[18] Roman wall painting supplies images evocative of possible folk performances. Persius' stork poking *a tergo*, a vivid gesture, recalls the War of the Pygmies and Cranes (Hom. *Il.* 3.3–6) and their representations such as storks or cranes poking pigmies in the buttocks; compare Persius' *o Iane, a tergo quem nulla ciconia pinsit* (58).[19] In some depictions, pygmies wear conical hats, suggesting that Persius' folk imagery derived partly from the street-comedy of a *sannio* (cf. *sannae*, "the grimace of a clown," *Sat.* 1.62).[20] Persius' elite patron (*o patricius sanguis*, 61) fails to watch behind him and is therefore vulnerable precisely where the elite male body was not to be penetrated. This "penetration" is not "real"; it is a fantasy of what hidden ridicule *a tergo*, "from the rear" (*Sat.* 1.58), can do to elite male "face." This fantasized anal penetration is particularly salient for Satire 1, a poem otherwise replete with phobic evocations of the specters of effeminacy and sex between men. Defense of hyperbolic elite male dignity (ego) would require a bi-frontal deformity of psyche, metaphorical eyes in the back of the head (*Sat.* 1.61–62).[21]

Augustine on Varro's Janus

When Varro organized pagan gods according to phases of human sexual reproduction starting from Janus, he provided Augustine an object for satiric attack *a tergo* (*CD* 6.9). Augustine performs upon pagan Janus the ridicule feared by elite males, but supposedly thwarted by dicephaly. At *City of God* 7.2, Augustine summarizes Varro's description:

> For, first of all, Janus himself opens an approach to receiving seed [*aditum aperit recipiendo semini*], when an embryo is conceived. It is from there that all those divine works take their beginning, distributed bit by bit to little deities. Saturn is there too, because of the seed [*semen*] itself. There too is Liber, who relieves the male of seed by pouring it out [*marem effuso semine liberat*]. There is also Libera, whom they also call Venus, who confers this same benefit upon the female, so that even she too will feel relief in the emission of seed [*ut etiam ipsa emisso semine liberetur*].[22]

Pagans specified other deities watching over sexual reproduction and bodily maturation, but Janus' "door" performs the passive function of *receiving* Saturn's *semen*. "Door" for the ancients was a euphemism for both *vagina* and *anus*.[23] So, by claiming, as Augustine does, that "Janus supplies an approach [*aditum*] and door [*ianuam*], so to speak, for *semen*" and that " 'select' Saturn supplies *semen* itself,"[24] Varro enables the interpretation that Janus provides an orifice for Saturn's *semen*.

While we might imagine Janus as opening mother earth or a woman's vagina to receive *semen*,[25] the traditional pairing of Janus and Saturn suggests another interpretion. The pairing of two male deities, Janus and Saturn, and Janus' possession of a "backdoor" (*posticum, postica*[26])—i.e., in his double gated shrine—implies an alternative receptacle of seed that is confounded with a mouth. Janus' epithet *Consivius* may have suggested this sexual interpretation.[27] As Augustine suggests, Janus is the *seminis admissor,* "receiver of seed," while Saturn is the *seminis dator vel sator,* the "giver or sower of seed" (*CD.* 7.3). Who produced this fantasy? Ancient pagans, suggests Augustine, men whom he later calls "seekers of every disgrace" (*CD* 7.4); perhaps scholars had already interpreted Janus sexually. Nevertheless, Augustine speaks facetiously about failing to find opprobrium in Janus (*CD* 7.4):

> As for Janus, nothing that would suggest his lack of (sexual) integrity [*probrum*] easily [*non mihi facile*] occurs to me; and perhaps he would have been the type who lived rather innocently and rather removed from crimes and outrages [*innocentius vixerit et a facinoribus flagitiisque remotius*]. In kindness he received exiled Saturn; he divided his kingdom with his guest, so that they founded individual communities—the one the Janiculum, the other Saturnia. But those [pagans] with an appetite for every vice [*omnis dedecoris appetitores*] in the worship of the gods, made him unsightly [*turpem*], whose life they found less unseemly [*minus turpem*] through a monstrous deformity [*monstrosa deformitate*] of his image—by making him now two-faced, now four-faced, two-fold so to speak. Or, since very many "select" deities had lost "face" [*amisserant frontem*] by perpetrating shameful acts [*erubescenda perpetrando*], did they want Janus, perhaps, to appear "more faced" [*frontosior*] as much as he was more innocent?[28]

Like Persius' Janus, Augustine himself looks behind Varro's Janus, knowingly wary of a "pagan" sexual depravity symbolized, yet concealed (screened), by Janus' physical deformity.[29] Augustine feigns his own innocence of this sexual knowledge while insinuating that pagan "seekers of every disgrace" (*omnis dedecoris appetitores*) constructed the "monstrous [moral] deformity"[30] of Janus' two heads as "ugly" compensation for his lack of moral ugliness. Yet, as Augustine had implied, Janus' mouth-anus was open to receiving semen. Janus' two heads suggest his innocent surveillance of his own "face" or dignity (sexual integrity), so that he would have "more face" than other gods, but the faces also provide "cover," concealing moral deviance, or so Augustine seems to imply. Augustine's fantasy of pagans prowling ("cruising") for sex (*appetitores*), even among the gods, makes Janus' dicephaly screen pagan shame—*probrum, facinoribus flagitiisque, turpem, erubescenda.*"[31]

Janus and Fearful Uncertainty: The Author-Reader Relation?

Persius and Augustine partially expose Janus' psychosocial function in Roman elite male subjectivity. His bodily deformity represents not physical, but mental splitting, especially in relations between men, interpreted through male anxiety or fear of "penetrative" criticism. When Ovid appeals to Janus before Germanicus (*F.* 1.63–70, 1.283–89), he also draws precise attention to Janus' two-headedness, as if focusing on this deformity, already noticed at the inauguration (63–88, above). After pondering Janus' dicephaly (89–92, above), Ovid recounts how such contemplation had caused Janus' "appearance"—both his apparition and his form (93–100):

> haec ego cum sumptis agitarem mente tabellis,
>   lucidior visa est quam fuit ante *domus*.
> tum sacer *ancipiti mirandus imagine* Ianus
>   *bina* repens oculis obtulit *ora* meis.
> extimui sensique metu riguisse capillos,
>   et gelidum subito frigore pectus erat.
> ille tenens baculum dextra clavemque sinistra
>   edidit hos nobis ore priore sonos:

> When, after taking up my writing tablets, I was considering such things in my mind, the house appeared brighter than it was. Then holy Janus, a

marvel with his double-headed image, brought to my eyes his paired faces. I was scared out of my mind and felt my hair grow stiff with fear, and my heart went cold with a sudden chill. Holding a staff in his right hand, a key in his left, that [god] issued to me such sounds from his front mouth. . . .

Janus' response follows (101–44). Given that Ovid is representing Janus' apparition, the illumination of the house (*domus,* 89–96) and Ovid's "shocked" stiffened hair are not surprising (97–8); divine epiphanies often inspire fear.[32] Far more surprising are Ovid's continued remarks about Janus' two heads and two mouths (95–96: *tum sacer ancipiti mirandus imagine Ianus/ bina repens oculis obtulit ora meis*). Twoheadedness is the true marvel (*ancipiti mirandus imagine*) "behind" the conventional fear. Anxious curiosity while contemplating Janus' deformity is what prompted Ovid's apparition.

Indeed, Janus' epiphany initiates a "dialogue" between Ovid's fear and inquisitiveness, because Janus' "appearance" answers Ovid's curiosity about deformity and yet augments his fear (stiffening hair, chilling heart, 97–98), resulting in a cognitive dissonance (*haec ego cum sumptis agitarem mente tabellis,* 93). The effects of fear (*extimui,* 97) answer Janus' "appearance." This is, of course, a psychical phenomenon. *Mente* (93) marks the mental medium of Ovid's excitation and the subsequent dialogue of mental voices (transcribed into words, now rendered "audible" by recitation): Janus instructs Ovid, "With fear put aside, poet-seer working on the days, perceive my words *mentally*" ("take my expressions in your mind," *voces percipe mente meas,* 102).[33]

Ovid's fear before Janus' "appearance" may initiate deferred interpretation of the fear that Ovid had expressed before Germanicus in the dedication where he sought the prince's numinous guidance of the poem's "path." Ovid vacated the position of authorial control and sought Germanicus' control of his poem as answer to his fearful uncertaintly. Ovid surrendered to Germancius' *peaceful* mastery, seeking his *"pacified* face" (*pacato voltu,* 3), and prayed, "give yourself to me *placidly*" (*da mihi te placidum,* 17). Now we find that Janus controls access to Peace (*Pax*) within his *placidis tectis* (121) and becomes *pacatus* himself when talking with Ovid (146); As we will see, Janus mediates Peace (285–88) and, standing at the gate of heaven, Janus also mediates prayers to other gods (126–25, 122–44, 171–76; see below). So, what Ovid wants from Germanicus must pass through Janus. Might Janus provide an approach or "door" (so to speak) mediating the uncertainty of the relation between Ovid's relation to his (elite male) readership, especially the ideal reader Germanicus, whom Ovid addresses at the beginning and end of the Janus episode in close association with both Janus and Peace (*otia*, 63–70; *Pax*, 285–88)?[34] Might Janus' (be)hindsight embody Ovid's anxious wariness in his own relation to this Roman audience, especially Germanicus? If Janus serves to mark this wariness, Janus' uncanny dicephaly might "screen" (cover, yet represent) the circumstances of Ovid's own hesitant compositional desires.

The word *domus* at 1.94 helps to "situate" the ideological circumstances of Ovid's encounter with Janus. While interpretable as Ovid's own home, *domus* here more likely refers to the home of a consul just inaugurated, because that is where prominent citizens went to perform their *officium*, specifically the New Year's day *salutatio* before the inaugural ceremony and party afterward. From exile Ovid twice imagines visiting the homes of men elected consuls on their inauguration days (*Ex P.* 4.4, Sextus Pompeius cos. 14 CE; 4.9, Graecinus, cos. suff. 16 CE).[35] Moreover, Ovid wrote those poems during the time he was revising the *Fasti*. But Ovid does not specify a "real" *domus* at 1.94. Rather, he seems to maintain a broader appeal by addressing Janus as doorman at the portal of the celestial palace or house of heaven, a house emblematic of every door of every house of every potential patron. On the other hand, the heavenly house of the Palatine Hill, the *domus Augusta*, was where Augustus had lived as ruler, and was the one that Tiberius inherited in 14 and to which Germanicus was to succeed as heir. The ceremonial circumstances of inauguration day (January 1) entailed a performance of ritual exchanges at houses of patrons—exchanges of New Year's blessings, New Year's gifts (*stenae*), and kisses (*Ex P.* 4.9.13). Janus and Ovid engage in a verbal transaction that conveys the meaning of these exchanges, a kind of literary surrogacy for their face-to-face performance (cf. *Ex P.* 4.9.11–14).

Janus as Primal Fantasy: An Origin of (Male) Subjectivity

Janus' apparition answers Ovid's fundamental question, "What god shall I say you are, biform Janus?" Which is to say, "What do you mean by assuming a biform?" One can see Janus' two heads, but what do they *really* mean? What is the dicephaly of Roman Janus getting at? This *"Che vuoi?"* questions how the anomaly of Janus' two-headedness belongs to the symbolic, divine, dimension of inaugural ceremonies.[36] Persius and Augustine-Varro provided their readers with answers, both lodged in elite male psychosocial hesitancy, reflecting a kind of "hysteria" answering antagonisms between men (envy, rivalry, etc.) and uncertainties about what other men *really* think and want. Again, might Janus' "appearance" in the *Fasti* figure Ovid's uncertainty, as a wavering, distant exile, about what his audience *really* wants and, conversely, his audience's (specifically Germanicus') uncertainty about what Ovid *really* intends, not only by his fantasy of seeing Janus, but also by the unfinished *Fasti* as a fragment of a whole seeking an "answer" from his audience?

How does Ovid's Janus explain his dicephaly? His answer is a fantasy: a reported numinous phenomenon answering Ovid's initial "noumenal" or intellectual curiosity (*F.* 1.101–44). Janus' words merge cosmological myth and autobiography (103–12):

> me Chaos antiqui (nam sum res prisca) vocabant:
>> aspice quam longi temporis acta canam.
> lucidus hic aer et quae tria corpora restant,
>> ignis, aquae, tellus, unus acervus erat.
> ut semel haec rerum secessit lite suarum
>> inque novas abiit massa soluta domos,
> flamma petit altum, propior locus aera cepit,
>> sederunt medio terra fretumque solo.
> tunc ego, qui fueram globus et sine imagine moles,
>> in faciem redii dignaque membra deo.

Me the ancestors used to call "Chaos" (for I am a very ancient thing). See how I sing the events of distant time. The clear Air here and the three bodies that remain—Fire, Waters, and Earth—used to be one heap. When once this mass was dissolved and separated into new houses because of conflict over their affairs, Flame went above; the next spot took the Air; Earth and Sea settled on the ground in the middle. Then I, who had been globular matter without image, had recourse to face and limbs worthy of a god.

Janus here answers Ovid's "*Che vuoi?*" by narrating his own conception, his own birth from Chaos to assume his anomalous physique (111–12). As Slavoj Zizek has stated it, fantasy "always involves an impossible gaze by means of which the subject is already present at the act of his/her own conception."[37] What is so compelling about such "primal fantasy" is that the subject's fantasy gaze is informed by models of birth and development iterated in culture's basic sciences, myths, legends, and traditions. Culture provides the "setting" for the subject's retroactive formation of experience.[38] Janus' narrative response to "What does your dicephaly *really* mean?" aligns Janus' culturally informed, "autobiographical," tale of his own "birth" (what's behind Janus' "personae" or personality) with a cosmological narrative from ancient physical science merged with a Romanized mythology of the origin of gods. As Barchiesi has emphasized, Janus alludes to Hesiod's epic "Birth of the Gods" (*Theogonia*) as well as Callimachus' elegiac poem on "Origins" (*Aitia*).[39] Ovid's Janus, as Chaos (a *res antiqua* revealing acts of distant time, 103–4), resituates the physics and mythology of cosmic birth in terms of a Roman symbolic tradition. I will return below to this Romanization of universal origin.

But first we should note that Janus' "gaze" at his own birth answers Ovid's "*Che vuoi?*" by "getting behind himself," as if he could in memory travel back before his genesis to witness his birth. Janus provides his before and his after "shots," two "photographic" images, so to speak, testifying to a change made by a mysterious "cutting" segregating elements in a scene of antagonism (*lite*, 107). His "before" figures a *Chaos* (103), an *acervus* or heap of bodies (*corpora* 105), a "mass" (*massa* 108), a globular pile (*ego, qui fueram globus et sine imagine moles*, 111)—an orgy of elements, a collective. His "after" depicts articulated, "properly" spaced, ranked, and regimented *corpora* (105–6, 109–10), a scene showing him with "face and limbs worthy of a god" (*in faciem redii dignaque membra deo*, 112), both a cosmological and "cosmetological" *imago* (111), a portrait (or mask) screening him now as worthy of viewing. But whose gaze is this? For whose gaze was the "after" imago formed? Who judges the propriety of Janus' "after," his trim new body? For whose gaze was the raw material separated into "seemly" design? Was it for Janus himself? This question poses a humorous contrast between Janus' self-view and Ovid's view of him as external spectacle of deformity. For some other *deus* (112)?[40] Perhaps it does not matter, because antagonism, *lis* (107), is the genuine origin of all appearances, an origin of a whole "world" of relations.

One consequence of "antagonism" as origin of Janus' dicephaly is that as a fantasy Janus does not portray an escape from regulation or some overthrow of the status quo. Quite the contrary, his birth story retroactively imagines what amounts to Law and Order (the symbolic order of things) imposes upon the mass(es), upon what "I" was "before me," to created "me" as subject. Thus, Janus entered the Symbolic order (as do all subjects). The "retroactivity" of Janus' narrative gaze upon his own "conception" enables (be)hindsight, reflexivity that is somatized in two-headedness, helping him conceive the scene of his own conception, a primal (primordial) fantasy of origin.[41] Yet Janus' humorous understatement confesses that he retains a latently chaotic element (113): "Even now, as a small mark of my formerly confused figure, what is before on me and what is behind on me seems the same [*idem*]." *Idem*, the base word for "identity," marks a continuation of elemental "confusion" in Janus that links his "before" to his "after." This "identity" is, however, an underlying persistence of former uncertainty, despite manifest change, confusion that resists periodizing or historicizing before and behind (after) as "facets" of Janus.

Janus' narrative response to Ovid's *"Che vuoi?"* encourages a retroactive trajectory of reading. Re-read, the inauguration presented prior to Janus' appearance, but occurring logically after his "birth," anticipates the antagonism in the narration of the cause of Janus' birth. As noted above, that ritual scene articulates a sameness in the coloration and harmonization of the senses at the same time as the ritual outcome is the installation of Roman authority (empire) at the origin of the Roman year (Janus, the *anni origo*, 65). Antagonism was also latent at the inauguration (73, *lis* in the courts and markets of the Forum Romanum), but it was suppressed for the sake of a ceremony of governance. What both the inauguration and Janus' narration of his own birth do is articulate the ceremonial "birth" of Roman Law and Order (consuls) and national feeling, a "proper" enjoyment (felicity). The ceremonial merger of Law and Enjoyment recreate Roman (male) subjectivity at the ambivalent scene of Roman harmony, yet antagonism and uncertainty (cf. the Forum)—poised between ordered governance and confused threatening rabble—at the site of division between "before" (the old year, chaos) and "after" (the new Year, cosmos).

Potential antagonism or conflict also governs Janus' symbolism for everyday social exchanges. We have seen that antagonism (*lis*, 107), which individuated Janus' "face(s)" and his sense of worth in acquiring "face," caused elements to separate (*secessit, abiit*) into "houses" (*domos*, 107–8). Janus' double face (111–12) now enables his role (*officium*) as interface between the *domos* or houses (115–16, 125–26, and 133–46). His unresolved facial deformity offers an ambivalent or double response toward social antagonism.[42] Janus' two faces emerged precisely to address (in bodily fantasy) the shifting, closing and opening, of relations between the elemental *domi* of the cosmos (117–18). As Janus explains it, with his two faces, he has the job and authority (*officium*,

115–20, esp. 116; 126) of guarding the vast universe and its axis or "hinge" (*cardo*). He stands at a major seam or fissure of universal structure, at the doors of Heaven (125, 139–40). Janus' spectral dicephaly sutures the split. He conceals the hostilities, yet there is sometimes passage through Janus: Jupiter, ruler of the universe, comes and goes via Janus at heaven's gate (126). His duty as guard at the interface between heaven and earth is similar to that of doors and doormen at mortal thresholds (133–46) controlling interpenetration even between domestic (private) space of the *domus* and the public sphere (136–37). As we have seen, Ovid addresses Janus at some *domus*, whether material or symbolic (93–94, above)

Ovid, Janus, and (Homo)social Intercourse

In the context of the New Year's *salutatio*, Ovid addresses Janus, the doorman, to secure social relations through exchange of symbols or "token" discourse on New Year's Day. Ovid's queries and Janus' explanations of the customary holiday blessings and gift exchanges (*strenae*) exact, yet contract, "meaning" not only for relations between men generally, but also for Ovid's poem specifically. The token discourse between Ovid and Janus stations the text as a token passed within the same homosocial economy that it describes.

Ovid is able to develop this "economy" by drawing upon Janus' associations with banking in Rome and by obliquely developing the god's function as "broker" not only of mortal relations with gods, but also of relations between men. Consider how the two began to interact after Janus had finished his initial speech (145–48):

> [Janus] had spoken: and by his facial expression, he agreed that he would not be difficult with me if I wanted to ask (for) more. I gathered courage, and, and, without terror, thanked the god, and, *staring at the ground*, I spoke more words. . . . [43]

"More" (*plura*, 145 and 148) is thematic. Ovid performs its meaning in the length of the first question that he poses to the god. Ovid asks a two-line question (149–50), but appends a ten-line commentary (151–60) that luxuriantly describes the emergence of buds, grasses, and young animals in spring as indicating a natural beginning of the year.

Ovid's earthward gaze while describing spring seems a gesture of modesty before the powerful deity, suggesting "humility" (or human affinity for the "lower" elements in nature such as the *humus* or earth), but it may betray his thematic interest in the sexuality and fertility of nature then developed in his commentary.[44] Janus' brief response rebuffs Ovid's long commentary (161–64):

> I had made inquiry at length [*multis (verbis)*]; not lingering at length [*non multis moratus*], he [Janus] put his words into two verses like this:

> "Its shortest day [*bruma*] is the first of the new sun and the most recent of the old sun: Phoebus and the year follow the same principle."[45]

Ovid and Janus thus offer conflicting approaches to the year's beginning. Ovid imagines a shift of New Year to spring, observing the year's renewal in the fertility of the earth. At the spring planting, the ground isn't closed over with icy hardness and so allows penetration (*patitur*) by the plow blade (159–60).[46] Undeterred, however, by Ovid's lengthy ecphrasis of spring, the god *curtly* asserts a less sensual, more sterile, and mathematically precise design—the year and the sun begin their course together at midwinter on the *shortest* day of the year (*bruma*, from *brevissima*).[47]

From the next exchange we learn in retrospect that this initial *conflict* between Ovid and Janus is symbolic (165–70) because Ovid next wonders why New Year's Day is not without *antagonism* (*cur non sine litibus esset/ prima dies*, 165–66), as if he had just experienced conflict with Janus. Janus explains that samples of verbal conflict are "performed" on New Year's Day as a "libation" (*quisque suas artes ob idem delibat agendo*), a gesture to avoid an omen of inactivity (*inertia*) for the whole year (note the pun on *ars* and *iners*, 167–68). Ovid's ecphrasis of spring makes an offering of his own craft—*suas artes* (*his solitum opus*, 170), the type of poetry that will appear later in the *Fasti*, such as ecphrases of spring in March (by Mars) and April (praising Venus).[48] Janus' "epigram" provides a sample of another *ars*, astronomy in the brief epigrams that will periodically appear in the poem. The "conflict" between Ovid and Janus anticipates, by token gesture, conflicting meanings in the rest of the *Fasti*.

Yet, this "token" of friendly antagonism is merely a subtype of other auspicious exchanges between men on New Year's Day. Men also exchanged blessings and gifts to symbolize enjoyment of felicity, expressing mutual yet competitive (emulous) desire for prosperity in daily social and economic relations. The ritual exchanges prompt attention to the libidinal quality of relations between men, i.e., a desire for cooperative, yet competitive, relations between each other.

Janus' role as "doorman" at the gate of heaven and as "broker" of desire is crucial to the operation of this "economy." Janus proclaims that mortal prayers, good wishes, and other "offerings"—all expressing mortal "desires"—must pass by or through him—i.e., his double-door shrine or "mouths"—before even reaching other intended deities. These gods are imagined to reside beyond the gate in the "heavenly palace" (*caelestis aula*) that Janus says he watches (*F.* 1.133–44).[49] In this regard, Janus' office (*officium*, 1.115–26) is a post not unlike that of men in proximity to the imperial family who brokered access to the *aula* or court of the emperor and his family. Offers of gifts (bribes) open access to the *domus*—the "private," yet politically powerful, domain of the emperor (*domus Augusta*) or other elite patrons.[50] Consequently, the *strenae* (New Year's gifts[51]) discussed by Janus and Ovid are exchanged within a libidinal economy that Janus mediates in a manner like that of the imperial court (cf. Janus as doorman at the *aula caelestis*), a grand version of patronage conducted at the homes of many elites. The rituals of patronage include the *salutatio* at the door.

Cash Gifts and the Economy of Desire

Besides kindly prayers or blessings for divine favor (*alternas preces*, 175–82), the *strenae* (gifts) that Janus and Ovid overtly discuss include sweet foods (dates, figs, and honey, 185–88) and a *stips*, a cash donation of coins (189–26). When Ovid asks why this *stips* is exchanged (189–90), Janus describes how money has a sweetness, like the dates and honey (191–94) that lure a kind of alimentary desire (195–96):

> In time, the love grew which now is the greatest—that *for possessions* [*amor habendi*]: it hardly has room to advance further.[52]

The language *tempore crevit amor* (1.195) is the same as that describing the love between Pyramus and Thisbe (*Met.* 4.60). Mad lust for wealth (*opum furiosa cupido*) shapes Janus' version of Roman economic history (1.211–12):

> Both wealth and the mad lust for wealth grew [*opum furiosa cupido*], and, though people may possess very many things, they seek more [*plura*].[53]

Janus' economic moralizing is standard in Roman satire and historiography,[54] to decry degradation of values through the corrupting influence of new wealth from empire. Yet, whatever indignation one may
discern in Janus' explanation, he is inconsistent or ambivalent about it.
After all, his two faces look backward to ancient parsimony, and forward to future gain.

However, even Janus' chronology of greed's development is inconsistent. He says that even in the age of Saturn (1.194)—traditionally, a
nostalgic age of simple farming and virtuous poverty[55]—he hardly
knew anyone who did not think profits (*lucra*) were sweet (*dulcia*).[56] At
the same time, Janus also describes a time of simple poverty when
Romulus ruled or when the early consuls drove a plow like everyone
else (197–98). Poverty and agricultural simplicity are arch symbols of
communitas, i.e., a lack of class distinction and shared understanding
between men—a communal feeling invoked by the inauguration of the
new year (see *F.* 1.199–209).[57]

However, Janus hints at greed's presence even during the archaic
period of simple agricultural poverty (suggestive of self-restraint)
when he uses lexical witticisms to situate the origin of Roman financial
language within the agricultural milieu.[58] These figures indicate perhaps ideological stakes in representing the agricultural, therefore virtuous, origins of wealth (e.g., *pecunia*, "money," derives from *pecus*,
"herd"). Janus' strong association with banking and the merchant
economy suggest otherwise.[59] Here, we see how Janus' two heads symbolize his ability to "screen" the "nature and causes of wealth" by
inserting opposing moral and economic values into each other, revers-
ing the diachronic order of values in a quite inconsistent, synchronic
presentation of his own libidinal conflict. Janus' "conflict of values"
reaches a climax when he describes a "diseased" desire of wealth in
conspicuous consumption (1.209–18):

Yet, after the Fortune of this place raised its head and Rome reached
[*tetigit*] the gods by the top of her head, both wealth and a furious desire
of wealth grew, and, although people possess very much, they seek out
more. People compete [*certant*] to find out how they may consume, and
how to get it again once it's consumed, and these spirals [*vices*] are nour-
ishment for vices [*vitiis*]: In this way seawater with which a belly has
been swollen is thirsted for more when it's been drunk more. Now values
are in the valuable: economic status [*census*] gets (you) offices [*honores*], it
gets (you) connections [*amicitias*]. In anything, the poor man is
despised.[60]

The imagery of Rome desiring and "touching" (*tetigit*) the gods mirrors the envious rivalry among men in conspicuous consumption. Competition (*certant*) produces wealth and privilege, which lead to greater and greater desire for wealth and social distinctions. Essential to all this wrangling is competitive, yet mimetic, desire between men for the same goal—wealth and status distinction or *census* (217). While Janus medicalizes excess desire as morbid, uncontrolled, "thirst" (215–16),[61] the resulting wealth produces a social mobility that Janus himself enjoys (see below), although it contradicts his nostalgic idealization of simple poverty among the early elite.[62] As Janus remarks, wealth or census status (social class) produces political offices and friends in the right places (*honores* and *amicitias*, 217–18).

Janus realizes, however, that he has strayed from Ovid's question—why coins are given as New Year's gifts (219–20)—precisely while he is commenting on wealth as social leverage (the transformation of economic into social capital). So, Janus now refocuses upon the *stips*, the coins, as an omen of a prosperous New Year.[63] But Janus digresses again, remarking that there are two types of coins used as *stips*—old bronze types and new gold ones. The two metals again represent a conflict of values similar to the earlier discussion and similar to, yet different from, the traditional Hesiodic Golden and Bronze ages. Here the conflict is between two types of nobility—nobility of idealized values (agricultural simplicity and poverty) symbolized by the cheaper old bronze coin, and a nobility of wealth symbolized by the newer gold coin. Old bronzes (the *as*, probably bearing the double head of Janus on its obverse and a ship's prow on the reverse; 229–34) recall the good old days, while the newer gold coins (*aureus*) evoke the contemporary influx of wealth.

But historicization of ethics is not fully resolved for Janus, who says that, for the sake of good omen, he accepts either coin; indeed, the modern gold coin grants *better* omen (221–22). In other words, in his brokerage of access to gods, omens are no different from political offices and friendships; more cash buys more access. It is here, as a broker of access to divine favor through two different monetary standards, that Janus most vividly implicates himself in libidinal antagonism. Janus vacillates between the public rhetoric of "traditional values" (e.g., *paupertas*) and his practical self-interest in promoting a better image of himself among other gods and men (221–26):

> They once used to give bronzes: now the omen is better in the gold, and
> the defeated old coinage has yielded to the new. The temple is delighting

me too—the gold one—although I approve of the ancient one: *the grandiosity [of the golden ones] suits a god.* I praise the ancients, but I find our era gainful: yet, either custom is equally worth cultivating.[64]

Two-headed Janus has a highly ambivalent desire for dignity. But gold coins and a newly rebuilt gold temple[65] bolster Janus' *maiestas*—his grandiose image proper to his godhood (1.224).[66] Indeed, we have already seen that Janus was self-conscious about his appearance and social role: as he shifted from Chaos to Cosmos, he acquired "face and limbs worthy of a god" (1.112). He also derives esteem from his doorman's position before heaven's palace (*foribus caeli*, 125; *caelestis ianitor aulae*, 139): "Jupiter himself comes and goes by my office" (Janus' control of heaven's *aditus* and *limina*, 1.126, 175–76).

In short, Janus is quite aware of competition between men—the investments that they make in friendship with each other at the same time as they compete for status—and he knows how he can benefit in the process. Thus, Janus' explanation associates the *stips* with these latent competitive desires hidden beneath an outward show of "communitas," symbolized by free-flowing gift-exchange on New Year's Day.

Janus-head coins with a ship's prow on the reverse, a very old, common type, were often used for the New Year's *strena*. However, the Janus-head on the obverse and the ship's prow on the reverse make them an emblem situating homosocial relations at the center of Rome's libidinal economy. Ovid asks precisely about the "impressions" stamped on the coins (1.229–30): "I've learned many things indeed, but why has a ship-form been embossed on one side of the bronze and on the other a two-headed form?" What are apparently two questions pertain to one dynamic, the *relationship* between Janus' dicephaly and the ship. Janus' two-headed image hardly awaited Janus' interpretation (231). Ovid's question must pursue the relationship between the ship and the Janus-obverse (between "two sides of the same coin") that is explicable through the *relationship* between Janus and Saturn (233–54).

In fact, Janus says that posterity stamped the prow on the coin "witnessing to the advent of the divine guest" (239–40). Moreover, Janus emphasizes that Saturn was an exile (*pererrata . . . orbe*, 234), and whereas Jupiter, his son, had expelled him from heaven, Janus received him (*hac ego Saturnum memini tellure receptum*, 235). Saturn "hides" in Latium (from *latere*, to hide, also at Verg. *Aen.*8.322; Serv. *ad loc.*). In other accounts, Janus even shares his rule at the site of Rome, with Saturn settling on the hill that will become the Capitoline and he on the Janiculum. Saturn in turn teaches inhabitants seed-planting and harvesting (cf. his sickle; *falcifer, F.* 1.234) and minting of coinage. Then, after Saturn's departure, Janus (*F.* 1.239 reads *posteritas*) stamped a coin bearing images commemorating their relationship—Janus double-head and a ship's prow.[67] Ovid's Janus alludes broadly to this background by emphasizing his reception of the exiled Saturn into *hospitium,* i.e., as *hospes* (*hospitis adventum testificata dei,* 240).[68]

The coin functions as *token* or proof of this *hospitium: hospitis adventum testificata dei* (cf. 240). This implies that Janus' double-headed coin that was given as *strena*—omen of goodwill—on New Year's also functions as a "symbol" or *sumbolon* (σύμβολον; Latin, *tessera hospitalis*) of this bond, an object whose two halves constitute a symbol of a bond. The partners broke the *sumbolon* into two parts; each partner retained his half as proof of belonging to the guest-friendship or other contract. There is some evidence that coins sometimes provided these tokens. Janus-headed coins were definitely halved, but usually to produce small change rather than explicitly to form a bond. The split Janus-head enabled the halving, each part bearing one of Janus' faces. Horace may allude to the "halving" of coins when he uses financial language addressing the ship (*navis*) carrying away Vergil on his way to Greece, calling Vergil *animae dimidium meae,* "one-half of my soul" *creditum,* "credited," to the ship (Hor. *Odes* 1.3.5–8).[69] But even the halving of coins to make small change attests, in material abstraction, participation in a shared symbolic system. This practice of halving coinage shows how the market functions as a scene of unconscious "social thought" prior to (conscious) social thought, particularly in the ideal of cash as symbolic of status position. The dialogue between Ovid and Janus exposes elements of this material abstraction of social thinking.[70]

The New Year's *strena* was also important to imperial ideology, specifically to the relation between Augustus and the people. On New Year's during the reign of Augustus people of all social orders used to donate to him a *strena* on the Capitoline Hill, even when he was absent from Rome. From that very large sum of cash, Augustus then purchased expensive statues of deities that were erected at crossroad shrines dedicated to the *Lares et Genius Augusti,* protective deities drawn directly from the Domus Augusta but distributed throughout the city, drawing the city into the metaphor of one "household." Tiberius had an entirely different attitude toward the New Year's *strena* and the reciprocity its gift giving required; Tiberius limited the gift giving to only one day, January 1, and he stayed away from Rome on

New Year's Day to avoid taking any *strena* and having to *re*pay it in multiples, as Augustus had.[71]

A Sweet Taste in Your Mouth: Janus and Oral Exchange

Sweet foods were a kind of *strena*, highlighting another figurative representation of desire in the Janus episode, that of oral consumption. As we will see, oral consumption—eating—alludes to the mouth and the palate, metaphors that pagans offered to explain the structures of both the cosmos and of Janus' two faces (throat and mouth framing the oral cavity). At the same time, Ovid's interaction with Janus implicates a sensuality within these cosmic references. This sensuality highlights a figurative interplay between mouths—tongues, tastes, oral expressions, and oral incorporations.[72]

Oral consumption of sweets serves as an *omen* for the year in an alimentary analogy. Ovid had questioned Janus about these sweets (*dulcia*) before asking about the *stips* (185–88):

> I [Ovid] said, "What's the intent of giving the date, wrinkled fig, and the light-colored honey in a white jar?" He said, "omen is the reason," so that the sweet flavor may follow events and the year may finish the path begun.

Janus' analogy between the sweet taste of the foods and the year's "journey" (*ut res sapor ille sequatur/ et peragat coeptum dulcis ut annus iter*) mimics Ovid's prayer that Germanicus guide Ovid's reins so that "under your auspices the year may go felicitously (*auspice te felix totus ut annus eat*, 26). Of course, the proper path (*iter*) of sweets is alimentary: this meaning—that food travels the path it began—is implied by the hyperbaton of *et peragat* (after *sequatur*) and *dulcis* (modifying *sapor*). Following this analogy, the course of the year would be comparable to the digestive tract (*iter*). As we have seen, Janus also uses alimentation (thirst) as a metaphor for the desire and consumption of cash (1.213–16[73]). Thus, the *strenae*, whether sweets or coins, entice an "appetite" for "consumption." Food and cash gifts are appetizers that symbolically indulge human digestion to prefigure prosperity at the "mouth" or doors of Janus.

Janus may have already associated this alimentary symbolism with ritual at his door/mouth. At 1.125–32, Janus says a priest (*sacerdos*, 127, *rex sacrorum* perhaps) offers him seed cakes (*liba*) and salted grain (*farraque mixta sale,* 128), and gives him ceremonial epithets referring to his alternate "opening" and "closing" (1.125–32). Janus claims these epithets are funny (*nomina ridebis,* 129). What is the joke? The priest seems to insert (*imponit,* "put in," 128) the seed cakes and salted, ground grain-seed (*mola salsa*) into his "mouth"/gate. Then Janus opens and closes. "Open" (*Patulcius*) and "Closed" (*Clusius*) are rustic, ritual epithets (cf. *rudis illa vetustas,* 131) which seem jokingly to refer to chewing (opening-closing the mouth/gate) in "alternate functions" (*alternas vices*).[74] Thus, Janus has earlier referred to his own "ritual" consumption. Yet, there is another interpretation: the possible insertion of *semina* or seeds—cf. Varro's symbolic interpretation (ap. Augustine) for Janus. The grains of *mola salsa* inserted into Janus are *semina,* seeds, symbolic of human and agricultural fertility. Janus opens to receive the seeds in the cakes and in the salted grain, much as Varro describes Janus as the receiver of Saturn's seed (*semen*). Ominous of fertility, these seeds intimate sexuality and reproductive felicity.[75]

Aside from the seed offerings, men give Janus two other consumable goods, wine and incense. When Ovid asks about these, he learns that they broker an entrance for men's prayers to the celestial palace (1.171–77), where Janus stands watch (*praesideo foribus caeli,* 1.125; *caelestis ianior aulae,* 1.139). The offerings create an opening for desires verbalized in prayers, which explains why, at the end of Ovid's *vota pro salute* (65–69), he urges Janus, " . . . unbolt the bright temples [*templa*] with your nod" (70).

This opening of *templa* for entrance of prayers—mortal desires—entails attention to sounds of sacrifice in ritual space void of conflict (*F.* 1.71–74), while fires glow on hearths to burn incense (75–78). Here the altar fire issues a crackling noise and sweet smell (75–76) and a quavering beam of light. These sensations convey mortal prayers in burnt incense to the gold-ornamented temples (77–78). The event communicates through auditory puns in ritual form. The fire's tongue-like articulations of light and sound "verbalize" (*verberat,* "whip," but cf. *verba,* "words") mortal prayers into the gold/ears (*aurum-aures*) of divine temples, as if, via similarity of sound, "temples" of stone make resonate the "temples" of mortal minds (cf. Lucr., *De rerum natura* 5.103, *in pectus templaque mentis*) whose desires are transferred to gods via divine *aures* or "ears," suggested by the *aurum* or "gold" of the shrines. Ovid returns to this semiotic transformation of prayer at 175–82, where he asks Janus:

"But why are joyful expressions spoken on your Kalends, and why do we give and receive reciprocal prayers?"

Then, leaning upon his cane [*baculo*], which he was wielding in his right hand, he said:

"Omens are usually in beginnings. You turn your anxious ears [*aures*] to the first utterances, and an augur interprets the bird that's first seen. Temples [*templa*] and ears [*aures*] of the gods are open [i.e., on the Kalends of January] and no tongue conceives impotent prayers; *words have weight* [*dictaque pondus habent*]."

As Frazer noted, Ovid here refers to a mode of divination known as "cledonism," from the Greek κλήδων, "an omen or presage contained in a word or sound." According to Cicero (*De div.* 1.102–4) such omens involve "telling" aural wordplays that adumbrate alternate latent meaning within events, not unlike those in the opening inaugural setting (*aurum/aures* and *templa* of heaven, earth, and mind).[76] We have already seen Janus use such aural wordplays in his economic history to contrast nostalgic poverty and lust for wealth. Indeed, in the last couplet (183–84), Janus constructs a verbal omen in the relationship between tongue (*lingua*, 181) and ear (*aures*, 181), and describes "ears" and "temples" (*templa*) as "open" to ominous sound or words.

These "ominous" prayers for prosperity possess a type of fertility (181–82). On Janus' Kalends (New Year's), the tongue does not "conceive" ineffective prayers (*nec lingua caducas/ concipit ulla preces*, 181–82). On the Kalends of January, words have weight (*pondus*). *Concipit* can refer to reproductive and cognitive conception.[77] So while *pondus* alludes to the "weight" of blessings exchanged at New Year's, *concipit* suggests that this weight "carries," in part, a colloquially "pregnant" meaning[78]—especially as those blessings, like the following gifts, seek fertility and prosperity. In other words, in ritual thinking, such prayers and blessings have cognitive and divine resonance as they "seed" mortal and divine minds with prosperous and prospering attitudes.

Touching and the Kiss

The social function of exchanging blessings on New Year's is confirmed by Ovid's response to the god, where he says, "I 'touched,' not the god, but his words." This language of "touch" suggests Ovid's emotional attraction to what Janus has said, that language has ominous *pondus*, weight or substance (183–84):

Janus stopped [speaking]. I did not leave a long silence, but I touched
upon [*tetigi*] his final words with my own.[79]

Ovid's follow-up question engages Janus reciprocally (*verbis . . . verba
meis*, 184) beginning just after or simultaneously with the end of Janus'
statement (*nec longa silentia feci*, 183). Ovid "touched" Janus' words
(*tetigi*, 184). *Tetigi* attributes a tactile connotation to Ovid's verbal relation to Janus. The word *tango* could suggest sexual or sensuous contact
as used, for example, by Propertius and Ovid.[80]

Janus has already alluded to the receptivity of his "temples" to
blessings—emphasizing presumably his mouth/gate—and has
marked the weighty substance of words (181–84). In his following
question, Ovid "touches upon" Janus' suggestion of oral omens, referring to sweet flavor (*sapor*, 185–89). Might the verbal exchange between
Ovid and Janus allude to potential oral communication between them,
but metaphorically passed between mouths, by figurative extension
from words? Ovid and Janus become more relaxed with each other
through the ritual exchange of words between them. However, kisses
also belonged to everyday relations between men. At the morning
greeting or *salutatio*, clients, but also relatively equal "friends" (*amici*),
would go to the homes of elite men (potential patrons and friends) to
await the opening of the doors in the morning, when they would
exchange wishes for *salus* (welfare, cf. *salutatio*). Ovid imagines going to
Graecinus' home and greeting him with a kiss on the day of his inauguration as consul (*Ex P.* 4.9.13). Among "friends" (*amici*), an exchange
of kisses on the mouth attended this exchange of gifts and blessings.
The kiss distinguished levels of friendship, distinguishing them from
the more distanced persons.[81]

This everyday ritual had its annual "origin" on New Year's Day.
That day's *salutatio* performed an omen for good relations for the
whole year. The exchange of *strenae*, both sweets and coins, on that day
was combined with kisses and utterance of blessings (cf. *salutatio*).
Exchanges of these "sweeteners" of homosocial relations are precisely
the topics of discussion between Ovid and Janus. But if kissing was a
common social ritual, and Ovid is alluding to it, why is he so coy?
Tiberius' prohibition of the daily kisses (*cotidiana oscula*) might explain
it in part. Suetonius introduces it in the same sentence with Tiberius'
limiting the *strena* to one day (Suet. *Tib.* 34). Both regulations function
together with Tiberius' notorious parsimony in funding public games
to portray him as misanthropic.[82] Moreover, Ovid has repeatedly
referred to Janus' mouth. The first references occur precisely at the

moment of theophany (95–6):

> tum sacer *ancipiti* mirandus *imagine* Ianus
> *bina* repens oculis obtulit *ora* meis.

And (99–100):

> ille tenens baculum dextra clausaque sinistra
> edidit hos nobis *ore priore* sonos.

Perhaps these are references to Janus' faces, but these faces have mouths (*ora*) producing sound, oral speech. Janus himself indirectly refers to his mouth as orifice of oral consumption, rather than speech, at 127–32 (above).

But what is most important is Ovid's intimate focus of narration upon the "tactile" nature of words (above) and upon Janus' lips. At *Fasti* 1.253–56, precisely at the interchange between Janus' words and Ovid's, there is ambiguity about lips and where or how they are "pressed":

> "nil mihi cum bello: pacem postesque tuebar,
>   et," clavem ostendens, "haec" ait "arma gero."
> *presserat ora* deus. tunc sic ego *nostra resolvi,*
>   voce mea voces eliciente dei.

> He [Janus] said, "I used to have nothing to do with war: peace and posts I used to watch, and," showing me his key, "such are the weapons I wield." The god had *pressed his lips.* Then, in this way, I *loosened mine,* my voice luring out the statements of the god.

True, the poet is orchestrating a shift in speaker, from Janus to Ovid: Janus "had closed his mouth" and Ovid "opened his own." Pressing his upper to his lower lip would make sense for closure of Janus' mouth (*presserat ora deus,* 255). But this is not exactly what Ovid says. Why did the poet write *presserat* ("had pressed") and not *clauserat* ("had closed") if that is precisely what he meant? Imprecision enables semantic ambiguity. After Janus had pressed his *ora,* mouth or lips, Ovid relaxed or opened (*resolvi*) his own mouth in the interchange between them.[83] The oral exchange is, of course, a metaphor representing the divine inspiration of the poet. Ovid seems to appropriate those figures that Propertius deploys in elegy 3.3, where the elegist in a

dream of Helicon places his small mouth on the large gushing fountains from which the epic poet Ennius drank (3.3.5–6); but after
Calliope "touches" him and orally instructs him (37–38, 39–50), she
trickles water from the aqueduct of the elegiac poet Philetas into the
elegist's mouth (3.3.51–52).

So, in overlapping his words with Janus' while asking about the
sweets, Ovid alludes to oral exchanges between men, but symbolically
transacted with Janus as divine "source" and model. But Ovid intimates these divine kisses for a special aim, literary production.[84] The
sweet taste of honey, dates, and figs, as well as "sweet" words, would
have been on the lips (*ora*) of men as they performed ritual exchanges
on New Year's Day.[85]

Heads or Tales?

Endowed with rich associations with watercourses, Janus could access
"underground" channels covered by pavement in the Forum
Romanum, and then cause that water to seethe up from below the
market surface. These hydraulics enable Ovid to appropriate the gate-
way shrine of the two-headed god figuratively as a "primal" (first)
source of poetic inspiration (1.255–76).[86] So while remaining an "interface" between the poet and his elite male audience, Janus models for
Ovid a latent "art" of seething explosiveness that Ovid may then
"mouth" as inspiration. One might imagine the inspirational transfer
occurring via the metaphor of the "kiss" suggested above. Janus' art of
producing seething poetic water (268) would then pass from Janus'
mouth to Ovid's (cf. reported dialogue), affecting the exile's poetry
with an oscillating uncertainty between antagonism and cooperation,
aggressivity and passivity (cf. passive aggression).

Janus' underground watercourse "surfaces" thematically after
Janus nostalgically laments[87] lost enjoyment of the Golden-Age community, when gods, including Saturn, still mingled on earth with
humans (243–50) and Shame was guiding the people instead of fear
and violence (*proque metu . . . sine vi*, 251); rules were unecessary (252).
Janus says (253–54): "I had nothing to do with war [*nihil mihi cum
bello*]: I used to protect peace [*Pax*] and the doorposts, and," showing
his key [*clavem*], " I wield such weapons as these" [*haec . . . arma gero*].
Janus does display a "weapon" (*arma*), his key (254). Implicitly, the key
symbolizes peace, not war. But how can his key function as a weapon
(*arma*)? Ovid's following question (257–58) seems strategically to "elic-

it" (*voce mea voces eliciente dei*, 256) from Janus a response partially contradicting his own peaceful pose (255–62).

Janus then digressively answers Ovid, reportedly by recounting the legend of the Sabine War and Tarpeia, of a fickle watchman who betrayed the secret entry or gate to the fortress. Janus ascribes desire for jewelry (armbands) as Tarpeia's motive, but Propertius (4.4) had made Tarpeia's motive lust for the Sabine chief, Titus Tatius, and shaped the story after a *paraclausithyron*, an erotic scene of a locked door (the city gate), here penetrated by Tatius.[88] After Propertius 4.4, mention of Tarpeia would easily have evoked his ordering of the tale around "the warfare of love" metaphor, and perhaps would influence how readers would interpret Janus' defense of his impenetrability against Tatius' *arma*, which Ovid directly quotes (263–76):[89]

"inde, velut nunc est, per quem descenditis," inquit
    "arduus in valles per fora clivus erat.
et iam contigerat portam, Saturnia cuius
    dempserat oppositas invidiosa seras;
cum tanto veritus committere numine pugnam,
    ipse meae movi callidus *artis opus*,
*ora*que, qua pollens ope sum, *fontana reclusi*,
    sumque repentinas *eiaculatus* aquas.
ante tamen madidis subieci *sulpura* venis,
    clauderet ut Tatio fervidus umor iter.
cuius ut utilitas pulsis percepta Sabinis,
    quae fuerat, tuto reddita forma loco est;
ara mihi posita est parvo coniuncta sacello:
    haec adolet flammis cum strue farra suis."

"From there," he said, "there was a steep path just as now through the forums by which you descend into the valley. And already he had come into contact with the gate, the opposed bolts of which the envious daughter of Saturn had removed. Fearing to join battle with so great a deity, I cleverly set in motion the work of my art: I unlocked my fountain's orifices, in which resource I'm powerful. And I suddenly shot out water. But first, I cast sulfur in the watery channels so that seething water would close off Tatius' pathway. When its effectiveness had been perceived in driving away the Sabines, the form that had existed earlier was returned to the secured location; an altar was placed next to a small shrine: with its flames this [altar] burns and smells of grain and cake."

Here, Janus boasts an altar erected beside his small shrine to honor his participation in the Sabine War (275–76), when his key functioned as his weapon: it opened his gate/mouth to spew sulfuric waters that blocked hostile entry through his gate (perhaps across the forum, the *Porta Ianualis*), which Saturn's daughter (Juno) had opened.[90]

Interpreted through the narrative frame of the Tarpeia story and the sexual metaphor of doors or gates, Janus' aggressive expulsion of sulfurous water implies a potentially scatological self-defense. Fortress gates were often eroticized as vulnerable points of entry into the fantasized "body" of the city.[91] While in Greek or Latin "gate" or "door" could euphemistically mean "vagina," in Latin usage "gate" more often referred to the anus or *culus*.[92] Ovid's dialogue with Janus jestingly implies anxious associations between *ianus* and anus; Andrew Wallace-Hadrill has observed a possible trend in ancient usage away from the older word *fornix* in favor of *arcus* or *ianus*, due to popular salacious associations of *fornix* with *fornicatio*. Ovid's text would then be attaching a similarly popular connotation to *ianus*.[93] At 245–46, Janus describes his settlement on the Janiculum:

> arx mea collis erat, quem volgo nomine nostro
> nuncupat haec aetas Ianiculumque vocat.

> My citadel was the hill that this era vulgarly hails by my name and calls Iani-culum.

In popular usage, the names of things useful to humans commonly bore the names of gods providing them[94]: Ceres-grain, Bacchus-wine. But Ianus? The word *vulgo* (245) indicates that readers might interpret the naming of Janus' hill (*Iani collis*) by salacious popular usage such as Wallace-Hadrill observed with *fornix* ("arch"; cf. fornication). The pun *Iani-culum*, "ass of Janus" (or Anus-ass) would not be the only such punning compounds on *culus* ("ass").[95] Here it would allude to Janus' "rear" wariness discussed above; the *Ianiculum* was a lookout over a vulnerable point in Rome's defenses.[96]

In Janus' Sabine tale, *contigerat* ("had touched," 265), the verb referring to the enemy's first "contact" with the *porta Ianualis*, can also carry erotic meaning—from erotic touch to sexual intercourse.[97] Janus' anxiety is indicated by the fact that the sequential order of his words obscures the grammatical subject of *contigerat*. When the verb appears, the last potential subjects that Ovid had mentioned in his narrative summary include not just Tarpeia (*levis custos armillis capta*, 261), but tellingly Tatius (260) and the Sabines (261–2, *Sabinos . . . tacitos*), who are interested in "reaching" or "touching" Janus' gate to penetrate it. Moreover, it is the arms of Oebalian Tatius (*Oebalii . . . arma Tati*, 260; Tatius, 272) that Janus thwarts, not Tarpeia.[98]

Then, as if to avoid placing Tatius at his gate, Janus quickly introduces *Saturnia*, the hated (*invidiosa*) daughter of Saturn (Juno), to remove the bolts from the *porta Ianualis*, the gate of Romulus' defenses facing Janus' shrine across the forum (265–66). The shift to Saturnia transfers agency from a mortal male penetrating Janus' gate to a divine female.

But Janus does not directly attack Juno. He fears that prospect. So, instead, he uses subterfuge, his clever "oral" art (*sumque repentinas eiaculatus aquas*, 267–68)—opening his *ora* or orifices suddenly to ejaculate sulfurous water (269–70). This water has ambiguous powers. It could purify, either despite or probably because of its odor (Vitr. 8.2.8).[99] Janus blocks Tatius' entry through his gate (i.e., *Porta Ianualis*) by spewing sulfuric water (271) that has a "fervid" or seething quality (*fervidus*, 272). Other sources explicitly describe the water as boiling (e.g., *Met.* 14.772–804).[100] But the *Fasti* and *Metamorphoses* are the only sources identifying sulfur in Janus' watery expulsion. Since the *Fasti* does not mention fire, the chief feature of Janus' water (271) might be its smell rather than its boiling temperature. This would imply that Janus Geminus (in the Forum) could marshal a flood against Tatius and the Sabines by unlocking underground brooks and the Cloaca Maxima, the great sewer-drain of the settlement. The sulfurous association—smell, taste, or otherwise—may be associated with underground springs, but it may also be linked with the widely known Forum flooding and a resulting regurgitation—"backup"—of Tiber waters through the sewer system of Rome, especially the Cloaca Maxima.[101] That would block access. A flood deep enough for boats swamped Rome in 15 CE, while Ovid was revising the *Fasti* (Dio 57.14.7).[102] The Velabrum and the Forum valley were long famous for flooding.[103]

The proximity of Janus Geminus to Venus "of the Cloaca" (Cloacina) may explain Venus' association with Janus in the *Metamorphoses*—through subterranean waters. Both deities sanctify the paving-over of streams and sewer channels. On the other hand, some traditions linked the foundation of both shrines with the peace treaty between Romulus and Tatius (Romans and Sabines). In this tradition, the shrine of Cloacina (*cluere, purgare*, to purify) commemorated the site of the ritual purification of bloodshed. Janus' sulfurous emission might also be significant as an agent of purification (fending off Tatius). The final

treaty between the Romans and the Sabines was supposedly conclud-
ed in the Forum at the Comitium along the Sacra Via. Janus'
door/shrine would then mark a point of transition from war to peace,
via purification (Venus Cloacina) and Janus' portal.[104] Moreover, his
two heads symbolize the two parties (Romulus-Tatius; Romans-
Sabines) who swore to the peace agreement. Thus Janus betokens a
peaceful merger between them (Serv. *ad Aen.* 12.198) or a portal of transition (cf. rites of passage) between war and peace between men.[105]

This symbolism indirectly shapes how Ovid's dialogue with Janus
betokens the poet's relation to his ideal male reader, Germanicus.
Overall, what "screens" that desired relation with the prince is Ovid's
negotiation with Janus and Janus' allusion to two contrary commu-
nicative styles. One is sweet, like the New Year's *strenae*, the blessings
and the (implied) kisses; the other is a caustic, sulfuric, or foul-
smelling flood ordinarily concealed "underground." This flood provides a way to block hostile penetration into a closed interior akin to
war; by contrast, sweet oral exchanges augment a bond akin to peace.
These contrary models of oral exchange reflect the uncertain oscillation of antagonistic and cooperative communications in a male
homosocial milieu. Thus readers might imagine the flood emitted from
Janus and the *strenae* as supplying two different kinds of poetic style
and inspiration through which Ovid might communicate with his
readers. In their discursive symbolism, these images of Janus in
Roman ritual and the Roman landscape partially displace the conventional fountains as sources of inspiration. Indeed, the Heliconian landscape of the Muses is deferred to the opening of "May," Book 5.[106]

The language at the crossing between speakers at 255–56 orchestrates slippage between discourse and watercourse: "The god had
pressed his lips. Then I loosened mine so, my voice luring the voice of
the god (*presserat ora deus. tunc sic ego nostra resolvi,/ voce mea voces eliciente dei*). While *elicio* sometimes suggests a "raising up" or "conjur-
ing" (cf. Jupiter Elicius, *F.* 3.327; Tib. 1.2.46; Plin. *H. N.* 28.104), Ovid
uses it in Janus' Sabine tale at *Met.* 14.789–90 to say the nymphs "*drew
out* the veins and streams of their fountain" (*venasque et flumina fontis/
elicuere sui*, 789–90). Flood and discourse are thus analogously "elicit-
ed" (cf. Hor. *S.* 1.4.11, 1.10.50–64). In fact, *elicio* can often be used to
describe the luring of resources or phenomena out of dumb, difficult
nature, by magic or art; by analogy, the verb *elicere* can mean the drawing out of passionate expressions that seem bound within the body of
an individual. It also connotes the drawing out of a force or expression
that the material source is "reluctant" (or opposed) to produce. That is

what Ovid does by asking Janus questions; he "draws out" from him latent "rivers" of discourse that flow and digress from their point of inquiry, modeling a mode of social commentary, if not resistance.[107]

This watery imagery also applies to Germanicus, who possesses great *flumina* of poetic talent (*F.* 1.24); this is the "river" that Ovid channels by eliciting Germanicus' critical help or response to the *Fasti*. For example, Ovid observes and perhaps envies precisely the position Salanus has as Germanicus' companion (*comes*) in rhetorical recitation (*Ex P.* 2.5.45–46): "when you [Salanus] are speaking, at once an urge arises in him [Germanicus]: he has you to elicit with your words his words" (*te dicente prius fit protinus impetus illi:/ teque habet elicias qui sua verba tuis*). The key issue is desired face-to-face reciprocity (cf. repetition at *F.* 1.256, *voce mea voces eliciente dei*, and 184, *sed tetigi verbis ultima verba meis*). Moreover, Ovid made a point of using the word *impetus*, "urge" or "drive" (cf. *Ex P.* 2.5.45), to describe Germanicus' "move" or "attack" upon Ovid's *artes* (1.24; ch. 2). That same *impetus* produces the prince's great *flumina* of talent (1.23–24). But here (268) the word *ars* describes Janus' flooding the field of combat with a sulfurous watery defense. The image carries negative implications for the quality of Germanicus' poetry, but Janus' watery/fiery oral defense recalls a benefit of Germanicus' discourse already observed (1.21–22): "For we perceived the eloquence of your cultivated mouth when its utterances offered legal defense [*civica arma*] of the quaking defendants." Janus' defensive *ars* retroactively recalls the peaceful aid Ovid wants from Germanicus (ch. 2). Later, *artes* will describe Cacus' vomiting of fire, his defensive resource against Hercules (*F.* 571–78).

In the *Fasti*, Janus embodies a complex of relations negotiated through exchanges of grain-seed, cakes, prayers, blessings for prosperous fertility, sweets, and coins. Janus may even broker "kisses"— tokens of elite male intimacy or bond. One is not to force penetration of Janus. His eruption of sulfurous water suggests he can be explosive (259–72). Instead, one verbally solicits him (255–56) and brokers for peace (121–22, 283–84) using blessings, offerings, sweets, and cash.

Ovid, Germanicus, and the Missing Half

Perhaps what Ovid *really* wants is to reach Peace (closed within Janus' shrine, 121–22) but not unleash *arma* (277; perhaps Janus' flood above), when finally he asks (277–78), "But why do you hide in peace, and you are opened when war is waged?" Janus answers specifically that he is open in war to receive "returns," but under the Caesarian deity (*Caesario . . . numine*), he "will be closed for a long time" (282). Janus seems here to acknowledge Germanicus' presence (63–64), and proceeds, after Ovid's dialogue with him, to grant both Ovid and Germanicus access to Peace. Mention of *Caesareum numen* as securing Peace would then anticipate Ovid's praise of Germanicus' triumph over Germany (285–86, declared by the Senate on January 1, 15 CE, finally celebrated May 27, 17), which would provide an external context from which the fantasy scene develops.[108]

Ovid seems to be negotiating Janus' reception of Germanicus' and, in fantasy, his own peaceful "return" (*reditus*, 279–80), figured as Janus' opening his door for them to Peace, not War (283–88):

> dixit, et attollens oculos diversa videntes
>   aspexit toto quicquid in orbe fuit:
> Pax erat, et vestri, Germanice, causa triumphi,
>   tradiderat famulas iam tibi Rhenus aquas.
> Iane, fac aeternos Pacem Pacisque ministros,
>   neve suum praesta deserat auctor opus.

> He spoke, and, lifting his eyes that look upon opposite things, he saw whatever was in all the world: there was Peace and, Germanicus, the cause of your triumph, the Rhine had now given up to you his waters as household slave-girls. Janus, make Peace and the attendants of Peace eternal, and ensure that the author [of Peace] does not abandon his work.

Scholars have noticed the contradiction in the function of Janus' door: he closes to imprison wars and opens to release Peace freely at 121–24, but here he opens to release wars and closes to retain Peace.[109] Consistency is not a hallmark of Janus' personality, but some evidence suggests (cf. *F.* 3.781–82) that the shrine of Janus Geminus supported or contained a statue of Pax purchased with the New Year's *strena* in 10 BCE (Dio 54.35.1–2; Suet. *Aug.* 57).[110] The important point is that Janus grants access to an imagined complete enjoyment illustrated by celebratory triumphs and by Peace as an object of desire. If Ovid's poem screens a fantasy *paraclausithyron*, Janus is rather like Hermes in Aristophanes' *Peace* (*Eirene*), petitioned by Ovid playing a part rather like Trygaeus', i.e., asking the gods to release Peace for human enjoyment.[111] As a shared object of desire for both Germanicus and Ovid, Pax recalls how, at the end of Aristophanes' *Lysistrata,* personified *Diallagê,* or Reconciliation, desired and shared by both Spartans and Athenians, provides the medium of peace between them. Mortals must vigilantly secure Peace, a symbolic "woman," from thefts of enjoyment. In the *Fasti,* Ovid and Germanicus are to be servants or escorts of *Pax* on earth (287–88): "Janus, make Peace and her attendants eternal, and take care that the author does not abandon his work." Janus warily (looking both ways, 283–84) plays a deceptive doorman in a different kind of elegiac *paraclausithyron* (locked doorway scene) tacitly granting access to "Peace" within the Roman *domus.* For as Janus informs Ovid, as doorman of heaven he can, when he is pleased (implicitly, given gifts), release Peace to walk (implicitly earthly) paths (121–22). After carefully looking around the world (cf. Jupiter's gaze, 1.85–86), Janus permits Ovid and Germanicus access to Peace (*Pax erat,* 285), securing the felicity that Ovid tells Germanicus that Janus is announcing for him at 63–64. Peace is the feminine object—personified abstract of male desire—trafficked and secured between men, grounding homosocial relations.

Ovid's brokering with Janus enacts the poet's desire for a relation with his male readership; in the revision of 15–17 CE, this becomes a desire for the aid of Germanicus. By discussing with Janus the varied New Year's gift-exchanges that express longing for mutual felicity (*strenae*), Ovid invokes models by which his poetic "exchange" with Janus constitutes, at least after exilic revision, just such a *strena*—an "ominous" gift[112]—of poetic discourse from an exile (cf. Saturn) offered to Germanicus (1.3–4, *excipe . . . hoc opus;* 5–6, *officioque . . . en tibi devoto;* 63, 285–86). We might then imagine the broken *Fasti* functioning socially as half of a *symbolon*—a Janus-headed half-coin, or a portion of a whole symbol for Ovid's desired relation to his fantasized other half of enjoyment stolen by exile. The partner controlling the "other" half, together with Ovid, is to share the work of Peace (*suum opus,* 288), figured most immediately in the composition—completion—of the *Fasti* itself. The missing half of the *Fasti*—its absence—ultimately cannot escape "symbolizing" Ovid's desire (the absence) for this relationality in "reality." As a halved *symbolon,* the *Fasti* was (probably) never made whole. Thus, the apparition of two-headed Janus, embodying the "merged" partners of a bond, stages an Ovidian fantasy or desire for completion.

In retrospect, therefore, Janus' two-headedness symbolizes in part a desired, though wary, male homosocial bond between the exiled author and his reader. Guardian of felicitous completion of the year and Peace, Janus provides a literary and visual symbol of this uncertain literary and social bond between men and a careful emblem of a prospective textual completion that Ovid supposedly seeks with Germanicus himself (ch. 2). Janus' two-headed form seems, in fact, to screen a Roman version of the original double-sided, two-faced humans that the character Aristophanes describes in Plato's *Symposium* (189a–193d). Zeus splits them apart due to their terrifying strength and ambition. Weakening them, this splitting causes them to relate to each other in a way that Aristophanes compares to a broken *symbolon* (191d); it causes mortals to feel a passionate lack, longing, or sexual drive (*eros*) for their matching other half. Of course, in Plato's *Symposium*, the social *symbolon* is homoerotic. However, Zeus' splitting of the original humans and their enjoyment is comparable in the *Fasti* to Ovid's loss of social-literary enjoyment and the fracturing of the *Fasti* by the exile imposed by Augustus. Ovid's half-*Fasti* and his interaction with Janus stage a fantasy of desire or longing for a remediation of this literary-social fracture. [113]

CHAPTER FOUR

Monthly Prefaces and the Symbolic Screen

t he calendar provides a convenient structure for Ovid to account for "himself" before Germanicus and other readers [1] because it evokes, in its symbolic chain, the fantasy supports that helped Roman subjects make sense of their lives, find enjoyment, and manage traumatic events (changes, gains and losses, etc.) from birth through adolescence, to marriage and military service, to illness and death by fitting these changes into a communal symbolic order. Thus, the calendar acts as a locus of mediation, as a fantasy "screen," between cooperative and competitive desires.

Ovid's encounter with Janus in January (ch. 3) "opens the door" (1.171–74) to a continuing, but broken, series of fantasy scenarios in which Ovid meets gods. In these prefatory scenes, Ovid, as former erotic elegist, tries (perhaps facetiously) to reconcile his erotic play with Rome's symbolic order through fantasy encounters with the supposedly divine, but conflicting, authorities that supported the calendar's guidance of temporal order (cf. *iura,* 1.38, 45). But Ovid's presentation of conflicting meaning de-naturalizes the calendar as a fantasy-support of meaning. This encourages readers to go "behind the scenes" to assess both Ovid and the calendar's symbolic order. By inviting the ideal reader (Germanicus) to govern and judge him and his work, Ovid engages a wider elite male readership (their critical thinking) in a (Lacanian) "going through the fantasy." That process involves a modified reckoning or "settling of accounts" between them, through imagined exchange over the symbolic meaning of the months. As Slavoj Zizek has noted, "going through the fantasy" would not ultimately involve a totalizing symbolic interpretation of Ovid's text or the calendar's symbolic order. Such a goal—an absence—would constantly recede or be filled with new fantasies (ideologies). Yet, interpretation of the symbolic is the immediate process or path (the aim) necessary to "go through the fantasy," to reach a point where the author and reader recognize antagonism as that which fantasy covers.[2]

To observe this "going through the fantasy," the following analysis tracks such a reversal by the author and his elite (male) readership by reference to symbolic month-names and an idealized male life-course that the names imply. First, the discussion will introduce some metaphorical coordinates of elite male maturation—a kind of temporal syntax or order of (male) life. Crucially, "becoming a [real] man" here entails an age-appropriate shift from supposedly frivolous to "responsible" objects of desire. This shift in objects widens the social scope and impact of male homosocial relations by metaphorically extending its desired object—a position held by "woman" in erotic elegy[3]—to include a variety of sublimated objects of deferred enjoyment. This model of "maturation" enables Ovid's projection of his shift from elegy's frivolous erotic themes to more serious, national passions expressed in the high genres of tragedy, epic and, perhaps, civic elegy (the *Fasti*). While not exhaustive, the metaphorical structures presented here—*militia, census,* and Hercules as idealized model of the heroic male—screen conventional masculinity known to Ovid, Germanicus, and other (elite male) readers.

Following this survey of structures of elite male life, a sequential analysis will interpret the remaining prefaces, from February to June, as autobiographical episodes, in which Ovid progressively "screens" his calendar composition as a relation between his own "elegiac" desire and the "epic" order of elite masculinity. In these scenarios Ovid attempts a literary path toward "correct" elite manhood symbolized by the epic genre, but also, by this deviance from the right path, invites reader "correction" of himself and his poem (cf. *derige navis iter,* 1.4; *rege habenas,* 1.25). However, Ovid's ambivalent, avoidant, behavior— his knowing failure—also performs a civic service: he engages male readers in rival interpretations of the fantasy structures supporting the ideology of elite masculinity.

Symbolic Structures and Elite Male Life

Military service (*militia*), the *census,* and the tale of Hercules' life provide metaphorical "nodal points"—points of ideological "(mis)-match," or antagonism, between Ovid and his (male) readership—framing variable approaches to enjoyment, from the elegiac mistress to matrons and Vestal Virgins. These structures frame Ovid's self-presentation as the authorial subject (I-speaker) and provide coordinates within which he "screens" his desire of reader reception and response.[4]

Militia

Recent scholarship has examined the thematic use of *arma* (war and weaponry) in the *Fasti* as formal references to the epic genre, rather than as an ideological practice (*militia*) in which elite males earned desired esteem for *virtus,* manly honor, from other men by showing courage and self-mastery on the battlefield. The moralizing use of epic literature in elite male education encouraged male identification with epic heroes and military heroism expressed in social practice.[5]

Rather than interpret *arma* in the *Fasti,* as some have done, as turning elegy away from its prior erotic history, I argue that the inclusion of *arma* in the *Fasti* helps Ovid "publicize" or broaden eroticism thematically into a key venue of male civic identity. This expansion exposes unruly libidinal forces within male citizen identity that are screened, that is, concealed, by the fantasy of heroic self-control within a supposedly stable symbolic order. Obvious military references (*arma, signa, militia*) appear in the prefaces from the start. For example, the dedication depends upon Ovid's libidinal inversion of quasi-military *devotio* (1.5–6) to Germanicus, a famed triumphant general (15–17 CE; ch. 2). Similar (quasi-erotic) inversions of military symbols appear in subsequent prefaces, such as Janus' use of his unusual *artis opus,* or "work of art" (his sulfuring flooding), as a defense against Tatius' entry through a gate (ch. 3).

Sequential interpretation of the prefaces will interpret Ovid's references to *militia* as deriving symbolic force from the envelopment of *militia* within male citizenship defined by the Roman *census.* Moreover, *arma* cannot be cleanly separated from idealized tales of an heroic life-path, such as that of Hercules.[6]

Census: Ovidius Eques

The Roman *census* or "appraisal" defined citizen males physically, financially, and morally. Traditionally two censors, elected for five-year terms, counted male heads of households; the heads of households rendered a report (*rationem vitae*, Suet. *Aug.* 39) of their property and the number of persons in their households (including wife, children, and slaves); and they were then ranked as plebeian, equestrian, or senatorial, based primarily upon property qualifications (equestrians: 400,000 sesterces; senators: one million under Augustus), but also upon birth, record of public office, and morality. Moral character could be challenged on the basis of written or oral denunciations of one's behavior in public office or in domestic affairs; however, in rendering an account of his life, the citizen-subject could defend his character by citing his public service to the state, family, or gods.[7]

Augustus developed these censorial functions by creating new offices for selected aristocratic commissioners, who could aid in the complex reviews of citizens. Greater social expectations and fewer numbers enabled censorial reviewers to focus more exacting attention on the morality of the elite classes threatened with possible marks of *infamia* or *nota* (disgrace) and various punishments, including demotion of class rank. While plebeians were reviewed in the Campus Martius, outside the city boundary, in military "centuries," senators and equestrians were reviewed inside the city in the *lectio senatus* and the *recognitio equitum* was held in the Forum. While they did not form in military formation, equestrians wore cavalry gear at their review, which took place every five years, and each led his horse before censorial officers. In Ovid's day, the emperor and a commission conducted a "testing" every July 15 of knights in a mounted parade, the *transvectio equitum*.[8] These public events "staged" the *equites* (equestrians or knights), symbolically linking them to their horse (*equus*) as an emblem of their class within a quasi-military ranking.

Ovid's poetry frequently refers to the poet's equestrian status,[9] to his sitting in the first fourteen rows of theater seats reserved for *equites* (*F.* 4.377–86), and to his service in the initial judicial offices of an equestrian public career.[10] As an *eques* in exile, Ovid fantasizes celebrating a

German victory (*Tr.* 4.2.15–16) and imagines participating in Graecinus' inaugural procession (*Ponto* 4.9.17–8). Equestrian status was the
honorific position from which exile notionally degraded Ovid and his
household (*Tr.* 2.109–14). More importantly, the initial lines of *Tristia* 2
describe how Ovid's poetry has recently caused Caesar (retroactively)
to criticize him and his morals (*carmina fecerunt ut me moresque notaret*,
Tr. 2.7), although Ovid had frequently passed before Augustus at the
equestrian review without incurring any censorious "mark" (*Tr.*
2.89–90, 541–42). The verb *notare* (*Tr.* 2.7) refers technically to marking
moral disrepute at the *recognitio* (*nota* is the corresponding noun). Censorious readers seem to have swayed the emperor against Ovid (*Tr.*
2.277–78).[11] *Tristia* 2.541–46 specifically frames Ovid's *Fasti* as a work
that, for an equestrian (male) poet, should fulfill censorial expectations
of public service (*Tr.* 2.547–52), but exile has broken the *Fasti*. Retroactively, exile might seem to have been directed at the *Fasti* and less at an
apparently intact *Ars amatoria*.

The dedication of the *Fasti* refers to *recognitio* when Ovid, submitting the poem to Germanicus' critical guidance, states (*F.* 1.7–8): "You
will review [*recognosces*] rituals unearthed from old annals and how,
deservedly, each day *was marked*" (*merito quaeque notata dies*). The verb
recognoscere technically designated the censorial review of Roman
"knights." Such review seems metaphorically to frame critical reading
of the *Fasti*, as if prior to full publication. Thus Ovid would be exposing
the process of "censorship."[12] The phrase "undergo judgment" (*iudicium . . . subitura*, 19–20) echoes Suetonius' description of elite young
men, early in Tiberius' reign, who willingly "underwent" (*subire*) the
judgment (*iudicium*) of infamy (*infamia, nota*). This censorial "review" in
court supplemented the regular census procedures: some young elites
flouted decorum, receiving "a *nota* of an infamous judgment" (in
court), demoting them to the rank of *infames* ("infamous"), in order to
preempt imposition of exile and to continue performing in ignoble
fashion as gladiators or actors. Ovid's participle *notata* (*F.* 1.7–8 above)
recalls *nota*, the censorial mark of ignominy demoting elite citizens of
suspect character.[13]

Moreover, Germanicus, as the *princeps* before whom Ovid's Page is
to "undergo" judgment (*F.* 1.19–20), is not the emperor, but perhaps
princeps iuvenum, "leader of the youth," a title ascribed to the emper-
or's heirs (*Pont.* 2.5.41–42; cf. *Pont.* 2.1.61–2, *iuvenum belloque togaque
maxime*), shortened to *princeps* (cf. *Pont.* 2.5.55 *facundia principe
digna*).[14] Germanicus was leader of the *iuvenes* who symbolized the

next generation of the ruling class, and were representative of Ovid's class, *equites*, in state ceremonials.[15] Thus as *princeps iuvenum* (*Pont.* 2.5.41–42) and model for the young *equites* (Suet. *Aug.* 34), Germanicus was also figurative patron of the *equites*, which partially explains why Ovid submits his text to Germanicus' review (*F.* 1.19–20). As *princeps iuvenum,* he supervises *recognitio* of Ovid's text (*rege vatis habenas,* 1.26), much as he could easily have served as one of the censorial administrators helping Augustus review each *ratio vitae,* "account of life," that knights submitted (cf. *pagina iudicium . . . subitura/principis,* 1.19–20).[16]

The prefaces of the *Fasti* follow a scheme or *ratio* by which to "account for" elite male life, in which any *error,* or deviance from moral uprightness and manly class honor, was seriously scrutinized. Consider the figurative use of *error* immediately after Ovid dedicates the poem to Germanicus (1.27–44). Here Ovid introduces the calendar scheme of Romulus, the founder of Rome and Rome's first calendar (1.27–32). Two vocatives—Romulus and Caesar—signal Ovid's double address:

> tempora digereret cum conditor Urbis, in anno
>   constituit menses quinque bis esse suo.
> scilicet arma magis quam sidera, Romule, noras,
>   curaque finitimos vincere maior erat.
> est tamen et *ratio,* Caesar, quae moverit illum,
>   *errorem*que suum quo tueatur habet.

When the Founder of the City was organizing a calendar, he established ten months in his year. Romulus, you of course knew weapons better than stars and conquering neighbors was your greater worry. Yet, Caesar, there is also a systematic *account* that motivated him and he has a way to defend his *error* so that he may be watchful.

Romulus' calendar was astronomically erroneous, but Ovid defends Romulus' *error* before Caesar, the "inspector" (1.19), by rendering a *ratio* (an *account,* or "guiding principle"; cf. the *ratio vitae* at *recognitio,* above).[17] The *ratio* for Romulus' *error*—his year of ten rather than twelve months—thematizes human biology: the length of time it took an infant to gestate and the proper time a widow would mourn her deceased husband (1.33–36). Thus, biology of birth and rituals of death determined the length of Romulus' annual *ratio.* Male life phases articulate months within Romulus' year. His first two months honor his "birth." Claiming that Mars had fathered him personally (*ipsius pater*, 40), Romulus named the first month "March," for Mars, a god of fertility as well as war. Venus as mother of Aeneas was a more distant progenitor of Romulus' family. But as goddess of erotic desire, she is also an immediate cause of sex and offspring; she is *generis princeps*, "first [or model] of reproduction [or family]" (40).[18] The next two months, May and June, reflect elite male age-classes in the *census*. The name "May" (*Maius*) honors the "elders" or *maiores*, while June honors the younger males (the *iuniores* or *iuvenes*). This temporal order of months gives honorific priority to the elders, inverting chronology (*F.* 1.41–42, 5.427–28, 6.65–88, esp. 83–88).[19] Romulus next used ordinal numbers to "note" the "crowd" (*turba*) of months that followed (*F.* 1.42: *quae sequitur, numero turba notata fuit*), from Quintilis (fifth) to December ("tenth"). These months mirror the hierarchy of Romulus' society: the broad "counting" of the "mass that follows them" is not unlike the *census* itself—a counting and ranking of the free male citizen body, their dependents and property. Indeed, in the March preface (*F.* 3.127–34) Ovid describes Romulus' inventory of ten months on the model of the *census*, the counting, of male citizens in military formation—an implicit parallel between a monthly *ratio* of time and the hierarchical accounting of citizens.

Ovid, Hercules, and Heroic Identity

Hercules' twelve labors provided another fantasy-support for the ideology of masculinity in Rome, much as it did in Greece. In some localities, Hercules' rites protected males entering manhood.[20] But the *Fasti* vividly exploits three narrative features of Hercules' life. First, Books 1, 2, 5, and 6 present several tales of Hercules' adventures in Latium while herding the cattle of Geryon from Spain.[21] These scenes contribute toward a second motif, life as a long path of labors eventually rewarded in the afterlife. References to the hero's progress screen the author's compositional progress on his *Fasti*. A third feature, the famous "Choice of Hercules," or "Hercules at the Crossroad," locates the hero as a youth just entering manhood and choosing between two "ways" of life, that of manly honor (*Virtus*) and that of immediate enjoyment (*Vitium*). Through the interweaving of these features, Ovid encourages the reader to examine him, in part, as an elegiac "Hercules."

Tracking Ovid's references to *labor*, especially his own and Hercules' incomplete *labor*, suggests how readers can interpret the former love elegist as struggling with his own Herculean feat(s) in composing his *Fasti*. Both Janus and Mars call Ovid "a work-burdened bard of the days" (*vates operose dierum*, 1.101, 3.177)²² and, at the end of Book 1 (723–24), Ovid describes the progress of his "work" (*labor*): "But now the *first part of my labor has been completed*, and the booklet has an end with its month" (*sed iam prima mei pars est exacta laboris*). Hercules visited Chiron and Achilles with "*part of his labors completed . . .* almost the final commands awaited the hero" (*F.* 5.387–88, above). Ovid aims to complete his labors, as did Mater Matuta (*defuncta laboribus*, 6.541).

As Hercules endured twelve labors, so is Ovid composing twelve month-books, negotiating divine powers along the way (cf. Numa "mastering" Jupiter Elicius, 3.327–47; Aristeus, Proteus, 1.368–80; Carmentis-Cranae, the *Striges*, 6.131–68). ²³ The *Fasti* as poetic *labor* is the idea behind *F.* 5.693–96, where Ovid asks Mercury to tell at what time Phoebus (the Sun) enters Gemini and Mercury responds: "When you'll see that just as many days of the month are left as are feats of Herculean labor" (*"cum totidem de mense dies superesse videbis / quot sunt Herculei facta laboris" ait*). Mercury's response alludes to the laboriousness of Ovid's project and implies an analogy between time units in Ovid's *Fasti* and Hercules' labors.

Ovid's desire for an end to his labor at the end of only his sixth book seems premature. Ovid falters along his path of labor. A reference to aging precedes (6.771–78): "Time is fading and I'm getting older with the silent years. And, rein unrestrained, days are fleeing" (*tempora labuntur, tacitisque senescimus annis, / et fugiunt freno non remorante dies*). At 6.795 Ovid mentions that there are just as many days left of the month as there are *Parcae*, or Fates, the deities who determine the span and quality of life, even of gods. Ovid, a mortal, tracks a path of death.²⁴

Then at 6.797–800, Hercules makes his final appearance in the last passage of the extant *Fasti*, recounting the origin of the temple of Hercules Musarum or Hercules' association with the Muses:

> tempus Iuleis cras est natale Kalendis:
>   Pierides, *coeptis addite summa meis.*
> dicite, Pierides, quis vos addixerit isti
>   cui dedit invitas victa noverca manus.

Tomorrow is the birthday for the Kalends of July: Pierides, add the summation to my beginnings. Pierides, tell who assigned you [the Muses] to that man [Hercules], to whom the conquered mother-in-law [Juno] submitted her unwilling authority.

Summa (798) refers to a summation, conclusion, perhaps not just of this book, but of the entire *Fasti*. The Muses are to add the final "sum" to Ovid's accounting. Ovid conjoins the word *summa* with *laborum* in a letter to his friend Atticus, referring to the innumerable "sum of my labors," suggestive of Herculean labors in a poem lamenting his exilic suffering (*Ponto* 2.7.29; cf. *summa malorum*, *Tr.* 5.7.7). But *summa* sometimes modifies *manus*, the "final touch," the finishing hand," which the *Metamorphoses* needed (*Tr.* 3.14.21–22). Pompeius Macer's *summa manus* implies he completed Homer by composing a "prequel" to the *Iliad* (*Pont.* 2.10.13–14; *Am.* 2.18.1–2; *Pont.* 4.16.5–6). This compositional "completion" of one man's work by another lies behind Sabinus' composition of elegiac letters from Ovid's heroines (*Heroides; Pont.* 4.16.13–14, *Am.* 2.18.27–28). At *F.* 6.798, Ovid invites the Muses to consummate his *dimidium* (half-work).

By contrast with Ovid, Hercules has finished his work. At *F.* 6.797–800 Juno has submitted her authority (*manus*) to Hercules, relinquished her resentment, and ceased punishing him. Hercules is imagined in heaven after reconciliation with Juno, after apotheosis and marriage to Hebe, celebrated in a heavenly banquet among the Muses, a motif known in Hellenistic art.[25]

The temple of Hercules Musarum depicts Hercules among statues of the Muses and holding a lyre rewarded, at least with enjoyment of poetry, after completion of his labors (6.812).[26] Located along the triumphal route, this temple symbolically rewards military *labores*, especially of a triumphant general (cf. M. Fulvius Nobilior's triumph, creation of the temple, 189 BCE; and his calendar displayed there; ch. 1). Germanicus had been delaying completion of his German campaign and its symbolic end in an expected triumph (*Pont.* 4.13.45; declared in 15 CE, celebrated 17). Some readers might imagine an identification of Germanicus with Hercules, recalling the popular identification of Augustus or Aeneas with Hercules.[27] Ovid's friend Carus, personal tutor of Germanicus' sons while their father was in Germany (*Pont.* 4.13.47–48), had composed an epic on Hercules that illustrated the strengths (*vires*) of Hercules (also Carus' poetic strength, *Pont.* 4.13.11–12). Ovid expects Carus will also compose a poem on their father's approaching triumph (*Pont.* 4.13.46).[28] Since Ovid also associates his own poetic labors with Herculean efforts, rewards for Germanicus and Hercules, but also for Ovid if he completes his *Fasti*, symbolically converge at the temple where Nobilior displayed his calendar (ch. 1).

But completion is a prerequisite for reward. As Hesiod states, Hercules completed his labors and won marriage to Hebe-Juventas (6.65–89), symbol of eternal uninterrupted enjoyment of Youth (*Theog.* 950–55):

> *Having concluded his grievous labors* [τελέσας στονόεντας ἀέθλους, 951], Herakles, daring son of fair-ankled Alcmene, made Hebe, child of Great Zeus and golden-sandaled Hera, his modest wife on snowy Olympus—blessed! *Since he completed his great work* [μέγα ἔργον . . . ἀνύσσας, 954] and (now) dwells amongst the immortals, unvexed and ageless all his days.

Hesiod emphasizes that marriage to Hebe and living eternally with gods result from Hercules' completion of his labors (951), his "great work" (954). In the preface of June (6.79–82), Juventas herself highlights her marriage to Hercules (as does Ovid, 6.65), but her antagonism with mother Juno is far from the blissful reward promised (see below). Unresolved antagonism increasingly threatens to "undo" completion of Ovid's poetic opus (cf. ἔργον, *Theog.* 954, *Iane . . . neve suum praesta deserat auctor opus*, 1.288; 2.4). The question becomes whether the ideological antagonisms encountered during Ovid's labors are too great for (his) manhood (cf. *incipe maius opus*, *Am.* 3.1.24; *grandius opus urget*, 3.1.70; also *F.* 2.123, 4.948; Verg. *Aen.* 7.45).

Most influential for this symbolism of manly labor are the first and last poems of Ovid's final book of the *Amores* (3.1, 3.15). Here Ovid situates himself as an erotic poetry maturing, or trying to go beyond, his youthful erotic poetry—his *iuvenilia* (*Tr.* 2.339, 5.1.7; Fabius Maximus, *Pont.* 3.3.29)—by placing himself in a well-known allegorical scene, "Hercules at the Crossroad" or the "Choice of Hercules" (derived from Prodicus, a fifth-century sophist).[29]

In the philosophical version, Hercules, on the cusp of entering manhood, goes to an isolated locale where he sees and is asked to choose one of two "ways" of life, either the long laborious road of manly honor (*virtus*) rewarded with bliss after death (or apotheosis) or the "short circuit" of manhood in immediate enjoyment (*vitium*) and then nothingness or suffering after death. Hercules' symbolic choice directs the trajectory of his life of labors. The figure of Virtue embodies the mature male's "correct" relation to enjoyment, deferring pleasure while enduring a life of labor and reaching a reward in the end, while Vice embodies male moral weakness, a lack of self-control in the face of feminizing immediate pleasures, and a perverse relation toward civic manhood.

But in *Amores* 3.1, Ovid faces a choice between two genres, Tragedy (poetry of kings and heroes) and Elegy (poetry of dalliance in the pleasure of erotic affairs). Echoing the philosophical binary, the personified genres present female bodies that are more stoutly masculine (Tragedy) or more seductively feminine (Elegy) to suit their stature in the hierarchy of genres.[30] Tragedy specifically presses Ovid, "Begin a greater work" (*incipe maius opus, Am.* 3.1.24), one more suited to men than girls (25, 27). But far from imitating Hercules, Ovid leaves aside Tragedy (the literary surrogate for *Virtus*) for immediate enjoyment of Elegy, thus delaying conventional maturation. However, by *Amores* 3.15, Ovid has commanded Venus and Amor to remove their standards from his "field" (*campus;* 16–17): his "great steeds" (*magnis equis*)—perhaps symbolizing his equestrian social status (cf. *eques, Am.* 3.15.5–6)—are galloping upon an *area maior,* a "greater range" (3.15.18), pursing the *maius* or *grandius opus* urged in *Am.* 3.1.

February through June: the Sequence of Prefaces

February and Deviation

In the preface to "February" Ovid comments on the growing size of his *Fasti* as a *maius opus,* portraying its composition as literary maturation blending aspects of Hercules' life-path with military service and the census:

> Ianus habet finem. cum carmine *crescit* et Annus:
>   alter ut hic mensis, sic liber alter eat.
> nunc primum *velis,* elegi, *maioribus* itis:
>   *exiguum,* memini, nuper eratis *opus.*
> *ipse ego* vos habui faciles in amore ministros,
>   cum lusit numeris *prima iuventa* suis.
> *idem sacra cano* signataque tempora fastis:

ecquis ad haec illinc crederet esse *viam?*
haec mea militia est; ferimus quae possumus arma,
   dextraque non omni munere nostra vacat.
si mihi non valido torquentur pila lacerto
   nec bellatoris terga premuntur equi,
nec galea tegimur, nec acuto cingimur ense
   (his habilis telis quilibet esse potest),
at tua *prosequimur* studioso pectore, Caesar,
   nomina, per titulos *ingredimurque* tuos.
ergo ades et placido paulum *mea munera* voltu
   respice, pacando siquid ab hoste *vacat.*

Janus [January] has an end. The Year *grows* along with the poem: just as the second month goes here, so let a second book go. Now for the first time, Elegies, you go with *bigger* sail-cloths: you were recently, as I recall, a *little* work. *I myself* had you as compliant ministers in love, when *my early youth* frolicked to its own rhythms. *I, the same person,* am singing the rituals and the events marked in the calendars: who would believe there is a path from those themes to these. *These [rituals] are my military service.* We are carrying what weapons we can, and my right arm is not at leisure from all public service. Although pikes aren't hurled by me with a strong arm, though the back of a war horse is not pressed, though I'm not protected by a helmet and not girded with a sharp sword (anyone could be handy with such weapons), still, Caesar, I'm following your name. I am advancing in accord with your titles. So, attend and look back at my public service with a calm face for a little while, if there's any leisure from pacifying the enemy.

Here Ovid organizes his developing use of Elegies along a path, *via* (9), stretching two-directionally between *amor* (5) and *sacra* (7) and, beyond the *sacra,* to *militia* (9). This *via* splits the two themes of erotic elegy's *militia amoris,* the warfare of love, into two separate objects.[31] This is a binary found in the "Choice of Hercules," dichotomizing manly honor and (perverse) enjoyment, here formulated as *sacra militia* and *amor.*

   Imagery of physical growth and life-phase (*crescit,* 1; *velis maioribus,* 3; *exiguum opus,* 4; *prima iuventa,* 6) suggests how maturation informs this *via.* Ovid's formerly small elegies are growing into manlier ones, sporting *maioribus velis,* bigger "sails," a word Cicero used for the flowing togas of Catiline's effeminate youths (*Cat.* 2.10.2). Yet Ovid mainly refers to a poetic ship (1.4). Moreover, elegies are no longer an *exiguum*

opus, a little work. Yet Ovid does not yet say his elegies are a *grandius* or
maius opus, such as Tragedy projected (*Am.* 3.1.24, 70). They seem to be
at an "awkward, in-between, stage"—a transition associated with adolescence or, as Ovid says, "earliest youth" (*prima iuventa*, 6; cf. Cic.
Cael.), when greater expectations of public life are impressed upon
youths, although frolicking in erotic desire is also expected, within
limits.

Implicitly, youthful elegies now are entering manhood and helping
Ovid to create sacred calendar poetry (7) and to perform his *militia*
(9)—officially the duty of all citizen males. Moreover, Ovid seems cur-
rently to travel this *via* or path of life unidirectionally toward greater
responsibilities and away from youthful frivolity. Immediate enjoyment had been associated with earlier erotic elegy and the elegist's
conventional choice to refuse, despite his elite equestrian status, military and government service to indulge in erotic enjoyment.[32] Here the
sacra provide a mediating screen between *militia* and *amor*.

A similar model for Ovid's poetic "maturation" appears in *Tristia* 2.
Describing with irony how, as a youth, Vergil had without punishment
composed bucolic love themes (*hic idem . . . ignes / bucolicis iuvenis
luserat . . .* 537–38; cf. *ipse ego . . . in amore . . . cum lusit . . . prima iuventa
. . . , F.* 2.5–6), Ovid contrasts his situation (*Tr.* 2.539–52):

> nos quoque iam pridem scripto peccavimus isto:
>   supplicium patitur non nova culpa novum;
> *carminaque edideram, cum te delicta notantem*
>   *praeterii totiens inreprehensus eques.*
> ergo quae *iuvenis* mihi non nocitura putavi
>   scripta parum prudens, nunc nocuere *seni.*
> sera redundavit veteris vindicta libelli,
>   distat et a meriti tempore poena sui.
> *ne tamen omne meum credas opus esse remissum,*
>   saepe dedi nostrae *grandia vela* rati.
> sex ego *Fastorum* scripsi totidemque libellos,
>   *cumque suo finem mense volumen habet,*
> *idque tuo nuper scriptum sub nomine, Caesar,*
>   *et tibi sacratum sors mea rupit opus.*

I too erred a long time ago in that type of writing: hardly a new fault, it
suffers a new punishment [exile]; I had produced the poetry, when as a
knight I went past you without censure, while you were marking lapses.
So, what writings I *as a youth* imprudently thought would not harm me,

now have harmed me in *old age*. The punishment for that earlier book has returned late but in excess and the punishment is distant from the time of the mistake. Still, *so you do not think that all my work is negligent*, I did put *grand sails* on my ship. I composed six and the same number books of the *Fasti*, and with its month the book roll has its end. *And my lot [exile] broke (off) this work, Caesar, written recently under your name and dedicated to you.*

The descriptions of the *Fasti* in the *Tristia* and the February preface are quite similar: each month ends with its book roll (*volumen, Tr.* 2.550; *liber, F.* 2.1–2), and the *Fasti* is dedicated to "Caesar" (*scriptum sub nomine, Caesar, Tr.* 2.551; *tua prosequimur . . . , Caesar, / nomina,* etc.," *F.* 2.15–16). Both passages share an emphasis on the author's youth contrasted with maturity (*Tr.* 2.538, Vergil's youth; *Tr.* 2.543–44, Ovid's youth vs. maturity; *F.* 2.5–7, Ovid's youthful elegy). Stylistically, *hic idem*, referring to young Vergil at *Tr.* 2.53, echoes Ovid's self-designations at *F.* 2.5 (*ipse ego*) and 2.7 (*idem sacra cano*). But most compellingly, Ovid characterizes the *Fasti* in *Tristia* 2 as showing that "not every work of mine is negligent" (*remissum*, 547). The *Fasti* is placed in Ovid's senior years (*seni*, 544), that is, when he is no longer a *iuvenis* (*Tr.* 2.543; cf. Vergil *iuvenis*, 538). The large sails symbolize maturation: Ovid placed *grandia vela*, "huge sails," on the *Fasti* (*velis maioribus* at *F.* 2.3; cf. *grandia vela, Tr.* 2.548).

However, Ovid composed scenes with erotic appeal late into his life in both the *Metamorphoses* and *Fasti*. He stresses in *Tristia* 2 not so much that the *Fasti* is compliant with duty, but that it is "not negligent" or lazy—i.e., it does not fail to engage *grandia* or *maiora*, themes suited to manhood in Rome (*F.* 2.15–16, *Tr.* 2.551). Ovid was fifty or fifty-one years old, thus no longer in his *prima iuventa*, when he was exiled. His thematic change mimes a social aging of his poetic persona. But incompletion of the *Fasti* suggests incomplete maturation and a problematizing of manhood's path.[33]

Moreover, Ovid's mature chronological age (cf. *seni, Tr.* 2.544) would seem at odds with his pretending to perform *militia* (*F.* 2.9–18), the obligation of *iuvenes* (cf. *F.* 2.6; *Tr.* 2.543). *Militia* was expected of equestrian males wishing to advance in public careers and was highly defined (*militia equestris*).[34] Ovid was aware of the status of men who had earned equestrian status through *militia* vis-à-vis those who, like himself, might serve in the courts (*F.* 4. 377–86; *Amores* 3.8). From exile (*Tr.* 4.1.71) Ovid recalls how "when a youth, I fled the bitter fighting of military service," only now to face it in old age on the frontier.

But in what sense is Ovid fulfilling his *militia* symbolically? He alludes to, but simultaneously denies, riding a war horse and wielding weapons (*F.* 2.9–14), substituting elegy for the instruments of war. The writing of elegy about the *sacra* symbolically replaces required military service, a subject of the *recognitio equitum.* But how can Ovid's sacral poetry substitute for *militia?* The verb *vacat* at *F.* 2.10 and 18 frames Ovid's poetic *militia* as a *vacatio militiae,* an excuse from military service, granted *in exchange for* rendering other state services.[35] *Vacatio militiae* could be granted to *pontifices, augures,* and their children in local towns (*CIL* 2.05439, sect. 66; *Lex Coloniae Genitivae Iuliae Ursonensis*). Even men reporting divine encounters, as did P. Vatinius (reporting an epiphany of Castor and Pollux revealing the defeat of Perses), could be rewarded "by the senate with land and release from military service" (Cic. *ND* 2.2.6).[36] So, a former "erotic" elegist now claims elegiac treatment of sacral themes as services done for *vacatio militiae* (*munera:* 9–10, 17–18). Perhaps the *sacra* offered are also entertaining diversions, such as the *ludi* or games associated with the Roman *iuvenes,* events that Caesar would view when he, too, was free from fighting the enemy (2.18).[37]

Several features of the February preface characterize ritual elegies as substitutes for *arma.* Ovid performs his *militia* without weaponry (2.9–14). Warriors without weapons were characterized as *nudus,* "naked," equivalent to *inermis* ("unarmed"). Yet, *nudus* might describe various states of undress: no clothes; only a *tunicus;* or just a *cinctus* or *succinctorium,* a loincloth (cf. the Greek *perizoma*).[38] Propertius had described Rome's first *militia* as without proper weapons, performed "nude" (*proelia nuda*). The *Luperci* wielding their *sacra,* the *verbera saetosa,* i.e., shaggy (goat-hide) lashes, repeat the model (Prop. 4.1.25–28); they represent the origin of Roman military history in a rustic milieu characterized by scant clothing and improvised weaponry (whips and stakes).[39]

Comparably, in *Fasti* 2.9–14, Ovid says he carries the weapons he can (9), not those of a proper *miles.* In fact, he lists what he is *not* wearing. Ovid is implicitly *nudus,* relatively disarmed, in his *militia.* Later, the nudity of the *Luperci,* the young equestrian celebrants of the Lupercalia, will play a vivid part in Ovid's depiction of the *Lupercalia* (*F.* 2.267–380; ch. 6). Language celebrating the *Lupercalia* retroactively supports identifying Ovid's maturing elegies with youths at the Lupercalia (Feb. 15) wielding goatskin whips, racing "naked" around the Palatine, and striking passersby. In the February preface, Ovid anticipates the *Lupercalia* by suggesting a sacral role for his elegies as the weapons he can wield despite being otherwise *nudus.* In this

month, elegies conveying *sacra* might imply that the personified Elegies, or the poet, wield *sacra* in the manner of the rustic goat-hide
whips (Prop. 4.1.25–28), which are signs of both warfare and play.

At *Fasti* 2.287–88, Ovid describes Faunus-Pan as ordering the *Luperci* to go naked (*ipse deus nudus nudos iubet ire ministros*, 287). Already at
2.5–6 Ovid characterizes his elegies as compliant *ministros* in words
anticipating Pan's own ordering: *ipse ego vos habui faciles in amore ministros*. The poet thus implicitly commands his elegies as Pan-Faunus
does his Luperci. Ovid's elegiac *ministri*, once serving love-making,
now celebrate the *sacra* of February (cf. *Lupercalia*). All subsequent uses
of *ministri* in *Fasti* 2 refer to the *Luperci*. The expression *iubet ire ministros* (287; cf. 268, *Fauni sacra bicornis eunt*), describing Faunus' command to the *Luperci*, includes the verb *ire*. Ovid uses that verb to
command his Elegy at 2.3: *nunc primum velis, Elegi, maioribus itis*,
refined at 2.2: *alter ut hic mensis, sic liber alter eat.*[40] Ovid's phrases "Let
another book go" and "Now, Elegies, you go with larger sails" echo in
part the language of *propemptika* and in part a sailing metaphor common to poetry. However, as the brief preface unfolds, it becomes
apparent that Ovid's book of February proceeds with Elegi who can
convey *sacra* much as the Luperci carry their *februa*.

In this sense, Ovid's maturing Elegies perform *sacra* as a screen for
the poet's own maturation (2.5–6); notably the *Lupercalia* was a cult of
elite male maturation,[41] although entertaining erotic play continues in
public rites serving publicly sanctioned eroticism. *Lusit* at 2.6 (describing the frolicking of Ovid's early youth) echoes the erotic play of the
Luperci (Varro at Tert. *De spect.* 53).[42]

But the chief effect of lines 15–16 is to direct this literary performance of sacral, perhaps "Lupercalian," *militia* to the gaze of Caesar
(2.15–18):

> at *tua* prosequimur studioso pectore, Caesar,
>   *nomina,* per *titulos* ingredimurque tuos.
> ergo ades et placido paulum *mea munera* voltu
>   *respice,* pacando siquid ab hoste vacat.

> Still, Caesar, I'm following your name. I am advancing in accord with
> your titles. So, attend and look back at my public service with a calm
> face for a little while, if there's any leisure from pacifying the enemy.

Here Ovid says that he will "pursue" or "celebrate at length" (*prosequimur*, 15) Caesar's name as a theme. But he does not merely claim to

praise Caesar; he also "identifies" Caesar's name, *nomina*, and *titulos* (16) as marking the symbolic position from where his elegiac *munus* or *militia* is being observed (*respice*, 18).

However, Ovid pursues an unexpected etymological "origin" for the name *Caesar* that relates it to the month's chief festival, the Lupercalia, deriving Caesar from *caedere*, to "beat," "whip," or "flog." This etymology is specific to the *Lupercalia* and to a *praenomen* "Kaeso" used only by members of the Fabii and Quinctii, two families supplying *ministri Luperci* at the cult's origin (Serv. *ad Aen.* 8.343, *februis caedere*, to strike with the goat-hide whips).[43] However, in 45 BCE a third cult group for the Lupercalia was begun, the Iuliani, headed by Marcus Antonius.[44]

By "following through" thematically on "Caesar" as name (*prosequimur tua nomina*), Ovid indicates pursuit of the etymology of "Caesar." Placed just before the vocative *Caesar* and modifying *prosequimur* adverbially, the preceding ablative phrase *studioso pectore* ("with a zealous/studious intent") indicates a "studied" meaning at stake. In other words, Ovid refers to the celebration of Caesar's names and titles, not just elsewhere, but also here, in relation to Ovid's Lupercalian *militia*. Retroactively, Caesar's "name" or reputation seems "whipped up" by celebration of Ovid's elegies, and so Ovid appears to progress into manhood "in accord with" the meaning of Caesar's name (*per titulos ingredimurque tuos*), verbally "quipping" to draw Caesar's attention.

Ovid's playful misidentification of Caesar's name and excessive imitation of the meaning of "Caesar" might authorize the poet's own erotic play within the symbolic order of a calendar dominated by a family whose patriarch exiled him (cf. *pater patriae* at *F.* 2.119–44).[45] This playful (mis)identification of Caesar's name might then imply that Caesar is not the only gaze for which Ovid provides his exhibition (*munera*). Caesar could be lured into watching or interacting with Ovid (*mea munera respice*, 2.17–18). The wider Roman (male) audience could then watch the interaction between the two.

March and April: Two "Failed" Tests?

In the February preface, Ovid's overidentification with the gaze of "Caesar" provides him the cover of choosing manly honor over erotic pleasure: he "matures" to *sacra* and *militia*. But behind that screen, Ovid extends erotic play by formulating from the calendar itself a

"Lupercalian" elegy that can erode distinctions between *amor* and *militia* and maintain an elegiac *militia amoris* that the "Choice of Hercules" would separate between virtue and vice.

The merger of *militia* and *amor* continues in the prefaces of March and April. Representing two contradictory origins of the male subject and his life-story, both months and their patron deities (Mars and Venus) configure different imagined origins (primal fantasies) for the birth of the nation. While Venus, patroness of April, was the first in birth, family, or reproduction (*haec generis princeps*), Mars, patron of March, was the father of Romulus himself (*ipsius ille pater,* 1.39–40). Mars and Venus thus symbolize paradigmatic sexual differences: manhood-womanhood, war-sex, father-mother.

Yet Mars and Venus also figure binary options within the "Choice of Hercules," which confronts the male subject with a forced choice between Virtue (manly honor) and Vice (sexual and other enjoyments). That forced binary founds an awareness within the subject of society's proper or improper relation to enjoyment. However, the binary of Hercules' Choice did not force a "choice" in the February preface: his "Lupercalian" elegy blends *amor* and *militia*. In the March and April prefaces, Ovid again responds creatively to this psycho-social binary between Virtue and Vice by exposing its inconsistencies.

Diverting Enjoyment: Mars, Ars, and Ovid

As discussed earlier (ch. 2), Ovid and his elegiac calendar poem become receptacles for Mars' divine "seed" of inspiration comparable to Rhea Silvia and her twins. In effect, Ovid and the poem become objects of Mars' (surplus) enjoyment. But how does Ovid divert Mars' attention from war to aiding the *Fasti*, Ovid's object of enjoyment in treating the Roman calendar? Observations here focus on how Ovid's cultivated diversion, even "entertainment," of the god, mollifies Mars' physical antagonism in military prowess, rendering *virtus* (manly honor) more cultured and less threatening (perhaps more "feminine"), and turns him toward antagonism in the cultural symbolism of calendars. Ovid draws Mars from a less cultured, yet properly Roman, defensive hardness toward Ovid (as poet) and his "tender arts" (3.1–6, *ingenuis artibus;* 3.99–110; cf. 2.857–64) toward participation in Ovid's "strange camp" (3.173; cf. Prop. 4.1.135).

Being at leisure from war is a prerequisite for pursuit of surplus enjoyment. In the February preface, *vacatio militiae* freed Ovid (2.10) to

substitute Lupercalian elegies for *militia*, to divert Caesar (*mea munera
. . . respice*, 2.17–18), "if there's leisure" (*si vacat*) from pacifying the
enemy in war (2.18). In the March preface, Ovid cites Minerva as Mars'
leisured, yet competitive, model for displacing *arma* for the "tender
arts":

> ipse vides manibus peragi *fera bella* Minervae:
> num minus *ingenuis artibus* illa *vacat?*

> You yourself see that fierce wars are completed by the hands of Minerva.
> None the less, isn't she at leisure for tender arts?

Minerva takes leave from wars (*vacat*, 6) to enjoy "tender arts."[46] Here
vacat introduces Minerva's periodic shift from *arma* to "tender arts,"
ingenuae artes (3.5–6). Apparently Ovid wants Mars to be free (*vacat*) to
engage in *ingenuis artibus*, and he later invites Mars to search other calendars for months named after "Mars," " . . . if, by chance, you are free
[*quod si forte vacas*]" (3.87–88).[47]

Education in *ingenuae artes* can reflect one's tender character or render savage dispositions *mollior*, "softer," perhaps "more effeminate."
Ingenuae artes exercise civilizing influences, saving the overly masculine, hostile, or barbarian from savagery.[48] Ovid had included these
ingenuae artes or *bonae artes* in the education of young male lovers in
the City (*Ars.* 2.121–22: *nec levis ingenuas pectus coluisse per artes; Ars*
1.459–60, *bonae artes*). *Artes ingenuae* also mark superior social class:
Ovid contrasted his own *artes ingenuae* as an equestrian of inherited
wealth, status, and liberal education, with the crude violence and cash
of a rival for his mistress, who had freshly acquired equestrian rank
through the *militiae equestres* (military posts), earning him cash and
rank (*Amores* 3.8.1–38, esp. 1–8).

In a letter from exile to Salanus (Germanicus' training companion in
oratory), Ovid cites *ars ingenua* at the center of relations between himself, Salanus, and Germanicus (*Pont.* 2.5.65–66, cf. *F.* 1.22–23). Such
artes of literary creation are both *sacra* and *militia*, "rites of fellow sol-
diering that must be preserved" (*commilitii sacra tuenda*, 2.5.72).

Mars, Competition and the Rhetoric of Size

Likewise, in the March preface, Ovid verbally softens Mars' potential
violence through homosocial collaboration in these *artibus ingenuis*,

precisely the communal "rites" warranting Ovid's letter to Salanus concerning Germanicus. But in the March prefaces, Mars first needs to be at leisure, which is why Ovid recounts Mars' rape of Rhea Silvia, a sex story illustrating what he can do without actual weaponry (*inermis*, 3.8). This flatters Mars' male pride, thus winning his goodwill. Mars' fertility—the fathering of twins—is also a point of pride. Flattery diverts the god's attention from war. However, for some readers, rehearsing the story of Mars' rape of the Vestal Virgin Silvia (3.9–48) will highlight Mars' rape as aberrant behavior (see below). Ovid then augments Mars' pride in fatherhood, by narrating the birth and upbringing of his sons Romulus and Remus (3.49–58),[49] a tale culminating in Romulus' founding of Rome (69–72). Romulus himself is now a *pater*, "father of the City" (*pater urbis*, 71–72), swearing to provide symbolic proofs (*pignora multa dabo*, 73–74) that Mars was his father, by honoring Mars with the first month of his calendar. "March" would interest Mars as an honor accruing to him from his son.[50]

However, Ovid then focuses Mars' attention upon calendars by cataloging various other states, Latin and Greek (3.79–86, 87–98), that promoted their nation's military superiority through the symbolism of a month named after Mars. Romulus' calendar surpassed these, at least in making Mars' month the first (*F.* 3.97–98; cf. 1.29–30). This catalogue encourages Mars' pride. Moreover, inviting Mars to examine foreign calendars, if he is at leisure (*quod si forte vacas, peregrinos inspice fastos*, 3.87–88), tempts the war god into a more scholarly, leisured posture, diverting him from violent savagery (cf. *ferae genti*, 86) and war as a "studied" object of desire (*studium*, 3.80), toward practices of peace (cf. 3.173, *studiis pacis*) and more sophisticated methods of calendar construction for more subtle social ends. Ovid depicts these sophisticated, astronomical methods in an unflattering comparison of Romulus' calendar and Greek calendars (3.99–134). At 99–100, Ovid notes, " . . . the ancients [Romans] didn't have as many Kalends (month beginnings) as now: that year was *smaller* (*minor*) by two months" (cf. *F.* 1.27–32, above).[51]

For the competitive ego, size matters, and it encourages Mars' rivalry with more refined "Hellenic" knowledge (3.101–10). Greeks outpaced Romans in eloquence and other refined pursuits (101–2), including astronomy (105–10). Romulus and the early Romans were unaware of the divine star-signs. Instead, they considered fighting a form of eloquence and their military standards as divine signs. They were concerned with military conquest and military-censorial organization (1.29–30, 3.111–34). The contrast of Greek and Roman might prick Roman ethnocentric pride; Ovid even modifies Horace's famous tag by saying, "not yet had Greece surrendered conquered arts to her conquerors" (*F.* 3.101–2).[52]

At 119–20, Ovid expands his critique of the early Roman lack of knowledge, noting how much *shorter* Romulus' year was than the Greek year: "Therefore, minds untaught and still lacking rational understanding used a five-year cycle *smaller* [*lustra minora*] by ten months [than ours today]." This rhetoric of size goads Mars' male pride with a subtext: "the Greek calendar year was bigger than your son Romulus.'" Both uses of *minor* (3.100, 120) imply that the "Greek" solar year (adopted by Julius Caesar in Rome) is *larger, longer,* or *greater* than Romulus'. Ovid continues prodding Mars by telling him that Numa and then Julius Caesar had to reform his son Romulus' calendar by adding days to lengthen the year (3.151–52, 163–66).

Julius Caesar offers a competitor for Mars and Romulus (3.155–66). As Ovid notes (3.157–58): "That god [Divus Julius] and author of so great a lineage did not believe such matters [calendar] were *lesser* [*minora*] than his duties [*officiis*]."[53] Implicitly, Ovid is asserting, "Julius Caesar, who became a god, did not think the calendar was beneath his public duty. What about you, Mars?" Moreover, Julius Caesar tried to correct Romulus' original persistent error, a correction that Numa had attempted (*sed tamen errabant etiam nunc tempora*, 3.155). Such competition guides Mars to rivalry with Divus Julius, "that god" (*ille deus,* 3.157) who not only reformed the calendar to proper size, but was also the "father of so great a lineage," including the emperor Augustus and the Julii (*tantaeque propaginis auctor*, 3.157), and rivaling that of Mars and Romulus (2.119–44). Caesar even ventured imaginatively into heaven before death while mapping the heavens for his calendar reform (3.159–60; 1.295–310, esp. 307–10).

The rhetoric of size and the competition between Caesar and Mars help "Ovid" maneuver the god into contributing to his elegiac calendar. But his contribution to the Fasti's *ingenuae artes* (3.6) would soften the god into a figure resembling Minerva, another competitor.[54] Reflecting "tender arts," Ovid's calendar poem is an object of surplus enjoyment luring Mars into collaboration, but also competition.

March and the Screen of Diversion

Ovid leaves unresolved a certain unsettling moral dissonance. By telling a second story of rape (the Sabine women, 3.167–258), mirroring

Ovid's (Silvia's rape, 3.9), Mars, the prototype of proper manhood, provides an account of himself and his son (Rome's founder) violating Augustus' legalistic appropriation of traditionally domestic law and family control from heads of household to the state. This ethical contradiction is wholly relevant, because at *Fasti* 2.139–40 Ovid directly compares Romulus and Augustus on precisely this point—rape—and implicitly references Augustan marriage laws: *tu* [Romulus] *rapis, hic* [Augustus as *pater patriae*] *castas duce se iubet esse maritas.*[55] *Duce se*, "with himself as a model," may refer to Augustus' exile of both his daughter and granddaughter, who had been caught in alleged adulteries (Vell. 100.3–5, Suet. *Aug.* 65.).[56] Moreover, rumors reported Augustus' own enjoyment of deflowering virgins (Suet. *Aug.* 71, cf. 69). In defense of his erotic elegy, Ovid cites Ennius' revered epic, the *Annales*, as capable of rousing a woman to the point of weakness with its tale of Silvia raped by Mars (*Tr.* 2.259–60). Indeed, near the beginning of his *Ars amatoria* (1.101–32) Ovid cited Romulus' rape of the Sabine Women (a story told widely) as a model of behavior (1.131–32): "Romulus, you knew how to grant 'compensation' [Sabine Women] to your soldiers. If you gave me 'compensation' like that, I'd be a soldier."

This poses an interpretive problem for Ovid's elite male readers. Is rape at the foundation of Rome an "error" needing "correction"? These narrated fantasies of rape ground features of Roman "manhood" and "womanhood" (gender), that is, what men can do and women suffer. Could one possibly eradicate them from cultural memory?

The problem of rape at Rome's foundation is related to a broader issue: Ovid's sexual diversion of Mars from a military posture to forms of literary "enjoyment." According to one interpretation of the Choice of Hercules, Ovid's elegiac diversion might lead Mars from manly honor toward vice. Although Mars suitably explains his month's first ritual, the content and style of that explanation is either against the law (rape) or disturbing within Augustan cultural norms (Ovid's "penetration" by Mars; ch. 2). Such a narrative might therefore substantiate some readers' fears of vice in Ovid's elegiac calendar.

To others, however, Ovid might seem to use Mars' position within Roman culture to uncover contradictions within the symbolic order. Yet that message, too, is screened behind "diversion" or "entertainment," a mode of enjoyment that equally reveals and conceals ideology. Ovid took great pains to point out the moral license granted to public entertainments (staged mimes and pantomimes), thus undermining the legitimacy of moral criticism of his poetry as a reason for his exile (*Tr.* 2.479–520). Part of that entertainment in the March preface is

Mars' entry into Ovid's *nova castra,* his "strange camp," as a new form of *militia amoris,* marked by homoerotic innuendos (ch. 2). As Mars says (3.175–76): "and the undertaking is not a bother: to divert oneself [*morari*] in this way is a delight." Later in "March" (3.615–16), *mora* is the word that Aeneas uses to describe his diverting delay at Carthage, which the gods criticized.[57]

Ovid screens Mars' dilatory digression with the model (dis)order in the heavens. In constructing his revised, longer calendar, Caesar had marked out periodic "diversions" or "pauses" in the sun's path, solstices and equinoxes (*moras solis*), "where the Sun would go backward upon his own signs [constellations of the zodiac]" (161–62). An unusual expression for the winter and summer solstices and the spring and fall equinoxes,[58] *moras solis* ascribes to the sun moments of temporizing delay, entertainment, and regression (*mora,* literally "delay"), where the sun slows and turns direction, "retreating," in a sense. Retroactively, behind the astronomical screen, Mars seems to select Ovid's "delays of the sun" as a point of identification authorizing the god's dalliance with Ovid.

Mars' amusement in explaining why matrons worship him (cf. *iuvat in hac quoque parte morari,* 3.175) becomes evident in his luxurious elaboration of alternative etiologies.[59] Eventually realizing his prolixity, Mars comments retrospectively upon the inspirational "load" (*onus*) that he has given Ovid (3.249–50):

> Why do I *delay* and *load* your spirit with different explanations [*quid moror et variis onero tua pectora causis*]? *Look! What you're seeking is standing out in front of your eyes* [*eminet ante oculos quod petis ecce tuos*]. My mother likes brides: my mother's crowd throngs around me. Such a pious reason as this especially suits me.

Moror, "to delay" or "divert," signals Mars' entertaining "loitering" with Ovid. Yet *onero* recalls duty, as well as *onus,* "the burden," or *semen* in a woman's womb or "pregnancy," classifiable among beneficial labors with the *sacra,* military duties, public offices, and so on. Mars impregnates Ovid and his *Fasti* with multiple seeds, a grander poetic burden than earlier erotic elegy.[60] Innuendo supports this view. What does Ovid both seek (*quod petis*) and see (*eminet ante oculos . . . ecce tuos*)? Perhaps it is the phallic spear, the one object repeatedly observed in Mars' hand (*F.* 3.1, 8, 104, 172, 198, 225–32),[61] standing before Ovid's eyes, which won the Sabine women; it is likewise a magical implement of fertility (cf. Minerva, 3.7, as model for planting the spear, ch. 2).

Mars' spear provides a symbolic, "instrumental cause" of his potency in poetry and biology (*hasta*, 3.1, 172). Mars shows what Ovid wants (*quod petis*)—i.e., what causes matrons to worship him—standing out (*eminet*) before Ovid's eyes (*ante oculos. . . . ecce tuos*, 250). This gesture may indicate his spear as the instrument of his military manhood enabling rape of the Sabines and subsequent fertility, both biological and poetic. Ovid, too, wants what the spear symbolizes; his trajectory through the prefaces is toward *arma*, but on his own elegiac conditions. Thus, Mars answers Ovid as he did Romulus: "What you seek (my) weapon will grant" (*quod petis arma dabunt*, 3.198).[62]

April, Venus, and the Calendar Screen

Mars and Venus were frequently conjoined in Roman art and literature, a pairing traceable to Homer's *Odyssey* (8.267–367), where at the Phaeacian banquet a bard sings of Aphrodite and Ares caught in illicit lovemaking. The proem to Lucretius' didactic epic, *De rerum natura*, vividly described the seductive power of Venus' erotic kiss to placate Mars' violent urges (Lucr. 1.1–47), and Ovid alluded to their "juncture" before and after exile.[63] So, a reader might easily suspect that, in his encounter with Venus in the April preface, Ovid might mediate a juncture between Venus and Mars, prefigured in their adjoining months of March and April (*F.* 4.57–60, 133–34; 1.39–40).

The discussion here suggests that Ovid uses March and April to screen *militia amoris* as a response to polarities in the "Choice of Hercules" between adult male deferral of enjoyment (virtue) and boyish, even feminine, indulgence (vice). Ovid's elegiac art has already "seduced" Mars, divine figure of manly prowess (*Virtus*), into sharing with Ovid the "tender arts" (*ingenuis artibus*), whereby Mars "impregnates" Ovid and his calendar poem with divine inspiration. Now, in the April preface, Ovid encourages retrospection upon that seduction of Mars, from the position of Venus within the calendar's symbolic order. In the April preface, Ovid and Venus also look back toward the epilogue of the *Amores* (3.15), where Ovid had dramatically chosen to "mature" by dismissing Venus and taking up more serious genres, such as tragedy (*Medea*), epic (*Metamorphoses*), and perhaps the *Fasti* itself (*Tr.* 2.547–62).

This retrospection upon Ovid's "choice" of adult masculinity in *Amores* 3.15 and the February and March prefaces encourage readers to look behind the months and their maturational symbolism as screening (concealing yet revealing) Ovid's creative return to Venus amid a fundamental cultural antagonism in which Mars and Venus symbolize a basic incommensurability ("mismatch") between gendered positions of Roman national enjoyment. Ovid "sides" with Venus in this irremediable conflict within the ethics of masculinity in Roman (and Julio-Claudian) culture.[64]

Venus, Ovid, and Cultural Antagonism

Much of the April preface (*F.* 4.19–132) engages this cultural antagonism through an "academic" screen, by siding with Venus in an antiquarian debate over whether the month of April symbolizes "Venus" or other rival concepts (4.85–130, anticipated by 19–84). But the preface begins with Ovid resolving his own prior antagonism with Venus. At 4.1–18, Ovid is "returning" to Venus, "the mother of twin Loves" (*geminorum mater Amorum, F.* 4.1; cf. *Am.* 3.15.1, *tenerorum mater Amorum*), after he had parted ways with her in *Am.* 3.15, commanding her, "Recruit a new poet" (*quaere novum vatem*, 3.15.1), and "Tear away your golden standards from my ground" (*aurea de campo vellite signa meo*, 3.15.16), as if she were a military force dominating Ovid's literary power (*ingenium*; cf. *Am.* 3.1.25). Ovid declares, "a greater area should be trodden by my big horses" (*pulsanda est magnis area maior equis*, 3.15.18). He was finally entering the "space" of manhood's "greater work."

In the brief preamble (4.1–18), Ovid seems on the one hand like an equestrian youth having undergone the *transvectio* (above, and *eques*, *Am.* 3.15.6) and returning home to his poetic mother Venus to display his new manhood. He has sung "grander things" with Mars (*maiora*, 4.3; *area maior*, 4.10), the divine patron in Augustan Rome of males taking up the *toga virilis* and enrolling in the military (Dio 55.10.2).[65] On the other hand, Ovid explicitly resubmits to Venus as her "soldier" of *militia amoris*. While at *Am.* 3.15.16 Ovid ordered removal of Venus' *signa*, he implies at *F.* 4.7 that he never really abandoned them (*saucius an sanus numquid tua signa reliqui?*). While it is true that his poetic steeds now tread the *area maior* required of him as a man (*Am.* 3.15.18; *F.* 4.10), he still has Venus as his *propositum opus*, his "intended labor" (*F.* 4.8), implying the sexual libido lying beneath the "grander things" of adult male poetry (*maiora*, 4.3).

Ovid returns to "mother Venus" in a direction contrary to "progress" along an idealized path of maturation. He goes back to his (literary) source or mother, after having used elegy to seduce Mars, the god of manhood (*virtus*) toward erotic themes and "mother(s)" (*Matronalia*, March 1, and his mother Juno; *F.* 3.170, 245–52). Venus is *always* Ovid's work (*semper, F.* 4.8). His poetry represents the "real" workings of Venus screened in and behind grander parts of the symbolic order (4.7–10).

Caesar and Venereal Contagion

Ovid is easily reconciled with Venus, who transfers her "inspiration" to him by touching his brows (*tempora*) with a myrtle branch, her sacred plant.[66] Through this *touching* (*contigit,* 16), Ovid receives a vision (*sensimus,* 17) of the origins of days in Venus' month. He then turns to pass the "contagion" on to Caesar (4.19–22):

> siqua tamen *pars* te de fastis *tangere* debet,
>   Caesar, in Aprili quod *tuearis* habes:
> hic ad te magna descendit *imagine* mensis,
>   et fit adoptiva nobilitate *tuus.*

> But, Caesar, if any part of the calendar ought to *touch* you, you get something to *observe* in April: here, for you, a month descends in a *grand image*, and becomes *yours* because of family nobility obtained through adoption [Germanicus was Claudian, but adopted into the Julii].

Ovid's language of "touch" (*contigit,* 4.16; *tangere,* 19; cf. *texit,* "covered," 143) alludes to an affect that Venus inspires by the touch of myrtle (*sensimus,* 4.17; *sensit,* 143). Now that affect passes to Caesar via Ovid's metaphorical language conveying erotic innuendo (*pars* and *tangere,* 4.19).[67] As Venus' *vates* (4.14, 16), Ovid "transfers" (traffics) her or her significance in April to "Caesar" (*tuus,* 22).[68]

But Ovid's emphasis on Venus' "important image" (*magna imago*) screens her civic role as Genetrix or mother of Caesar's family, as represented in dynastic statuary (cf. *magna . . . imagine,* 4.21).[69] Yet, behind that image, Romulus named April after Venus, "because she had been *received at many stages* of his family" (*gradibus multis in gente receptam,* 4.27). This "reception" implies in the (Caesarian and Roman) family tree (4.31–56)—from Dardanus, son of Electra, down to Romulus and Remus, son of Ilia (Silvia)—repeated female acceptance of *venus* or sexual intercourse and reproduction outside legitimate marriage (Electra and Jupiter, 31–32; Venus and Anchises, 35–36, 123–24; Silvia, as Ilia, 55–56). While most individuals that Ovid names are "Julian" kings of Alba, references to females track sexual transgressions between gods and mortals and major geographic migrations of the family. The maternal in this lineage implicitly tracks a sometimes illicit, but creative, sexuality or *venus* "at many degrees in the family tree" (4.27).

Aphrodite and Greek Heroes

However, as Ovid later notes (4.85–90), some ancient scholars contended that *Aprilis* did not honor Venus, but derived instead from "opening," *aperire* (see below).[70] At 61–84, Ovid preempts this demotion of Venus by celebrating her birth from sea-foam, ἄφρος, and the multiple migrations of Greek heroes to Italy over her sea (*F.* 4.131–32, 18), importing her cult along with Hellenic culture (4.61–84).[71] Italy's reception of both Greeks heroes and their "Aphrodite" (sexual adventures) went hand in hand with producing local lineages around Italy.[72]

Ovid here manipulates Hellenism in a game of male rivalry with Venus' critics, played specifically through calendar interpretation and its application to cultural competition. On the surface, Greek culture works as it did in the March preface in Ovid's dealings with Mars. Greeks possess cultural priority and mediate a Roman desire for cultural distinction and dominance. Ovid pricks cultural egos by resituating Roman cult and culture within "Greater Greece" (*Graecia Maior,* 64) and Hellenic "precedent" (cf. *F.* 3.101–9). But Ovid does so with a purpose, to bolster the prominence of Venus within Roman cult and culture, thus preempting the arguments of interpreters demoting her. So, Ovid's brief history of Hellenic migration offers an "academic" screen behind which unfolds a male homosocial cultural polemic over the place of Venus (erotic desire) within the Augustan symbolic order, exemplified by April in the calendar.

The antagonism is "personal" as well as cultural. The catalogue cites the names of many heroes—Hercules, Evander, Odysseus, Halaesus, Antenor, and Diomedes—but culminates with the pair Aeneas and the little-known Solimus, a *comes* ("comrade") of Aeneas and founder of Ovid's native Sulmo (4.79–80). As companion exiles or refugees—one weaker, the other stronger—Solimus (*comes*, 79) and Aeneas indirectly model an heroic male pair, reflecting what Ovid desires with his ideal reader, Caesar (Germanicus).[73] This bond between Ovid and Caesar is signaled by the "touch" (i.e., the cult) of mother Venus that they share, as discussed above.

However, Ovid's thought of Aeneas and Solimus, who end their exile from Troy by founding Ovid's two "homes" (Sulmo and Rome), leads the poet into a lament over his current distant exile in his address to Germanicus (4.81–82). But he then suppresses his "Muse" (83) once he realizes the impropriety of singing the *sacra* sadly (84). Exile might also recall the alleged reasons for Ovid's exile—his *error* and his *Ars amatoria*.

Thus Ovid confronts not simply his exile, but the whole moralizing "disciplinary arena" of manhood (*area maior*, 4.9–10; *Am.* 3.15.17–18) censuring the presence of sexuality (*venus*) in his elegiac poetry (*Am.* 3.1, *Rem.* 357–96), where its erotic themes allegedly "caused" immoral behavior (*Tr.* 2). By being an embodiment of sexual enjoyment, Venus becomes a vexing, ironic figure between Roman men. Imperial rule entails her prominence as dynastic "mother"; but Ovid's erotic elegy had cultivated her as pleasure. Caesar, Ovid, and various male readers share her, but view her differently and shape her for different purposes. "Venus" thereby screens different male fantasies of desire.

Venus, Invidious Antagonism, and Ovidian "Care of the Self"

Rival etiologies conceal, yet reveal, this antagonism. At *F.* 4.85–132, Ovid suggests that envy (*livor*, 85), which had motivated moral criticism of Ovid's erotic poetry (*Rem.* 365, 369, 389–90), has also caused some to want to strip Venus of the honor of the name of April.[74] This censoriousness extends even to calendar interpretation by substituting a rival explanation of the month"s name: Spring "opens" (*aperit*, cf. *Aprilis*) all things as its warmth loosens the stiff chill of the earth and allows plants to grow (87–88). Ovid is claiming that, by appropriating from Venus' power these phenomena of spring, some scholars rob or begrudge the cultural value of Venus and of Ovid himself as her bard.[75]

The rest of the April preface, a hymn to Venus,[76] defends her in this cultural polemic. As in the March preface, "size matters" but Venus' mastery differs from Mars' (4.91–98):

illa quidem totum dignissima temperat orbem,
   illa tenet nullo *regna minora* deo,
iuraque dat caelo, terrae, natalibus undis,
   perque suos initus continet omne genus.
illa deos omnes (longum est numerare) creavit,
   illa satis causas arboribusque dedit,
illa rudes animos hominum contraxit in unum,
   et docuit iungi cum pare quemque sua.

It is she [Venus] indeed who most worthily tempers the whole world. She controls *domains lesser than no god,* and she issues laws to heaven, earth, her native seas, and she continues every breed of animal through her "entry." She created all the gods (it's too long to enumerate them), she gave the origins to seedlings and trees, and she drew together the rude minds of mankind into a unity, and taught them how each could be joined with his own mate.

Venus "tempers" the world.[77] The phrase "she controls domains lesser than no god" (*nullo regna minora deo,* 92; cf. *ius maius,* 118) implies that Venus' power rivals other, supposedly nonerotic powers. Her "rule" stretches into the animate universe (heaven, earth, sea, 93) by bestowing upon it an urge to "join" the self with another inspiring "culture" among humans (97–98).

As at *Ars amatoria* 2.477–78, *blanda Voluptas* or pleasure—another name for Venus—is the origin of cultivated human life. Pleasure is the very reason that creatures of every sort "come together" (99–100). But the examples follow the principle that a show of feminine allure softens the approach of an aggressive male. Venus softens male ferocity (*deposita . . . feritate,* 4.103). Although one can contradict this argument that Venus softens violence (cf. *Ars* 2.477),[78] Ovid here asserts that Venus' *voluptas* exerts a civilizing influence upon human males (107–8):

prima [vis] feros habitus homini detraxit: ab illa
   venerunt *cultus* mundaque *cura sui.*

This power [sexual urge, Venus] first removed from man feral deportment: from that power came *cultivation and tidy care of the self.*

While Venus' pleasure promotes reproduction in animals, it also creates self-awareness in the human male, *cura sui,* or "care of the self."[79] As interpreted by Michel Foucault (*History of Sexuality,* vol. 3), *cura sui* refers to a philosophical and cultural turn in the early empire toward moral self-reflection in addition to self-control of the "things of Aphrodite" (*aphrodisia*), a complementary discourse of mutual monogamy within marriage. Contemporary Augustan marriage and moral legislation augmented anxiety over the sexual deportment of men and appropriated to the state authority over sexual morality.[80] So, a restrictive turn seems to have contributed to Ovid's exile.

But this moralizing anxiety existed in tension with enjoyment. In this cultural antagonism, Ovid does not associate his "care of the [male] self" with the practices that Foucault described—pensive moral anxiety over pleasure. Far from it. Indeed, Ovid extols Venus in the sense of a sexual urge or act of pleasure. When relayed (deferred) through symbolic, prolonged quests for pleasure—i.e., surplus enjoyment—she is mother of all civilized cultivation (4.107–14). Venus and the pursuit of pleasure (*studio placendi,* 113) motivated the origin of thousands of arts and sciences (*artes,* 113).[81] Ovid's prime example of articulate culture (*eloquium,* 111) is love poetry and its classic scene, the locked door (*paraclausithyron*) so prominent in Roman elegy (109–14).[82] Consequently, Ovid's rhetorical construction of rivalry (*Livor,* 85–86, 115–16) between scholars contesting the meaning of "April" implies conflicting ideologies toward enjoyment or pleasure (*voluptas,* 99) from *Venus,* which Ovid cites as fundamental to self-knowledge (*cura sui*).[83]

Venus (un)Covered: The Myrtle Screen of Desire

The debate over the month's name is but an academic screen for antagonism over sexual desire within the symbolic order of the calendar. Venus' claim to a place within that order rests upon more than Romulus' legendary creation of March and April to honor his symbolic parents (4.57–60). Events on the Kalends of April dramatize how public cults "screen" antagonistic ideas of sexual morality. Ovid's handling of these cults encourages (male) readers to recognize, whatever their views, their own symbolic relation to "sex" (*venus*).

"Looking" is everything on April 1, as it is in elegy generally (cf. Prop. 1.3). First, Venus—i.e., her statue—takes a bath, either as part of her toilette or as a ritual repeating her birth from the sea.[84] As priestly-poet directing ritual, Ovid commands women—both prostitutes (134) and respectable matrons and daughters-in-law (133)—to remove Venus' jewelry, bathe her, then re-adorn her with jewelry and fresh flowers (4.135–38). While these events lure male looks, they occur "under" or behind a sacred "screen" of myrtle (*sub viridi myrto*, 139), which itself frames the visual event. To justify his command, Ovid recounts the origin of Venus' use of myrtle (141–44):

> litore siccabat rorantes nuda capillos:
> *viderunt satyri, turba proterva, deam.*
> *sensit* et opposita *texit sua corpora myrto:*
> *tuta fuit* facto, vosque referre iubet.

> She [Venus] was naked and drying her wet hair on the seashore. *Satyrs— that naughty band—saw the goddess.* She *sensed* it and *screened her body* by placing *myrtle* in the way: by that act she was *watched over* and orders you [the matrons and wives] to repeat the act.

Myrtle screened (*texit*, 143) the feminine "venereal" body as a "subtext" for male eyes. Mythic baths of goddesses sometimes ended in the death of males looking at their bodies (cf. Artemis-Diana and Actaeon). Not here. Venus realized (*sensit*, 143) the presence of the male gaze and used myrtle as a defense, confounding their senses, yet exploiting the presence of that gaze to promote her value. In some stories of her birth, Aphrodite-Venus *touches* the Satyrs with myrtle as if to drive them mad (they dance wildly) with a desire that renders them senseless.[85] Venus was safe using the myrtle (*tuta fuit facto*, 144) and advises mortal Roman women to do the same (143–44): the myrtle screen interrupts male looks at women's bodies, setting both within a symbolic cult(ural) event that augments feminine allure, inviting yet blocking further male looking.

   Myrtle, mediating the sexual anxiety of the culture, acts in this ritual scene like Ovid's language, that is, as a screen through which *venus,* sex, can be seen. A touch with myrtle and the words *coeptum perfice . . . opus* (4.15–16) are Venus' symbolic answer to Ovid's language, brokering his return to, reconciliation with, and inspiration by her in the opening scene (4.15–18). That initial language anticipates Venus' cult of the Kalends celebrating the primal origin, the birth, of "venereal" allure (4.133–44). Repeated words or the recurrence of related verbal forms affirm a formal recurrence of Venus as "experience" of the gaze (*sensimus*, 17; *sensit*, 143) of watching (over) or being watched (over)— leered at or protected—especially when Ovid transmits his contagion to Caesar (*te . . . tangere debet,* 19) in the form of a month dedicated to Venus, which the prince may "observe" (*in Aprili quod tuearis habes,* 20;

cf. *tuta fuit facto*, 144) metaphorically as a *magna imago* that he inherits from the Julian family (21–22; cf. *marmoreo . . . collo*, 135). The satyrs saw (*viderunt satyri*, 142), but so did Romulus (*hoc pater Iliades . . . vidit*, 23–24). Implicitly, Ovid and Caesar do so as well. Ovid thus alludes to Venus as a central power of (male) experience established within the "original" calendar and an important image and principle for Caesar to maintain (20). Venus is central to the *error* of Romulus' calendar (*F.* 1.32) and to the poetic *error* resulting in Ovid's exile.[86] So, within the mythical scene of Venus' bath or birth, the naughty band of Satyrs (*satyri, turba proterva*) take up a potential position for Ovid, Germanicus, or other (male) readers looking at (or for) Venus and inspired by a varied, fragmented "vision" of her.[87]

But Ovid's Kalends of April offers women a bathing option, less sublime than the myrtle-screen bath: supplicating the goddess *Fortuna Virilis* (Manhood's Fortune or Fortune from Manhood) and stripping naked at the men's bathing complexes. Ovid's contemporary Verrius Flaccus reports in his *Fasti Praenestini* that women make supplication on April 1, but that the "lower-class" women (*humiliores*) enter the men's bathing complexes, "because in them men are naked in that part of the body where the favor of women is desired."[88] But Ovid does not label these women as *humiliores*; the lack of a moralizing label constructs the day's events as subject to women's choice. In fact, all women (cf. *cunctas*, 147), or at least those willing to strip, could offer incense in the baths to Fortuna Virilis. The place receives them completely naked (*posito velamine*, 147) and *sees* every sort of bodily flaw (*vitium nudi corporis omne videt*, 148). Here women conceal their "flaws" (cf. *error*) from men with little more than a few grains of incense, for which Fortuna Virilis "stands in front" of women (*praestet*, 150) and screens (*celet, tegat*, 149) any *vitium* or flaw (4.147–50). Thus, the Kalends of April also holds erotic opportunities for men outside of wedlock and, perhaps, financial opportunities for women (prostitution) in the men's baths.[89]

But other rituals on the Kalends of April allude to wifely chastity, marital conflict, and restored marital harmony.[90] The drinking of ground poppy seed in milk, a marriage ceremony, recalls Venus' marriage to her husband Vulcan (*Aen.* 8.370–406), not her infidelity with Mars, her often mentioned extramarital consort in Rome (*F.* 4.57–58, 129–30, 153–54; their love triangle at *Tr.* 2.255–56). Women supplicate Venus as "Verticordia," or Heart-Change, to give them competitive beauty, good morals, and a good reputation (4.155–56) to "turn" their husbands back to them, as Ovid seems to have returned to Venus in the opening scene (4.1–18).[91]

Thus, Venus' Kalends captures multiple antagonistic male views of woman (madonna-whore), symbolic (fantasy) constructions screening a direct view of Venus in her glory. Yet the erotic allure remains behind these different (male) screens for desired objects, whether they are virtuous wives or prostitutes. Implicitly, Ovid's combined celebration of these rites on the Kalends could erode the distinction between virtue and vice. Such moral variety within the calendar might again invite debate among Ovid's readers about the significance of Venus.

May and June: The "Family" as Disciplinary Scene

March obviously precedes April in the calendar, and Ovid's "greater task" at hand (composing an elegiac calendar) will "progress" according to that chronology. But this temporal sequence provides the pretext for Ovid's avoidance of martial literary duties (epic), evident in his eroticizing Mars and in his "return" to Venus, the mother of erotic elegy, whom at the end of the *Amores* he had forsaken in order to take up a "greater task." Censorious readers might interpret Ovid's return to Venus as resumption of "error," or "regression," away from the burden of adult masculinity (*virtus*), back to indulgence (vice). In the prefaces of May and June, additional scenes of divine encounter reiterate the "primal fantasy" of the Choice of Hercules, which organizes the "origin" of adult masculinity in the forced choice between Virtue and Vice. By repeatedly returning to this scenario, Ovid revisits the ideological supports of "proper" manhood (*virtus*), by which his authorial identity and "error" were judged.

Managing the Divine Family: The End of April

The prefaces of May and June allude to Prodicus' "Choice of Hercules" via *Amores* 3.1 and mythic variations (Paris' Judgment), but complicate the notion of choice so as to demonstrate the irresolvable conflict of the burden that Ovid faces. The last vignette of April (4.943–54, April 28–30) anticipates these complexities. Here, Ovid chooses between two objects of celebration: the Games of Flora starting April 28 (*Ludi Florales* or *Floralia* lasting to May 3)[92] and the altar and statue of Vesta that Augustus installed in his Palatine house that same day (after becoming Pontifex Maximus on March 6, 12 BCE)[93]:

After Phrygian Aurora has left Assaracus' brother [Tithonus, Aurora's aging husband] and has lifted her ray in its immense globe, a goddess arrives with her hair braided with a crown of a thousand flowers [Flora] and the *stage keeps her custom of (sexually) freer jesting*. Flora's ritual also passes over onto the Kalends of May: I'll look to it again at that time, *now a grander work is pressing me [grandius urget opus]*.

Vesta, seize the day [April 28]: Vesta has been received within the threshold of her *male relative [cognati . . . limine]*; so the just fathers [senators] ruled. Phoebus [Apollo] has a section of the house. Another part cedes to Vesta. He [the relative] himself, the third one, holds what is left over from them. Stand Palatine laurel trees, and may the house stand, protected by the oak [wreath]: one house holds three eternal deities.[94]

Here Ovid chooses between Flora and Vesta. Vesta, the goddess protecting the state hearth, was associated with chastity through the Vestal Virgins (her priestesses). By contrast, Flora, goddess of flowers, sexuality, and fertility, was associated with prostitutes who stripped and performed erotic mimes at her *ludi scaenici* (theater shows, 4.746; 5.183, *ludis iocosis, theatris*, 189, 331–34).[95]

Thus, Ovid here faces a choice analogous to that between Virtue and Vice. Vesta symbolizes a facet of idealized manhood (*virtus*), its supposed self-control or deferral of sexual and other enjoyments, while Flora represents banqueting and immediate indulgence in enjoyment (Vice), a lack of restraint (5.331–34). Topography made the binary choice obvious: Flora's temple (*aedes*) on the Aventine Hill stood near (*iuxta*) the Circus Maximus,[96] facing the House of Augustus on the Palatine Hill. These two cults of conflicting morality were within view of each other across the Circus valley. As if choosing virtue over vice, Ovid defers celebration of Flora to relate how Augustus (Vesta's male relative, or *cognatus*) installed the chaste goddess Vesta as a "family member" within his household.

Allusion to the "Choice of Hercules" screens this literary choice as one of manly honor. Ovid delays celebrating Flora's festival (until May 2, F. 5.182–378), because a "bigger piece is pressing," *grandius urget opus* (4. 948), which is lifted from the last line of *Amores* 3.1 where, facing a "Herculean choice" between Tragedy and Elegy, Ovid tells Tragedy, the grander genre, to wait (*Am.* 3.1.67–70):

"Tragedy, give a poet a little time. You are an *unending labor [labor aeternus]*; what she [Elegy] wants is but brief [i.e., sex]." Persuaded, she [Tragedy] gave me leave—while there's time, may my tender Loves hurry [with sex]; a 'bigger piece' is pushing from the rear (*a tergo grandius urget opus!*)![97]

At *Am.* 3.1.70 the phrase, "from the rear" (*a tergo*), precedes the clause *grandius urget opus*.[98] Tragedy, a rather phallic "female" surrogate for *Virtus* ("manliness"), prods Ovid from the rear (*a tergo*) with her "staff" (*thyrsus*), toward a *maius opus* (*Am.* 3.1.23–4).[99] In *Amores* 3.1, Ovid's reaction is perverse or at least obstinate; Tragedy's staff at his rear motivates the poet to make "love" faster with Elegy.

But at the end of "April," celebrating Vesta aligns with the *grandius opus*, and Flora is equivalent to Elegy-Vice. Ovid chooses to celebrate Vesta first: if he did not, the *domus Augusta* would approach *a tergo*. But Ovid's is a Janus-like approach (1.66, 92; Ch. 3)[100] to the pressing *grandius opus* (*F.* 4.948). While Ovid has chosen first to celebrate Vesta's worship within the House of Augustus, his six-line treatment of her is "short" (4.949–54) compared with Flora's deferred 196-line passage (*grandius opus*, 5.183–378). Ovid endorses Flora with a personal "signature" (*sphragis*) at the end of the Flora episode, associating his name *Naso*, "nose," with smelling—enjoyment—of Flora, "Flower" (5.375–78). Thus, Ovid's earlier choice first to celebrate Augustus' domestic cult of Vesta screens a "latent" choice of Flora.

But Ovid's focus on the household of the emperor draws attention to Augustus' moral-domestic management. Regulation of the household was an elite male concern, especially regarding sexual behavior—both his own and that of members of his household. Even Augustus was subject to observation and gossip in this regard.[101] As Pontifex Maximus managing the Vestal Virgins, he was required to live in the *Domus Publica* (in the Forum Romanum near the "House of the Vestals"). But Augustus gave the *Domus Publica* to the Vestal Virgins, made his Palatine house "public," and installed there an altar and statue of Vesta.[102] The result was a tripartitioning of the House of Augustus among *three* deities—Apollo, Vesta, and Augustus himself—anticipating the divine choices in the May and June prefaces.[103]

Verbal repetitions signal retroactively from the May and June prefaces that the end of April anticipates the divine "tripartition" of the subsequent prefaces. In April, Ovid uses the word *pars* to describe the gods sharing the *domus Augusti*,[104] and he stresses (4.954) the numbers "three" and "one."[105] This numerical language reappears at the ends of the May and June prefaces: "Every *part* of the crowd [of nine Muses] had the same [number, i.e. three]," 5.110; "The stated explanation is *three*-fold," 6.97; and "*two* [goddesses] harm more than *one* helps,"

6.100.[106] These repetitions frame the conflicting female deities of the
May and June prefaces within a domestic scene of household management on a divine level, a "scene" recently broached at the end of
"April" by Ovid's mention of three deities within the House of Augustus, but anticipated by Janus, the doorman of the heavenly palace (*F.*
1.137–40, 125, 173–74; cf. 107–8).

May, June, and Antagonism within the Divine House

Both ancient philosophy and Roman custom posed the ideal male subject as master and manager of his household. Philosophical literature
often constructs scenes of dialogue between men consulting with each
other about such management: wives, mothers, and sexual pleasure
(slave boys or prostitutes) pose crises for male governance of self and
family.[107] Male homosocial "talks with a confidant, with friends, with a
guide or director" aid management. In fact, such a dialogue was precisely the context in which Socrates in Xenophon's *Memorabilia* cited
Prodicus' tale of Hercules at the crossroad (*Mem.* 2.1.20–34).

Several features of Ovid's May and June prefaces encourage comparison with a Herculean style choice. Ovid begins the May preface by
directly comparing himself to a traveler at a crossroad uncertain which
path to take (*F.* 5.1–6), the very setting of Hercules' choice in its famous
Pythagorean version (represented also by the Greek letter upsilon).
The main narrative portion of the June preface begins with Ovid
searching for the "origin" of June in an isolated grove near a bubbling
brook (6.9–16), as if metaphorically searching for a "source" for his eti-
ological "stream" of discourse (cf. Prop. 3.3.1–6, 13–27, 51–52). This setting of grove and fountain, while perhaps a commonplace (Prop.
4.4.3–6), mirrors the one in *Amores* 3.1.1–6 where Ovid had sought
what *opus* (6) he would take up and encountered Tragedy and Elegy in
a scene modeled on the "Choice of Hercules." Moreover, Ovid twice
compares his encounter with three goddesses (Juno, Juventas, and
Concordia) to the Judgment of Paris (6.13–16, 99–100), a variation
upon the allegorical diatribe also found in the Choice of Hercules.[108]

Sufficient clues may support interpreting the prefaces of May and
June through the screen of Hercules' Choice, but the form of these scenarios exceeds the simplistic dimensions of the Herculean model.
First, the number of choices that Ovid faces is greater than Hercules'
(three, not two), although it does not exceed Paris' (choosing "the
fairest" among Juno, Minerva, and Venus). Perhaps, as Ovid notes at

6.99–100, Paris, whose choice of Venus-Aphrodite started the Trojan War, offers an anti-heroic position in the fantasy, contrary to idealized Hercules.

Secondly, Ovid's choices allude not just to moral ideology in the abstract; some options are highly politicized features of contemporary imperial policy as enacted in contemporary social laws and religious iconography. We have already seen that Ovid earlier interpreted May and June as named after the two main age groups of elite males (1.41; cf. 5.55, 6.87), the *maiores*, or elders, and the *iuniores*, or juniors, an interpretation found in Fulvius Nobilior's calendar-commentary housed at the temple of Hercules and the Muses (Macr. *Sat.* 1.12.16; ch. 1).[109] In the preface to May, the muse Urania argues for this etymology, but it is contested by the the muse Polyhymnia, who argues that May is named after *Maiestas*, a personified essence of grandeur associated with lofty position, ideally modeled upon Jupiter's as ruler of the universe. *Maiestas* was important to imperial ideology and politics as the term applied to the divine essence of the state (*res publica*), the senate, or the emperor.[110]

These politics of the May and June scenarios are additionally complicated, because some of Ovid's choices are "personal" and thus might offend members of the imperial family. *Maiestas* could be linked with the person of the emperor (Ov. *Tr.* 2.511–12, below) or an imperial family member, such as Livia (*Pont.* 3.1.155–56). But Carole Newlands has observed how Ovid's June preface presents a disagreement between female members of the family of gods (Juno and Juventas) and the values of family harmony (Concordia personified) and that these goddesses have political importance for Rome.[111] This observation indicates the domestic antagonism operating within the scenes. Juno is mother of Juventas; Juventas is hostile to her mother; and Concordia celebrates the intermarriage of Sabines and Romans and symbolizes domestic and political harmony. But this mythical conflict could be "personalized" by linking these goddesses with female members of the imperial house, especially Livia, Augustus' wife. Vesta, the goddess installed in the Domus Augusta on April 28 (above), was associated with the public image of Livia, who was called Juno both in inscriptions and in Ovid's poetry, both the *Fasti* and elsewhere.[112] As for Juventas, Juno's daughter, Augustus rebuilt her temple in the Circus Maximus.[113] But Livia's ancestor M. Livius Salinator vowed the temple to Youth (manpower) at the Battle of the Metaurus River where he defeated Hasdrubal, Hannibal's brother (207 BCE).[114] While Concordia has a complex history as a deity of Roman class conflict and harmony, between the patrician-equestrian and plebeian social orders, she had been recently prominent in official "family" policies of Augustus[115] and represented domestic and conjugal harmony between the Claudian and Julian branches of the family, celebrated by Livia' construction of an altar or perhaps *aedes* to Concordia in her Porticus Liviae (*F.* 1.649–50, 6.637–38).[116]

Ovid's literary choices in these prefaces remain far more complicated than Hercules', also because Ovid leaves his points of decision—his crossroads—"undecided." Desire for divine cooperation may motivate Ovid's hesitancy in both scenes. In the May preface, he wants the support of all the Muses; he cannot forego the favor of those Muses whose views he would have to reject. In the June preface, Ovid seeks to avoid mimicking the choice of Paris and Troy's destruction renewed in contemporary Rome (6.15–18, 99–100; Prop. 4.1.47, *resurgentis Troiae*), a clear case of the poet recognizing that his literary choices can be judged through the screen of moralizing myth. But basically, he avoids what he interprets as Paris' mistake: offending two goddesses by preferring just one (the three being Juno, Juventas, and Concordia [6.100: *plus laedunt, quam iuvat una, duae*]).

For Which Gaze?

More important than explaining precisely why Ovid avoids decision making is the question (also not fully answerable), "For which gaze does Ovid produce these fantasy scenes of indecision"? These scenes revisit the ideological "origins" of these months, providing literary versions of "primal fantasies" elaborating ideological supports of contemporary male identity in the symbolic order of government and family.

By "gaze" I refer not to a particular person's "view" (such as Germanicus', Augustus', Tiberius', Livia's, or even Ovid's) which could be integrated into Ovid's rendering of May and June. Rather, his very indecision implies, or perhaps fashions, some uncertain point within the Roman symbolic order that cannot easily be integrated, a central irreducible antagonism. Ovid's iterations of the "Choice of Hercules"—his avoidance of choice in its precise terms—bespeaks a repeated confrontation with the fantasy formed around this antagonism. Moreover, by twice refusing to come to a decision (closure), Ovid perpetuates his presence before this antagonistic point, where he as subject is fixated by an "impossible gaze by means of which the subject is already present at the act of his/her own conception." The "conception" in question here is one of manhood conceived at a point of decision (castration; separation from enjoyment) at a kind of second birth.[117] Ovid's recurrence to the "Herculean Choice" and his attempted obviation or suspension of it in some sense act as a discordant "blot" revealing yet concealing, blocking, the spot from which this gaze emanates and delimits human (male) control, where Troy's Paris—everyman—must err, yet conceal his error, upon entrance into (symbolic) manhood.

By refusing to play the part of Paris (6.99–100), Ovid refuses the Law—the binary symbolic order that constructs the choice between virtue or vice, and screens "perception" through them. On one level, the encounters with three goddesses render the poet mesmerized or disempowered (castrated; de-authorized[118])—by itself, Ovid's indecision acts as a confusing stain, *vitium*, upon the *maius opus* of his manhood. But, on another level, that staining indecision, if deliberately produced, stations Ovid dramatically at a time just before committing an error à la Paris. From that position Ovid can envelop his reader in the simultaneous lack and surplus of meanings for the origins of May and June. Ovid remains at a loss, although a surplus of meanings is available (three deities and concepts in each month). As Ovid states when introducing the May preface (*F.* 5.6): "I don't know which way I should go and *the very abundance* [of explanations] *is harmful* [*copiaque ipsa nocet*]."[119] What we have is excess cultural enjoyment around potential antagonism.

Comparison between these scenarios complicates identification of the gaze for which Ovid displays indecision. Since the options in the May and June prefaces are entangled with each other, they have the effect of producing points of lateral perspective between the two scenarios. For example, *Maiestas* is political, yet "she" is personified and has esteemed "parents"—Honor and Reverence (5.23–26)—and friends who sit with her, Shame and Fear (5.29). Later, she holds Jupiter's scepter and sits beside him (5.45–46). But is that not where Juno, the first claimant for honor in June, should sit? She is both the wife and sister of Jupiter (6.27), queen of the gods (*regina*) or leader of the goddesses (*princeps dearum*, 6.37), who holds the scepter (6.38) and shares Jupiter's couch (*torus*, 6.33). *Maiestas* in May claims many of these attributes; she is herself rather like a political hussy, a usurper or rival (*paelex*, 6.35) for Juno's position. As Jupiter's concubine, Maia (the third claimant in May) bore Mercury. Mercury's son Evander brought to Latium the cults of Faunus (Lupercalia), Mercury (5.663–92), and

Maia (Mercury's mother, 5.81–106). Also, if Ovid chooses what he had earlier advocated as honoree for May, the "elders" (*maiores*, 1.41), then logically in June he should also advocate Juventas, representing *iuniores* or *iuvenes*. In addition to these demands, Juventas quarrels with her mother, Juno (6.67–74, 89–90). In these two prefaces, Ovid confronts complex contradictory pressures and intense jealousies among the goddesses. All these demands impact Ovid's authorial situation. If Ovid should choose one goddess in one scene, he would confront hostilities from the other scenes that threaten to confound a comprehensive order. Consequently, although meanings of the month-names are available in excess in the prefaces of May and June, there remains, ironically, a persistent lack of or desire for determined meaning that is screened by Ovid's own authorial failure.

Ovid does identify certain views from outside these scenes, and one can imagine these persons looking at, judging, and perhaps guiding Ovid's indecision. The poem's dedication invites Germanicus' critical scrutiny and guidance of the poem (1.1–26). In February, Ovid invites "Caesar" to view the poem (*respice*, 2.17–18). In the preamble to June (6.1–8), Ovid anticipates his ultimate indecision by inviting readers to choose: "This month also has uncertain reasons for its name: you yourself choose *what pleases you* from those reasons presented" (6.1–2). Ovid lures "you" to form meaning by choosing from the various reasons for the month name (*quae placeat . . . leges*, 6.2), thereby vacating a Paris-like position of male choice. Already in the opening of "May," Ovid addresses his audience: "*You*'re asking how I think the name was given to May" (5.1). At the end of the May preface, Ovid returns to his quandary with the question, "What should I do? Every faction [of Muses] has the same number" (5.107–8). We might imagine Ovid's wider (male) readership looking at the poet's indecision, judging him or wanting to advise.

Ovid's addresses to readers at the beginnings and endings of these prefaces turn the gaze of antagonism from within the uncanny scenarios (cf. the fear: *horrueram tacitoque animum pallore fatebar*, 6.19; cf. 1. 95–98) back upon the viewer-reader. While a reader may initially "look at" Ovid and judge, that reader also can soon become involved in the gaze itself—become a "Paris"—if he deigns to choose within the scene. If he fails to choose, that, too, subjects him to a failure or stain (*vitium*). Such a gaze is embodied in the symbolic (dis)order of the scene itself.

Conclusion: A Retrospective

In his handling of monthly prefaces, Ovid exposes *vitium*, not merely his own vice, but the flaw or crack in masculinity in the Roman symbolic order. The sequence of prefaces traces in part Ovid's attempted entry into adult male responsibility, in literary form, by undertaking a *maius opus*, a "greater work" celebrating the calendar in elegiac verse. But this process leads to Ovid's encounters with and attempted management of splintering antagonisms, until representation of that symbolic order—a *symbolon* or token of relation between men—breaks in half. This kernel of antagonism within Roman culture, screened in Ovid's various prefatory scenes, is only partially illumined by the scenarios of the "Choice of Hercules" or the "Judgment of Paris." These scenes variously iterate collapse of the fantasy of a monolithic masculinity facing a naïve difference between Virtue and Vice, a simplistic fantasy-choice where one can easily discern virtue (manly honor) and submit to its burden.[120]

Ovid's prefaces exploit the scene of heroic male choice to stage the irruption of antagonism within the symbolic order of the calendar, especially the May and June prefaces, where conflicting meanings gather and offer split, conflicting gazes that peer from behind Ovid's vacated locus of judgment toward readers examining Ovid's broken *Fasti*. That complex, multiple gaze of conflicting gods, then, might also draw an attentive audience into Ovid's impossible situation.

This placement of Ovid against such gaps in the calendar's symbolic order positions him as an author still working at the strategic points of symbolic breakage and conflict left by his exile. It is from this cleft in the calendar's symbolic order (Ovid's *symbolon*) that fantasies emerge to cover, or screen, the gap. This explains why various ideological readings of Ovid's *Fasti* are possible; they attempt to seal the "wound" in the symbolic—an impossibility (Ovid seems to show): there is always some stray image or power escaping the symbolic order and threatening to disrupt it. That element can approach *a tergo*; therefore, one should approach the symbolic warily, like a Janus, with two faces, or like Hecate Trivia, with three (1.141–42).

CHAPTER FIVE

Under the Imperial Name: Augustus and Ovid's "January" (Fasti, Book One)

a calendar screens mastery of time by presenting a field of signifiers referring to the order of things (e.g., months, days, seasons, astronomical movements, festivals, etc.). In the luni-solar Republican calendar, those signifiers "erred." Its year "wandered" from the solar cycle, fixed by winter and summer solstices and spring and fall equinoxes (e.g., Liv. 1.19; Ov. F. 1.163–64, 3.161–66; ch. 1). The Republican calendar required more intercalation than did the Julian solar calendar, and the pontifical college and senate determined the timing of that intercalation. Consequently, Rome's shift to Caesar's solar calendar had political symbolism. Reducing and regularizing intercalation to one day, Caesar's calendar transferred control from traditional elites (the pontifical college and the senate) to an "automatic" solar-astronomical mechanism, established by Caesar's one-man rule and monitored by bureaucratic, often foreign, professionals (astronomers). In other words, local negotiation among Republican elites over this temporal sliding, which would be a potential flaw in the new order, ended with installation of an imperial solar year. This new order of calendar-knowledge bolstered the new totalitarian rule.

The Julio-Claudian solar calendar was "imperial" in another sense: it included festivals honoring Julius Caesar, his heir Augustus and the Julio-Claudian dynasty. Just as the new solar calendar stabilized "veering" intercalation, new dynastic festivals grounded imperial power as its center of meaning, characterizing the Julio-Claudian family as shared symbolic support and goal of Rome's imperial destiny. Inscribed in calendar headings and festival entries, the imperial name marked the pivotal position of difference in the whole symbolic field.[1]

Identification of the calendar with the emperor's name grounded the way that it symbolically mediated other male identities. At *Tristia* 2.251–52, Ovid heralds the thematic importance of the imperial name in the *Fasti:* "My fate has broken that work [the *Fasti*], recently written under your name, Caesar [*scriptum sub nomine, Caesar*], and dedicated to you." This theme of *nomen* is implied in the poem's dedication when Ovid informs Germanicus that in the calendar poem "you will find your family's domestic festivals; often your (adoptive) father [Tiberius] and your grandfather [Augustus] are to be read (*saepe tibi pater est, saepe legendus avus*, 1.10). The poet iterates the theme in the preface of February (2.15–16): "Still I am celebrating with eager heart, Caesar, your names [*tua . . . nomina*], and I am advancing according to your titles [*per titulos . . . tuos*]." This chapter and the next examine how Ovid handles imperial epithets (*cognomina*) as a means of identifying the self within the symbolic order.

In these two chapters, interpretation turns from the level of months to that of days within January and February, focusing upon Ovid's celebration of *Augustus*, "Venerable," in January (January 15, the Ides, 1.587–616), and *pater patriae*, "father of the fatherland," in February (Feb. 5, the Nones, 2.119–144; ch. 6). Ovid's treatment of imperial *cognomina* enables readers to explore imperial name and reputation as part of the calendar's screen of symbolic order—as concealing, yet revealing, antagonisms and lack or failure of order. In both books the narrative functions of women, the feminine, and castration help to adumbrate another side of male fantasy—loss and its attempted recuperation.

Analysis here begins with observation of the key tropes by which Ovid represents the conflicting significance of the *nomen Augusti*, as site of stability, yet anxiety in Rome's imperial order: primarily *Augustus* as the *axis mundi*. The chapter then elaborates discussion in three parts. The first examines how Ovid characterizes the *nomen Augusti* in conflicting ways, as support of symbolic order, yet as object of male rivalry, potential failure, and, consequently, as a source of anxiety. The specter of animal "orality" and sacrifice in Ovid's *Agonalia* illustrates how the identities of Ovid and many of his readers offer a symbolic contrast to the structural dominance of the *nomen Augusti*. The second part suggests how *Augustus* as *axis mundi* bolsters a crucial metaphor in which astral notices in "January" act as markers enabling "foresighting" and "backsighting," processes by which readers generally construct symbolic order (meaning) in Ovid's poem. The chapter's third section explores how Ovid's handling of major festivals in "January" encourages conflicting, retroactive interpretation of the *Nomen Augusti* and Augustan ideological symbols such as Peace and Concord, dynastic fertility, and manly honor, which are now anxiously insecure after Augustus' death (14 CE).

Augustus as "Quilting Point": An Introduction

"January" (Book One) indicates the emperor's pivotal position by associating the name *Augustus*, an imperial *cognomen* heritable by Tiberius upon Augustus' death (Tac. *Ann*. 1.11–13; Suet. *Tib*. 26.2; Dio 57.2.1; 57.8.1–2),[2] with an instrument frequently used to construct structures of time and space, the *gnomon*. This Greek word refers to the shadow-pointer in ancient sundials which functioned as astronomical calendars as well, but use of the *gnomon* was not limited to sundials or astronomical calendars. By measuring the sun's shadow-length in different locations of the empire, ancient geographers calculated the earth's circumference, constructed latitude (north-south position on the earth's curvature), and mapped the empire. Locally, land surveyors used the *gnomon* to lay out the main boundaries of territories (centuriation), organize streets of new towns, and create local maps. *Gnomonike*, the systematic application of the *gnomon*, supported not only Caesarian construction of a solar calendar, but also an imperial project (managed by Agrippa) of mapping the world at both macro and micro levels. As Claude Nicolet has demonstrated, this effort enabled word-wide census and taxation, integrating far-flung localities into one imperial, bureaucratic network.[3]

A pivotal instrument of local, yet cosmic measurement of time and space, the *gnomon* provides an objective metaphor for the central position of "emperor" as the key signifier by which the subject could measure his difference—his identity—within the symbolic field, a function Lacan called a "quilting point" (*point de capiton*) of the symbolic order.[4] The *cognomen Augusti* acts as a "quilting point" of elite male identity, stationing "Augustus" within a network of cultural signifiers, much like the *gnomon* as a central axis indicated by its shadow other relative positions in a spatial-temporal system. As symbolic center (quilting point), *Augustus* pins down Roman cultural symbols like the calendar as "imperial" and helps identify the elite male subject's place within the ideological screen of imperial order: the title *Augustus* temporarily stabilizes semantic drift of cultural signifiers—allowing local, subjective variations, but orienting broad interpretation of self and others around imperial rule.

But Ovid does more in *Fasti*, Book One, than simply explicate the objective order of imperial rule. He also uses figurative language and sound-effects at a phonemic level (even outside of syntax) to herald potential deformations of that order. If the syntax and vocabulary of Ovid's poetry are a poetic screen of the calendar's objective order, then its figurative play of sounds apart from that order (produced on lips between words, between the lines of the register of writing) render an uncanny "voice," perceptible to subjective, antagonistic desires that have been excluded from the calendar's screen. In fact, it is the play of such sound-effects that suggests recognition of the *nomen Augusti* as a figurative *gnomon* of the imperial symbolic order.[5] However, this phonemic play, interpretable as an error (of the poet or the reader), also associates this quilting point with repression or concealment of other meanings.

I: What's in a Name?

Nomen Augusti *and* Anxious Male Identity

Ovid celebrates the senate's grant of the title Augustus to Octavian on the Ides of January (13th), one of three "pivot days" (with Kalends and Nones) halfway in the structure of a Roman month (ch. 1). All Ides were sacred to Jupiter (*F.* 1.56; Macr. *Sat.* 1.15.14–15, 18), and here a possible association, even equation, of the emperor with Jupiter (the emperor as Jupiter on earth) would not be unusual (*F.* 2.138–9).[6] What is unusual is Ovid's comment that the vitals of a *gelded* ram (*semimaris ovis*, 588) are offered to Jupiter on the Ides of January. Might sacrifice of a gelded ram be salient to interpretation of the *nomen Augusti?* This is a question to which I will return after discussing broad themes in Ovid's homage to the *nomen* (1.587–616).

After commenting on the gelded sacrifice, Ovid presents *Augustus* to Germanicus (590) as a name marking superiority in male rivalry for esteem (*contigerunt nulli nomina tanta viro*, 592). In the passage as a whole, the size of a man's conquests measures his relative stature among men (cf. *superbum*, 595). Special names acknowledge heroic stature by labeling a man's *geographic* contribution to "increasing"

Rome's *imperium*. Many *cognomina* derive from locations conquered and added to Rome's *imperium* (1.592–600). Their listing "maps" that imperium: Africa (Publius Scipio *Africanus*, 593), the Isaurians (Publius Servilius Vatia *Isauricus*, proconsul 78–74 BCE; F. 1.593–94); Crete (Quintus Caecilius Metellus *Creticus*, 69 BCE, 1.594); the Numidians (*Numidicus*, 1.595); Messana in Sicily (Manius Valerius Maximus Corvinus *Messalla*, 263 B.C.; 595); and Numantia in Spain (Publius Cornelius Scipio Africanus *Numantinus*, 133 BCE; 596).[7]

But names mark a man's stature in other ways. For example, some names mark scenes of hand-to-hand combat between two men (Torquatus and Corvinus) and derive from symbols or booty from that contest (necklaces, crows, 601–2). Secondly, relative status can be marked through degrees of linguistic comparison of an adjective. "The Great" (*Magnus*), Pompey's title, is the measure of his great deeds (603), but Caesar was "greater" (*maior*, 604), because he defeated Pompey (at Pharsalus). However, *Maximus*, a title belonging to the Fabii—the superlative "degree" (*gradus*, 605) of *magnus*—exhausted the capacity of *magnus* to indicate a further degree of fame (603–6). Thirdly, accumulation of *cognomina* was another practice but, Ovid observes, Caesar would gain as many names as there are nations in the world (599–600). Something more practical is needed. Besides these are all merely human honors.

Consequently, Ovid celebrates the emperor's title *Augustus* as marking the divine power underlying all heroic names—that of "increase" itself (*augere*), the divine force of the empire's growth.[8] "Increase" underlies manly accomplishment (*virtus*) and is associated with the augural blessing from "Heaven" or Jupiter that such men receive when taking the auspices before battle. The origin of *Augustus*, the title, was itself "augural" (587–616). *Augurium* (augury) and the adjective *augustus* are related words (611);[9] *templa*, the spaces of augural viewing, are called *augusta* (609),[10] and Jupiter or heaven uses his power to cause any kind of increase (612). Thus, the title *Augustus*— associated with heaven itself or Jupiter (*hic socium summo cum Iove nomen habet*, 608)—signifies Octavian's more than human stature or status (Dio 53.16.7–8). Ovid then prays that Jupiter will increase the supreme power and years of the Roman emperor (*augeat imperium nostri ducis, augeat annos*, 613), who here seems to be Tiberius, because the next couplet, revised after Augustus' death in 14 CE, concludes the vignette by praying (615–16) that the *heir* (*heres*) of so great a *cognomen* assume the burden of the world-order (*orbis onus*) with the *same* omen as his father (*pater*).

But the echo of *omen* in the word *cognomen* (615–16) suggests that Tiberius confronts his inherited burden of name and rule with a certain anxiety. The gods are "augurs" (*auspicibus deis*), while Tiberius is to take up world-wide governance and the name *Augustus* as his patrimony. But in the dedication (1.25–26), Ovid has asked Germanicus to act as *auspex*, so that the "whole year" (*totus annus*) or his whole *Fasti* (a representation of the *annus*) would proceed felicitously. At 615, *auspicibus* marks Germanicus' augural role as ideal reader of "signs," a role invoked already at 591–92, when Ovid urges him to read *carefully* (*perlege*) the noble *nomina*.[11]

The final couplet (615–16) focuses attention upon Tiberius' succession in 14–15 CE, when he not only exposed his reluctance to use his adoptive father's *cognomen* (*Augustus*) in Rome with the governing elite, but even showed (feigned) reluctance to accept the "burden" of imperial rule (cf. *F.* 1.533–34, discussed below; *Pont.* 4.13.27–28). Such hesitation was *in*auspicious, suggesting a potential gap or power vacuum at the "quilting point" of the symbolic order. *Augustus* remained the name for what or who might fill this gap.[12] According to Tacitus (*Ann.* 1.11.1–3), Tiberius feigned fear of "the burden of governing" a vast world-wide empire:

> . . . and he kept elaborating in various ways concerning the magnitude of supreme power [*magnitudine imperii*] and his own modesty, saying that only the mind of divine Augustus was *big enough to hold so great a mass* [*solam divi Augusti mentem tantae molis capacem*]; that although he himself had been relieved by Augustus in a portion of his worries, he had learned how lofty [*arduum*] and how subject to fortune is *the burden of governing all things* [*regendi cuncta onus*].

Tiberius' anxiety before *regendi cuncta onus* echoes Ovid's description of Tiberius hesitating to take up (*suscipiat*) the inherited *orbis onus*, ("burden of the world," *F.* 1.616). *Magnitudo imperii* in Tacitus recalls the *nomen* in Ovid (615) shared with highest heaven (*socium summo cum Iove nomen*, 608). In Tacitus Tiberius stresses Augustus' capacious mind holding the *tantae molis* (great mass) of world empire, much as in Ovid the title *Augustus* is *tantum* (1.592, 615; cf. earlier, 533–34, *caelesti mente* of the emperor).

Elsewhere in "January," Ovid uses *orbis* for the circuit or orb of heaven or the world within it. Many uses are associated with Janus and Jupiter's or Janus' cosmic supervision (*totum orbem* of Rome's, 85–86; Janus as *globus*, 111; custody of *mundus*, 119; defense of *totus orbis* 123–24). At the end of their encounter, Ovid describes how two-headed Janus' surveys the world (283–86):

> dixit, et attollens *oculos diversa videntes*
> aspexit *toto* quicquid in *orbe* fuit:
> Pax erat, et vestri, Germanice, causa triumphi,
> tradiderat famulas iam tibi Rhenus aquas.

He finished speaking and, lifting his eyes seeing in opposite directions, he observed whatever was in *all the world:* Peace was there and, Germanicus, the source of your triumph, the Rhine, had already surrendered to you his slave-girl waters.

Matching Jupiter's augury near the encounter's beginning (85–86), Janus' final gaze upon the world—looking simultaneously in two directions—suggests perception of two angles of view, two registers or symbolic fields.

But at 1.615–16, (in)auspiciousness in Tiberius' acceptance or refusal of the *nomen Augusti* and its *orbis onus* involves manly honor (*virtus*): "Such great names have befallen no man [*nulli viro*]." Heritable rank of manly honor, marked by a heritable *nomen,* defines male identity within the symbolic network of relative esteem. When Ovid celebrates the origin of *Germanicus,* his ideal reader's inherited *cognomen,* he evokes memory of the prince's biological father Drusus (Tiberius' brother, 597–98) and his manly honor:

> et mortem et nomen Druso Germania fecit;
> me miserum, virtus quam brevis illa fuit!

Germany caused both death and a name for Drusus; miserable me! How brief was that manhood!

Bestowed posthumously by the Senate in 9 BCE, the title *Germanicus* symbolized and defined Drusus' life and his manly reputation within Rome's symbolic order. *Germanicus* marked the addressee's father in a symbolic position relative to other men, including Augustus. But the loss of Varus' legion in Germany (9 CE) had caused anxiety: defeat had decreased, not increased, manly honor. So, inherited by the son, *Germanicus* also "marks" the symbolic position of Ovid's addressee, who was commanding armies in Germany and Gaul when Augustus died. He was commanding armies, while Ovid was revising the *Fasti* and Tiberius was hesitating before the *nomen Augusti* and its "burden of the world." Germanicus' campaigning aimed in part to rebuild Rome's manly honor, but also his own, adumbrated by his inherited title (cf. *F.* 1.245–86).[13]

Yet, *Germanicus* also has a meaning relative to the name *Augustus* that Tiberius facetiously hesitated to assume. Consequently, the *nomen Augusti* threatens to become an empty, yet persistent signifier of loss or lack of manhood. It could recall the loss of a particular individual, the deified first *Augustus*, who had stabilized the imperial order and whose death had left a symbolic gap where he had been. But more radically, if the *nomen Augusti* continued to be vacant, that gap could indicate a lack of manhood in Tiberius, other elite males, and in the Roman Empire as a whole.

The first couplet heralds this "castration" anxiety (1.587–88). Ovid remarks that the "chaste priest" (Flamen Dialis) offers to Great Jupiter the entrails (*viscera*) of a castrated ram (*semimaris . . . ovis*, 588). Sometimes gelded rams were offered to the divinized dead heroes; perhaps deceased Augustus is here identified with Jupiter (cf. 608; 650), portraying a lesser Jupiter such as Aeneas as *Iuppiter Indiges* at Lavinium (Jupiter's *cognomen* here is only *magnus*, 587, not *Optimus Maximus*).[14] But in addition, Ovid seems to commit a deliberate "error": he has already stated at 1.56 that a *grandior agna*, a larger ewe-lamb (female), is sacrificed to Jupiter on the Ides. This contradiction in the sex of the victim (*grandior agna* or *semimas ovis*) has drawn attention from modern scholars,[15] as should a second anomaly: Ovid dates to January 13 the anniversary of the *cognomen*, conferred by the Senate as reward to Octavian for defeating Antony and Cleopatra and restoring all the provinces to the Senate and the Roman People (1.589–90). But the Senate voted the title on January 16, not 13.[16] This shift of the anniversary to coincide with the Ides allows Ovid to associate the castrated sacrificial ram of its sacrifice with the *nomen Augusti*.

Acoustic Augury, Animal Mouths, and the Agonalia

Ovid's ideal reader Germanicus might "recognize" or discover (*recognosces*, 1.7, *invenies*, 9) other anomalous characterizations of his own family's rites; but, if so, how is he to interpret them? From where do these anomalous signs arise? Are they accidental? Merely convenient? Ovid invites Germanicus to observe carefully the *nomina* (591). How might Germanicus direct augural attention to the *omen* of manhood (nulli tanta nomina viro, 592) in the *nomen Augusti?*

The month's patron deity Janus indicates one method (ch.3): "kledonism," augury from sounds, words, names. On New Year's Day, one exchanges cheerful blessings, because there are *omina* in beginnings, and people turn *anxious ears* (*timidas aures*) toward initial utterances (*primam vocem,* 179) and an augur receives advice from the first bird seen (180). *Ears* and *temples* of the gods are open (181): "Words have *weight*" (*pondus,* 182). But already Janus' *first* appearance prompted Ovid to observe the god's dual body and mouth (*ancipiti imagine,* two-headed image, 95; *bina ora,* double face or mouth, 96).[17] That duality shapes *sound* (100): "[Janus] produced these sounds for me from his front mouth" (*edidit hos nobis ore priore sonos*). The repeating syllables of *ore* in the phrase *ore priore,* framed chiastically by [h]*os* and *sonos* suggests that Janus' two mouths produce split, stereo sounds—a front sound and another background sound behind him. Perhaps "heard" *sotto voce,* in undertone or soft aside, this "other" sound is "off-screen," apart from syntax and semantics.

For example, for the *Agonium* or *Agonalia* honoring Janus (Jan. 9, 1.317–456), Ovid offers an etymology of the cult name in Callimachean fashion and then a digressive explanation of why animals are sacrificed.[18] Off-screen wordplays and animal sounds provide signals of repressed desire natural to animals.[19]

Mouths ("orality") cause trouble for animals in these tales. In the longest example (391–440), the ass is sacrificed to Priapus, because it emitted uncannily timed brays, *intempestivos edidit ore sonos* (434)—diction strangely similar to that describing Janus' utterances: *edidit hos nobis ore priore sonos* (100). The ass's untimely braying alerts other gods to Priapus' attempted rape of the nymph Lotis, trumpeting Priapus' excess desire. Priapus unjustly blames the ass for his conceivably accidental braying and demands its sacrifice (1.391, 439–40). In a similar tale (6.319–48), the braying of an ass rescues Vesta, the virgin goddess of Rome, from Priapus' attack, "when he brayed with an untimely sound" (*intempestivo cum rudit ille sono,* 6.342). However, Vesta rewards asses with a holiday from work at millstones during the *Vestalia* (6.311, 318, 347–48).

Other animals are unjustly blamed for what they "mouth." Immediately after the Priapus tale, Ovid addresses birds (1.441–56) as "you who make nests, warm eggs with feathers, and *produce sweet tunes with pliant mouth*" (*et facili dulces editis ore modos,* 444), language recalling

Janus' "orality" and the ass's brazen mouth (*rauco ore*, 433–34). Birds reveal divine thoughts (*dique putant mentes vos aperire suas*, 446), with wings but also with *ore* (447–48). Consequently, the gods desire sacrifice of *indicis exta sui*, "the entrails of their own discloser" (450).

Other animals are sacrificed not for what passes out of, but what goes into their mouths. Pigs were the first sacrificial animals because (349–53): "Ceres found that in early spring her shoots, milky with young juices, had been *unearthed by the mouth* of the bristly pig" (*sata . . . eruta saetigerae comperit ore suis*). The notion of the oral object has shifted from narrated animal sounds (braying, birdsong) to animal mouths grasping the hidden or forbidden. While grain-shoots (*sata*) are food, their oral uncovering (*eruta ore*) suggests an agricultural metaphor of textuality and oral consumption of language.[20] Pigs and other animals "chew" the plants, so Ovid's readers can be viewed as consuming his poetry orally, that is, reading aloud its language and perceiving uncanny effects buried beneath the textual surface. Ovid has already used *eruta* (unearthed) in the dedication to describe what Germanicus will find in the poem: "You will read [or recognize] the *sacred unearthed* from the old annals" (*sacra recognosces annalibus eruta priscis*, 1.7). For Ceres, *sata* just beneath the earth's surface are her *sacra* (cf. the *Sementiva* below, 1.657–704). So, the sow discloses *sacra* from beneath Earth's "textual" surface just as birds expose the secrets of other gods in heaven.

Another possible shift in register from animal-sound to a metaphor of text and its reading[21] appears when Ovid explains why harmless sheep were first sacrificed: "a ewe-sheep wantonly plucked herbs that a devoted old woman customarily brought to gods of the countryside" (*verbenas improba carpsit,/ quas pia dis ruris ferre solebat anus*). Such sacral herbage, *verbenas*, sounds like sacral "verbiage" (*verba*); sacrifice then represses the sheep's wanton (*improba*) enjoyment of verbal-herbage. The sheep is a silent gatherer-reader, and semantically fecund sound-effects are latently available in Ovid's *verba*, in the *verbena* chewed in the sheep's mouth. Sacred *verba-verbenae* are "realized" in the reader's consuming lips in an imagined reading.[22] A reader mouthing the text might "recognize" the discovery (cf. *sacra recognosces annalibus eruta priscis*, 1.7).

But in Ovid's introduction to the *Agonalia*, his sympathetic identification with the animals unjustly sacrificed[23] reaches a climax by way of an eerie animal gaze. That identification begins with the very ram (*lanigerae coniuge . . . oris*, 334) sacrificed at the *Agonalia* to two-faced, two-mouthed Janus (317–18), figure of elite male wariness (ch. 3).

Various etymologies for the cult name (*nominis causa*, 319) alternate
points of view between the *minister* sacrificing the ram (319), the ram's
fear or anxiety (*metu*, 328), and Ovid's sympathy with the victim. [24]

Crucial to his sympathy is that the ram can "augur" his coming
death, because the knife, although coming from *behind* him, is reflected
before him in the holy water (327–28; cf. Janus' double-face; ch. 3). The
ram's foresight of the coming knife (*cultros*) echoes not only Pythagoras' description of sacrificed cows in the *Metaphorphoses* (*boves*,
15.120–42, esp. 134–35), but also Callimachus' description of cows
(βόες) "about to tear their hearts upon seeing the sharp knife in the
water" (*Aetia* fr. 75.10–11). But in the *Fasti* Ovid has shifted emphasis
from cows to the *Agonalia*-ram offered to two-headed Janus at the festival. Victim to Janus, this ram's anxious perception of impending death
suggests exiled Ovid's own identification with the sacrificial victim's
"gaze" returned, Janus-like, from the refractive surface of the sacred
water of the text[25]: the ram seeing his own impending death offers us an
uncanny gaze lurking within the screen of the sacral surface of the *Fasti*.
Either the ram or the knife "looks back" at readers, depending upon the
reader's angle of view (sympathies). Moreover, if Ovid aligns his own
perspective with that of the ram's, the author—an exile nearing death—
seems to look back at his imperial readers via this ritual screen. If so, the
ram's face and Ovid's are strangely merged. Thus, uncannily timed
ass's braying and other epiphenomena offer extra-syntactic signs leading augural readers beneath or beyond symbolic surfaces to off-screen
specters that animals grasp or express more immediately.

Lacanian theory addresses a similar phenomenon under "voice,"
one of the two libidinal objects (along with gaze) that Lacan added to
Freud's three (breasts, feces, phallus). Voice and gaze become objects
of desire when, to enter into culture—into the symbolic order and
one's very subjectivity—the individual must forsake direct, unmediat-
ed contact with desire. Lacanian "voice" refers not so much to the symbolic code of words, but to the interplay of their auditory units and to
acoustic and semantic effects "off the page" or "between the lines" that
arise from beyond the system of ordinary language, yet somehow partially intimate repressed desires can never be fully contained in the
symbolic.[26] The symbolic order provides the screen-background or context in which symbolic errors can indicate, as if by a "shadow," the
subject's excluded desires where epistemological errors, contradictions, or gaps appear in the symbolic. Such epiphenomena of the symbolic open the subject to specters of "other," excluded meanings
(desires) resonating beyond the symbolic screen.

Lacan's notion of "voice" resembles ancient rhetorical discussion about (mis)communication and audience identifications and misidentifications of words. When describing figured speech (*schema*), Quintilian comments on *kakemphaton*—an emphasis upon phonetic play (intentional or accidental) along a text's objective surface that unearths, in the listener's (mis)judgment, scandalous, sexual, or scatological meanings (*Inst.* 8.3.42–45). Ambiguous collocations of syllables (across words) provide opportunities for scandalous emphasis (8.3. 45–46). Pauses and stresses, either in delivery or in the audience's imagination (cf. 9.2.71), articulate unanticipated combinations or new word divisions at odds with objective divisions of words. Audience attention to such syllabic play forms new off-screen "words" apart from the surface syntax. For these listeners, sounds shift discourse toward what Quintilian calls obscene meaning (*obscenum intellectum*)—a scandalous stain upon the symbolic order. To illustrate this audience-phenomenon, Quintilian cites none other than Ovid: "[Apollo] thinks hidden things are better" (*quaeque latent meliora putat*, *Met.* 1.502, cited at *Inst.* 8.3.47). Here, the god looks at and beyond Daphne's surface, imagining Daphne's still more desirable, hidden features. The suspected, but hidden or adumbrated object—answering (excluded) desire—lures the god below surface screens. [27] Like a hungry sow, an inquiring reader who wants to know what Ovid means will unearth what is beneath the surface (cf. Ovid's reading-instructions at *Rem.* 359–60).

Kakemphaton is a subtype of "figured speech" (*eschematismene lexis*), which ancient rhetoricians theorized as simultaneously concealing and revealing meaning to divergent audiences. Figured speech thus acts in literature as a verbal "screen." Lacan's notion of "voice" concerns not just the objective, syntactical, or surface intention of a speaker, but how repressed desires, hidden even from the author or audience, can seemingly evoke untoward signs from outside or beyond conventional surface syntax. This is a meaning (desire) that is usually unsaid, repressed, but which the audience or reader directly experiences as a lurking phantom. Although, in terms of objective discourse, this recognition would be "mistaken," one's very error answers to a truth of desire. Voice concerns this subjective "angle" from which an individual or sub-group hears and construes meaning differently and "discovers" in some discursive fragment an excessive extra-syntactic kernel of unexpressed desire brought near the surface of conscious awareness by auditory echo. [28]

If the figured speech of Ovid's poetry is comparable to a fantasy screen, then "voice" corresponds to its phonemic play—(mis)recognition of meaning in that screen—that the reader-audience "mouths" or voices these sound-effects in oral reading in ways that may partially reveal desire and political meaning. Such phonemic ambiguity is heard "off-screen" in the juncture (*iunctura*) and disjuncture (*divisio*) of syllables or in homonyms (words that sound the same, but have different meanings). Not necessarily attributable to the work's objective surface (words or syntax), such "voices" are similar to what Michel Chion calls "acousmatic," voices or sounds in cinema, sounds not immediately locatable to an on-screen body, which here corresponds to the text.[29] However, acoustic events also appear in the ass's braying (*asellus*, 433), raised from another locale than the venue of Priapus' attempted rape of Lotis; that braying, intentionally or not, seems uncannily to mark the god's *obscena pars* (437).

Nomen Augusti and Acoustic Identification

Below I suggest that an acoustic echo between *Ovidius* and *ovis* reinforces Ovid's identification with the ram at the *Agonalia:* it suggests in his name a figurative transformation (*paranomasia*) seen throughout his works.[30] Such "mutations" of names are common in Ovid. For example, Ovid suspects the name *Agonalia* is a mutation, derived from Greek words (1.329–30) or from a Latin word for sheep (331–32) or simply from *agna* ("lamb," 325–26), rendering the festival's original name *Agnalia*, "so that one letter was removed from its proper place" (*una sit ut proprio littera dempta loco*). Of course, such playing with etymology and the sound of names is not unique. Ovid constantly exploits it. But he is particularly cognizant of phonetic mutation as caused by a social exchange. At *F.* 2.599–60, Lara (goddess Acca Larentia, the other of the Lares) is nicknamed Lala: "By chance there as a water-nymph, Lara by name, but she had an old name imposed due to [her?] 'error' [chattering], by repeating the first syllable (*la*) twice [*prima . . . dicta bis . . . syllaba*]." Her name is critique. Consonant change altered the cult-name *Remuria* (honoring dead Remus) into *Lemuria* (5.479–82), *lemures* being the phantom spirits of the ancestors, first of Remus. Vowel mutation screens an original scatological *Urion* (from *urina*) as *Orion* (5.535–56), recalling the act of urination shared by a mortal man and male gods in the miraculous conception and birth of Orion. Ovid recognizes that phonetic corruption is a residue of ancient interaction between Greeks and Latin-speakers. For example, he "augurs" (*vaticinor*) that April was derived from "Aphrodite," the

Greek name of Venus, explaining that Greeks, in Italy for a long time, produced the month-name (4.61–64). In Ovid's *Floralia* (May 2, 5.191–8), Flora, goddess of flowers, explains the "corruption" of her original name *Chloris* (Greek): "The Greek letter [X] was corrupted by the Latin sound of my name" (*corrupta Latino / nominis est nostri littera Graeca sono*, 5.199).[31] So, *chi* shifted to *phi*.

However, Ovid concludes his *Floralia* vignette with a mannerism that appears in his treatment of the name Augustus—a personal confrontation with a god's name. In concluding the *Floralia*, Ovid elaborates his own cognomen, *Naso*, meaning "Nose," to suggest his own perpetual olfactory consumption-inspiration (fragrance) in poetry from Flora or "Flower" (5.377–78): "I pray, [Flora], sprinkle my chest with your gifts [flowers], so that the song of Naso may flower in every age." In this poetic "seal" or *sphragis* (F. 5.377–78) "Nose" sets the author's identity in symbolic relation to Flora, an erotic goddess. This symbolic relation of "Nose" to "Flower" of inspiration suggests a "sphragistic" function for the first couplet of the *nomen Augusti* vignette (587–88).[32] That couplet begins with *Idibus* (the ablative form of *Idus*) and ends with *ovis*. Inverted and re-joined, these two separate words produce *ovis-idibus*. Rendered together, they echo the sound of the poet's family name *Ovidius* (Publius Ovidius Naso).

But why did Ovid set the words apart? The *sphragis* occurs on a "dividing" day in the month, the Ides. An important ancient etymology derived *Idus* (Ides) from an Etruscan word *iduare*, meaning, "to divide"; the Ides of January divides both the month and Ovid's name in half.[33] "Division" may be thematic since the Ides of January splits the *Carmentalia* into two distinct days, January 11 (F. 1.461–586) and January 15 (617–36), which Ovid treats immediately before and after the *nomen Augusti* passage (587–616). On this Ides, Ovid divides his own *nomen*, *Ovidius*, distributing its halves between *Idibus* and a castrated *ovis* whose entrails (*viscera*) were offered to "great Jupiter"—an act mirroring the ram sacrificed to Janus.

Ovid's prior sympathy with Janus' ram fearfully foreseeing his own sacrifice (knife reflected by water) anticipates this subjective identification of the author with the castrated ram. Another lure to reader scrutiny is *semimas*, synonym of *semivir*, connoting the castrating position of male subjectivity upon entry into a symbolic order. This word denotes a position relative to the *nomen Augusti*, the "quilting point," the mark of absolute manhood's difference within that order.[34] Perhaps the offering of a castrated ram to Jupiter (587–88) reflects the subjectively "castrating" effects of Ovid's exile, evident in the breaking of his *Fasti* (*Tr.*

2.551–52). Covertly expressed in acoustic effects alongside the overt *nomen Augusti*, Ovid's split *nomen* stations his identity within the Augustan symbolic order—as sacrifice to heroized "great Jupiter," a screen identity for Augustus. The castrated ram, initially a quizzical feature of the vignette, now begins to make sense as offering an angular "Ovidian" vantage point upon the *nomen Augusti* and suggests what can happen to a subject who approaches that quilting-point of the symbolic order where the emperor bears the burden of the world (*orbis onus*, 616). By hesitating to assume this position (*F.* 1.615–16, 1.531–34; *Pont.* 4.13.27–28), Tiberius threatens to open a gap in the symbolic order of things that no one could fill.

"Off-screen" acoustic play in the final couplet (1.615–16) symptomizes this social-political uncertainty. Acoustic repetition of syllables in the enjambment of *tanti cognominis heres/ omine* (615–16) primes "augural" attention. Fluid pronunciation joining the final words *orbis onus* can then imply *orbi sonus*, the "sound" or "utterance" of the "bereft" or "childless" (see below). Perhaps this *sound* (*sonus*) is of interest, because Latin *onus* is a homonym for Greek ὄνος, "ass." Association of "ass" with the name *Augustus* recalls the *omen* that Octavian encountered when advancing into battle at Actium[35] (defeating Antony and Cleopatra), an ominously named ass *Nikon* (Victor, in Greek) with his ominously *named* ass-driver *Eutychos* ("Lucky Man"; Suet. *Aug.* 96).[36] But as Ovid has noted, asses were sacrificed to Priapus, because one once brayed uncannily timed *sonos* (1.434), sounds "accidentally" calling humorous attention to Priapus' phallus (437–38: "all too much at the ready in his *obscene part* [*obscena parte*])." This phallic *onus/* ὄνος associated here with *Augustus* mirrors the castrated *ovis* identified with Ovid in the first couplet: Ovid's *Agonalia* heralds both animals as symbolizing unjust sacrifices.

These sound-plays on *onus-sonus-*ὄνος in the last couplet track the anxious shifting of the imperial burden of world-rule onto Tiberius at his accession. In Ovid's first *Carmentalia*, Arcadian Carmentis mentions this anxious shift of rule in her prophecy delivered while she and her son Evander approach their home in exile, the future site of Rome (529–34):

> tempus erit cum vos *orbem*que *tuebitur* idem,
>   et fient ipso sacra colente deo,
> et *penes Augustos* patriae tutela manebit:
>   hanc fas imperii frena tenere domum.
> inde nepos *natusque dei, licet ipse recuset,*

pondera caelesti mente paterna feret,
utque ego perpetuis olim sacrabor in aris,
   sic Augusta novum Iulia numen erit.

There will be a time when the same man will watch over you [Trojan
gods] and the world, and the sacred rites will be performed while a god
himself officiates, and the watch over the fatherland will stay with the
"Augustans": it is divinely sanctioned that this house keep the reins of
supreme power. Consequently the grandson and *the son of the god, though
he may refuse it, will bear the weight of his father with his heavenly mind,* and
just as I will be divinized some day upon everlasting altars, so Julia
Augusta will be a new divinity.

Carmentis portrays Tiberius, despite his refusal, as bearing *pondera
paterna,* "the burdens of his Father" (534), language evoking Aeneas
carrying Anchises (now *Divus Augustus*) and the Trojan *sacra,* but also
summarizing the emperor's duties: watching both the gods and the
world (*vos orbemque,* 529) and governing the world empire (*imperii
frena,* 532) with a heavenly mind (*caelesti mente,* 534).[37] The image of the
emperor's mind supporting the weight of rule (cf. *orbis onus,* 616) is that
of Atlas supporting the sphere of heaven (cf. the Farnese Atlas, an
imperial sculpture showing the Titan bearing the sphere of the heavens with constellations).[38]

   If the expression *orbis onus* implies the burdensome duty of the
emperor who "quilts" together the whole imperial order, then *onus-
ὄνος* might refer not merely to an animal, but to the "quilting" instrument, the central node of the empire. The word ὄνος also designated a
pole or post designed for turning, a capstan; a millstone or its upper
part called an "ass" (because this animal often turned it); by analogy
with such turning motion, a distaff or spindle could also be termed an
ὄνος.[39] Latin equivalents for this turning-post implement include *axis,
axon, axiculus,* or *sucula.*[40] However, it is perhaps by analogy with the
ὄνος-*axon,* that the upright in a sundial, its *axis,* could be called an *axon*
(Vitr. 9.7.5). Thus, the weighty polyvalent phrase *orbis onus* rephrases
axis mundi, the center of a cosmic empire.

   Tiberius is to take up a place before a divine labor or burden, like an
"ass" or an Atlas. This structural function of the emperor recalls Janus'
function (*officium,* 1.116, 126) at the *cardo mundi* (119–20): "In my control
alone is guardianship of the vast cosmos, and all authority over turning
it on its hinge is mine (*me penes est unum vasti custodia mundi, / et ius vertendi cardinis omne meum est*). This *cardo* (1.120) is the cosmic axis

around which the earth and heavens spin, but, as Augustine might point out (*CD* 6.7 of goddess *Cardea;* cf. *F.* 6.101–82 on Carna, Janus, and Cardo), its name also refers to a lowly thing, a door hinge. Janus' claim that *custodia* of the vast cosmos (*vasti custodia mundi*) rests "with me" (*me penes unum,* 119) anticipates Carmentis' prophecy that the *domus Augusta* will control the cosmos: the *tutela* of the fatherland and reins of supreme power are *Augustos penes,* "with the Augustans" (531). Janus himself symbolizes this generational transfer of power: Tiberius dedicated the temple of two-faced Janus in the Forum Boarium (ch. 3); Janus' double-herm aspect may betoken succession between men. [41] Nevertheless, the *nomen Augusti* labels the central place of imperial labor; *axis-ὄνος* provides a symbol of this quilting function in the symbolic order. It is the functional position from which Tiberius, or any emperor, as heir endures the inherited burden of governing a world-wide empire.

Augustus as Quilting Point: *Nomen* as *Gnomon*

This cosmic ὄνος or *axis mundi* was sometimes materialized in the form of a *gnomon,* the pointer of a sundial-calendar. These sundial-calendars were *simulacra* of the cosmos, because they were constructed as analogs of the cosmos' moving structure—the relation of the earth to the heavens upon a shared axis.[42] Whether used in a sundial or in land survey, the *gnomon* provided a visible form for the *axis,* exploiting the sun's shadow to orient and plot time or space (land) in a symbolic order traced by the sun's annual movement in heaven.

Augustus' construction ca. 10–9 BCE of a gigantic astronomical calendar, the *Horologium Augusti,* warrants interest in the *orbis onus* as allusion to an *axis mundi.* [43] In 10 BCE Augustus imported to Rome a 21.79 meter (71.5 feet) red-granite obelisk from Heliopolis, Egypt to serve as the sundial-calendar's *gnomon.* Symbolizing, as Ammianus Marcellinus says, "the pinnacle of all things" (*tamquam apex omnium,* 17.4.12), the obelisk towered over a huge dial paved in travertine where inlaid bronze bars formed lines indicating not only hours, but also astronomical information in Greek lettering—e.g., passage of the sun through houses of the zodiac, the winter and summer solstices, and the spring and fall equinoxes. Greek letters in bronze along one side of the meridian bar (with cross-hatching) indicated the twelve constellations in the zodiac (Parthenos-Virgo, Krios-Aries, Leo, Taurus) and refer to other celestial-meteorological phenomena (e.g., "The

Etesian winds cease" and "Beginning of Spring"). Around the base of the obelisk were mosaic depictions of the Winds.[44]

Symbolizing Augustus' defeat of Antony and Cleopatra, the *horologium* obelisk (booty or tribute from a conquered province; cf. Strabo 17.1.27) was not unlike the torque that Manlius "Torquatus" took in combat as spoils, symbolizing acquisition of manly honor (*virtus*) from another; it was also a reason for Manlius' "name" (601–2). Augustus' conquest and "return" of all the provinces to the Senate and the People and the Senate's bestowal of the *nomen Augusti* are the general circumstances to which the dedication on the obelisk's new base referred. In that inscription, the name *Augustus* appears in discernibly larger letters, alone on the second line. It identifies *Augustus* as the benefactor dedicating the obelisk above the base to the Sun-god, patron of Heliopolis (*Soli*),[45] "because Egypt was brought back into the power of the Roman People" (*Aegypto in potestatem Populi Romani redacta, CIL* 6.702).[46] This language recalls Augustus' own description of the circumstances in which the Senate gave him the epithet *Augustus* (*Res Gestae* 34):

> . . . *potitus rerum omnium,* rem publicam *ex mea potestate* in senatus populique Romani arbitrium transtuli. quo pro merito meo senatus consulto Augustus appellatus sum.

> *Having gained control of all affairs,* I transferred the state *from my power* into the judgment of the Senate and the Roman People. I was called *Augustus,* by a decree of the Senate, for this meritorious deed.

Ovid summarizes these circumstances at 1.589–90: "*Every province* was restored to our people and your grandfather was called by the name Augustus" (*reditaque est omnis populo provincia nostro/ et tuus Augusto nomine dictus avus*). Ovid's *redita* (589) recalls *redacta* on the obelisk's base. Ovid says *omnis provincia,* but the base mentions *Aegypto.* Both Ovid and the base also identify only the people (not the Senate) as recipient of the province(s), but Augustus emphasizes "all provinces," much as Ovid says "every province" (*omnis provincia*).

How are these circumstances for the bestowal of the *nomen Augusti* connected with the obelisk? Egypt is key. Egypt's conquest, mentioned on the obelisk's base, supplied a metonym for *omnis provincia,* as is indirectly shown by the cosmic dial below the obelisk. In the *Res Gestae,* the epithet *Augustus* rewards the emperor for all the provinces into which he had expanded Roman *imperium* or which he restored to

Roman rule (*RG* 26–33; Ov. *F.* 1.599–600). Prominent among them was Egypt (*RG* 27), where he had defeated his chief enemies, Antony and Cleopatra (30 BCE). This cardinal conquest had secured Octavian's domination over *omnis provincia* and the *nomen Augusti*. So, to commemorate Egypt's conquest twenty years later Augustus imported two obelisks, the first in Rome, and dedicated them to the Sun, placing one in the Circus Maximus, the other in the *horologium*.

A subsequent confirmation that indeed *nomen* and *gnomon* could be associated in a trope of identity appears in Petronius' *Satyricon* (ca. 54–66 CE). A rich freedman *Augustalis*,[47] Trimalchio imitates locally his imperial model, Augustus: at the end of an elaborate feast, Trimalchio reveals plans for his own tomb-complex to contain "a sundial [*horologium*] in the middle, so that whoever examines the time, whether he wants to or not, will read my *name*" (Petr. *Sat.* 71.11: *horologium in medio, ut quisquis horas inspiciet, velit nolit, nomen meum legat*). Trimalchio's *nomen* displaces the *gnomon* as "quilting point" in the symbolic order of time.[48] This *gnomon-nomen* in a sepulchral sundial suggests retroactively how Ovid could identify the *nomen Augusti* with the *gnomon* in Augustus' piazza-like *Horologium Augusti*.[49] In placing a sundial in a tomb complex, Trimalchio, an *Augustalis*, imitates his model, Augustus, and provides confirmation that Ovid was not alone in playfully associating *nomen* and *gnomon*.

While Ovid does not use the words *gnomon* and *obeliscus*, both are technical words of Greek origin, making them less amenable to use. But we must realize that *obeliscus* does not appear in any extant Latin until Pliny the Elder used it later in the first century, precisely to describe the sundial's *gnomon* (*H.N.* 36.64). Meanwhile, Latin had words to gloss this Greek term. Designating a variety of tall pointed markers besides turning-points in the circus,[50] *meta* had uses in land surveying and in boundary marking (see below). *Gnomon* is a technical term of geometry, geography and astronomy more common in Greek. In Latin it appears mainly in Roman technical writers, not in elegiac poetry (Vitr. 9. pr. 1, 1.3.1, 1.6.6, 9.7.2; Plin. *H.N.* 2.182, 6.212, 36.73). So, the absence of either term does not make a metaphorical *nomen-gnomon* less likely. Rather, Greek and Latin association of Augustus with the *orbis onus* or *axis mundi* and the cosmic ὄνος or "ass" emphasizes the emperor's centrality to the symbolic order, while integrating the usage into a wider ritual and mythological context established prior to the *nomen Augusti* passage. The metaphor of Augustus' *nomen* as *gnomon* provides a *simulacrum* of its "quilting" function in society.

II: Astronomers Surveying Heaven

Additional confirmation of the *nomen-gnomon* trope is implied elsewhere in the *Fasti* when Ovid deploys allusion to *gnomonike*, that is, the principles of the *gnomon* in charting time and space. Most relevant is *F.* 1.295–310, the "preface" praising astronomers who first charted the stars. Like any preface, it presents readers with the prime metaphors organizing the author's discourse. Here, the discourse concerned is Ovid's practice of marking days with notices of rising and setting constellations (*stellas,* 295; *signa,* 310). A crucial metaphor is surveying.[51]

In the first couplet, Ovid poses for himself the task of announcing the stars (*F.* 1.295–96: *stellas, ut quaeque oritur caditque / dicere*). He then blesses the souls of those who first cared to know the stars (*cognoscere,* 297) and "scale into the domains above" (*inque domus superas scandere cura fuit!* 298). Ovid disavows a physical assault on heaven, unlike Giants piling up Mt. Olympus, Ossa, and Pelion (307–8). Instead, Ovid observes how the spirits (*animae*) of astronomers use mental vision (*oculis mentis,* 305) to approach the stars (*sidera*) and subject the sky to their intellect (*aetheraque ingenio supposuere suo,* 306). How do they "subject" heaven? The verb *supposuere* implies that astronomers "*counterfeited* the sky with their ingenuity"—i.e., they deceptively substituted their intellectual representations, in which the huge dome of the sky, really above and around men, was transferred onto an object smaller than man, such as a sphere or map, and seemingly "beneath" the human view. Such objects fashioned an ideological fantasy of mastering heaven. Ovid mentions the spheres that Marcellus, the conqueror of Syracuse, imported to Rome among war booty (*F.* 6.277–78; *orbem,* 271; *onus,* 276; *globus,* 278; *figura poli,* 278; *sphaerae,* Cic. *Rep.*1.14.21–22); these were geocentric orreries designed by Archimedes—mechanical spheres showing the relative orbits of the sun, moon, the five planets, and the stars around the earth. Ovid's description of astronomers' *ingenium* (1.306) alludes to the ingenuity by which astronomers represented (or counterfeited) subjected heaven.[52]

In the final couplet, Ovid declares that he will follow the astronomers' model of "mapping" heaven (1.309–10): "Under such leadership, I will measure heaven [*caelum metabimur*], and I will place their days according to wandering signs [*signa*]." *Signa* is a perfectly common term for constellations and so renames *stellas* in the first line (95). But Ovid's use of *metabimur* (309) suggest a "measuring" of boundaries such as surveyors do on land or in military camps using

metae, temporary "boundary markers."[53] The verb *metabimur* thus adds
a layer of meaning to *signa*, so that *signa* allude to "boundary markers"
(as it commonly does in land surveying). Consequently, the clause
ponemus dies ad vaga signa (306) restates the action of *caelum metabimur*
(cf. *meta* and *signa* in Germanicus, *Aratea* 5–8).[54]

Ovid again alludes to *gnomonike* in the March preface, where he
explains to Mars the contrast between Greek astronomical knowledge
and Roman military practice (*F.* 3.99–112; 1.29–30). Romans had not yet
gained astronomical knowledge from conquest of Greece (101–2) and
thought a man was "skillful" (*disertus*), if he could throw *pila*, pikes
(103). *Pilum*, literally a pestle or pounding pole (cf. ὄνος, millstone),
was by extension a military spear. The feminine form, *pila*, denoting a
pestle, could also mean a pillar or "ball."[55] Such ambiguity (spear-
sphere) enables a transition in the next two couplets (105–8) to Greek
knowledge that "under the open heaven there are two poles" (cf. *gemi-
nos esse sub axe polos*, 106). Ignorant of heavens (*sidera libera, inobservata*,
111), early Romans did not consider astral *signa* divine (113), but
instead worshiped *signa*, military standards (112). These military *signa*
were made of hay bundles suspended from a tall pole called a *pertica*
(115–18). Moreover, kept in shrines centrally located in military camps,
they provided a symbolic "quilting-point" for the military structure
(legion). Significantly, the *pertica's* "suspension" of straw bundles
mimics astronomical structure: *signa* of heaven suspended from the
central cosmic axis or *polus*. Finally, as a surveyor's measuring rod (cf.
Prop. 4.1.130), the *pertica* (often ten feet long) figures not just as a
"quilting point" in military structure, but also in land survey. Land
surveyors used a rod called a *pertica*. But as either military standard or
surveyor's rod, *pertica* functions as a "quilting point" ordering a symbolic "field."[56]

At the end of the "astronomers" preface, Ovid promises to follow
astronomers (1.309) charting and ideologically mastering heaven.
These acts the verb *metabimur* characterizes as "land surveying." The
phrasing *stellas dicere* in the first couplet (1.295–96) gains meaning in
retrospect from *metabimur*, which implies that *stellae* are like *metae* or
more generically *signa* (*ponemus . . . ad vaga signa dies*), both terms in
ancient surveying manuals. Roman surveyors most commonly adjusted
boundaries using a *groma*, consisting of an upright pole (such as the *pertica*) topped by a rotating star-shaped attachment termed a *stella* ("star";
ἀστερίσκος). Plumb-lines hung from each arm. The *stella*-mechanism
turned to align "sightings" of both plumb-lines and *metae*, at distant
corners of land being demarcated.[57] From the perspective of *caelum*

metabimur, the earlier expression *stellas . . . dicere* (295–96) seems to borrow connotations from the surveyor's language *metas dictare* (and variations), referring to the rotating adjustment of the *stella*-mechanism atop the *groma* to view *metae* in alignment.[58] So, *stellas . . . dicere*, like *dies ad signa ponemus*, describes the action that Ovid performs when he measures out heaven (*caelum metabimur*) and declares days: he apportions time with rising and setting "signs," his metaphorical *metae-signa*.

One should compare Ovid and his astronomers mentally ascending and surveying heaven to the famous astronomer Meton in Aristophanes' *Birds* 992–1020.[59] Meton enters the sky, realm of birds, where Peisthetairos is establishing a new fantasy-empire that "screens" the relation between gods and men. Historically, around 433–32 BCE, Meton had erected a *gnomon*-like device on the Pnyx in Athens (*heliotropion*, perhaps only a pillar on a level platform) and used it as an astronomical calendar to observed shadow lengths at equinoxes and solstices and fashion a new mode of intercalation (19-year Metonic cycle). But Meton offers Peisthetairos other services (995–96): "I want to measure the air [γεωμετρῆσαι τὸν ἀέρα] and divide it for you into parcels [διελεῖν τε κατὰ γύας]." Peisthetairos even asks about Meton's odd instruments: "They are air-rods" (κανόνες ἀέρος, 999). Meton then offers to plan a capital city around a central market, from which streets extend like a star (*asteros*, 1007).[60]

The gnomon of Augustus' sundial was also an "aerial" *canon* or rod. The layout of grid-lines on the massive plaza-like face of Augustus' *Horologium* provided a prominent representation of the "surveyed" heavens placed beneath not merely the view, but even the feet of humans. Astronomical and weather notations on the sundial (cf. Caesar's *exactis notis*, 3.162) recall the *parapegmata* devised by the ingenuity of astronomers (1.305–6).[61] Celestial notices in Ovid's *Fasti* transpose such a visual representation of cosmic empire into a poetic register ordered around the *nomen Augusti*.

Stellar Notices, Gender, and the Nomen Augusti

However, despite the technical use of stars as objects of astronomy and geometry, the astral notices in Ovid's "January" often describe celestial phenomena as objects of a dreaming human view, but sometimes as uncanny animate beings directing a gaze at events on earth.[62] The first notice describes the dewy conditions of the third day before the Nones (January 3, counting inclusively) and the "posture" of Cancer, the

Crab, sinking below the western ocean (311–14). Likewise, on January 5 (Nones), a couplet (315–16) notes that "rains cast from black clouds will give you signs [*signa*], while the Lyre [a constellation] rises." Astral and weather phenomena supply visual, perhaps acoustic (thunder) objects of perception.

But a survey of signs surrounding the *Nomen Augusti* vignette reveals celestial phenomena hearing or seeing human actions from a place off-screen from human events. After the *Agonalia* (January 9, 317–456; above) shifts attention from meteorology (311–16) to images of "mouthing" animals, a two-line notice portrays a constellation possibly responding to these sacrifices (457–58):

> Meanwhile, a Dolphin, a bright constellation, is lifted over the sea and protrudes his mouth [*exserit ora*] from beneath his father Neptune's sea.

Like a dolphin emerging from the sea, the Dolphin's "mouth" appears above the horizon. But since animals are sacrificed because of their *ora* (the sow, sheep, ass, birds), one might wonder if the *ora* of this celestial animal, a dolphin, merely watches the events and remains mute. Might the stellar dolphin's *ora* protruding from "off-screen" emit a typical dolphin's high-pitched voice (laugh or scream?) curiously answering to other animal *ora*? An index of repressed desire (*F.* 2.81: dolphin, *occultis felix in amoribus index*), the Dolphin (whether mute or voiced) marks an uncanny off-screen sign in dialogue with the *Agonalia*.

The announcement on January 10 metaphorically ascribes to "midwinter" a position between past and future characteristics of prophetic vision and of Janus (459–60):

> The following day marks winter with its midpoint, and what will remain [of winter] will be equal to what has been passed by [*aequaque praeteritae quae superabit erit*].

Here Ovid thematically repeats Janus' foresight and hindsight (cf. Janus on the *bruma*, winter solstice, 1.162–63), anticipating prospective and retrospective views in the next two notices. [63] The first dates the *Carmentalia* to January 9 (461–62):

> The next bride of abandoned Tithonus will look upon [*prospiciet*] the ritual of the pontiff for the Arcadian goddess.

Aurora (the Dawn) abandons her aged husband (Tithonus) to watch (*prospiciet*) a major festival honoring Carmentis, the divinized prophet-ess and mother of Evander.[64]

Aurora's prospect upon the first *Carmentalia* on January 9 is answered by the Sun's retrospective view at 617–18 (Jan. 15):

> When the Titan [Sun] will look back at the completed Ides for the third time [*respiciet Titan actas ubi tertius Idus*], repeated rites will be performed for the Parrhasian goddess [Carmentis].

First, female Aurora will look forward to the first *Carmentalia* (*prospiciet*, 461); the male Titan will turn away from the second *Carmentalia* and look backwards toward the Ides (*respiciet*, 617). By their contrary view-points, these two animate celestial phenomena group the two *Carmentalia* around the *nomen Augusti* on the Ides. The contrast between Aurora's and the Sun's angles of view implies that they screen a thematic gender antagonism.

The cognomen Titan and Titan's "viewpoint" mentioned at 1.617 imply retrospectively the function of the *nomen Augusti* as metaphori-cal gnomon and "quilting point." Ovid uses the name Titan immedi-ately after the phrase *orbis onus* concludes the *nomen Augusti* passage (616). Titan here renames the god Sol, the Sun, to whom Augustus ded-icated the obelisk-gnomon. The name Titan alludes to the fact that Sol-Helios was the son of Hyperion, the sun-god among the Titans (gods born from Uranus, Heaven, and Terra, Earth). The name Titan also pro-vided the name *ad Titan* for the early church (San Lorenzo in Lucina) adjacent to that very obelisk.[65] Secondly, Ovid says that Titan "looks back at" or turns his attention to (*respiciet*) the events of the Ides (*actas Idus*), when Ovid chose to celebrate the *nomen Augusti* as "cosmic bur-den" or *orbis onus* (not the correct date, January 16; above). The verb *respiciet* designates the visual trajectory of the Sun who, as the *oculus mundi* (eye of the world), seems to look twice at (*respiciet*) the *nomen Augusti* as ὄνος or axis-gnomon. The sun's visual "double-take" (dou-bling back to examine the events of the Ides) seems to respect the Ides' division of the month, honor for Augustus, and the tropes of the previ-ous couplet. These tropes imply the symbolic function of the *nomen Augusti* as a cosmic-imperial "quilting point," a gnomon by which the temporal units of the *annus* are measured and Sol's own path is tracked and interrelated to earth.[66] If the *nomen Augusti* passage alludes to the shrine to Sol, the Solarium that Augustus dedicated with an imported obelisk-gnomon, then Ovid's celebration of the *nomen*

Augusti lures Titan Sol's attention, particularly since the Solarium functioned as a sundial/ calendar.

Astral epigrams surrounding the *nomen Augusti* express a backward and forward viewing, audition, and perhaps sound (Dolphin), apart from the main texts of the poem.[67] This forward and backward cognition mimics the process by which readers synthesize unfolding *stoicheia* (letters and syllables as acoustic units) into words, phrases, and clauses of discourse.[68] In Greek, *stoicheia* could label stars in heaven and the basic cosmic elements (*primordia:* earth, water, air, and fire; alternatively, atoms)—the elements composing and controlled by Janus (103–20; cf. Polyhymnia's version, 5.11–52). Ancient philosophy constructed an analogy between the combination, dissolution, and recombination of physical *stoicheia* (producing the world and its seasonal changes) and the articulating and rearticulating (Platonic collection and division) of syllabic *stoicheia* into meaningful discourse.[69] What resulted was a model of immanent, elemental *logos* (and wordplay). Through control of cosmic articulation, Janus is both a representation of cosmos and yet a gigantic oral cavity (*mundus, palatum,* οὐρανός), a model of cosmos as "mouth" from which *logos* emerges, a trope which Augustine found in Varro and mocked (*CD* 7.8; Ennius in Cic. *ND* 2.49). Ovid's Janus opens and closes a mouth/gate (*F.* 1.127–32) and reports his oral defense against Tatius (269–70).[70]

However, the play of *stoicheia* in the *Fasti*—acoustic units (syllables) as well as cosmic elements and star-patterns—invites readers to act as a *gnomon* of sorts, as a tongue or "reader" (*glossa* as *gnomon,* Xen. *Mem.* 1.4.5) that can "tell" the order of syllabic *stoicheia* by manipulating—mouthing—the *stoicheia* around the *orbis onus.* The *nomen Augusti* might then assume the proportion of Janus's *cardo mundi,* a *gnomon* casting the long shadow of Augustus' manly honor over the whole imperial order. That gnomonic shadow—also curiously called *stoicheion*[71]—articulates other men's relative positions within the imperial order.

Janus and Pax: Surveying Ovid's January

We have seen how Ovid develops "surveying" as a metaphor by which readers may re-conceptualize his poetry. This metaphor gains salience when interpreted together with the fore-sighting and back-sighting ascribed both to celestial phenomena and to two-faced Janus, who visually aligns (*perspicio,* 139) two directions simultaneously from the two gates of heaven (eastern and western horizon, 139–40; ch. 3). Proper use of the *groma* or *stella* and other surveying instruments (e.g., *dioptra*) required both "fore-sighting" and "back-sighting" to align straight borders and boundary-paths (*limites*).[72]

At the end of his encounter with Ovid, Janus, himself a cosmic figure, uses his "eyes that look in opposite directions" (283) to observe (*aspexit*) "whatever is in the whole world" (284). Sighting *Pax*, "Peace," he then celebrates the Rhine's surrender, a "cause of trumph" for Germanicus (*causa triumphi*, 1.283–88). Rome had built an altar to Augustus on the banks of the Rhine, a river forming the northern boundary of Rome's *imperium* (*ara Ubiorum*).[73] So, Janus' sighting of both Peace and the Rhine curiously anticipates Ovid's celebration of the Altar of Augustan Peace (*Ara Pacis Augustae*) at 709–22, just before the very "boundary" (*finis*) of Book One's last couplet on January 30 (723–24).

Janus' own fore- and aft-sighting of the *orbis terrarum* thus enacts a kind of metaphorical "survey" structuring the book, if not the whole work. Astral notices and the emperor's *nomen* provide additional *metae* by which the reader's eye aligns with that of Janus, a model for the reader. However, the *nomen Augusti* also provides a looming symbolic *gnomon*, a taller central marker or "quilting point" in the ordering of imperial time and space, articulating (measuring) all other positions within it.

This metaphor is supported by the fact that, in the Campus Martius, the obelisk-gnomon of the *Horologium* had a visual, if not astronomical relationship to the *Mausoleum Augusti* and the *Ara Pacis*. Different lines of sight linked the *gnomon*-obelisk with the dynastic Mausoleum (death) and the *Ara Pacis*, forming a right angle with the obelisk-gnomon at its center. More speculatively by one calculation, the shadow of the obelisk pointed to the door of the Altar of Peace (flanked by the "Mother Earth" image) on the fall equinox, September 23, Augustus' birthday. The *Ara Pacis* was dedicated on January 30, Livia's birthday (*F.* 1.709–22).[74] Thus, the landscape implied a fertile, cosmic "juncture" of imperial husband (*Augustus, gnomon*) and wife (Livia, *Ara Pacis*). This symbolic context "phallicized" the *gnomon* to imply the role of *Augustus* as dynastic "increaser" (cf. *augere*) of peaceful fertility secured by military *virtus* (cf. obscene trope, "the *gnomon* rises," Diog. *Epist.* 35).[75]

By celebrating the Ara Pacis at the book's "end" (*fine*, 1.710; *finem*, 724) and not on July 4, Ovid deliberately shaped the book's broad structure.[76] The choice guides readers retroactively. Looking back from the *Ara Pacis*, readers can "back-sight" the metaphorical alignment of ideological objects that screen imperial order. Janus, *stellae-metae, nomen-gnomon* are just the lineaments of this "order." Like Janus with his double viewpoint, the reader can double-back upon Ovid's presentation of Augustan ideological values.

III: Augustan Values and Manly (Dis)Honor

What else might the male eye see around Ovid's depiction of the *Ara Pacis Augustae*? The walls of the *Ara Pacis* itself screen fields of manly honor and political posts, but also imperial wives and children and agricultural fields, "fields" in which men worked to scatter seeds of their names, fields screening *semeia* (signs) as *semina*. Fields of flowering (agri)cultural seeds might act for Ovid as tropes for fields of mnemonic symbols of men's reputations, like literary texts, statues, and inscriptions, other fields in which men disseminated the "seed" of their *nomina*.[77] But from the *Ara Pacis* vignette (*F.* 1.709–722; Jan. 30), a retroactive eye can perceive between the *Nomen Augusti* vignette (587–616, Jan. 13) and the *Ara Pacis* not only this screen of Augustan values reflecting the precinct walls of the *Ara Pacis,* but also repressed off-screen voices.

Semeia, Semina, and Sementiva

For example, Ovid's *Sementiva,* a festival of seed-planting (1.657–704), evokes imagery of fertility like that of the *Ara Pacis Augustae.* One panel of the altar shows Pax, Ceres, or Tellus—a variously identified female holding two infants.[78] Agricultural and animal imagery in Ovid's *Sementiva* name animals (birds, ants) also found in the vegetal motifs in lower zones of the Ara Pacis.[79] Overall, Ovid's *Sementiva* offers a "Tellus-Ceres-Pax" panel of its own, suggestive of the Augustan Peace (704), securing agricultural fertility, seeded and protected by Augustan *virtus.*

But Ovid's language in the *Sementiva* "transfers" symbolic fertility of Earth (Tellus) and Grain (Ceres) to an agricultural parable of textuality.[80] Ovid begins by announcing that he could not find the *Sementiva,* although three times he unrolled his *"fasti* marking the times," *sig-*

nantes tempora fastos.[81] But a Muse informs Ovid that "this day is indicated," orally announced: *lux haec indicitur* (659). As "moveable" festival, the *Sementiva* is not fixed, "stated" or written in calendar-texts (*quid a fastis non stata sacra petis?* 660). Ovid here engages two symbolic spaces, one screened by text and the other "off-screen," a sub-textual symbolic "fertility" that offers an "earthy" temporal code (cf. Ovid at 1.147–64; and 4.85–114). The off-screen, oral declaration of the *Sementiva* and the verb *indicitur* ("is orally declared") recall the repressed voices of animal *indices*, "informers," the birds and ass (1.450, 6.346). Moreover, signs of planting, unseen in a calendar-text, help to "divine" the festival time (*certa tempora*, 661); these signs appear "off the books" (*a fastis non stata sacra*, 660) in *seminibus iactis*, in "tossing of seed" (662) and pregnant earth (*fetus ager*, 662). A sow could unearth with her mouth (*ore*) its undergrowth.[82] In farmland representing off-screen meaning (desire), *semina* provide *semeia* (Greek, "signs").

Anti-Fertility and the Second Carmentalia

Prior to the *Sementiva*, an untoward sound-play around the *nomen Augusti* vignette (1.587–616) has already heralded potential human infertility: as noted, the syllabic play *orbi sonus*, from *orbis onus* (616), suggests "sound of the childless." This sound-effect recalls the sacrifice of a castrated ram mentioned in the first couplet (*semimaris ovis*, 587–88). But some readers might object to this infelicity irrupting into the calendar poem's course toward fertile Peace (1.709–24), thereby blocking felicitous closure of the whole work (*auspice te felix totus ut annus eat*, 1.26; cf. closure of Janus' doors, sign of peace). However, this infelicity is endorsed by explicit reference to abortion in the second *Carmentalia* (January 15, 1.617–36).

As noted, this vignette begins with Titan-Sol looking back at (*respicit et*) the Ides and phallic "rise" of the *nomen Augusti* as *gnomon*, alluding to the *horologium* obelisk as offering to Sol himself. This representation of manhood (*virtus*) and male "name" (*nomen*) is countered by the second *Carmentalia*. In Ovid's version, women use abortion (conscious infertility) as a response to men's stripping them of honor: the honor of riding the *carpentum*, a type of carriage that (he says) was named after *Carmentis-Carmenta* (619–22, 6.603).[83] Deciding not to renew (*novare*) their husbands (*viros*) with offspring (621–22), women use abortion to ensure infertility (623–24):

neve daret partus, ictu temeraria caeco
visceribus crescens excutiebat *onus.*

And in order not to provide offspring, each rashly probed the growing
burden in her entrails with a secret striking.

Visceribus and *onus* (624) echo retroactively the first and last couplets of
the *nomen Augusti* passage, where Ovid mentions "entrails of the castrated ram" (*semimaris viscera ovis*, 587–88) and the "burden of the
world" (*orbis onus*, 615–16), associated with the *cognominis heres*.
Retroactively, the specter of abortion enables castration (588) and the
acoustic effect of *orbi sonus*, the "sound of a childless man" (606), to por-
tend infertility (abortion, miscarriage) in the second *Carmentalia*. This
off-screen specter addresses male fears not merely of female control
over the male esteem signaled by failed reproduction of offspring
(*novare viros*, 622), but loss of male potency.[84]

Endorsing this effect is the curious change in the meaning of *onus*
within the space of ten lines (616 and 624), from the burden of world-
mastery to the burden of male *semen* in a woman's womb (or *fetus*). At
624, women expel this seminal *onus* (cf. Silvia, 3.42), antagonistically
refusing "labor" within a male-controlled social order. The female
homosocial tactic thereby interrupts reproductive manhood (*virtus*).
The elite male social-sexual "burden" (to beget children, heirs) was
encouraged by Augustus in his moral laws. In a contemporary patriarchal context, women's abortion figuratively emasculated the male
albeit through masochistic means (cf. infanticide by Medea).[85]

This anxiety over abortion, infertility, and an heir enables a spectral
re-imaging of the symbolism of the *gnomon- Ara Pacis* complex. While,
together with the Mausoleum, these monuments screen the *nomen
Augusti* and dynastic continuity in Rome's topography, Ovid's handling of abortion interrupts a pure and simple screen of fertility with a
spectral intrusion transforming the *nomen-gnomon* into an instrument
of infertility: the needle-like shape of the obelisk jarringly recalls a nee-
dle-shaped instrument that, with a "hidden blow" (*ictu caeca*), a
woman might turn upon her own *viscera*.[86] This spectral refiguring of
ideology transforms the Augustan ideological landscape, symbolizing
Julio-Claudian fertility, into a scene of infertility, in which the *gnomon* or
its shadow approaching the Ara Pacis poses the specter of abortion.
This spectral answer is perhaps lured by the contradiction that Augus-

tus and Livia bore no children together, despite encouraging others to reproduce.

Concord as Ideological Screen

Antagonism between the sexes finds another screening ideology in the goddess *Concordia*, "Harmony" (*F.* 1.637–50). Ovid celebrates her refurbished temple in the Roman Forum (10 or 12 CE) on January 16, between the second *Carmentalia* and the *Sementiva*. But Ovid traces the temple's origin from Camillus and his forging of a bond between senatorial and plebeian leaders (*F.* 1.641–44). With his bond, Camillus controlled advocates of more open power-sharing and, thereby, strengthened military manpower. Even when symbolizing "harmony" in marriage, Concordia still represents male homosocial political relations. Concord herself stresses at *F.* 6.91–96 the settled union of Romulus and Tatius, forged from the rape/marriage of the Sabine women. *Concordia* screens ideological order, both revealing and concealing family, class, and national (ethnic) antagonisms. Such is the clash in the preface of June (6.89–90; ch. 4) between Juno and Juventas, that the appearance of *Concordia Augusta* suppresses Concordia's concealing role at 2.631–32. By contrast, Gnaeus Flavius exposed the calendar of legal days, angering equestrians and patricians (ch.1); yet he too tried, with much elite opposition, to capture control of the ideological screen of Concordia and by establishing his own shrine to Concord in the Forum.[87]

But, Ovid says, "the recent cause [of reconstruction] was even better [*melior*]" (1.645–48)—domestic harmony within the imperial house. As noted, Tiberius' reconstructed temple memorialized collaboration between brothers (sons of Livia), between himself and Drusus.[88] Tiberius rededicated Concord in his own and his brother's names. Yet prior to his brother's death (9 BCE), Tiberius published a letter in which Drusus urged attempts to persuade Augustus to restore a true republic; the release could damage Drusus' relationship to Augustus relative to Tiberius (Suet. *Tib.* 50). Concord screens this antagonism by bolstering a public ideology of fraternal *pietas* echoed in a subsequent epigram on Tiberius' refurbished Temple of Castor and Pollux (6 CE), divine brothers whom Ovid compares with imperial brothers Tiberius and Drusus (*F.* 1.705–8; Jan. 27).[89]

Temples to Concordia and Castor and Pollux also screen antagonism among the next generation of Claudian males, Tiberius (and his
son Drusus) and Drusus' sons (Germanicus and Claudius).[90] Drusus
(Germanicus' father, Tiberius' brother) had helped conquer Germany;
in fact, it killed him (1.597–98). Yet, it is Tiberius' conquest of Germany that is said to finance Concordia's refurbishment (645–48).[91]
Strategically placed references to Germany or the Rhine (1.597, 645;
Rhenus, 1.286) augment the competition over name (both *Germanicus*
and *Augustus*) and honor among Claudian males (Tiberius and Germanicus). The earliest phases of refurbishment already screened
Tiberius' antagonistic "Harmony" ("civility") at a critical time (7 BCE),
when Augustus was promoting Gaius and Lucius Caesar (sons of
Augustus' daughter Julia and Agrippa) as heirs displacing Tiberius.[92]
Tiberius' withdrawal to Rhodes in the next year until the death of
Gaius (4 CE, when Augustus adopted Tiberius) delayed rededication
of Concord's temple to 10 CE (perhaps 12 CE).[93]

Ovid's climactic elevation of Livia in the last couplet as "founder" of
Concord (*constituit*) in both her behavior and in an altar (*et rebus et ara*,
649) extends, yet alters Concord as screen of "family values." Livia's
altar of Concordia was publicly dedicated in the *Porticus Liviae* by
Tiberius and Livia in 7 BCE (see also *F.* 6.337–648).[94] It symbolized the
domestic loyalty of Tiberius and Livia to Augustus and the connection
between Claudians and Julians in marriage, a new form of marital or
familial Concord shaping the *domus Augusta* as dynasty.[95] Comparing
this description of Livia (*F.* 1.649–50) with others from exile (e.g., *Ex P.*
3.1.114–18: Ovid' wife is to plead before Livia), Herbert-Brown demonstrates that Ovid probably wrote the Concordia vignette after Augustus' death, in the early years of Tiberius' rule, after Augustus' will had
adopted Livia and attributed to her an unofficial authority, reminiscent
of Tiberius'.[96] By calling Livia "the only one found worthy of Jupiter's
bed" (1.649–50), Ovid not only identifies her as a "Juno" matching
Jupiter-Augustus (at 587–616, 608), but also elevates her above
Tiberius. By calling Livia Tiberius' *genetrix* (an epithet of Venus, no
mere *mater*),[97] Ovid grants Livia the status of quasi-divine matriarch,
source and rival for power and influence. So, at the vignette's climax,
Ovid calls attention to the marital bed—the sexual venue—in which
that harmony would have been forged.

Beyond merely celebrating the political "partnership" or the "ideological unity" between Tiberius and Livia,[98] the last couplet (649–50)
also screens an anxiously gendered "antagonism." That antagonism
suggests vulnerabilities that Tiberius faced in establishing his rule as

emperor and as a man controlling his own household on a par with other men in the Senate—as a man independent from his mother.

This antagonism between mother and son is not directly stated in Ovid's celebration of Tiberius' Concordia; rather, it is manifested in lexical anomalies. Verbs ascribe "official" action to Livia, not to Tiberius: where Livia *has established* Concordia (*constituit*, 649), Tiberius uses war-funds to "make" a temple (*fecisti*, 648). *Constituit* is more official and ceremonious, *fecisti* more generic. By "founding" Concord in her behavior (*rebus*), an altar (*ara*, 649, in the Porticus Liviae), and in bed with Jupiter-Augustus (*toro*, 650; a rather "elegiac" image), Livia broadcasts herself in "concord" with Augustus; she is *genetrix* of the *domus Augusta* and wife of Jupiter-Augustus. Livia embodies the Concordia that Tiberius worships (*quam colis ipse*, 648). Thus, Livia's "Concord" with Augustus "upstages" Tiberius' (above) and poses the specter of displacing Tiberius from the pinnacle of power, especially given Tiberius' tentative use the *nomen Augusti* among the Roman elite and his initial hesitancy to shoulder the burden of rule.[99]

Livia became *genetrix* of Tiberius not merely in biology, but in religious ideology. Inscriptions identify her not only with Juno, but Venus as genetrix and with Ceres celebrated in Ovid's *Sementiva*.[100] As Susan Fischler argues, these religious identities elevate Livia's importance in the symbolic order, in order to elevate the "patriarchal emperor": representing mother goddesses contributed to representation of the emperor as potent, fertile, and in control over his household.[101] Thus, imperial iconography can still "traffic in women" as symbols or symptoms of man (as gendered symbolic positions), especially the emperor as The Man. But Ovid's representation of Livia in the Concordia vignette complements Ovid's representation of abortion and castration. Together with Tiberius' hesitancy, they pose the specter of Tiberius' loss of control over symbolic "trafficking." As symptom or vehicle of power's (re)production, Livia threatens to master Tiberius and his patriarchal inheritance.

Mother and Son: Carmentis and Male Identity

The gendered antagonism of the second *Carmentalia* encourages a retrospective upon Ovid's first *Carmentalia* (1.461–586) as also portraying gender anxiety around relations between mother and son.[102] Ovid's treatment of the pair elaborates marginal details in Vergil's treatment of them. In *Aeneid* 8, Arcadian Evander is prompted by an altar to Carmentis at the *porta Carmentalis* to reminisce only briefly about his deceased but divinized mother (*Aen.* 8.333–41; Serv. *ad Aen.* 8.337). Ovid augments the mother-son relationship by staging in narrative fantasy the "primal scene" of Evander's separation from his mother and his entry into "manhood" at the Ara Maxima of Hercules—the symbolism indicated to Vergil's Aeneas by Evander and Pallas. By contrast with Vergil's monocular masculine perspective, Ovid's narrative provides both feminine and masculine viewpoints (Carmentis' and Hercules') from which to review the specter of Tiberius' wavering succession to imperial *virtus*.

Ovid's tale of Carmentis and Evander's exile from Arcadia to Latium provides several points of identification for exiled Ovid and his readers. Since identification is never unitary or consistent, it would be impossible to enumerate them all. However, Ovid derives Carmentis from *carmen*, meaning both poetry and divinatory incantation (467) while inviting the goddess to guide his sails (ship; *deriget mea vela*, 465–66), "so that the honor for you does not veer" (*ne tuus erret honor*, 468). This language echoes Ovid's request of Germanicus', "guide the course of my fearful ship" (*timidae derige navis iter*, 1.4). Carmentis' poetic relation to Ovid would then seem to repeat Germanicus,' indirectly identifying Carmentis and the prince. The ideal reader's projection of "Carmentis" might then mobilize his guidance of "Evandrian" Ovid during "exile." However, Ovid's reader will also learn that it is Carmentis' own frank divination—revelation of the gods' thoughts (she is *nimium vera*, 466; has *ore vero*, 474)—that offended a god, inspired revolution (*motus*, 474), and caused the exile of mother and son.[103] Offense to a god resulting in unjust divine anger recalls the accusatory conditions of Ovid's own exile (cf. *culpa* at *Tr.* 1.2.98, 1.3.38; 2.104, 208, 315, 540; 5.7.60; *Pont.* 1.6.25–26, 2.2.15, 2.3.45–46) and of animal sacrifices in Ovid's *Agnalia* (*culpa*, *F.* 1.361,480; *meritus* 1.8, 350, 483). Thus, Carmentis also provides a position of symbolic identification for Ovid. However, other readers might identify in Carmentis and Evander the mother-son relationship between Livia and Tiberius (*F.* 1.649 on Livia, Tiberius' *genetrix*), perhaps seeing in Evander's exile and despondency traces of Tiberius' withdrawal to Rhodes (6 BCE) and his subsequent return.

Carmentis' two speeches to her son (479–540) prompt more nuanced identifications with the characters. In her first discourse, Carmentis emboldens her son to endure misfortune "like a man" (479–96) and, in her second, foretells Rome's greatness, Julio-Claudian rule,

Livia as matriarch and Tiberius' hesitant succession (509–40). These two discourses represent the gender anxiety of mother-son relations with different ideological screens.

In the first speech, Carmentis first commands her weeping son (*flenti*): "Stop your tears, please—you must endure this (mis)fortune *like a man* [*viriliter*]." Evander was a youth (*iuvenis*, 477), which might sug- gest inexperience; now he must be a man (*vir*; cf. *viriliter*, 479). Car- mentis suggests that circumstances (*fortuna*) force manhood upon Evander. She controls Evander's male identity (manly honor) through language of male shame like that of Tullia, addressing her husband Tarquin (*F.* 6.587–88, 594: "If you are a man") or that of Livy's Lucretia (cf. Ovid's; below, chapter 6).[104]

Carmentis' language does what a paternal or male adviser would do—rally a son or male protégé to manly action (1.479–96): she cites multiple examples of male heroes—ideal models for Evander's identifi- cation—who overcame misfortune and suffering (487–94; cf. Anchises' 'fatherly guidance of Aeneas, *Aen.* 6; Ovid to Germanicus in the *nomen Augusti* passage). Carmentis urges her son to "conceive" (*concipit*) hope in his heart (*intra pectora*, 485–86) rather than fear, so that the unseason- able storm (*fera tempestas*, 495–96; *ista procella*, 488) will not engulf him if he follows the lead of *ingentes viros*, "great heroes" (488). In this moth- ering of male self-esteem, the prophetess Carmentis might also recall Livy's Tanaquil using prophetic interpretation to steer her husband (Liv. 1.34). Strengthened by his mother's words (*vocibus Evander firmata mente parentis*, 497), Evander sails toward Italy (498), but his mother has shaped this venture. By controlling the "rudder" (ship, *ratem*, 499) of Evander's desire of manly honor, Carmentis propels him into a narra- tive of exilic survival and journey to a new land, Italy.

But Ovid complicates this mother-son relation, using the symbols of sailing and the language of poetics (1.4, *derige navis iter*). It is "on the advice of learned Carmentis" (*docti monitu Carmentis*, 499) that Evan- der initially steers the ship up the Tiber River (499–500). Carmentis' frenzy upon seeing scattered huts leads to rival *manus*, "control," of the ship: she held back the *manus* (hand) of Evander guiding the ship (*regentis iter*, 504). In turn, she is barely contained "by the *manus* of Evander" (508) from leaping overboard trying to reach land. The scene stages struggle over authority, *manus* over a "ship of state"—a fore- boding of what will follow.

But, as the pair arrive, the prophetess Carmentis produces a different *carmen* screening the future of the primal landscape—a rich and power- ful Rome (cf. Janus' critique, 1.191–218)—through a dynastic ideology.

This vision of a future Rome (529–36, above) offers the reader a "primal" fantasy, a retroactively "past" position from which the reader assumes an impossible view of the deepest origin of Julio-Claudian rule (529–32), leading to Tiberius' succession (533) and even Livia's divine status as *Iulia Augusta* (535–36).

Carmentis cites a succession of "son" and "grandson" (*nepos natusque dei*, 533), language similar to that in Ovid's dedication (10) and the *nomen Augusti* passage (590, 616) and referring to male dynastic succession and honors that accrue to it, including the name *Augustus* itself. But Carmentis directly foretells Livia under the title *Julia Augusta* (536, bestowed by adoption in Augustus' will; Tac. *Ann.* 1.8). Predicting (and petitioning Evander for) her own worship at an altar (535), Ovid's Carmentis foresees herself as a model for the identity of *Julia Augusta*.[105] Implicitly, one could identify Evander (left to divinize her and erect her altars) with Livia's son and Augustus' heir, Tiberius. Livia's elevation as wife of Jupiter and founding altar to her own Concord with Jupiter-Augustus echoes Carmentis' vision of altars and worship (cf. *F.* 1.645–50).

However, at 531–32, Carmentis' prophecy of Julio-Claudian power anticipates portrayal of the *Nomen Augusti*—*axis mundi*, a "quilting point" in the imperial symbolic order—as a phallic object of male rivalry and world-wide empire: "And the watch over the fatherland will stay with the 'Augustans': it is divinely sanctioned that this house keep the reins of supreme power" (*et penes Augustos patriae tutela manebit: / hanc fas imperii frena tenere domum*). *Penes Augustos* offers the first use of *Augustus* in the *Fasti*. As a plural noun *Augustos* might anticipate Tiberius' succession as if there were two *Augusti*.[106] So, properly, *penes* is a preposition, meaning "in the house (power) of" the Augustans. But this preposition can be (mis)recognized as *penis*, or at least male fertility through which a lineage is (re)produced to make multiple "Augustuses" (*Augustos*, 531) within the *domum* (532). Arguments for this wordplay upon *penes* include the preposition's rarity and contexts in Ovid. The preposition occurs only three times in Ovid's poetry. The earliest is *Amores* 2.2.1: "Bagoas, in whom is the task of watching my mistress" (*quem penes est dominam servandi cura, Bagoa*). Bagoas is a eunuch (a castrated male guardian of a girl; *dominae cura*, 8; *custos*, 9) acting as doorman, who yet has control over Ovid's aim (thwarted by the eunuch: *Am.* 2.3). The second and only other use belongs to Janus' self-description as guardian of the *axis mundi* (*Fasti*, 1.119): "In my control alone is guardianship of the vast universe and the right of turning its hinge is all mine" (*me penes est unum vasti custo-*

dia mundi / et ius vertendi cardinis omne meum est). Janus' power is in controlling the *cardo* (axis, hinge, of the world), resembling the *gnomon*. In Carmentis' prophesy, the use of *penes* is more ambiguous, potentially allusive to penis-phallus. *Penes* as plural of *penis* modified by *Augustos* would suggest: "the guardianship of the fatherland waits Augustan penises"—i.e., "real men," such as would belong to and produce a dynastic lineage of *Augusti*.[107]

But Carmentis' control of Evander through harangue and dynastic prophecy ends at 541–52: "Nor was there a long delay: new homes rose and no other was greater in the Ausonian hills than the Arcadian" (*nec alter . . . Arcade maior erat*, 542), language of "greatness" anticipating the *Nomen Augusti* vignette (*Magne, maior, maxima*, 603–6). This "Arcadian" could refer to Carmentis or Evander, but Carmentis now becomes marginalized: she is not mentioned again until 583–86, where she antagonistically prophesies the death of Hercules, the male hero supplanting her in the narrative of her own *Carmentalia*.

Meanwhile (543–82), Ovid reports the same tale that Vergil's Evander tells Aeneas (*Aen.* 8; cf. Prop. 4.9). Killing the local "bad guy" (Cacus, who stole two of Hercules' cattle, 548; masculine figure of *Kakia* or Vice), Hercules built the *Ara Maxima* to himself (574–82), a cult which other sources state was open only to men (e.g., Prop. 4.9.65–70). Hercules preempts Carmentis' altar, becoming the heroic model of male honor apart from women.[108] Evander now follows Hercules' new cult. Why were women excluded? By some accounts because of Carmentis' resentment.[109] Gendered ritual antagonism colors Carmentis' prediction of Hercules' death ("the time is near when Earth will not need her Hercules anymore," 583–84). Her cult day receives only one couplet (585–86).

Hercules and Cacus' *Onus*

Ovid's tale of Hercules' killing of Cacus and retrieving his two bulls (*tauros duos*, 548) deploys "off-screen" acoustics to focus attention upon the nature of Hercules' manly "burden" or *onus*. The ugliness (*dira viro facies*, 553; *squalidaque humanis ossibus albet humus*, 558), incivility (*non leve finitimis hospitibusque malum*, 552), violent strength (*vires pro corpore*, 553), and size (*corpus grande*, 553–54) ascribed to Cacus and his subterranean cave provide a narrative of male virtue and vice, but off-screen effects emerge guiding discovery of untoward meanings. Cacus' cave screens orality: he lives in a cave that displays *ora* and *bracchia*, instruments of oration, above the entrance (557), not unlike Cicero's head and hands, spoils for Antony, affixed to the *rostrum* in the Forum (Dio 47.8.4). But off-screen, stolen bulls participate. When Hercules was about to depart, "the thefts [*furta*] issued a lowing [*mugitum*] with a raspy tone [*rauco sono*]" (560), the same sound quality as the ass bray (*rauco . . . intempestivos edidit ore sonos*, 434) heralding Priapus' attempted rape of Lotis. Hercules hears the "calling back" (*accipio revocamen*, 1.561, cf. 6.517–22) and retraces *the sound* (*vocem*, 561) back to the entrance of Cacus' huge cave, whose "façade" covers long recesses (*longis spelunca recessibus ingens*, 555) making it "hidden, barely discoverable by wild beast" (*abdita, vix ipsis invenienda feris*, 556). Thus, sound again enables discovery.

After Hercules gains access to the cave (563–68) and has fought with Cacus hand-to-hand (569–70), wordplay upon "orality" returns: "hardly brave" (*male fortis*, 571), Cacus resorts to "tricks of his father," Vulcan, god of fire (*Mulciber*, 554): Cacus vomits flames from his "resounding mouth" (*ore sonante*, 572), recalling Janus' spewing of sulfurous water from his *fontana ora* (1.267–72). In response, "Hercules takes him, and his three-knotted club, drawn up, sinks twelve times upon [or "in"] the man's up-turned up mouth [*adverso ore*]" (575–76). Hercules uses his phallic club to smash or plug Cacus' mouth, answering Cacus' oral arts (cf. *artes*, 571; *ore*, 572 and 576). Emblem of his divine-like power, Hercules' *clava* (*Priapeia* 20.5) is comparable with Priapus' *obscena pars* (*Pr.* 9.9) or wooden penis (Ov. *F.* 1.437; *Pr.* 6.2): they are instruments of divine potency.

Hercules gains access to what he wanted off-screen, in Cacus' cave, by performing a symbolic castration. Cacus "had blocked [screened, *praestruxerat*] his entrance with a bolt from a broken mountain" (*ille aditum fracti praestruxerat obice montis*, 563). This "bolt" (*obex*)[110] is an *opus* (564), a work or piece, that "barely would ten pairs of oxen have moved" (564). Pushing it with his shoulders, upon which "Heaven had sat" (565; Atlas' *onus*), Hercules moved the *vastum onus*, "the huge load" (566). Falling, it caused the ground to settle, "stricken by the weight of the mass" (*icta pondere molis*, 568).

Both *opus* (564) and *onus* (566) are euphemisms for the male genitals.[111] Cacus' *opus* is phallic-shaped, if it is the crag Evander describes for Aeneas at *Aeneid* 8.233–35:

> stabat acuta silex praecisis undique saxis
>   speluncae dorso insurgens, altissima visu,

dirarum nidis domus opportuna volucrum.

A pointed crag, with stone cut away all round, stood rising upon the
back of the cave, very lofty in appearance, an appropriate home for nests
of scavenger birds.

Vergil's Hercules struggles against (*nitens concussit*, 8.227) and rips this
pointed, towering crag away from the cave (*imis avulsam solvit radi-
cibus*, 8.227–28), pushing it over (*inde repente impulit*, 8.228–29), so that
it shakes the earth, as it does in the *Fasti* (*Aen.* 8.239–40; *F.* 567–68).

Cacus blocks Hercules' entry into his cave with his own symbolic
phallus. But Hercules removes it in pursuit of "secret" thefts (*furta*,
549, 560), "thefts" being a sexual euphemism in erotic elegy.[112] Hercules' *clava* defeats Cacus' symbolic phallus and fiery orality with a
sexualized violence that states a symbolic castration.[113] When Cacus'
phallic *onus-opus* (a discursive screen) is removed, Hercules retrieves
from Cacus' cave-orifice desired objects, two bulls, one of which Hercules sacrifices to his father Jupiter (548, 579), while dedicating an altar
to himself as Jupiter's son (*constituitque sibi*, 581; 1.579–82; cf. *Aen.*
8.271–75).[114]

Hercules' Bulls, the *Fasti*, and Ovid's Loss

In Ovid's version, the Hercules-Cacus story screens a primal fantasy,
an impossible view of the origin of anxious male identity and its institution at the Ara Maxima. Ovid portrays such psychological effects by
screening tension between symbolic figures (Evander and Hercules as
virtue; Cacus as vice) dramatizing loss (of cattle) and latent sound
effects (mooing cows) luring retroactive desire of recovery: Hercules
retraces bovine tracks by listening to bovine sounds. Thus, inarticulate,
off-screen lowing invites Hercules to topple Cacus' phallic bolt barring
entry to his cave.

In effect, Hercules' killing of Cacus and the removal of the bolt displaces Cacus from the symbolic "quilting point," his terrorizing local
dominance over male identity (*Cacus, Aventinae timor*, 1.551). By building the *Ara Maxima*, Hercules screens himself at the site of absolute,
fixed identity, the one controlling the symbolic "quilting point" of other
male identities. Consequently, by placing his Hercules-Cacus tale just
prior to the *nomen Augusti* vignette, Ovid anticipates the title *Augustus*

as the new ideological quilting point, the symbolic male identity ostensibly stabilizing and defining contemporary male identities.

Yet, context within the *Fasti* enables author and readers to interpret
variously the Hercules-Cacus tale. For example, Ovid's possible identification with sacrificial animals in the *Agonalia* might extend here to
the bull that Hercules has just saved but now deliberately sacrifices, a
seemingly illogical if not unjust act. If so, in the first part of the tale,
Hercules provides a complementary role of rescuer, one that exiled
Ovid implicitly invites Germanicus to perform. But other traits of Hercules invite readers to identify Ovid with the hero who "measured
out" (paces off) a world-wide journey (cf. 544: *emensus longi claviger
orbis iter*), a feat comparable to that of astronomers charting heaven.
Likewise, Ovid says, "I will measure heaven" (*caelum metabimur*, 309)
by designating days with sacral (289–94) and astral notices (295–310).
Ovid's is a *literary* journey he invites Germanicus to direct (1.4).

But, since Ovid travels a literary path, Hercules' sacrifice of one of
two rescued bulls (1.579) might refer to a possible sacrificial-poetic
loss, one of two halves of the *Fasti* or, more generally, the condition of
the poet and his *Fasti* in exile. But how? Tithing supplies a clue. At Hercules' *Ara Maxima*, men commonly struck agreements with each other
or bargained for Hercules' help by tithing a *loss* as offering to Hercules
(Dion. Hal. *Ant. Rom.* 1.40.6). Hercules' sacrifice of cattle (one tenth, by
some accounts) modeled this tithe. [115]

Hercules' sacrifice of one of two bulls is symmetrical with the condition of the *Fasti* as offering: only one half exists. This symmetry suggests that Ovid's Hercules screens in the register of narrative the poet's
literary sacrifice of half the *Fasti* given up for the god (*tibi sacratum, Tr.*
2.552), "under your name, Caesar" (*Tr.* 2. 551, *Augustus*). Such a "dedication" echoes the poem's rededication to Germanicus, where Ovid
describes the *Fasti* as "service . . . devoted to you" (*officio . . . tibi devoto*,
1.5–6), language of *devotio* having (self-)sacrificial connotations (ch. 2).
Representing sacrificial loss explains, at least in part, why at *Tr.* 2.549
Ovid reports ambiguously the number of month-books composed, six
or twelve (*sex ego Fastorum scripsi totidemque libellos*). The ambiguity
toys with the presence or absence of half the *Fasti* broken by exile (*sors
mea rupit opus, Tr.* 2.552).

Finally, the passage where Ovid celebrates the *Ara Maxima* and Hercules' sacrificial tithing is strategically located (*F.* 1.579–82), strangely
"before," if not "beneath," the "lofty" *nomen Augusti* in the next
vignette (*F.* 1.586–616). That vignette celebrates the emperor's position
as higher than *maximus* (603–6). Yet *Maximus* was a title ascribed in

contemporary Rome to the Fabii, patrons of Ovid. Placing Hercules' *Ara Maxima* "before" the imperial *nomen-gnomon* implies a comparison between Hercules and Augustus as figures controlling the symbolic "quilting point" of male identity.[116] Perhaps the *nomen* (*gnomon*) of Augustus surpasses that of Cacus and even Hercules' *Ara Maxima* as symbol of total mastery. In Ovid's "January," Tiberius' hesitation to control this "quilting point" opens a fracture or gap in the symbolic order that reflects in part Ovid's own uncertain condition in exile. Ovid's celebration of Hercules, the progenitor of the Fabii just prior to the *nomen Augusti*, can seem to bait rivalry between great men to control the "quilting point" figured in the calendar, a gendered antagonism between men continuing under new guises in "February."[117]

CHAPTER SIX

Patrimony and Transvestism in "February" (*Fasti,* Book Two)

t he previous chapter presented Ovid's "January" (Book 1) as offering angular views of the emperor's title *Augustus* as primary signifier within the Roman symbolic order. This chapter examines another title of the emperor, *Pater Patriae* or "Father of the Fatherland," as a focal point in Ovid's "February" (Book 2). I will discuss how anomalies of sexuality, gender, and poetic genre as "blots" require the reader to reexamine the book from a "transvestic" position in order to negotiate meaning in the book. Symbolic "transvestism" (cross-dressing), figured by incongruities of genre (elegy-epic) and gender (female-male), provides an "anomaly" implying a destabilizing, anamorphic view of the "Father of the Fatherland" as a "master signifier" grounding a symbolic father-son relation between the emperor and his male subjects.[1] Consequently, the following discussion centers upon Roman social-political notions of *pater,* generally signifying a split between a savior-sustainer (not necessarily a biological father) and a tyrant.

Ovid's representation of "transvestism" enables a "veiled strategy" by which to perceive and negotiate the meaning of the emperor in this split fatherhood. Generally, this transvestic strategy also entails a self-effacement or show of renunciation that screens or dissimulates contrary intentions. This dissimulation of "manhood," or transvestic "screen," enables meaning to "lie in wait" for the proper (deferred) time, to alter the symbolic order around the *pater.*[2] Staining proper masculine self-display, symbolic transvestism provides a blot or blind spot on the meaning of "February." To examine these transvestic features requires readers to assume a symbolic position angular to conventional signs of gender. From that position they can reexamine

Rome's *pater* and see, retroactively, the salvific benefits of a transvestic or feminine manhood (and the potential failure of simplistic male bravado), especially under the rule of a tyrannical *pater*.[3]

My analysis will proceed in three parts, generally following textual sequence. The first will focus upon a cluster of vignettes on and around the Nones of February (Feb. 5) celebrating the *Pater Patriae* (2.119–44). Star myths surrounding the *Pater Patriae*, "Arion and the Dolphin" (Feb. 3, 79–118) and "Callisto the Great Bear" (Ursa Major; Feb. 12, 153–92), frame Ovid's treatment of the *Pater Patriae* with "transvestic" portrayals of male and female characters suffering destitution of power and identity (symbolic castration) at the hands of dominant masculine libidos. The *Pater Patriae* passage at the center stands in anxious tension with these transvestic representations.

Attention then turns to the most prominent scene of transvestism in the *Fasti*, the story of "Hercules and Omphale," included to explain the nudity of the Luperci, the equestrian youths worshiping the god Faunus-Pan (Feb. 15; 267–474, esp. 303–58). Cross-dressed in Omphale's clothes, Hercules—ancestral father of the Fabii (a prominent Roman family, and thus potential patrons)—provides for the Fabii the "primal scene" of symbolic transvestism as a strategy concealing power behind a feminine screen. This screen enables surprise revelation of manhood.

Thirdly, I focus on Ovid's retelling of the "Lucretia and Brutus" legend (for the Regifugium, Feb. 24; 685–852) which situates castration-transvestism at the "birth" of the Roman Republic (851–52). Here symbolic transvestism enables recuperation of "manhood" (power) under the tyrannical rule of Tarquinius Superbus—the brutal, tyrannical Father, whose savage modes of enjoyment are imitated by his equally brutal son. In the final scene of the narrative, two other characters, Brutus the "fool" and submissive Lucretia, seem retroactively in fantasy to have formed transvestic responses to paternal cruelty and, though they do not directly communicate, to have acted in concert and with uncanny, deferred timing that rescues manly honor that had seemed lost.

Arion, Callisto, and Transvestism before the Father

Ovid situated his praise of the *Pater Patriae* in February within a context reminiscent of his celebration of the *nomen Augusti* in January. As

Verrius' *Fasti Praenestini* confirms, the Senate, the Equestrians, and the Roman people voted the title *Pater Patriae* on February 5, 2 BCE (2.127–28), the Nones of February, a monthly dividing day (ch. 1).⁴ Likewise, Ovid describes the *nomen Augusti* on a "dividing day," the Ides (13th) of January. But to produce this structural parallel, Ovid displaced the *nomen Augusti* from the date of its actual vote (ch. 5; Jan. 16: *Fasti Praen. Feriale Cum.*).⁵ This "error" enables Ovid to situate his *nomen Augusti* between two *Carmentalia*, which offer positions from which to review the *nomen Augusti* as phallic *gnomon* (obelisk), as symbolic object of gendered antagonisms—phallus-castration, fertility-infertility, male-female—within a dynastic politics of mother and son (Livia and Tiberius; ch. 5).

By contrast, Ovid celebrates the title *Pater Patriae* on its true date, February 5, yet provides again two surrounding positions from which to view that *cognomen*—two star myths, "Arion and the Dolphin" and "Callisto the Great Bear (Ursa Maior)." The narrative fates of the two main characters are framed by the gendered nature of their transvestic guises and by salvation as the trait of a virtuous *pater*.

Arion and the Dolphin

Ovid introduces his version of Herodotus' story of Arion riding a dolphin to explain the "flight" or sinking of the "Dolphin," a constellation.⁶ But first Ovid describes the dolphin as Neptune's "felicitous informer in secret love affairs" (*occultis felix in amoribus index*, 2.81). The dolphin might suggest playful phallic symbolism,⁷ but as *index* he also recalls birds described under Ovid's *Agonalia* (Jan. 9) as *indices* of divine thoughts (1.445–50), like the ass revealing Priapus' lust (6.345–46).

According to Ovid, Arion's fame had spread on land and sea (83) because of his music's power to control natural forces, reconcile predators and prey (84–90), and even enchant virginal Diana (Cynthia), as would Apollo, her brother (91–92).⁸ But, after touring Sicily and southern Italy (93–94), Arion was returning to Greece with his wealth (*opes*, 95–96), when the ship's captain and crew armed themselves against him (97–102; *districto . . . ense*, 99–100).

At this point, Ovid's voice interrupts the violent scene by addressing the captain in the second person (2.101–2): "What do you have to do with the sword? Sailor, govern the hesitant ship: your fingers should not hold such weapons" (*quid tibi cum gladio? dubiam rege, navita, pup-*

pem: / non haec sunt digitis arma tenenda tuis). Ovid's advice here—*dubi-am rege . . . puppem* (2.101)—parallels his request in the dedication that Germanicus guide his poetic ship (*timidae derige navis iter*, 1.4; *rege vatis habenas*, 1.26). Arion's fear (*metu pavidus*, 2.103) is comparable to Ovid's own (1.4, *timidae . . . navis*; 16, *deque meo pavidos excute corde metus*). This parallelism suggests that the relationship between Ovid and Germanicus may be analogous to that between Arion and the ship's captain.

Arion then models strategic escape for poet-musicians: "Quaking in fear, he said, 'I am not begging to remove death, but let me offer a little reply[9] by taking up the lyre'" (103–4). Using his lyre as a "weapon" against the armed men (cf. the captain fingering *arma*, 102), Arion exploits song as a delaying tactic that invites the mockery of his pirate attackers (105–10):

> They grant leave and they laugh at his delay [*ridentque moram*]: he takes up a chaplet that could adorn your hair, Apollo; he had donned a *gown* [*pallam*] double-dyed purple with Tyrian murex: the chord when struck with his thumb produced its sounds, just as a swan pierced in his gray temples by a hard quill sings in meters of lamentation.[10]

Arion's diversionary strategy includes delay (*mora*) to dress for the "part," an act of sartorial transformation that quotes the appearance of Apollo (106) as *citharoedus* in his distinctly feminine appearance.[11] Arion dons a crown[12] and a long purple dress (*palla*[13]). This dress and lyre offer a highly gendered contrast with the captain and sailors armed with weapons and threatening violence (*ense destricto*, 99; *arma-ta turba*, 100; *gladio*, 101; *arma*, 102; cf. *Aen.* 1.1. *arma virumque . . .*). Attic vase paintings illustrate the festive cross-dressing of lyre-players in Hellenic ritual traditions.[14] Musicians in effeminate garb appear in other parts of the *Fasti* as well.[15]

Here, Arion's feminine appearance supplements his "elegiac" lament (*flebilibus numeris*, 109).[16] He mourns his own death, as does the proverbial swan, to which he is compared (109–110); likewise Sappho of Lesbos in *Heroides* 15 abandons lyric meters for elegy, *elegiae flebile carmen* (*H.* 15.7). Arion's clothes and lament evoke the pirates' laughter, perhaps at his feminine garb and tears before death (105).

But their laughter is foiled when Arion suddenly (*protinus*, 111) leaps into sea: "People say a dolphin with a curved back put himself beneath the strange burden [Arion himself]" (113–14). It is as if Arion petitioned the love of this "index of secret desire [or lovemaking]" for rescue. Sappho also threatens to leap to her death from the Leucadian crag—a leap, like Arion's, into the sea. Also like Arion, Sappho asks for rescue, but she asks *Aura* (the wind) and winged *Amor* to support her weight (*pondus*, 178) and save her (*Her.* 15.177–80). The dolphin supports Arion's *onus* (114). The gods witness the dolphin's act of devotion (*facta pia*), and Jupiter turns him into a nine-star constellation (117–18).

Arion's "transvestism"—combining poetic weeping (*flebilibus carminibus*) with soft, feminine apparel and his seemingly suicidal leap—presents a weak male subject. But he uses this (elegiac) appearance to lure, and then reverse, derisive domination by armed piratical (epic) subjects, who suppose themselves dominant, and him a victim. The story can be read as a triumph of the elegiac poet facing an "epic," warlike crisis (the pirate's threat). But the notion of a ship and its captain had long been a metaphor for the State.[17] So, the association of Arion with Ovid's authorial persona might suggest an identification of the violent captain driving Arion overboard (99, 101) with an emperor or an imperial reader such as Germanicus, who betrayed or might betray Ovid in exile. However, Germanicus, the poem's revised addressee, could also identify (or be identified by other readers) with the dolphin, the *index in occultis amoribus*—a symbol of "disguised desires" for Ovid's rescue from a state and its helmsman (Augustus, Tiberius?) who fails to do his duty of protecting his passengers. The story provides a fantasy scene staging at least two conflicting positions for reader identification (pirate or dolphin, possibly a pirate). For at least some of Ovid's readers, a literary-political allegory would seem credible.[18]

But none of that is expressly stated. What seems more important than one single allegory is the story's conflicting libidinal dynamics, · ranging from Arion's musical power of pleasurable peace to piratical greed, and the dolphin's responsiveness to secret, salvific love indirectly expressed. What is exemplary about Arion as poet in these dynamics is his deferral of a manly, aggressive response behind a self-sacrificing "transvestic," dilatory display. Key to Arion's strategy is handling his "Lesbian lyre" (*Lesbida . . . lyram*, 2.83) in such a way that it seems to summon from beneath the waves a hidden amorous dolphin to the rescue.[19]

Callisto the Great Bear and Her Son (Feb. 12)

While gender-bending tactics help Arion escape domination, for other characters they are not so salubrious. At *Fasti* 2.153–92 (Feb. 12), Ovid relates the origin of the constellations Arctos (*Ursa Maior*) and Arctophylax (*Ursae Custos;* or bear's guard). While literal transvestism is absent from this version of the tale,[20] a kind of metaphorical "trans-gendering" operates in Callisto's discourse to secure her role as a virginal devotee and hunting companion of the goddess Diana, the divine virgin-huntress (155–62):

> With the group of wood nymphs and the huntress Diana, Callisto was a part of a sacred chorus. Touching the bow of the goddess, she said, "Bows that I am touching, be witnesses [*testes*] of my virginity." Cynthia praised [her] and said, "Keep the promised bonds and you will be the model of my comrades." She would have preserved her covenant [*foedera*], if she had not been beautiful. She was wary of humans; she has her crime from Jupiter.[21]

In another version (*Met.* 2.405–597), Jupiter crosses genders, as Diana, to lure Callisto into a sexual moment.[22] Jupiter's "transvestic" strategy of (homo-)sexual conquest implies a preexisting female homosocial, if not homosexual, dynamic. *Fasti* 2.157–58 dramatizes female homosocial relations. The *arcus*, bows, in the oath scene are not simply the literal bows of Diana, but also Callisto's symbolic *testes*,[23] an ambiguous word meaning "witnesses" or "testicles." The bow was itself a stock symbol of the phallus.[24] Here, Diana's *arcus* provide Callisto her metaphorical "witnesses," her means of patrolling her virginity, but also her phallic *testes*, in the absence of a father or a husband (158). Moreover, she "touches" them to swear loyalty to Diana in an oath or *foedus* (*promissa . . . foedera serva,* 159), a word recalling Catullus' bond with Lesbia.[25]

The performance "phallicizes" Diana and Callisto within a female homosocial group independent of definition or identity through male dominance and protection. Ovid's scripting of *testes* in the dialogue between them retains the language of male anatomy, but Callisto uses the homynym ironically (in a double-entendre) to (a)bridge anatomy and law and thereby elaborate in a binding oath her self-understanding in a female homosocial bond.[26]

Callisto's clever use of the language of oath is undermined in two ways. First, Jupiter, finding her beautiful, pursues and rapes her.[27] Then Diana observes Callisto's signs of deviance from her word. For example, when Diana invites the "Tegeaean virgin" (Callisto) to bathe with the troop, Callisto blushes at the "false sound of 'virgin'" (*erubuit falso virginis illa sono,* 168). We have already found false or uncannily timed sounds marking latent sexual meanings (ch. 5).[28] But here a "false note" marks Diana's application of *virgo* to Callisto, a word no longer matching the physical reality of her body—a kind of dissimulative language masking reality. Indeed, Callisto's blush is a legible sign of falsity.

Moreover, Callisto "hesitates" to unveil her body and bathe with the others, which produces "bad signs of slow delay" (*nymphae velamina ponunt;/ hanc pudet, et tardae dat mala signa morae,* 169–70). Arion also delayed, but in order to assume, not to remove, a dissimulative cover, in his case an effeminate persona. Callisto's swelling body informs on her (*indicio,* 172), thus beginning her loss of autonomy. By contrast, Arion's revelation begins his rescue upon the dolphin, an *index* of hidden love (281). Although Callisto swore devotion to Diana in the language of manhood (*testes*), Diana can read the signs of Callisto's falsity.

As for the word *pondus,* similar language in "January" (*onus, pondus*) refers to the fetus in the womb (1.623–4, aborted).[29] That language reappears later at 2.452 (a prayer to Juno Lucina for successful childbirth) in a context in which there has also been a "dubious sound" or discourse (Juno's oracle to let a goat enter the Roman women, 2.441–42).[30] "Weight" has already appeared as a theme in the transvestic tale of Arion; he was the weight (*onus*) riding the dolphin. Arion places "emphasis" upon the dolphin; he was the "strange burden" that the dolphin·supported and saved (*oneri novo,* 2.114).[31] But Arion's "sounds" (*lyricis sonis,* 94; *sonos,* 108)—his lament in effeminate Apollonian garb—provided a feminine performative pretext or cover for the "dolphin's" "recovery" of Arion's physical autonomy. The lyre, itself an unlikely match for "manly" *arma,* along with the dolphin, is Arion's phallic surprise, roused up with the "Lesbian lyre" (recalling Catullus and, perhaps, Sappho, at *F.* 2.82, *Lesbida . . . lyram*).[32]

So, by contrast with Arion and his lyre, Callisto with her bow seems ironically trapped in an inescapable, gendered hierarchy of power. With the birth of her son, Callisto sheds the weapons that she has named her *testes* (158) and had used to protect her bodily independence (*virginitas,* 158) from male penetration—a symbolic castration. Weapons pass instead to her son Arcas/ Arctophylax upon his reaching manhood (183–84). Encountering his bear-mother, he "would have unknowingly pierced her with his sharp javelin" (*hanc puer ignarus iaculo fixisset acuto,* 187), if Jupiter had not "snatched" (*raptus*) both into the houses of heaven as constellations.[33]

Discipline between women reinforces male hierarchy. Diana's expulsion of pregnant Callisto from the virginal group distinguishes virgin from non-virgin (173–74). Juno's transformation of "beautiful" Callisto (Gr. *kalliste*) into a frightful bear (179–82) separates matron from rival concubine (*paelex*). The permanent prohibition on the constellation's "bathing" in Ocean[34]—a kind of banishment—retroactively interprets stellar motion as social law, so that Callisto's beauty is also spoiled by an excessive feminine toilette; as a bear, she now lacks *cultus* (cf. *cura sui*, 4.108).[35] Imposition of such an internal hierarchy among women displaces blame (*crimen*) from male power (Jupiter) onto an innocent "feminine" scapegoat (or bear-monster, 177–78[36]) and aids the return of the phallic weapon to the masculine order.

Transgendering effects in Callisto's tale reflect Ovid's role as poet. Callisto's pregnancy with Jupiter's divine seed, bearing its burden or weight, and her birth and eventual "banishment" (not to touch Ocean, 191–92) recall Ovid's appropriation of pregnancy as poetic metaphor for producing his *Fasti*. In his exilic poetry, Ovid repeatedly uses the Bear constellation to identify his distant location on the Black Sea in the far north near the Great Bear.[37] Callisto and Ovid are both exiles of sorts: there is symmetry between Ovid's exile across the sea and Callisto's expulsion from Diana's chorus and her exclusion from the sea. So Callisto's "castration" could symbolize Ovid's own "trauma" to his ability to communicate: due to its height, Callisto's bear-constellation could see both Ovid (*Tr.* 3.11.7–8) and his wife (*Tr.* 4.3.1–20) and, in fantasy, pass messages between them. Thus, Callisto's constellation functions as a symbolic "cover" for Ovid in savage exile.

Poetic Failure, Salvation, and the *Pater Patriae* (the Nones)

From the Kalends to the Ides, the major vignettes allude to demise and salvific agency (of Jupiter or the emperor), although some hint at Jupiter's power to destroy (Callisto; Lala-Larentia, later at 585–616). Ovid's celebration of the title *Pater Patriae* on the Nones (*Fasti* 2.119–44) stands in an indirect, highly rhetorical relationship to surrounding vignettes oscillating between loss and salvation. Key is the meaning of *pater* in Roman civic life.

Naming a public hero a *pater* or *parens* did not signify that the *pater* was a biological father, but was a "savior" to whom one owed one's life. Originally, the civic *pater* had rescued another man in battle—he had restored life (or lives) from the brink of death. By calling his savior a *pater*, a man signaled a debt of reverence and obedience that a son would owe his biological father. Debt, burden (*onus*), and obligation describe the "son's" relation to this social *pater*. The classic example was Quintus Fabius Maximus, the very man Ovid heralded on the Ides (2.241–42) for saving the state from Hannibal by his delaying tactics.[38] During the Second Punic War, Fabius, as dictator, saved from annihilation the army of M. Minucius Rufus, his *magister equitum*. Upon rescue, Minucius called Fabius his *pater* to signal that he and his army owed their lives and obedience to Fabius' guiding authority.[39] Applied in the late Republic to Romulus as founder, the title *parens patriae* or *Pater Patriae* labeled men who had founded communities or saved citizens or the whole state. The title became an object of elite male rivalry from Cicero to Julius Caesar and then Augustus.[40]

Various references to death and rescue surrounding Ovid's Nones of February indirectly signal the defining action of a *pater*. But such salvation imposes a burden of obligation in return.[41] At 2.119–26 Ovid begins celebrating Augustus as *Pater Patriae*, but expresses anxiety about his ability to bear the weight of this obligation. In 125–26 Ovid expresses it directly: the topic, suited for "heroic verse," has "such great weight" (*tantum ponderis*). Other couplets express the same obligation indirectly (*accumulatur honor*, 122; *maioraque viribus urgent*, 123; *tantum ponderis*, 125–26): basically, Ovid fears faltering in his obligation to the civic *pater*.[42]

"Burden" is present also in the first couplet (119–20), in a pun recalling a similar wordplay at the end of Ovid's celebration of the *nomen Augusti* (1.615–16). Here, *mille sonos* can produce an auditory effect, *mil(l)es -onos*, implying, "Now is my *soldier-burden*, and I would wish to have within me, Homer, your heart with which Achilles was commemorated." This pun emphasizes Ovid's military burden, as proclaimed in the month's preface: "This is my warfare: I carry the weapons I can" (*haec mea militia est; ferimus quae possumus arma*, 2.9; ch. 3).

What is so martial about the *Pater Patriae* theme? Homer has used his epic voice in the *Iliad* to commemorate, specifically, how Achilles learned to moderate his wrath. Ovid suffered Augustus' wrath in exile. Moreover, it is in *Tristia* 2 (Ovid's self-defense from exile) where the poet most often names Augustus as *Pater Patriae* and defends his poetry, while urging the emperor to moderate his wrath.[43] Ovid's "military" burden may be like that of the embassy to Achilles (*Iliad* 9), sent to appease the anger of Achilles.

The poetic weightiness of praising the *Pater Patriae* also recalls the immediately preceding episode, where Arion, dressed in effeminate garb, sang an "elegiac" lament of his own demise, then leapt into the sea to face his death, only to be rescued by a dolphin which in response "put himself with his curved back beneath a strange burden [*oneri . . . novo*]" (113–14). The Arion episode provides a position from which to view Ovid as exiled elegist praising the *Pater Patriae* in (inexplicit) desire of his own rescue from exile. In the *Pater Patriae* passage, might Ovid seek a saving "dolphin"—a kind of rescue—in one of his readers, who, like dolphins, are responsive to song?

But Ovid may secure a wider salvific response by doubting (tongue-in-cheek) his own tone (*sonos*, 119), inspiration (*pectus*, 120), and style of expression (*praecipuo ore*, 124)—a manly Homeric style worthy of an Achilles—and by longing for those qualities of an epic poet that he claims to lack.[44] Perhaps, like a *pater*, Ovid's elite male readers would have such qualities to rescue, sustain, or guide Ovid as he carries this burden in poetry (cf. Germanicus, *F*. 1.1–26, esp. 17: *da mihi te placidum, dederis in carmina vires*). During exilic revisions, that support would implicitly extend to rescue from exile. But whether or not readers actually "rescue" him, Ovid's professed weakness places his quavering praise of the *Pater Patriae* as a bait of helplessness. Might this scenario of personal weakness before imperial strength screen a lack or desire that Ovid or others experienced in the symbolic order of imperial Rome? Might the title of *pater* not screen a split between substance and mere name or language of fatherliness, i.e., the inconsistency between pardoning enemies (rescuing them from death, 143) and leaving Ovid a poet poised, like Arion, on the edge of death in exile? If not, the pose of personal and poetic weakness before imperial strength at least insinuates to Ovid's reading public a displacement of the *onus* of response from Ovid, the symbolic son, to the emperor, the symbolic father.

Pater Patriae and Gender Strategies

By announcing his potential failure to bear in elegy his epic burden with proper tone, Ovid enables perception of nonconformity in his celebration of the *Pater Patriae*. The following three epigrams contain brief meteorological notices (145–46, 147–48; 149–52) with anamorphic, "aerial" vantage points upon Ovid's professed failure (*defuit ingenium*, 123). These meteorological phenomena act as "diacritical signs" antic-

ipating uncertain "atmospheric" relations between Ovid and his audience (the emperor and other elite males in Rome) surrounding his panegyric of the *pater.*

The first two signs appear on the same day as the *Pater Patriae* (Feb.
5, the Nones; 145–48). First, the "Idean Boy" projects himself (*eminet*)
above the horizon, revealing himself down to his belly (*tenus eminet
alvo*) and pours out water mixed with nectar (145–46). This reference
identifies "Aquarius" with Ganymede, the Trojan youth whom Jupiter
loved and abducted as his "catamite" and water server. The abduction
of Ganymede thus "elevates" him from his mortal status[45] to heaven in
the service of Jupiter, to whom Augustus is compared as *Pater Patriae.*[46]
Here, the catamite Ganymede, a server at Jupiter's table, embodies one
prospect for a poet, as an elite yet exiled Roman male. The water
poured by Ganymede-Aquarius is parallel to the panegyric poetry of
the elegist.[47]

The following couplet (147–48) heralds the blowing of Zephyrus'
"softer" breeze; it is *mollior* than the bitter north wind of Boreas, from
whom some shrink away (*horrere*). The contrast may allude to elegiac
poetry versus epic, but *mollior* can also mean "more seductive" or
more effeminate.[48] Again, a concept of the yielding, weak, or effeminate marks the day of the *Pater Patriae,* supporting some suspicions in
Ovid's readership of the poet's self-abasement and flattery, or else a
hope for a gentler imperial response. Together, both Ganymede-
Aquarius (145–46) and Zephyrus (147–48) signal a "softer," yet more
effeminate "atmospheric" response of Jupiter-Augustus, the *pater.*[49]
This "atmosphere" agrees with the portrayal of the poet Arion immediately preceding the *Pater Patriae* passage—he is dressed in effeminate dress and performing for the violent sailors at his death—only to
be rescued by the dolphin, which signals in an astronomical "sign"
Ovid's desire for rescue (cf. Venus' and Cupid's rescue of fish,
2.453–74). But in the next group of couplets (assigned to Feb. 10), even
as Ovid observes the coming of spring (149–50), he warns his audience
not to be deceived, because wintry signs of "cold" linger and "resist"
(*ne fallere tamen, restant tibi frigora, restant, / magnaque discedens signa
reliquit hiems,* 151–52). Contrary chilly indications ominously remain
resistant to the "softer" signs that precede (148).

Meteorological signs of *mollitia* and transvestism surrounding the
Pater Patriae passage provide vantage points for Ovid's failure of
manly strength to bear his poetic burden (123). An additional observation indicates *mollitia* in his treatment of the *Pater Patriae:* Ovid invokes

Homer (119–20) by using the epithet *Maeonide*. Although *Maeonides/Maeonis* can describe generically Lydian persons and things, it appears only three times in Ovid's *Fasti*, all in Book Two. This address to Homer is the first. The other two appear later in Ovid's celebration of the Lupercalia; they both refer to the Lydian queen Omphale (310, 352) in the most prominent example of transvestism in the entire *Fasti*.[50] There Faunus, the Roman Pan, attempts to rape Hercules, the ancestor of the important Fabii family, cross-dressed as Omphale *Maeonis*. *Maeonis* herself, that is, Omphale cross-dressed as Hercules, wears his lion skin and holds his club as weapon.

Parentatio: the Fabii, Hercules, and the Lupercalia

A period of nine days beginning with the Ides of February (and a tale of the death of 306 Fabii) and lasting until the *Feralia* on February 21 centers, in Ovid's presentation, upon the *Lupercalia* on February 15. The period was called by a name related to "fathers" or forebears, the *Parentatio*, when families offered ancestor worship at the family tombs and ghosts could make contact with the living. Ovid's rendering revisits the "fathers" and Roman cultural patrimony in ways that fashion angular views regarding dominant structures of military *virtus*, that is, manly honor derived from daring aggressive action compared to humble inactivity. Ovid's use of transvestism in his Lupercalia, once a family cult of the Fabii,[51] to explain the nudity of the young male Luperci embodies an anxiety or split over the disposition of manhood.

The Ides and Fabian Manhood

Ovid locates remembrance of the Etruscan slaughter of 306 Fabii in battle on an unusual date, the Ides of February (13th; 195–242). Here Ovid offers a nuanced treatment of what the historian Livy describes (2.48–50)[52]—how "a single house had taken up the might and burden [*vires et onus*] of the city" (F. 2.197) by fighting the war against Veii.[53] This unusual date reflects Ovid's use of the tale to indicate the "primal scene" of an almost biological instinct among contemporary Fabian descendants for deferred or withdrawn manhood.[54] This delay or screening of manliness (*virtus*) from rash action enables an anamorphic view of simplistic notions of manhood founded on aggressive, violent daring.

Although the Fabii were a noble soldiery (*miles generosus*), any one of whom could have been a general or leader (199–200), they all perished in an ambush due to their lack of foresight (cf. *provida cura*, 2.60): they did not suspect treachery by weaker forces. Similes of the lion (209–12), boar (231–34), and flooding river (219–24) describe the bravado of the Fabii in elevated epic style, yet provide the setting for Fabian heedlessness.[55] The Etruscans learned they could not defeat the Fabii openly (*aperte*), so they cleverly hid in the wooded margins of a field (*campus*), while leaving a few men and stray farm animals to lure the pillaging forces. They then ambush the Fabii (213–14). Directly addressing the Fabii, Ovid contrasts their noble but naïve bravado (*simplex nobilitas*, 226; *virtus*, 227) with the deceptive concealment of the Etruscans (225–30) in language that could also describe a dissimulative rhetorical attack.[56]

In their *simplex nobilitas* and naive manhood (*virtus*), the Fabii have rashly taken up a burden proper to a whole city, marched out to war, and all perished in one day (235–36), thus almost destroying the whole family. Why? Because the Fabii naively interpret the discursive field (*campus*) as harboring no threat to themselves; they misread the signs. Yet Ovid asks (230), "What is at hand that may remain in a miserable crisis?" Ovid answers (as does Livy) that a Fabian "boy" (*puer*) was left behind. He was "still not capable in arms" (239), nor was he sexually potent yet—he was *impubes* (239). This *puer* eventually sires the lineage that begat the famous Q. Fabius Cunctator who saved Rome by "delaying" tactics, eluding and deceiving Hannibal in the Second Punic War.[57]

The direct *virtus* of the 306 Fabii was pragmatically weak. But the Fabian descendants differ from their ancestors; caution and clever delay replaced rash bravado, as is shown in Ovid's final address to a "Fabius Maximus" who saves by delaying (2.241–42). As Byron Harries and Alessandro Barchiesi have observed, Ovid here alludes to two different Fabii Maximii—Q. Fabius Maximus Cunctator (the delayer) and Ovid's contemporary patron Paullus Fabius Maximus.[58] This double reference is implied by Ovid's exilic attribution of Herculean *simplicitas* to Paullus at *Ex P.* 3.3.100 (cf. *simplex nobilitas* at *F.* 2.226),[59] and his celebration of Paullus' lineage from one Fabian survivor (*Ex P.* 1.2.2–3).[60] Harries also notes[61] that, like his famous ancestor, Paullus himself "delayed" marriage, perhaps until Marcia, a cousin of Augustus,[62] was of marriageable age. This was a strategic deferral, because marriage into the imperial *domus* could grant access to wealth, privileges, and favors at court. However, at more than thirty years of age, Paullus was scandalously old for a Roman male to defer marriage, especially in view of Augustus' marriage laws. Syme gingerly implies one interpretation: "Some may be tempted to surmise a distaste for women"—a statement "screening" desire for men.[63] Although social politics may explain marital delay, that politics does not absolve the aging bachelor of suspicions. If he lacked desire for women, strategic benefit would prove a strong lure to matrimony. Suspicions of Paullus' marital delay would be consonant with the specter later in Book 2 of cross-dressed Hercules. Hercules was the family progenitor, whose transvestism lures Faunus into bed (*F.* 2.303–58; see below).[64] As Harries notes, the Fabian *gens* had multiple problems reproducing sufficient heirs to continue their lineage,[65] which implies the "congenital" character of reproductive deferral within the family.

In another "sign" perhaps implying (hetero-)sexual dithering, Ovid calls the sole surviving Fabian *puer impubes*. Livy writes that he was "almost a man, left behind because of his age" (*prope puberem aetate relictum*); he does not say *puer* (Liv. 2.50.11). Ovid's description is both more elegiac and more ambiguous. *Puer* can mean an elegiac lover. *Impubes* may describe a "celibate" male deferring sexual contact with women as long as possible,[66] or else "beardless" or "youthful," qualities that one can produce artificially so as to extend a youthful appearance (cf. *pueri delicati* and *cinaedi*).[67] Ovid's *adhuc non utilis armis*, "still not ready for arms," is not in Livy, but mirrors Ovid's self-description in the preface of Book 2 (*F.* 2.9–16), where Ovid dithers in performing his *militia* (see chapter 4), and anticipates his eroticized lure to Mars' "seminal contribution" to the poem, as shown by the god's sexual prowess (*his officiis . . . virilibus aptus*, 3.169).[68]

This Fabian *puer* at 2.239 was preceded at 145 by the constellation Aquarius, Ganymede, the catamite of Jupiter.[69] Festus records a specific anecdote about an ancestor of Ovid's Paullus, a descendant of the famous Cunctator. Q. Fabius Maximus (cos.116 BCE; censor, 108) was called "Ivory" (unblemished; fair-skinned) and *pullus Iovis*, "Jupiter's chicken" because, supposedly, lightning had struck his buttocks. The campy language implied that Jupiter had raped him, since he had boyish good looks[70] and thus might be compared to Ganymede.

Ovid recounts the story of the Fabian clan on the Ides of February in ways that subtly develop themes of gender nonconformity already discussed. While the battle scene emphasizes the clan's near destruction in brash male bravado, reproductive salvation comes, ironically, in the implied dithering of a Fabian *puer* left in Rome. Implicitly, gender-bending or maturational deviance in the renunciation of male bravado (*simplex nobilitas* and naïve *virtus*) can enable greater control of impulsive libido on the battlefield and, if Harries is right, in sexual matters too. Fabian dilatoriness is comparable to that of effeminized Arion. The regressive dithering of Ovid himself in the prefaces of the *Fasti* may mirror the resistance of some elites, particularly equestrians, to Augustan marriage laws. Overall, the Fabian story advocates concealing one's masculine "weaponry" or manhood (*virtus*) to prepare for a surprise revelation.

Raven, Crater, and Water Snake: Augural Reading (Feb. 14)

The implication is that Ovid's *Fasti* offers the reader flattering surfaces, which may conceal potential resistance beneath an ambivalent, passive-aggressive discourse. Temporally, that discourse has the trait of narrative delay and digression. But such a dilatory tactic has its risks before power, the star myth on February 14 suggests.

Here Ovid reworks themes of delay and dissimulation while explaining the juncture of three constellations, the Raven, Crater, and Water Snake (2.243–66).[71] Commanded by Apollo to bring water for rites honoring his father Jupiter (2.247), the raven, potentially symbolizing the poet, is distracted by his desire for figs growing in a tree. The figs are not yet ripe, so the raven waits until they are sweet and then eats until he is satisfied (249, 256). However, since he has delayed his task for days if not weeks, the raven now attempts a clever substitute in the form of an entertaining pun that can be thought to fulfill Apollo's command: he provides the god a *hydrus* or water snake (257) for the holy water that Apollo requires.[72]

The *hydrus* fulfills the *imperium*, the "command," of Apollo (255) by way of a cryptic bilingual trope that enables the water snake to be interpreted as a rebus, that is, as an enigmatic visual emblem screening both Apollo's command and its fulfillment/nonfulfillment. First, it is as if the raven has associated the idea of *imperium* with the "crater" or bowl that Apollo had given him to carry the water (251). This association occurs, it seems, by way of a Greek equivalent of imperium, κράτος, which sounds similar to the Greek word for bowl, κρατήρ. Strategically, the raven now transforms his original task by substituting a water snake or *hydrus* for the original bowl and its attendant command (κρατήρ and κράτος). The word *hydrus*, which the raven calls *vivarum obsessor aquarum*, the "container"—that is, "holder," "haunter," or "blockade"—of living, running water (259), recalls a *hydria*, a water pitcher.

How does the snake screen for us the fulfillment of Apollo's command and yet its nonfulfillment? The snake's writhing body and its name, interpreted as "water holder," symbolize, but they do not actually provide, what Apollo wants—that is, the water container holding "living" water according to his command. This screening is evident in the actual encounter because, just when the raven presents the water snake to Apollo, he re-presents the snake in words (259–60) as " . . . the cause of my delay, a holder [or blockade] of living waters: he held [or contained, *tenuit*] the fountains and my duty." However, the snake-trope also screens the raven's disobedience. Instead of actual sacral water, he offers a humorous trope as a fictive compliance,[73] deflecting his delay from direct attention; behind the pun is enjoyment of ripening figs, an ancient metaphor of enjoyment, particularly sexual enjoyment.[74] As punishment, Apollo forbids the raven to drink any water while figs ripen. This prohibition recalls the ban on Calllisto, the constellation of the Great Bear, bathing in Ocean and might evoke, for some readers, Ovid's exile, as would transforming these star clusters into symbolic texts of warning. The whole narrative provides a vantage point upon the risks of delay and dissimulative screens before a clever but powerful augural reader like Apollo (cf. Germanicus as Clarian Apollo, 1.19–20).[75] This risk of delay and subterfuge counterbalances the death of the Fabii in their hasty surface interpretations of the battle scene, but also the salvific potential of later Fabian delay and avoiding direct attack (*F.* 2.193–242).

Nudity and Transvestism in Ovid's *Lupercalia* (Feb. 15)

Male nudity and its adornment are major concerns in Ovid's *Lupercalia*,[76] a festival dedicated to the god Faunus, the protector and fertilizer (cf. *pater*) of flocks both human and animal.[77] At the festival, select equestrian youths called *Luperci* ran around the Palatine; they whipped human bystanders to purify them from evils and to promote eroticism and fertility. The *Luperci* were originally naked, except for a goat-hide cape, although there were changes over time.[78]

The fact that Ovid spends over half the vignette explaining nudity (267–380) attests anxiety over concealment and disclosure within "February."[79] First, Ovid explains nudity as suited to running and as a vestige of Faunus, or Pan's, wild simplicity among primitive people who wore no clothes and toughened their bodies by living outdoors (284–302). The first explanation of the nudity of the Luperci and their god Faunus is that they reenact a prior human condition, recalling the hardened endurance of savage, bare bodies in the wild; ritual nudity recalls this primitive uncivilized condition (291–300).[80] Despite the festival's prehistoric origin, this explanation is "Greek": Evander imported the cult from Arcadia (279–82). Indeed, the next two explanations demonstrate that Ovid is not interested in the primitive origins of nudity, but in its currency as a social practice.

Yet, the second explanation of nudity, discussed below, contains the story of "Hercules and Omphale" and their cross-dressing. This explanation along with the first (deriving the Lupercalia from Arcadia; 5.97–104) Ovid calls "foreign" (*peregrinis*, 359). However, to balance these, Ovid introduces a third "Latin" origin (*adde peregrini causas, mea Musa, Latinas*, 359), drawing the nudity of the Luperci from a competition that arose between youthful Romulus and Remus during the Lupercalian sacrifice to Faunus. The pair with their band of followers (cf. the two colleges of Luperci) were preparing sacrificial meat for Faunus (361–64) when suddenly a shepherd reported a cattle-raid (369–70). Romulus, followed by the Quinctii (or Quinctilii or Quintiliani) and Remus, by the Fabii, raced off (in some versions, with strips of the sacrificial hides as weapons). Remus and the Fabii, not Rome's founder Romulus, defeated the cattle thieves and returned victorious to eat the meat before Romulus returned. One version that Plutarch cites (that of Gaius Acilius, a Roman senator who wrote a history of Rome in Greek in the 140s) states that Romulus and Remus stripped naked so that sweat would not impede their chasing the raiders.[81] Ovid is the only source[82] for the story that Romulus, Remus, and the pastoral youth (*iuventus*, 365) were sunning their naked bodies (*corpora nuda*, 366) in a *campus*, the current Roman term for *palaestra*,[83] and were testing their strength with bars, javelins, and weights (367–68), which recalls Vergil, *Georgics* 2.531–34.[84]

In this so-called "Latin" tale, Ovid explains nudity at the Lupercalia, ironically, by way of contemporary Hellenizing practices, thus triggering some Roman anxiety about them.[85] In the most orthodox discourse of conservative Roman values, *gymnasium-palaestra* signified Greek luxuriousness and extravagance: *gymnasium* required expenditure of leisure or free time (*otium*) to cultivate the appearance of one's body, which exposed the elite male body to an objectifying gaze in the *campus*, and provided (it was thought) opportunities in which male bodies might be subject to sexual attention by women, or perhaps by other men. The very suggestion of a man being a male's sexual object could prompt moralizing attacks by political enemies.[86]

If overt male nakedness prompts fear of male "deviance," then Ovid's second explanation exploits the other extreme, that is, layers of overly cultivated, effeminate clothing. Where the naked body might signify rustic simplicity, overrefined dress could suggest effete luxury. The rustic uprightness of male nudity is located at the juncture between the first and second explanations.

The first lines of this second explanation (the Hercules-Omphale tale, 2.303–12) portray Faunus, the god who has just been associated with man's savage origins, admiring and acquiring a taste for such effeminate finery:

> But [to explain] why especially Faunus should flee from clothes a story full of old joking is passed down. By chance, the young Tirynthian [Hercules] was going as a companion of his mistress [*comes dominae*]: Faunus saw both from a high ridge; he saw and he got heated, and he said, "Mountain deities, I have nothing to do with you: He(re) is my passion." She was going with hair poured down over her shoulders in perfumed locks, the Maeonian, worthy to be seen with her golden bosom: the golden umbrella was repelling the warm sun, but Herculean hands were holding it up.

Interpreters typically assume that Faunus desires Omphale; but Hercules is as much Faunus' desired object as she is. The first character to appear is Hercules (305). Omphale is second. As line 306 shows (*vidit ab excelso Faunus utrumque iugo*), the verb *vidit* is first, so its object is deferred, and that object is "both" of them (*utrum*), not just Omphale. Furthermore, Faunus rejects his mountain deities, saying, "*Hic meus ardor erit.*" The expression is ambiguous, but it can mean "He is my passion," as well as "This is my passion." Perhaps it could mean, "Such" or "Here is my passion." But for the clause to mean, "*She* is my passion," requires one to presume the gender object of Faunus' object of passion.

Initial vivid description of Omphale's perfumed hair (309–10) and her parasol (311) would confirm for some readers Faunus' heterosexual trajectory. But in the deferred relative clause (312: *quae tamen Herculeae sustinuere manum*), "Herculean hands" intrude beneath the parasol and it is this image (311–12) that draws the attention of the poet, tracking Faunus' view of the ensuing transvestism (313–25). First

(313–16), Ovid provides a setting with rather artificial, yet religious, features—a grove of Bacchus (*nemus*), a vineyard (*vineta*), and a grotto with a brook marking the entrance. The acts of cross-dressing (in 317–26) stress the high contrast between the sheer finery of feminine clothes on Hercules's massive build; in their incongruity, the tunic and girdle (319–20) only highlight his man's waist (321) and his "man-hands" (*magnas . . . manus*, 322), as do the armbands on his "man-arms" (323), and shoes on his "man-feet" (324). Omphale's cross-dressing draws less attention than Hercules': she dons the club, lion skin, and quiver—all in a single couplet (325–26).

The pair then have a banquet and "give their bodies to sleep" on separate but adjacent couches (327–28), for, Ovid says, they are preparing rituals for the "discoverer of the vine" (Bacchus), the type they would perform at dawn after refraining from sex. This sets the stage for Faunus' venture into the grotto, apparently for *amor*, described as *improbus*, shameless (*quid non amor improbus audet?* 331).[87]

However, cross-dressing (317–26) obscures Faunus' object. Ovid's description has provided a clearly perceptible gender binary in corporeal and sartorial signs of rough and soft textures. But night falls (331) and, in the darkness, the "rash adulterer" strays about (*huc illuc temerarius errat adulter*, 335) but uses his hands cautiously to guide him. (*et praefert cautas subsequiturque manus*, 336).

Most interpreters assume that Faunus tracks only the surface clothing—that is, that he is looking for Omphale and misconstrues Omphale's clothes for Omphale herself. This places Faunus in the role of the simple reader of the gendered "texts," as signified by a metaphor of textiles. But if Hercules appeared first (305), and Faunus saw them both (306) and declared, "*hic ardor erit*" (308), and, furthermore, if he saw the cross-dressing itself (which possibility is not excluded), then he would conceivably want Hercules, not Omphale. Alternatively, perhaps a preferable interpretation would be that Faunus may want the *cultus* or soft finery and additionally whoever presents him or herself in a culturally defined position as *mollis* or soft (e.g., *utrumque*, 306); the soft clothes (344–45) contrast with the rough naked bodies of rustic men hardened to the elements (189–302). The god of a country populace "devoid of art" (*artis ad huc expers et rude volgus*, 292), Faunus aspires "to be" a cultivated personage, yet his libidinal impulse takes the form of a desire "to have" and control sexually the person who presents a soft and cultivated external impression. The prospect of controlling and sexually penetrating the masculine Hercules, presenting signs of some vulnerability, might increase in

Faunus a sexual desire for Hercules. Omphale provides support for Faunus' fantasy by providing the signs of Hercules' weakness.

Ovid evokes humor by the contrast between Faunus' erotic groping and the epic simile for his fearful shrinking from the rough, bristly hide of the lion: he is like a traveler coming upon a snake and stepping back (341–42). But when he touches the *velamina mollia* (343–44), Faunus "is deceived by the lying symbol" (*mendaci decipiturque nota*). The *velamina mollia* are the symbol, but what does this mean to him? That Hercules is Omphale? But he saw them both and perhaps saw them cross-dressing. Faunus gets onto the bed with Hercules and achieves an erection (*et tumidum cornu durius inguen erat*, 346). Ovid describes what Faunus seems to feel while lifting the hem of the dress and seeing legs coarse with hair like his own: (*horrebant densis aspera crura pilis*, 348). The reader has earlier seen that Faunus was afraid and drew back his hand from the hairy lion's hide (*hirstua vellera*, 339–40). Why can't Faunus feel Hercules' hairy "man-legs"? Or does he feel them and not care? Ovid's verb *horrebant*, describing Hercules' prickly, hairy legs, conjures a possible readerly feeling of "horror" at the imminent specter of male homosexuality.

Judgment might ensue, but where does the onus for the act lie? With the typical explanation that it is just an accidental result of Faunus' misreading? But in what way was it a misreading? One would think that if Faunus desired Omphale, he would draw back at this point in homosexual "panic," as in the structurally analogous wall paintings where Priapus glimpses the male genitalia of Hermaphroditus.[88] But he does not. Hercules repels Faunus, just when Faunus was "attempting the rest" (*cetera temptantem*, 349)—referring perhaps to genital groping or intercourse, given Ovid's vivid emphasis on Faunus' "swollen groin, harder than horn" (346).

If the humorous "horror" resulted from Faunus' misreading, what did he misread? The *velamina mollia* probably did not deceive him into mistaking Hercules for Omphale (343–44). Rather they may have indicated (falsely) that Hercules was psychosexually *mollis*, i.e., soft or able to be dominated sexually.[89] In Roman popular thought, if not actual law, males who cross-dressed or wore effeminate garb were thought to be advertising for sexual penetration and "deserved what they got" (Sen. *Contr.* 5.6). Ovid himself describes effeminate grooming as typical of lascivious girls and "any man who wants to have a man" (*Ars am.* 1.523–34). Clothes can unmake a man: while cross-dressed, Hercules presents himself, no matter how muscular or hairy beneath, as sexually yielding.

But the ultimate signal problematizing Faunus' desire for women, naked or clothed, is his call for naked men, not women, to attend his ritual. If Faunus wanted women like Omphale, why did he not require their attendance? Ovid says (357–58), "Deluded by clothes, Faunus does not like clothes that deceive the eyes."[90] From one perspective this means that he was deceived by the surface of the yielding feminine-appearing (elegiac) text(ure), which channeled his lust toward the concealed body of (epic) Hercules. Based upon Hercules' soft attire, Faunus mistakenly inferred Hercules' passive sexual desire, despite obvious secondary sexual characteristics of the hero's body (bristly hair on his legs, 349). These signs indicate that the sex of Hercules' body is of little concern to Faunus. Moreover, Pan, Faunus' Greek equivalent, has male objects of desire, such as Daphnis, famous in pastoral poetry, whom Pan loves and teaches to play the (Pan) pipes.[91] But the same words can mean that Faunus doesn't like clothes because all clothes deceive him. Therefore, a desire for naked men could explain why Faunus invites naked men to participate. That view would also add irony to laughter and explain an asymmetry of hexameter and pentameter at 355–56. While in the hexameter all the male characters (Hercules, *ministri*, 317, "those who [*qui*] saw [Faunus] lying there") laugh at dejected Faunus (355), in the pentameter the Lydian *puella* (Omphale) laughs at her "lover" (*ridet amatorem Lyda puella suum*, 356). If Omphale is the *puella* and *domina* of Hercules (305; typical elegiac language), then Hercules is her lover; she laughs, partially, at Hercules, because her clothes have inverted his gender hierarchy and placed the he-man in the position of a sexual object. The lack of sexual exchange between the pair might also suggest to Faunus Hercules' lack of manhood despite his anatomy.

Faunus himself appears like Aurora, blushing "Dawn" (an amorous female deity prone to abducting young men[92]): to open the Lupercalia, Ovid cites Aurora as observing (*aspicit*) the naked Luperci (2.267–8), a vantage point of desire perhaps similar to Faunus' at 306 (*vidit ab excelso . . . iugo*).[93] In the vignette's first couplet, Aurora's gaze introduces the erotic look at the male body. Absolute nudity may have ceased by the time of Augustus, but, apparently, Luperci still wore only a small loincloth (*perizoma*). However, as T. P. Wiseman has suggested, Augustus "may have taken it [covering] still further" and introduced a longer apron—reflecting contemporary anxiety about elite male bodies.[94] One reason to suspect this change is that the emperor was aware of the sexual dangers to young men, because he forbade *imberbi*, "beardless ones," from the ritual. Usually *imberbi* are interpreted as young men

without facial hair, but they could also signify *cinaedi* or *androgyni* who
assumed feminine dress and depilated themselves to achieve a boyish
look. Ovid's explanation of the traditional nakedness of the Luperci
reflects this "cinaedic" possibility—a milieu of cultural anxiety over
male identity, and vulnerability to sexual penetration.[95] Ovid's treatment shows that, dressed in soft "elegiac" raiment, even heroes as
manly as Hercules invite penetrative interpreters; they become objects
of critical perception.

Together, cross-dressed Hercules and Omphale enact a fantasy
scene in which signs of masculinity and femininity are exchanged
between men, here between Hercules and Faunus (a male homosocial
exchange). While Hercules typically conjures images of overt masculine heroism associated with traditional depictions of him and his
labors, his cross-dressing with Omphale "stains" that masculine hardness or impenetrability of body (cf. Hercules and Cacus in Ovid's January; ch. 5) with traces of penetrable feminine softness suggesting a
blot or vulnerable spot on Hercules' masculinity (cf. *vitium*, vice,
crack). That blot of the feminine both produces and is produced by a
male erotic view, here that of Pan-Faunus, initially outside his
"object"—i.e., the whole fantasy scenario. But soon Faunus is drawn
by the signs themselves (that is, by the stain or blot of Hercules' femininity) into a staging of his own desire: Faunus positions himself over
Hercules in answer. This staging of Faunus' desire becomes a mythic
scene modeling the negotiation of literary meaning between the (male)
reader and the overlay of Ovid's elegiac calendar poem

The Tarquins, Brutus, and Gender: the *Regifugium* (Feb. 24)

The last major festival of *Fasti* 2 is the *Regifugium* (Feb. 24; 2.685–852),
recalling the "Running out of the King," the expulsion of the Tarquin
dynasty from Rome in 509 BCE and the creation of a republic governed
by two annually elected consuls.[96] Ovid follows Roman historiographers (especially Livy) when he explains this political revolution as
caused by the rape of Lucretia by Sextus Tarquinius, the youngest son
of King Tarquinius Superbus.[97] But Ovid's manner of retelling this legend can be viewed from the position required by earlier transvestic
images and their unstable interplay of signs of gender and power (cf.
Hercules-Omphale above). This "angled view" enables an observation

of subtle powers of gender and sex within ideological fantasy that render fantasy dangerous to persons and institutions, especially when wielding dynastic rule.

Moreover, scholars have observed that Lucretia's role in the legend is that of a woman "trafficked" between prominent men.[98] Her chaste identity and its violation symbolize the elite male dignity of her father and husband. Her rape dramatizes the regal violation of free male autonomy, restored to dignity by the exile of the king. While Ovid may exploit this political symbolism, his unique treatment emphasizes a split between surface and depth in communication and in the psychosocial dynamics between characters.[99] He thereby exposes the instabilities of reading gendered surfaces as a libidinal process underlying politics. In Ovid's version deceptions and miscommunication between characters expose flaws in naïve social conventions that are unable to contain repressed libidinal forces that erupt and extrude through the rents in a fragile social fabric.[100]

Ovid's Lucretia narrative (*F.* 2.852–53) contains a series of smaller episodes. Narrative reversals in each hinge on artificial (mis)communication. The first episode recounts the deceptive artifice of two covert texts that Tarquinius Superbus and the youngest of his three sons, Sextus, use when capturing Gabii, a town near Rome (691–710). Two narrative phases present these two Gabine "texts."

Gabii

In the first phase, Sextus came to the enemy at night in his true identity as the son of the king, but falsely characterizing his relationship to his father. Claiming that Superbus and his brothers (694) had sent him into exile, Sextus asserted that Tarquin "lacerated my backside with a cruel lash" (*Tarquinius qui mea' crudeli laceravit verbere terga,* 695). As Ovid comments, "in order to be able to say this, he had endured a beating" (*dicere ut hoc posset, verbera passus erat,* 696). By moonlight (*luna fuit,* 697), the Gabii "look at the young man and they sheath their swords (697; drawn at 693, *nudarant gladios*), and, when his clothes are removed, they indeed see a scarred backside."[101] Sextus' self-abasing exposure reveals his apparently abused body and evokes Gabine pity ("[the Gabii] even cry"; *flent quoque,* 699). They beg him to supervise the war effort along with them against his abusive father. "That clever fellow nodded 'yes' to the ignorant men" (*callidus ignaris adnuit ille viris,* 700).

Sextus' backside is a supporting document bearing "notations" or marks (*notata*)[102] made by *verbera*, whose phonetical similarity to *verba*, "words," suggests a kind of discourse. This displaying of Sextus' body is absent from Livy (1.53.4–11). Ovid's Sextus strips to reveal this falsified, yet true, "document." The connotations of this discourse are libidinal: whipping in the Lupercalia episode symbolized sexual penetration; as a fertility measure, women present their backsides (*terga*) to the lashes of the Luperci as a substitute for sex with a "sacred goat" (*F.* 2.425–52, esp. 441–46). So, why would a man manufacture such signs of submission on his body? The Gabii fail to discern textual surface from depth.

In the second phase, Sextus sends a friend to ask his father how to destroy the Gabii (701–2). Tarquin responds with an act of "gardening"[103]: he mows down the tallest lilies using his cane (*virga*, 706). When the messenger reports the action, Sextus says, "I discern my father's commands" (*filius* "*agnosco iussa parentis*" *ait*, 708). Without delay (*nec mora*, 2.709), Sextus kills all the Gabine leaders. This renders the town walls "naked and defenseless" (*nuda*, 710) and vulnerable to Tarquinian conquest. Thus, the false presentation of Sextus' debased, passive body conceals and prepares for his eventual active aggression.

The first and second texts complement each other in deceiving the Gabii. The first text lures the Gabii into a positive identification with Sextus as fellow victim of the cruel father-tyrant, while the debasement of Sextus offers a treacherous sign of a split between father and son. That text's simulation of father-son disaffection provides "cover" for subsequent covert communication between father and son over the method of destroying the Gabii.

The Snake Omen

The second episode (2.711–20) contains three enigmatic "texts," each commenting on a prior action. First, an ominous snake (*anguis*)[104] emerges between the palace altars and grabs entrails from extinguished fires—a divine comment on the rule of the Tarquins (711–12). Secondly, when consulted, Apollo at Delphi offers an enigmatic response: "the prince who has given kisses to his mother will be the victor," that is, successor to Superbus (713–14).[105] Thirdly, interpretations split between the mundane and the unusual. Others (the Tarquin brothers) brought hurried kisses to their human mother (715–16). But Brutus was "a wise imitator of a fool" (*stulti sapiens imitator*, 717) to keep himself "safe from your traps, grim Tarquin the Proud" (*tutus ab insidiis, dire Superbe, tuis,* 718). Brutus (meaning "fool") pretended to have "turned his foot" (720) and fell flat, kissing mother Earth (719).

Brutus dissimulates his interpretation of the oracle, and thus his participation in power, by presenting a "faltering" buffoonery that draws laughter proper to a *stultus,* a character in comedy.[106] The flawed abject persona covers a deeper understanding and enables "Brutus" to survive and eventually to reveal "himself" as a real man at the end of the larger narrative frame founding the Republic. In a sense, his technique, like that of transvestic Arion and Hercules, reserves his manly strength which is concealed behind a flawed textual cover or mask.[107]

Ardea

In the third episode, the siege of Ardea, another town near Rome (2.721–24), causes long periods of delay or idleness for the troops (*longas moras*), during which Sextus Tarquin hosts a banquet for his elite male comrades (725). There comes a verbal exchange among the men concerning "mutual concern" between husbands and wives (725–30):

> Tarquinius iuvenis socios dapibusque meroque
>   accipit; ex illis rege creatus ait:
> "dum nos sollicitos pigro tenet Ardea bello,
>   nec sinit ad patrios arma referre deos,
> *ecquid in officio torus est socialis?* et ecquid
>   coniugibus nostris *mutua cura* sumus?"

> The young Tarquin receives his compatriots in feasting and drinking; among these men, the son of the king said: "While Ardea keeps us anxious in her slow war and does not allow us to bring weapons home, is the bed of alliance at all in our duty? And are we at all a shared concern for our wives?"

Scholars limit the reference of Sextus' question to whether or not the wives of the men are being chaste (729–30); but Sextus frames marital relations in broader, almost philosophical terms—whether both husbands and wives, when separated geographically for a long time (as in this siege), have mutual obligation to monogamy (*ecquid in officio torus est socialis,* 2.729[108]) that reflects reciprocal affection (*mutua cura*). The phrase *mutua cura* seems drawn from Stoic discourse which valorized reciprocal love and mutual monogamy between spouses, a "new" understanding of "companionate marriage" (part of a longer historical development), evident by the first century BCE.[109] Prompted by Sextus' moralizing question, the men compete in showing solicitude (*cura*) for their wives (733–36).

> quisque suam laudat: studiis certamina crescunt,
>   et fervet multo linguaque corque mero.
> surgit cui dederat clarum Collatia nomen:
>   "non opus est *verbis*, credite *rebus*" ait.

Each praises his wife: the contest increases with zeal, and the tongue and heart boil with much wine. He rises, the one to whom Collatia had bestowed a famous name; he says: "There is no need of words; believe in deeds."

Thus we are to understand each man competing to offer hyperbolic rival panegyrics of his "wife" as a way to display his *cura* for her before other men. Each man's discursive "wife" may or may not be an illusory text. Words need testing by the real (*verbis, rebus*, 730), the contrast framing Ovid's contemplation of Augustus as *pater patriae* (*nomen* 127–28; *res*, 129).

At Livy's banquet, Collatinus barely mentions love and marriage at all; he is a more traditional Roman male than Ovid's, concerned with wifely chastity as a mask of his esteem.[110] Ovid's Sextus[111] introduces *mutua cura* as a modern "marital" relation that still channels latent libidinal interests of the male homosocial group. His moralizing discourse seems to publicize *male* affection for wives as a possible ideal of manhood, i.e., within their duties as men (*in officio*, 729). Yet, competition in "publishing" wives[112] suggests that it is male honor that motivates the display of this affection.

Hidden libidinal dynamics are indicated when Ovid's Sextus uses language alluding ambivalently to the siege at Ardea and male leisure. Such language intimates sublimated libido by splitting Sextus' language between a morally "correct" surface discourse and an erotic subtext of which he himself may not be aware.[113] That impulse appears in covert sexual diction. For example, the deferral (*longas . . . moras*, 722) of attaining the desired object, Ardea, keeps the men *sollicitos*, "troubled," "full of anxiety," which may also mean sexually stimulated or aroused.[114] The very name Ardea recalls *ardor*, the burning desire of

Faunus for the yielding finery of Hercules/Omphale (above, 331). Ovid has often emphasized the libidinal tension created by delaying gratification, lingering between desire and consummation (quickly grabbing a desired object; e.g., the Fabii and the Raven). Here, delay in the siege leads to drunken leisure, which stretches the libidinal drives of the men. But the men cannot take their "weapons" (*arma*)[115] home yet, at least not permanently (they do subsequently venture to see two women, but briefly). Sextus' final question *"ecquid in officio torus est socialis?"* suggests the play of his sexual impulse beneath the language of mutual monogamy. His phrase seems to ask, "Is the bed of alliance at all in our duty?"[116] In this reading, *socialis* refers back to *socii* (725), the male homosocial group whom he is entertaining. Sextus' *"coniugibus nostris mutua cura sumus?"* might ask, "Are we a love 'on loan' for our wives"—implying the opposite of "mutual" monogamy—i.e., mutual or shared sex, as a commodity to be borrowed (*mutua*).[117]

Whatever meaning the reader gleans from Sextus' words, suffering long separation[118] from wives poses the uncertainty of desire and affection in the marital relation, which emerges in ambiguous language. However, such innuendos are only potential seeds of a libido that can be most easily perceived retroactively from later events. Collatinus' declaration, "There is no need of words, trust in deeds," refers to a possible split between the men's outward discourses (*verbis*) and the reality (*rebus*, 734). But whose words and whose reality?

Women: Vice and Virtue

When the men go to Rome, they see a polarized view of womanhood that recapitulates the traditional "choice" between vice and virtue in male ethical subjectivity (cf. ch. 4). In comparison with Livy (1.57.8–11), Ovid elaborates extensively the psychology of this ethical/unethical viewership of women and Lucretia's place as an "object" of virtue within it. Sextus' wife, the "daughter-in-law of the king" (739), strikes a pose as Vice, staying up all night indulging in unmixed wine (*mero*) as the men do (725, 732; 740; Livy 1.57.9). By contrast, Lucretia presents the picture of Virtue: the men find baskets of soft wool (*lana mollis*) beside Lucretia's marital bed (741–42).[119] Her female house-slaves card wool by lamplight (743–44), while she urges completion of a cloak to send to her husband (745–46). The men overhear Lucretia saying (747–54):

quid tamen auditis (nam plura audire potestis)?
quantum de bello dicitur esse super?
postmodo victa cades: melioribus, Ardea, restas,
    improba, quae nostros cogis abesse viros.
sint tantum reduces. sed enim temerarius ille
    est meus, et stricto qualibet ense ruit.
mens abit et morior, quotiens pugnantis imago
    me subit, et gelidum pectora frigus habet.

Still, what do you hear—for you can hear more [than I can]? How much
war is left? Beaten, you will fall shortly; Ardea, you resist better men,
you unruly one who are compelling our men to be absent. Just let them
be returned. But in truth mine is that rash one, and he rushes off wher-
ever he pleases with his sword drawn and ready. My mind goes adrift,
and I just die whenever the image of a fighter [warrior] steals upon me,
and icy numbness takes over my heart.

Her voice breaking with tears, Lucretia lets her weaving fall and low-
ers her gaze toward her lap (2.755–56). Weaving a cloak to be sent to a
soldier-husband busies the wife left at home (745–46),[120] sublimating or
distracting her desire in the absence of her man to produce a text(ile)
that reinforces a bond between them; the *lacerna* is a *mutua cura*.[121] But
while weaving, she desires to hear about her husband.[122] The softness
of Lucretia's wool (*lana mollis*, 742) and faintness of her voice (*tenui
sono*, 744) imply an elegiac poetics recalling portrayals of other elegiac
women separated from men (cf. Prop. 1.4).[123]

   But despite her dutiful marital confinement, libido still plays
beneath the surface of Lucretia's activities and speech. For Lucretia,
war (*bellum*), the arch theme of epic, is a force that separates men from
their wives. Separation augments desire by deferral; she asks how
much more war remains. In fact, by addressing Ardea, she personifies
the town as an interloper, ascribing to the city the adjective *improba*,
"perverse" or "wanton," a direct contrast with her own probity that
again recalls Faunus' *improbus amor* (331) creeping into the "chaste"
cave of Hercules and Omphale and his declaration of *ardor* (308).
Indeed, Lucretia's Ardea recalls Sextus'.[124] She experiences a fantasy
image of a warrior (*pugnantis imago*, 753) whose military prowess and
rash assault make her swoon (755–56). Perhaps this is a melodramatic,
almost humorous, portrayal of a naïve, dependent, isolated female,
one that was passé in Ovid's day. Yet from this persona Lucretia

"stages" a contrasting fantasy (military) man—her husband, perhaps, although she never says "husband" (not *coniunx* nor even *vir;* see below). That isolated life of the woman weaving was one in which Augustus wanted to enclose his daughter and granddaughter (both named Julia), but to no success; they were both caught in adultery.[125]

Furthermore, Lucretia is suspiciously self-conscious or frantic about her chastity (her urgency about completing the cloak, 745–46). Perhaps this is because her controlled persona is on the verge of cracking or losing self-control under the pressure of deferred longing (cf. *longas moras,* 722). Thus we find references to her thoughts straying (*mens abit,* 753) and her "dying" or fainting (*et morior,* 753) when the *imago* of her ideal warrior "steals" upon her. This obsessional libidinal image creeps upon (*subit*) her unawares; it prefigures Sextus, the rape, and her death. In the ancient psychology of desire, this is a *phantasia,* or sense impression, of armed warriors at siege (cf. scenes in tragedy and epic of women ravished) that she keeps and "replays," prompted by the image of *improba Ardea* (749–50).[126] Thus, Lucretia's mind leaves her—it splits from her—revealing a fissure between an outward display of chastity (in traditional activities and a naïve moral discourse apparently praising warriors) and her inner erotic desire seeking expression. Here we witness another outward discourse of gender propriety, a fragile tissue splitting to reveal a libidinal reality beneath— *verba* versus *res* (734)—somewhat like the splitting of Omphale's garb on Hercules' robust body.

But the very anxiety of Lucretia's chastity, her near failure to restrain her desire, is itself attractive to her male voyeurs (757–58). Will it lure her ideal warrior? Her husband, Collatinus, breaks into the scene to rescue her by supporting the "burden" of her desire (759–60): "Her husband said, 'Come, and put aside your anxiety.' she came to life again and hung, a sweet burden, from the neck of her man" (*"pone metum, veni" coniunx ait; illa revixit, / deque viri collo dulce pependit onus,* 760). Collatinus' interruption implies that he fulfills Lucretia's desire for a hero, her *pugnantis imago.* But does he?

Sextus and His Re-presentation of "Lucretia"

Starting from the banquet at Ardea, Ovid has increasingly portrayed libidinal dynamics operating beneath scenes that, in Livy, lack explicit psychological treatment. Lucretia's revelation of her fantasy warrior suggests psychic departure from moralizing ideals, and inspires

Sextus' inner "conception of fires" (*furiales. . . . ignes concipit*, 761–62).[127] In lines 763–66, Ovid highlights the features of Lucretia's physical appearance (763–64) and her verbal expression (765–66) that caused Sextus to be "ravished by hidden desire" (*caeco raptus amore furit*, 762). But other men saw and heard the same admirable features. What makes Sextus a special member of Lucretia's voyeuristic "audience" is his apperception of these features within a subjective interpretation of them: Sextus (mis)perceives and (mis)interprets her desire through the code of his own fantasy. Lucretia's form and gestures may present stimuli, but Sextus *re-presents* them to himself the next day back at the camp (767–68). At 769–78, Sextus rehearses her features:

> carpitur attonitos *absentis imagine* sensus
>   ille; recordanti plura magisque placent.
> *sic* sedit, *sic* culta fuit, *sic* stamina nevit,
>   *iniectae collo sic iacuere co*mae,
> *hos* habuit voltus, *haec* illi verba fuerunt,
>   *hic* color, *haec* facies, *hic* decor oris erat.
> ut solet a magno fluctus languescere flatu,
>   sed tamen a vento, qui fuit, unda tumet,
> *sic*, quamvis *aberat placitae praesentia formae*,
>   quem dederat *praesens forma, manebat amor*.

His senses are in thrall to an image of a woman who is absent; more and more her features please him the more he recollects them. This is how she sat; this is how she was adorned; this is how she spun thread; and this is how her tossed hair lay on her neck. She had such expressions, such words she had, such a complexion, such a face, such was the charm of her mouth. Just as an ocean wave usually subsides after a huge wind-blast, but still a surge swells after the wind, such was the lingering desire that an appearance had given when present, although the presence of the pleasing form was absent.

Sextus' swirling fantasy image of absent Lucretia stands in place of her presence. The dynamics of short, choppy clauses represent Sextus' "imagination" of the absent woman (*absentis imagine*, 769). The anaphora of *sic* (771–72) and repetition of demonstratives beginning with "h" (773–74) mark mimetic or deictic gestures, performed in Sextus' mind (if not with his body), re-presenting to or within himself, impersonating Lucretia's absent appearance and voice. While anaphora can signal powerful emotion, this device is exaggerated by additional auditory repetitions, such as *decor oris* at 774 or, at 772, "in*iec*tae co*llo* sic *iac*uere co*m*ae." These repeated sounds and semantic stems carry the "tossing" of hair to excess (*-iec-t* . . . *iac-;* . . . *col-* and *com-*).

The vocal "singsong" and gestural play mark a split between Sextus' male body and his inner femininity. Sextus' male psyche is portrayed as under the "sway" of the image of a woman. Livy labels Sextus' femininity directly (1.58.3); Ovid has Sextus "perform" (manifest) it.[128] By re-presenting Lucretia's image to himself, Sextus loses masculine self-control, a lack of mastery portrayed in the simile of liquid fluctuation in Sextus' psyche (775–76).[129] Moreover, Ovid has rendered two opposite-sex characters (Lucretia and Sextus) in hypergendered style. In re-presenting Lucretia's *imago*—her mask— Sextus performs a female impersonation (*fictio personarum*) in his psyche or in soliloquy,[130] an interior, and thus secluded, version of "drag," which the Hercules-Omphale tale exteriorizes.

Yet, as the narrative proceeds, Sextus' hyperbolic performance shifts in answer to Lucretia's *imago* of an ideal warrior (*pugnantis imago,* 753) "rushing" about with his "sword drawn" (751–52). Lucretia has described her ideal warrior as *ille temerarius* (751), precisely as Ovid described Faunus creeping into bed with Hercules (*temerarius adulter,* 335); Lucretia's *imago* of a warrior creeps up on her (*subit,* 753–54). Both Sextus and Lucretia are ecstatic over idealized, hypergendered fantasies (*imago,* 753; *imagine,* 769) that compensate for the distance and delay caused by Ardea (721–22; Lucretia's *Ardea improba,* 749–50). This is the libidinal context in which Sextus "burns" (*ardet,* 779) and, "roused by goads of desire" (779), retraces the distance from Ardea to Rome and to Lucretia. He seems to assume she is sending a furtive message of desire.[131] Sextus emphasizes the boldness that the action will require (781–83), citing the "daring" deception of the Gabii as his model (*audebimus ultima,* 781; *audentes,* 782; *cepimus audendo Gabios quoque,* 783), which again recalls Faunus venturing into bed with Hercules (*quid non amor improbus audet?* 331).

Armed with a sword (*ense latus cinxit,* 784), Sextus poses himself in the place of Lucretia's *pugnantis imago,* the ideal warrior who rashly (*temerarius,* 751) rushes everywhere "with drawn sword" (*stricto ense,* 752). But was Lucretia not referring to her husband? She never specified her husband (e.g., with *meus vir, coniunx*), but she did describe the men (*viri,* plural) besieging Ardea (750), and she says somewhat generically, "Mine is that rash one, and he rushes everywhere with his sword drawn" (751–52). Moreover, she faints when the "image of a fighting man" occurs to her. *She* never specifies *her* Collatinus or *her* husband (*coniunx*), but it is *Ovid* who says, "Her husband said" (*coniunx ait*, 759) when Collatinus "rescues" her from her desire.

Perhaps Lucretia was constructing a fantasy "scenario" of a besieging warrior, into which she projects her husband.[132] This implies her unexpected simultaneous identification with and envy of wicked (*improba*) Ardea "being besieged." But such fantasy is libidinal (in the absence of men), so not strictly confined to marital boundaries. Sextus will soon pose in the role of the brash, sword-wielding soldier in fulfillment of fantasy, in a way that flatters him and his self-image as daring. But it is all a miscommunication.

Rape

The rape (785–812) develops out of these misperceptions.[133] "How much error is in the mind!" (*quantum animis erroris inest!* 789), Ovid says after narrating Sextus' entry into Collatinus' house (785) as a guest and kinsman (both are Tarquins), although he was an enemy (*hostis ut hospes*, 787).[134] But this exclamation also anticipates that Lucretia, "unaware of things, unfortunately prepares a feast for her own enemy" (*parat inscia rerum infelix epulas hostibus illa suis*, 789–90). Is she unaware or careless of signals sent? Personal preparation of the banquet suggests close contact with Sextus. In conservative Roman orthodoxy, any approach of a man to a woman could be (mis)interpreted as an insult to her chastity and her husband's (or father's) honor.[135] But Sextus is supposed to be her relative. Perhaps Lucretia's personal service to her "enemy" is a point of irony; but, in the context of Sextus' tacit, so unknown, fantasy, it provides an erotic (mis)cue, one absent from Livy's version, where he is entertained "by people ignorant of the plan" (*ab ignaris consilii*, Liv. 1.58.2). In Ovid's version, Lucretia may be unaware of Sextus' sexual intention, but Sextus is also unaware of the risk that his intention depends upon a fantasy image of Lucretia as one who desires a fantasy warrior-lover.

In the rape scene, fantasy and lack of frank communication enable misunderstandings of desire. Tracking the sword (phallus) suggests the play of imagination from Sextus' perspective. In a totally dark house (792), Sextus "rises and frees his sword from a golden scabbard [*aurata vagina*] and comes, chaste bride, into your bedroom."[136] This vividly erotic description of the sword and Ovid's repeated references to it are absent from Livy's version. Resting on her bed (*torus*, 795),

Sextus says, "Lucretia, a sword is with me, and it's me, Tarquin, speaking" (*ferrum, Lucretia, mecum est . . . Tarquiniusque loquor*, 795–96). Livy
gives his Sextus similar, yet different, words (1.58.2): "Silence, Lucretia! I am Sextus Tarquinius; a sword is in my hand; you will die if you
emit a sound." Livy's Sextus threatens to kill Lucretia immediately.
While Ovid's Sextus emphasizes his *speaking* with Lucretia (*Tarquinius
. . . loquor*, 796), Livy's emphasizes his identity (*Sex. Tarquinius sum*,
1.58.2). In Ovid's version, the erotic longing, performed in monologues
by Lucretia and Sextus, provides an angular position from which to re-
examine alternative, subtextual renderings of desire beneath Livy's
events; they reveal a secret, internal *mise-en-scène* of prohibited
libido.[137]

From one perspective, Ovid's Sextus seems to be playing out an
erotic fantasy he thinks Lucretia desires. The sword was an attribute of
her fantasy warrior (753–54). Ovid carefully reports that Sextus
brought it with him to Rome (784) and describes his "unsheathing" it in
erotic terms (793–94). By announcing that he has it with him (*mecum*,
795) and by identifying himself as Tarquin (796), Sextus can seem to
place himself in the role of Lucretia's ideal bold warrior (*temerarius ille*,
751–52); he has heard her fantasy and now rushes with his sword at
the ready, donning the *imago* of a besieger "creeping upon" Lucretia
(*subit*, 753–54). It is as if Sextus thinks that he is playing along with her
scenario and that she is somehow supposed to know this. So he has
brought a sword (phallus) as a prop for the warrior fantasy.

But a sword can be used in violence; and Sextus' possible role-play-
ing slips into that reality, because Lucretia is unaware that Tarquin is
playing out a fantasy (he may not be "playing") or that he thinks the
fantasy is hers as well. But in response to Sextus' initial advance, Lucretia says nothing (*illa nihil*, 797). Ovid states she lacks voice and power to
speak; has no thought (*neque . . . aliquid toto pectore mentis habet*, 798);
and trembles like a lamb caught by a wolf, an epic simile evoking that
heroic genre and its gender binary (799–800). Yet, it would be difficult
for Sextus to interpret "nothing" (nondiscourse) because, within the
fantasy scenario (warrior ravishment), speechless trembling would
conform to the feminine "victim" role (e.g., the woman ravished in a
siege). On the other hand, Ovid's short deliberative questions (801–3)
represent Lucretia's subjective wavering between fearful alternatives
(or are they Ovid's questions?). Nevertheless, none of her thoughts
engage objective dialogue with Sextus as he fondles her breasts (804).
Again, indirection and the failure of blunt communication create room
for Sextus' fantasy.

Returning to Sextus (805–10), Ovid calls him *amans hostis* (805), a "loving enemy" or "enemy lover," precisely the role that Sextus fantasizes that Lucretia desires. This fantasy could motivate the pleas, promises of money, and threats *(precibus pretioque minisque,* 805); but the distinction between open communication and fantasy collapses at 807 when Sextus says, *nil agis; eripiam . . . per crimina vitam,* which on one level, means, as A. J. Boyle translates, "No use, . . . I'll kill and defame you."[138] Another meaning would be, "You're not performing at all [*nil agis*], . . . I'll rob your life amid accusations." The point is that *agere* also means to perform or act a role.[139] The clause, "I'll rob your life amid accusations," should be read with the following passage (808–9), "I, an adulterer, will be a false [or concealed] eyewitness of adultery; I'll kill a male slave, with whom you'll be reported to have been caught in the act."[140] These words can be read in two ways. Either Lucretia's unresponsiveness frustrates Sextus' initial fantasy and, in turn, he threatens to shame her; or the initial fantasy falters (*nil agis,* 807) and Sextus switches to a fictional melodramatic scenario familiar in adultery mimes, one that pretends to involve voyeurism: he will have witnessed adultery,[141] yet is himself an adulterer who kills a slave who probably witnessed him in adultery with Lucretia.

Lucretia and Male Actors

With Sextus' threat of moral defamation, any distinction between fictional scenario and reality collapses. Sextus has been a clever performer in risky scenarios from the beginning of Ovid's Regifugium (Gabii), but in this scenario Lucretia is not lured into enactment of his libidinal fantasy (contrast the Gabii), even after she submits to rape under a threat of moral defamation.

At the end of the narrative, it is Lucretia who anticipates, even orchestrates, the ensuing course of events, that is, to induce males to action within her own fantasy scenario. And Brutus assists. In contrast with Livy's version (1.58.7–10), where Lucretia makes direct accusations against Sextus, Ovid's Lucretia never directly states what happened or what she desires. Instead, she manipulates her self-representation, the "cultivation of herself" (dress and gesture), to shape emotional responses from the men around her. She summons her father and husband from Ardea, who cease delay (815–16). Then, she dresses for her role in the ensuing public drama by donning mourning clothes (817), which prompt her father and husband to ask for whose funeral (*exsequias*) she is preparing (818)—a detail absent from Livy. Ovid's Lucretia is attired for her final public "performance" at her own funeral at 847 (*fertur in exsequias*) and her pivotal role in public fantasy.

In response to her father's and husband's inquiries, Lucretia is silent (819), hides her face (819–20), cries (820), and tries and fails to speak three times (823). Then, in answer to a request that she give *a hint* (*orant indicet* 821–22), does not lift her eyes (823–24), but says (825–26): "Will I have to do even this for Tarquin? Shall I myself, unfortunate though I am—shall I *deliver a monologue* [*eloquar*] about my disgrace [*dedecus*]?" In hyperbolic contrast with *indicet* (mere hinting), Lucretia's twice-repeated *eloquar* (evoking oratory) suggests her sarcasm about having to depart from feminine decorum—reticence—to proclaim out loud her disgrace, when her husband and father should simply be able to "tell."[142] Part of the game is sartorial. By contrast with Ovid's Lucretia, Livy's is not wearing mourning clothes as subtextual clue; instead, she names "Sextus" as the perpetrator, mentions her lost chastity, and refers graphically to "tracks" of another man in Collatinus' bed (Liv. 1.58.7–8). Exacting an oath of vengeance, Livy's Lucretia bluntly challenges the manhood of her father, husband, and their companions, Valerius and Brutus (1.58.7): "Sextus Tarquinius is the enemy who, as a guest last night, armed with force, stole pleasure deadly to me *and to him, if you are real men* [*mihi sibique, si vos viri estis, pestiferum . . . gaudium*]." In Ovid, Lucretia's verb *eloquar* expresses her frustration with the cognitive impotence of her father and husband in reading signs: they have not yet conjectured what she intends.

When Ovid's Lucretia does give vague indications (*Tarquinio*, 825, is not enough; her husband is a Tarquinius) and then blushes (827–28), her father and husband pardon her on the grounds that she was compelled. But their pardon in Ovid's version frustrates preservation of her fame (810, 826, 833–34), because her father and husband do not blame Sextus; they lack proper male dignity—a sense that Sextus has insulted their male identity by raping a woman connected to them.[143] So they are inert. In orthodox custom, a husband or father is supposed to be tempted to kill not merely the man, but even the wife or daughter involved (cf. Verginia and her father; Liv. 3.44–58). But in Ovid, the men whom Lucretia should expect to protect her honor are far from doing that, much less threatening Sextus. By contrast, in Livy 1.58.9, all the men in attendance (the father, Publius Valerius; Collatinus, the husband; and Brutus) not only acquit Lucretia, but also blame the "author of the violation" (*in auctorem delicti*) and swear an oath to

Lucretia to wreak vengeance. When Ovid's Lucretia stabs herself with a concealed sword or dagger (*celato ferro*, 831), she evidently has anticipated suicide as a self-empowering "act" preserving her reputation (*fama*)—the story that people will tell about her. Such narrative planning would complement her wearing mourning clothes for her own death.[144] The concealed sword and suicide write the conclusion.

But "she" in fantasy still performs. When Ovid's Lucretia falls, she makes sure she falls nobly (833–34: *tum quoque iam moriens ne non procumbat honeste / respicit: haec etiam cura cadentis erat*). Her dying is careful—perhaps overly careful: she still cares about the impression on male eyes (810) and thus her future "publication." *Decorum* is everything to her (*decor*, 764, 774; *dedecus* 826). The decorum of modest gesture and speech fitted to her gendered limits emerges in the "too-perfect" nod of assent from her lock of hair (845–46). This contrasts with Livy (1.58.11), where Lucretia falls forward, onto her own wound, suggesting a directness that matches her blunt speech. More importantly, Lucretia's concern for decorum in Ovid's version contrasts with the behavior of her husband and father (835–36), who lie on her body and groan aloud over the shared loss, "oblivious of appearances" (*obliti decoris*, 836), a rather unmanly display of uncontrolled emotion. In Livy (1.59.1), the husband and father exercise restraint, although they engage in conventional mourning gestures (*illis luctu occupatis*, 1.59.1).

Lucretia's husband and father are not her champions, her ideal warrior-rescuer, nor was Sextus. She herself has "manhood," the iron blade, concealed in her clothes. Tracking this sword tracks "manhood" (the phallus) and the emergence of surprise autonomy. Using this concealed sword, Lucretia kills herself, rather than accept lost sexual integrity. This dramatic act demonstrates that she is a "matron of a manly spirit" (*animi matrona virilis*, 2.847). By wielding the sword herself, Lucretia silences her own discourse, latent within the decorum of her feminine body. But the idiot "Brutus" becomes her hero when he removes from Lucretia's half-dead body the dagger with which she had stabbed herself (837–38). By taking the sword from her body, Brutus reveals his "manhood" (844), as if manhood could be transferred with the sword from Lucretia to Brutus. When Brutus wields that same sword, it enables a match or fit between a repressed inner character and his outward male body, which emboldens him to frank public speech in the forum (2.839–50). It is then that he "uttered fearless tones from his menacing mouth" (*edidit impavidos ore minante sonos*, 2.840)—a speech in which Brutus in fact says that "manhood has been dissimulated for long enough" (*iam satis est virtus dissimulata diu*, 2.844).[145] The publication (cf. *edidit*, 840) of these sonorous words enacts Brutus' simultaneous acquisition of public voice and manhood, refashioning him as an autonomous male citizen encouraging *virtus* in other men against tyranny.

The success of Brutus' deferred manhood derives from its temporizing latency and strategic timing of voice.[146] Brutus has been temporizing or delaying revelation of his male autonomy—appearing foolish, withdrawing from violent Tarquinian politics in the manner of one not a real man. But, given the proper timing, the public voice of the wise-fool—a stock description of a Socratic ironist (cf. 717: *Brutus erat stulti sapiens imitator*)—elevates the latent meaning of Lucretia's dead body to a public, surface meaning by publicizing her symbolic wound (849) and elaborating upon it verbally to rouse public opinion against Tarquin's rule (849–52).

Transvestism, "Feminine Manhood," and Two Fathers

Transvestism generally exceeds the everyday boundaries of gender in the symbolic order, rousing cultural anxieties arising from what Marjorie Garber called "category crisis."[147] For this reason, it can function for readers as did castration and abortion in "January," that is, as a kind of troubling blot or stumbling block. To look into that blot is to take up a position from which to re-examine the book of "February," so that readers might observe previously occluded textures, images, and meanings.

This psychosocial negotiation of gender—a process within the individual—poses for Ovid's male readers the specter, or strategic prospect, of their own Janus-like self-awareness (ch. 3), gendered bilaterally between masculine and feminine. This is not unlike Plato's depiction of Aristophanes explaining the origin of sex and gender through fantasy "androgynes," the original rotund humans with two faces, usually combining both sexes in one body (Plato, *Symp.* 189d–193d).[148] The stories about the pairs Hercules-Omphale and Lucretia-Brutus elaborate extended narrative scenarios eliciting from readers something of this awareness, already primed by "transvestic" images of Callisto, Arion, and Juno Sospita.[149] Ovid's mythological characters maintain a sartorial explicitness that is lost in the transition to the historical legend of Lucretia and Brutus. Yet even there Ovid's language maintains a transvestic sense of "category crisis" experienced in the tension between the fantasy of gender distinction and its collapse under the rule of the tyrant Tarquinius Superbus and his son Sextus. In the context of tyranny, Brutus' feminine manhood and Lucretia's manly womanhood may still exceed the everyday social order, but prove strategically salvific for the autonomy of Rome's male citizenry.

In all these transvestic scenarios, what is at stake (and threatened) is male autonomy. Female bodies and feminine traits donned by males (even Ovid's elegy itself) are trafficked to enact permutations of masculine symbolic identity, an idea not unlike Maria Wyke's observations about females portrayed in prior erotic elegy.[150] Indeed, Lucretia and her suicide were cited by Roman men as exemplary models for manly honor.[151] Lucretia's rape symbolizes, in ideological fantasy, the rape of the men's esteem. Her act, or Brutus', offers alternative modes to its restoration.

Lucretia and other female characters and transvestic guises of femininity provide fantasy supports to male recuperation of manhood. The major threat to male autonomy in *Fasti* 2 is being caught between two fathers—i.e., two aspects of an imperial ruler as *pater* with *patria potestas,* who can sustain one's life or destroy it.[152] In February, the specter of a tyrannical vicious Father is embodied by the character Tarquinius Superbus. Yet there is desire of benevolent rescuing fathers—either senators or, if possible, depending upon allegiances, Julius Caesar as *parens patriae* (Suet. *Jul.* 85) and later Augustus as *Pater Patriae.*[153] Fatherhood in February is Janus-like, shifting uncertainly between a Father of a stable symbolic order: one who appears to remain within boundaries and maintains, while benefiting from, the laws of the symbolic order; and another Father, who obscenely and without justifying himself exerts his tyrannical power to rape, or exploit every desire and take enjoyment.

In "February" Jupiter has this split paternal identity, raping (Callisto, 2.153–92) and silencing (Tacita-Lala-Larentia, 2.571–616). *Pater Patriae,* like *Augustus,* is a title Octavian shares with Jupiter: Ovid says that while "Jupiter has the name in the high ether, you [Augustus] have the name over the earth. You are father of men; that one, of the gods" (131–32).[154] The comparison with Romulus (133–44) should not exclude attention to the wider equation with Jupiter (cf. 1.607–8, 649–50) and the tales of Jupiter's violent desires, set beside his ability to save.

In *Tristia* 2, this assimilation of Jupiter and Augustus as *Pater Patriae* is the basis upon which Ovid pleads for mercy (33–40); Jupiter's anger can be softened and his lightning bolt can be turned. Can the emperor's? Ovid invites Augustus to follow the merciful way of the chief god who shares the title of *pater* and relents. In exile Ovid faces a double bind between a father-sustainer and father-destroyer that *Fasti* 2 elaborates, but indirectly.[155] Indirect, dilatory strategies of communication reflect the weakened position of male subjects within tyranny.[156] That verbal strategy perhaps reflects the once autonomous male's assumption in fantasy of the position of "woman" as subject to the master or Father, a kind of transvestic or submissive position from which to recuperate manhood.

Ovid and Broken Form: Three Views

e xile, a symbolic death, broke the *Fasti* (*Tr.* 2.549–52, cf. 555–60, 9 CE): "This work, Caesar [Augustus], written under your name and dedicated to you, my fate has broken [*hoc* . . . / . . . *mea sors rupit opus*]." The fractured *Fasti* reflects this "death," because it lacks the completion that the "living" author—present in Rome—might give it.[1] Yet, by revising the *Fasti* in his last years, Ovid looks back to a point prior to "death," that is, to his fantasized Roman origin. Here three views suggest how Ovid's *Fasti* communicates as a half-dead, broken form.

Between Two Deaths[2]

If Ovid is symbolically dead (exiled), yet poetically alive by returning to poetry (*Tristia, Epistulae ex Ponto,* the *Fasti* under completion), then two kinds of symbolic (non)existence—as citizen and poet—are pitted, temporally, against an impending physical death. The hinge of this double symbolic death—exile—has preceded Ovid's physical death, so that Ovid's calendar poem can seem to convey a spectral voice returning to civic-poetic life from beyond symbolic death. The *Fasti* can do this as a poetic calendar conveying the rites screening Ovid's Roman identity (ch. 1). In this sense, Ovid's return to the *Fasti* enacts his attempted return from the edge of death or manifests itself as an emanation from the living dead.

In his status as exile, Ovid partly borrows the quality of a *sacer* (an accursed man), a *devotus,* as he calls his poem, screening his own identity as dedicated, almost as a sacrifice, to Germanicus (1.5–7; ch. 2). This self-sacrificial pose of the poem (and poet) recalls sacrificial animals he treats at length for the *Agonalia* (1.317–458; ch. 5). As sacrifice, Ovid's view is angular or indirect, like that of the ram looking into holy water and seeing, indirectly, the knife that will cause his death. Or perhaps his voice in the *Fasti* is uncannily timed, like the ass's bray marking the sexual adventure of Priapus or indiscreet like the song of birds divulging the secrets of the gods. Like a sacrifice, Ovid is marked with death, but not dead yet. His words have *omen,* so perhaps readers might listen.

Dimidium Vestri Voti: Between Two Halves

Another way to view the fractured *Fasti* is, as chapter 3 has suggested, as a *dimidium,* a half, comparable to a Janus-coin of the Republic (bronze *as*) that was not uncommonly halved, each with a head. Somewhat comparable would be the Hellenic custom of two men forming guest-friendship (*xenia;* cf. Lat. *hospitium*) and splitting a *symbolon.* In this case, the half-*Fasti* figures as a social relation to another or the splitting of a shared object between two halves of a relation, that is, between Ovid and his reader.[3]

Ovid uses *dimidium* generally to refer to division between two people by death. The *Tristia* uses it three times. At *Tr.* 1.2.37–44 Ovid describes how his devoted wife grieves over his exile and wished to go with him, but he says he is glad that he did not allow her to board the ship, so that he "would not have to die twice" (42), noting that, now, "though I may die" (*ut peream*), "I will at least survive in a half portion" (*dimidia certe parte superstes ero,* 44). Thus, exile split Ovid between his entombment in exile and his existence through intimate contacts in Rome, here his wife. Across the divide of exile, Ovid's (male) readership also stands in the symbolic position of his wife, his "other half."

But Ovid is not alone in being split between two; so is the aging Augustus. At *Tr.* 2.175–76, *dimidium* appears twice in a description of Augustus as having two, split presences: "and while you look back, as if present, at the City with half of yourself [*dimidioque tui*], you are far away with the other half [*dimidio*] and are waging savage wars." One recalls Janus' two faces and Homer's description of the attention of prudent leaders (ch. 3). But the emperor, too, is drawing near to death and uses surrogates: in a later passage (*Tr.* 2.229–30), this halving becomes a splitting of social function, concealed by the unity of the name *Caesar:* "Now Germany feels you a young man in your son, and Caesar faces wars in place of great Caesar." Augustus' successor, Tiberius, occupies the symbolic position (and power) of the dying father, fighting campaigns under the emperor's *nomen* and *auspicia,* acting in his place.

Within the *Fasti, dimidium* appears four times, once in "April" and three times in "May." All these uses appear in narratives describing the loss, or "death," of half of one's ultimate desire or life. At *F.* 4.587–88 Ceres has searched the globe for her missing daughter Proserpina, who was brokered by Jupiter in marriage to his brother Pluto. Having learned from the Sun of her abduction, Ceres pleads with Jupiter: "If you recall from what god [i.e., Jupiter himself] Proserpina was born to me, she ought to have half of your concern" (*dimidium curae debet habere tuae,* 588). Since Proserpina has eaten a pomegranate seed and Ceres threatens to stay in the underworld with her daughter, Jupiter promises that Proserpina will be in heaven "for twice three months," or *half* the year. That half-year might reflect the length of the *Fasti* and Ovid's exile, both split between life and death.

Likewise, at *F.* 5.693–720, the twins Castor and Pollux try to abduct the daughters of Leucippus, betrothed to the brothers Idas and Lynceus, who resist them. Castor dies in the fighting (709–10). Therefore, Pollux petitions Jupiter (5.717–18): "The heaven which you are giving me alone, divide for two; *the half portion will be greater than the whole reward*" (*quod mihi das uni caelum, partire duobus; dimidium toto munere maius erit*). Ovid states, "He redeemed his brother by taking his place (i.e., in the underworld for half the year)" (*alterna fratrem statione redemit,* 719). They shared the same womb and now share the same divinity, literally, a half-portion of heaven. Readers might align life-death division with the exiled Ovid and the *Fasti* divided between life and death.

Earlier in the book, under his explanation of the *Lemuria* on May 9 (5.419–92; from *Remuria,* 479–84), Ovid reports (as Mercury reportly told him) that funeral rites for the murdered Remus had been performed improperly (*et male veloci iusta solute Remo,* 452) and that at night the ghost of Remus, Romulus' twin, appeared to Faustulus and Acca, their parents. The ghost's first words were (459–60): "Look, I am the half, and the other side, of your hope [*en ego dimidium vestri parsque altera voti*]. See how I am, and how I was just recently!" Again twins figure as *dimidia*, but here not of each other but of their foster parents' hope or longing for the future. Remus symbolizes the excluded—what was screened by Romulus' imposition of Law, a symbolic order of things that was symbolized by Romulus' token city wall, the *pomerium*, and his ban on anyone indicating defiance and interrupting its circuit by leaping over it. Remus was not accommodated to Romulus' order. He is the repressed alternative between two deaths, physically dead, but still symbolically "alive" and returning as a ghost. While the ritual (Lemuria-Remuria) screens off reemergence of a "Remus," Ovid's poetry re-evokes Remus' ghost or shadow (*umbra*, 457) as the dark double, the sacrificed, lost alternative latent in the symbolic order of Rome. Some readers examining the *Fasti* with a view to Ovid's exile might align Romulus' ghostly return with Ovid or his *Fasti* as a *dimidium*, or a portion reflecting symbolic death (exile) and Ovid's exclusion from the symbolic order. Others might respond to Ovid's half-*Fasti* as a broken, excluded potential calendar which functions as a ghostly testimony of the subjective moral and political rivalry among men in late Augustan and early Tiberian Rome. This antagonism, which ordinarily is concealed by the illusory wholeness of typical inscribed calendars, led, in the case of Ovid, to his physical and psychological loss, or death, through his absence from Rome. The half-*Fasti* offers in poetry a specter of this personal, political, and cultural loss.

To such readers, the loss of half the poem's form or beauty may be signaled at the Kalends of "May" (5.111–28) at 5.121–22: a she-goat was feeding the infant Jupiter milk, but "broke a horn on a tree" (*fregit in arbore cornu*, 5.121); she was thus denied "a half portion of her beauty" (*dimidia parte decoris*, 5.122). Almathea reuses the broken horn as a *rhyton* filled with fruit to feed Jupiter. Might this represent the sort of readerly response that Ovid seeks, that is, to pick up his broken work? To revitalize the broken?

Such readings explore brokenness as a sign of desire for a whole or an answer to desire. This notion of "the half" or *dimidium*, answered by one's relation to another, might then configure the zone of fantasy, where the poem, as an exilic work in progress, coordinates a desired relation to another half, a reader. The *dimidium* of the *Fasti* is a blot or apparent flaw that assumes a design—projects an ominous meaning— when the reader assumes an angular, anamorphic view toward it against the background of an imagined "whole," the symbolic screen of what Ovid and his calendar could have been.

Imperfectum

A third way to look at incompletion of the *Fasti* is that it engages readers in their own staging of Ovid as poet in exile beyond the edge of life and death and beyond the borders of the empire. By inviting readers to look into the blots on the poem, the *Fasti* might recall Michelangelo's *non finito* works, such as his "Slave," figures that seem to be emerging from rough nature. These "unfinished" works seem simultaneously to be incomplete in a conventional sense, yet complete as sign of sublime artistic process near the edge of death, where its very lineaments seek to exceed or struggle with that very limit of man. Ovid's dedication to Germanicus (ch. 2) and his subsequent monthly prefaces (chs. 3–4) invite readers into his own process of fashioning his poetic calendar over against readers' ideas of what the calendar means, what the proper meanings of rituals are. [4] Exile's break indicates that line of "death" against which Ovid struggles.

But how might readers have responded to such incompletion? In his *Natural History*, Pliny suggests a possible openness to such a subjective, anamorphic position of the viewer toward what he calls *imperfecta*, the unfinished works of deceased artists. He says that they evoke greater admiration than finished works (*H.N.* 35.145):

> illud vero perquam rarum ac memoria dignum est suprema opera artificum *imperfecta*sque tabulas, sicut Irim Aristidis, Tyndaridas Nicomachi, Mediam Timomachi et quam diximus Venerem Apellis, in maiore admiratione esse quam *perfecta*, quippe in is *liniamenta reliqua* ipsaeque cogitationes artificum spectantur, atque in lenocinio commendationis *dolor* est manus, cum id ageret, exstinctae.

> It is an exceedingly rare thing, and worthy of memory, that the last works of artists and their pictures left incomplete—such as the *Iris* of Aristides, the *Children of Tyndareus* of Nikomachos, the *Medeia* of Timomachus, and the *Aphrodite* of Apelles, as I mentioned—are held in greater admiration than their completed pieces; to be sure, in them [incomplete works] outlines remaining and the very plans of the artists are seen, and sorrowful longing for the hand that perished while doing it serves as an enticement to praise.

Ovid's admiring readership might position his *Fasti* as an *imperfectum opus*, like those that Pliny describes. While "trace outlines" (*liniamenta reliqua*) hint at the fuller concepts of the great deceased artist, as marked by his unique "handling" of a motif (*manus*), the viewer's desire for the artist and the whole work (the *perfectum*) elevates the *imperfecta* into the space of fantasy where viewer desire moves through the coordinates of remaining form, from idea toward consummation.[5]

As Pliny says, "The very thoughts of the artists are seen." But viewer desire is never fulfilled. The work will remain unfinished, forever showing an absence of completion, a gap which the viewer tries to fill with his own fantasy of the whole.[6] As a *non finito*, the *Fasti* stands poised between conception and materialization. That tension of life-death in the *Fasti* invites readers, through desire for Ovid or for poetic completion, to take up angular views toward Ovid, the text, and the poem's missing half, to imagine how Ovid and his *Fasti* might continue beyond the line of "death" where the exiled poet still struggles with a late Augustan and early Tiberian symbolic order.

NOTES

Introduction

1. The lost *Mênes* or *Months* by Simias of Rhodes and the lost *Names of the Months according to Nation and Cities* by Callimachus (Santini 1975: 8n7; J. Miller 1982: 400; Fränkel 1915: 140–41; Powell 1925: 109–20; Lesky 1963: 725n1). On the structural influences of Callimachus' *Aetia* on Ovid's *Fasti*: J. Miller 1982: 381 with n.44 and 400. Sabinus, Ovid's friend, wrote an *imperfectum . . . dierum . . . opus* (P. 4.16.13–16).

2. For Syme 1978: 22 composition began after 1 BCE; like Herbert-Brown 1994: 230–33, I view the half-poem, based on Ovid's statement (*Tr.* 2.549–52) to have been interrupted by exile, then revised afterwards. For dates of revision, 15–16 CE, see Herbert-Brown 1994: 186 and n21, and 206–12; Syme 1979: 194; mid-17 CE. Retrospective-prospective references to Germanicus' German triumph: *F.* 1.63–70, 279–81, awarded January 1, 15 CE, but celebrated only in May 26, 17 (Tac. *Ann.* 1.55.1; Tac. *Ann.* 2.41 with *Fasti Amit.*, Degrassi 1963: 462). Newlands 1995a: 3–5; Herbert-Brown 1994, passim, esp. 173–78; Alton, Wormel, and Courtney 1988: vi–vii. Questioning whether dedication to Germanicus displaced one to Augustus: J. Miller 1991: 143–44; Fränkel 1945: 239–40.

3. Newlands 1995a: 18 observes a narrative across the *Fasti* "from optimism to disillusionment," reflecting "disenchantment with a political system." Herbert-Brown 1994 interprets the *Fasti* as pro-Augustan panegyric seeking exilic return, so excluding oppositional rhetoric. Herbert-Brown has criticized anti-Augustan attempts to connect passages across the poem as subjective violations of ancient rules of ritual exegesis.

4. Structural confinements of elegiac meters: Heinze 1919: 75–76. Its negative effect on the *Fasti*: Barsby 1978: 27–29; Otis 1966: 4–44; Wilkinson 1955: 268–79; Kenney and Clausen 1982: 428–30; J. Miller 1982: 440, J. Miller 1983: 160; Mack 1988: 30. Questioning the rigidity of Heinze's epic-elegy distinctions are Little 1970, Brunner 1971, and Hinds 1987.

5. Heinze 1919 contrasted the elliptical versus full style of Ovid's elegiac and epic narrative. For critique, Little 1970. This generic contrast influenced Otis' assessment of the epic features of narrative in the *Metamorphoses* versus elegiac style. For a refinement of genre as a system of signs, rather than a rigid polarity, see Hinds 1987 and 1992.

230   Notes to Introduction

6. Merli 2000 usefully articulates how epic (*arma*) aids Ovid's fundamental renovation of the elegiac genre in the *Fasti*.

7. A similar authorial trajectory forward: Prop. 3.5. Skinner 1997 comments on the move from erotic play to political responsibility.

8. Religious-political ideology and the *Fasti:* Fantham 1983 and 1985 (e.g.), J. Miller 1991, Newlands 1995a, Herbert-Brown 1994, Barchiesi 1997a. Augustan religious revival: Beard, North, and Price 1998, 1: 167–210; Galinsky 1996: 288–31 (esp. 288–312); Zanker 1988 (passim), but esp. 265–95 (private sphere); Silberberg-Peirce 1980.

9. Extant calendars collected in Degrassi 1963 demonstrate this frequency.

10. Feeney 1998:123–36 and Rüpke 1994 argue that the *Fasti* in commentative function is literature about the calendar, distinct from calendars. Ch. 1 suggests erosion of this distinction in calendars as commentative social form (screen): as Zizek suggests (1989, 1993: 200–37; in Wright and Wright 1999: 52–86, 87–101), fantasy-screen is the basis of "nation" and ideology.

11. Lacan 1978: 107.

12. Ibid.

13. Mimicry, the human screen and the quote (Seminar XI): Lacan 1978: 91–119, 107. Silverman 1992: 125–26, esp. 147–54 clearly explains "screen," observing in Lacanian diagrams a coincidence of screen and cultural images appearing on it and finding in "playing" with the screen a potential "arena for political contestation" (150).

14. Silverman 1992: 151 on Lacan's linkage of gaze and spectacle in Seminar XI (1978: 74–75). Cf. Lacan 1978: 83: "From the moment that this gaze appears, the subject tries to adapt himself to it."

15. This question Zizek directs to the fantasy scene or narrativization, which screens (suggests, but conceals) fundamental antagonism (at Wright and Wright 1999: 87–101, esp. 93), this fantasy he had described as a screen of desire (1989: 118–21).

16. Primal or original fantasies: Farmer 2000: 55; Laplanche-Pontalis 1968: 11, 17; Zizek ("Fantasy as an Ideological Category") in Wright and Wright 1999: 93 applied to fantasy in ideology.

17. Farmer 2000: 55 (quotes); Laplanche and Pontalis 1968: 18; Zizek ("The Spectre of Ideology") in Wright and Wright 1999: 63–65 on rituals externalizing beliefs; Zizek 1993: 200–37 ("Enjoy Your Nation as Yourself!"), esp. 201–5; 201: "If we are asked how we recognize the presence of this [Nation-]Thing, the only consistent answer is that the Thing is present in that elusive entity called 'our way of life.' All we can do is enumerate disconnected fragments of the way our community organizes its feasts, its rituals of mating, its initiation ceremonies, in short, all the details by which is made visible the unique way a community *organizes its enjoyment*" (original emphasis).

18. Farmer 2000: 56.

19. Zizek 1999b. Cf. at F. 5.459–60 (discussed ch. 3), where murdered Remus' ghostly apparition which appears to Acca and Faustulus describes himself thus: "Look I'm the *half-portion* and other side of your hope, discern what I was and what I am now" (*en ego dimidium vestri parsque altera voti,/ cernite sim qualis, qui modo qualis eram!*)

20. Sedgwick 1985: 2 acknowledges using "desire" in the psychoanalytic sense of libido "for the affective or social force, the glue, even when its manifestation is hostility or hatred or something less emotively charged, that shapes an important relationship."

21. Ibid.: 1–27.

22. See Corbeill 1997, 2002 on variant ideology displayed through gesture and speech style.

23. On these practices of Roman literary recitation and critique at banquets and recitation halls, see Johnson 2000 and Dupont 1997, 1999.

24. Anamorphosis: Lacan 1978: 79–90; 1989: 98–100 (on the "ideological anamorphosis");" Zizek 1991 (esp. 88–106), 2001: 139–40.

25. Libidinal views of visuality: e.g., Benton 2002; Fredrick 1995, 2002; Koloski and Ostrow 1997; Morales 1996. Literature: Fitzgerald 1995; Fredrick 1997, 1999; Greene 1998; Janan 1994, 2001; Robin 1993; Segal 1994; Wyke 1995; Lee-Stecum 2000 in Fear 2000; P.-A. Miller and Platter 1999.

26. Herbert-Brown 1994 has an extensive, insightful, chapter on Germanicus in the *Fasti*. Barchiesi 1997a and Newlands 1995a also treat the issue. But these examinations do not concern gender in Ovid's address to Germanicus.

27. See essays in Hallett and Skinner 1997. Williams 1999 elaborates Roman elite male orthodoxy: penetrating (orally or anally), not receiving.

28. Psychoanalytic theory applied to literary and film influence my approach to male subjectivity: Silverman 1992, Edelman 1991. Also Sedgwick 1985, 1990; Fuss 1995.

29. Expectations of elite male civic and military careers contrasted with indulgence of love elegists: Lyne 1980: 1–18; Griffin 1985. Cf. Plautus' comedies: E. Segal 1987: 15–98.

Chapter One

1. Of his forty-four *fasti anni* (or *annales*) Degrassi 1963, superseding Mommsen 1893: 202–339, identifies one pre-Julian (*Fasti Antiates Maiores*), 21 Augustan, 8 Tiberian, 10 generally Julio-Claudian, 2 uncertain, and 2 late antique (*Fasti Furii Filocali*, 354 BCE; *Fasti Polemii Silvii*, 449 CE). Rüpke 1995 offers additional finds and recent commentary. See Michels 1967 on structure. For a large illustrated calendar beneath Santa Maria Maggiore in Rome (dating from late second century to Constantine): Coarelli 1984: 181–89; Salzman 1981; Magi 1972.

2. *Fasti Antiates Maiores:* Degrassi 1963: 1–28.

3. For *Fasti Amiterni*, ibid.: 185–200.

4. Michels 1967: 84–89 ("Nundinal Letters and *Nundinae*") and 191–206 ("*Nundinae* and *Trinum Nundinum*"), noting, for example, the *Lex Caecilia Didia* of 98 BCE that required the passage of a *trinum nundinum* (25 days) between the *promulgatio* and *rogatio* of a law. Scullard 1981: 43–44.

5. F marks *dies fasti* "on which the legal process known as *lege agere* or *legis actio* might take place," when the *praetor urbanus* was permitted (*fas est*) to use the words *do, dico, addico* (essential to traditional legal *formulae* for pronouncements of law, *ius dicere,* part of *legis actio*). N marks days when it was "not permitted" (*nefas*) for the praetor to utter these verbs. *Iuris dictio* was "the preliminary part of a civil case in which the praetor has to determine the *ius* or point of law involved" (Michels 1967: 51). According to Michels (1967: 68–83, 113), NP marked *feriae* (holiday for civil courts and from labor) celebrated by the state for the benefit of the people (*pro populo;* Festus 284L) at public expense (*sacerdotes publici* presided). Rüpke 1995: 259–60 has argued that NP means *nefas piaculum* (meaning that *iurisdictio* is not permitted and that there is a rite of expiation).

6. See Michels 1967: 29–30. *Dies endotercisus* (EN) was *nefastus* during a morning sacrifice, but the end of such a day was also *nefastus*, while the final offering of the victim was being made. The time between was considered *fastus*. Two days (March 24 and May

24) are marked with *Q.R.C.F.*, which stands for *Quando Rex Comitiavit Fas (est)*; it becomes *fastus* once the *rex sacrorum* performs the act (*comitiavit*; meaning uncertain). *QSDF* stands for *Quando Stercus Delatum (est) Fas (est)* (June 15, Ov. *F.* 6.711–14; Varro, *Ling.* 6.32; Fest. 466L; *Fasti Antiates Maiores*, Degrassi 1963: 12 and 471).

7. Michels 1967: 19 with n26 used the term "dividing days" to distinguish Kalendae, Nones, and Idus, which divide the time of each month.

8. For Mommsen 1893: 283–84 the two letter sizes referred to two historical layers, Numan and post-Numan (also Degrassi 1963: xxiii–xxiv). Michels 1967: 93–94, 132–36, and 207–10 proposed that large letters indicate the public ritual's importance.

9. Michels 1967: 21 (neuter plural adjectives and use of popular festival names).

10. Langer 1979: 79–102 ("Discursive Forms and Presentational Forms"); rpt. in Innis 1985: 87–107. Langer stresses that linear language is only one mode of articulation.

11. Austin 1962.

12. Michels 1967: 24. Use of genitive and dative (mistaken for ablative on page 383): Degrassi 1963: 370.

13. Beard 1987 identifies in the calendar a (Saussurean) linguistic contrast between the "paradigmatic" and the "syntagmatic"; cf. Langer 1979 on the contrast of presentational and discursive (above).

14. Small-letter notes in the *Fasti Praenestini* define terms of the calendar scheme, such as *fasti, nefasti, kalendae*, etc., but the *Fasti Praenestini* is an aberration among extant calendars because of its size. Most calendars could not afford to waste the marble.

15. From internal evidence, Degrassi 1963: 1, 28 dates the *Fasti Antiates Maiores* to the period between 84 and 55 BCE.

16. Michels 1967 is fundamental. Herbert-Brown 1994: 15–26 emphasizes Caesarian and Augustan influence upon the calendar. For chronographic concerns: Samuel 1972. On the early political significance of the Roman calendar: Taylor 1971 and Liebeschuetz 1979: 20–21.

17. Text: Degrassi 1963: 110–11, 327.

18. Varr. *L.L.* 6.27; Macr. *Sat.* 1.15.9–12, 14–18; Serv. 8.654 (on *Curiam Calabram*).

19. Romulus' 10-month year of 304 days: Michels 1967: 122 citing Macr. *Sat.* 1.12.1–14.15 and Censor. *De die nat.* 20; also Ov. *F.* 1.27–28; Gell. 3.16.16; Solin. 1.35; Serv. *Georg.* 1.43; Lyd. *Mens.* 1.16 (9 Wuensch).

20. All the 45 named days of the calendar followed the Nones, with the exception of the *Poplifugia*, July 5: Michels 1967: 120. On the ontent of the announcement of the *rex sacrorum*: Michels 1967: 19–20, 112, 130, 136.

21. Michels 1967; Scullard 1981: 42–44 discuss these old oral ceremonies of monthly calendar presentation. Degrassi 1963: 327–30 collects ancient written evidence for them, including Macrob. *Sat.* 1.15.9–21 and Serv. *A.* 8.654, and Fest. 176L (*Nonas*) and 93L (*Idulis ovis*); the Julian and early Augustan scholar Varro, *Ling.* 6.27–28; Verr. Flacc. *Fasti Praenestini* (on Jan. 1); and Ovid (*F.* 1.588–89).

22. For intercalation in the pre-Julian calendar: Michels 1967: 16–18.

23. Ibid.: 123–26 discusses how the sources retroactively ascribe to the Roman's priestly king Pythagorean mathematical interests, probably around the first decades of the second c. BCE.

24. On Numa's calendar, Liv. 1.19.5–7 (e.g., 1.19.7: *nefastos dies fastosque fecit, quia aliquando nihil cum populo agi utile futurum erat*).

25. Liv. 1.19.4: *qui cum descendere ad animos sine aliquo commento miraculi non posset, simulat sibi cum dea Egeria congressus nocturnos esse; eius se monitu quae acceptissima dis essent sacra instituere, sacerdotes suos cuique deorum praeficere.*

26. According to *F.* 3.151–54, Pythagoras (the Samian) or "his Egeria" taught Numa

Pompilius *Egeria sive monente sua* (154). Egeria as "wife of Numa": Ov. *F.* 3.261–62. Livy's *congressus nocturnos* allows sexual interpretation of *descendere*. For the obscene meaning of *descendere, TLL* 465.78–83, citing Varro, *RR* 2.7.9. Verg. *Georg.* 2.326 (*aether in gremium laetae descendit*; cf. Tert. *Nat.* 2.12), Juv. 11.164. *Descendere* meaning *penetrare, infigi: TLL* 650.62–80; metaphorical meaning derived from weaponry, *TLL* 648.15–30.

27. For the "female body" as brokering male civic relations, see Joshel 1992a on Lucretia and Verginia.

28. Livy 1.32.2 (esp. *omnia ea ex commentariis regis pontificem in album relata proponere in publico iubet*). *Fasti* within Ancus' display: Mommsen 1893: 284; Degrassi 1963: xix.

29. Michels 1967: 16.

30. Cicero reports (*Rep.* 1.25) that the *annales maximi* contained the record of an eclipse on the Nones of June at the end of the fifth century (400 BCE by some reckonings). Michels 1967: 126 reasons from this notice that, at the end of the fifth century, the Roman months seem no longer to have been determined by appearance of the crescent.

31. Ov. *F.* 2.53–54 attests decemviral calendar activities, but misinterprets the fact that, before the *decemviri*, the year ended with February, i.e., the year began with March (Michels 1967: 128–29). On the decemvirs, Liv. 3.32–33, 4.3; Dion. Hal. 10.3.

32. See Michels 1949 and 1967: 119–30. Varro ap. Macr. *Sat.* 1.13.21 claims that a law referring to intercalation from the consulships of L. Pinarius and Furius (472 BCE) was inscribed on a bronze column (Degrassi 1963: xx), but Michels suggests it referred to lunar intercalation.

33. Michels 1967: 128–29 and 97–101 on a shift in the year's beginning, starting in 450 BCE with the institution of a lunisolar calendar and 22-day intercalation, attributed falsely to 153 BCE, when the consuls merely started to enter office on January 1 (Michels 1967: 97 citing Liv. *Per.* 47; *Fasti Praen.* Jan. 1; Cassiodorus). Other authorities attesting the original beginning in March: Atta ap. Serv. *Georg.* 1.43; Varr. *L. L.* 6.33; Cic. *De leg.* 2.54; Ov. *F.* 1.39–44, 3.135–52; Festus 136L; Plut. *Q.R.* 19; Censor. *De die nat.* 20; Macrob. *Sat.* 1.12.5–7.

34. Michels 1967: 99–101, 129; esp. 100 on possible Roman use of the *arx*, used for observation of the crescent for lunar months, for this solar observation. Ov. *F.* 3.135–44 attests the rituals of March, signifying it as the original beginning.

35. Cn. Flavius, *RE* no 15. Cic. *ad Att.* 6.1.8 (claims that the Twelve Tables were concealed or faded). Degrassi 1963: xix–xx refers to the possible publication of a calendar in the Twelve Tables (produced by the decemvirs in 451–50 BCE, Livy 3.32–34).

36. For the *fasti* of Gnaeus Flavius see Michels 1967: 108–18, also 211 and 213. Ancient sources include (besides Cic. *Att.* 6.1.8) Cic. *Mur.* 25; Liv. 9.46.5; Val. Max. 2.5.2; Plin. *H.N.* 33.17–19; and Lucius Piso ap. Gell. 7.9 (on Flavius' election as curule aedile).

37. Livy 1.19.7 attributes the legal designations to Numa. Flavius either gained access to a legible tablet and copied it or over time carefully took notes. *Dig.* 1.2.2.7 claims that as censor in 312 BCE Appius Claudius Caecus drew up a book of *legis actiones* and calendar and that Gnaeus Flavius covertly gained access to it and published it.

38. The view of Michels 1967: 110–11, 129–30.

39. Scheid 1992; Varr. *L.L.* 6.27–28. The *Fasti Praen.* (Kalends, January) uses present tense (Degrassi 1963: 111).

40. See Liv. 9.45 and Val. Max. 2.5.2 for the calendar of *dies fasti/nefasti* and the *legis actiones* kept secret among the *sacra* of the *pontifices* (also cited above). *Dig.* 1.2.2.7 links the calendar and the *legis actiones* with Appius Claudius Caecus' censorship in 312 BCE, but the *legis actiones* are said to have formed the *Ius Flavianum;* see Michels 1967: 108 and 108n49. Also Gell. 6.9. Valerius Maximus (2.5.2) claims the pontifices kept the *ius civile* secret for many centuries among the *sacra caerimoniasque eorum inmortalium;* this

Livy confirms (9.46). For the religious-class dynamics, see Cic. *Mur.* 25; Cic. *Att.* 1.6.8; *De or.* 1.46.186.

41. For this notion of mimetic desire or mimetic rivalry, see Girard 1965 and 1977.

42. For anger of the nobles, see Val. Max. 9.3.3 (casting away gold rings) and 2.5.2; Cic. *Att.* 6.9, *Mur.* 25; Liv. 9.46 (the curule chair, rings); Plin. *H.N.* 33.6; and Gell. 6.9.

43. Livy 9.46 and Val. Max. 2.5.2 discuss Flavius' calendar in the context of his contested right to pursue the curule aedileship; nobles rejected him because, as a mere clerk (a civil servant)—servile labor from the nobleman's viewpoint—he could not stand for higher political office. The mixture of two roles would diminish the stature (cf. *dignitas* or *maiestas*) of the higher office, but Flavius avoided this "technicality" and was elected when he swore not to act as record keeper.

44. One of Livy's sources (Liv. 9.46), Licinius Macer, had asserted that Cn. Flavius was tribune, *triumvir nocturnus,* and afterward one of the three commissioners (*triumviri*) for settling a colony.

45. L. Cornelius Scipio Barbatus (s.v. *RE* no. 343): epitaph on a sarcophagus from the "Tomb of the Scipios," Rome (*CIL* 1², 6–7).

46. Liv. 9.46.6; Plin. *H.N.* 33.19. Varr. *L.L.* 6.61: "For a sacred temple is dedicated by utterance by a magistrate when a pontifex dictates the formula [for the magistrate to repeat]" (*enim aedis sacra a magistratu pontifice praeeunte, dicendo dedicatur*). *OLD praeeo* 3 ("to dictate a religious or sim. formula"); it seems to mean "to repeat."

47. As Livy explains (9.46), Appius Claudius the Censor had helped to elect Flavius by distributing lowborn citizen voters in the electoral tribes, erasing class distinction. Removal of rings and ornaments symbolized a lament for the destruction of class distinction (Plin. *H.N.* 33.19; Val. Max. 9.33; and above).

48. M. Fulvius Nobilior, s.v. *RE* no. 91. Varr. *L. L.* 6.33; Censor. *De die nat.* 22.9; 20.2, 20.4; Lyd. *Ostent.* 16a; and Macr. *Sat.* 1.12.16 (quoted above). See Degrassi 1963: xx; Mommsen 1893 (*CIL* 1².1): 285.

49. Richardson 1992: 187 ("Hercules Musarum, Aedes"), built after 189 (Nobilior's victory in Ambracia) and probably after Nobilior's triumph in 187. See Platner 1929: 255. But how soon after? Eumenius (*Pro instaurandis scholis* in *Paneg. Latini*. 9.7.3 Baehrens) says Nobilior used censorial funds to build it; Nobilior held the censorship in 179 BCE. Martina 1981: 49–54 and Sauron 1994: 84 84n5 hold to a date of 179 BCE.

50. Fulvius' calendar commentary may have appeared first in separate form as a book roll and then in a visual display: Michels 1967: 125n18. Clay statues of the Muses: Pliny, *H. N.* 35.66; Ov. *F.* 6.797–812. Platner 1929: 255 and Richardson 1992: 187 ("Hercules Musarum, Aedes"). Hercules with Lyre as *Musagetes:* Ov. *A.A.* 3. 167–68; *F.* 6.812; Coinage of Q. Pomponius Musa, 66 BCE in Moeus 1981: 4, pl. 3

51. Numa's shrine to the Muses moved to temple of Honos et Virtus, then the temple of Hercules Musarum: Serv. *A.* 1.8. Another object from Syracuse in the Temple of Virtus was a planetary sphere built by Archimedes; another sphere of Archimedes he retained in his family collection (Cic. *De re pub.* 1.22; Sauron 1994: 90, 86n10).

52. Conte 1994b: 83.

53. Conte 1994b: 79 on Ennius' *Annales* as allusion to the *Annales Maximi*. Whitened board of *annales maximi* and the calendar: Seek 1885; Frier 1979. Conte 1994b: 17 and Schwabe 1891: 105–8, sections 74–76. Cat. *Orig.* fr. 77 (Peter) = Gell. *N.A.* 2.28.6; Cic. *De or.* 2.52; Serv. *Aen.* 1.373.

54. Cic. *Rep.* 1.25: *annales* record eclipse of 400 BCE on the Nones of June, a specific date. Recorded *prodigia*, which Cato observes (at. Gell. 2.28.6) as characteristic of the

annales, make sense only if they record the dates. Cf. Obsequens' (4th cent. CE) *Liber Prodigiorum,* prodigies from Livy's history.

55. Seek 1885: the Pontifex Maximus organized his annual record using the calendar scheme.

56. The view of Sauron 1994: 90; more hesitancy by Platner 1929: 255 (Hercules Musarum) and Richardson 1994: 187. The modern dispute about date hinges on funding sources—*ex manubiis* (booty) as Cicero says, *Arch.* 27; or *ex pecunia censoria,* referring to Fulvius' censorship, as Eumenius says, *Panegyrici Latini* 9.[4].7–8 (= Eumenius, *Pro Instaur. Scholis* 7–9).

57. For this quarrel, 187 BCE, between M. Fulvius Nobilior and M. Aemilius Lepidus over Fulvius' triumph, postponed by two years: Liv. 29.4–5. Its resolution: Livy 40.46 (with Caecilius Metellus' speech). Cic. *Tusc.* 1.3 (Fulvius brought poets with him into Aetolia).

58. Hercules as symbol of masculinity: e.g., Loraux 1990: 21–52. Hercules' role as triumphant conqueror is well known. Sauron 1994: 85–86 emphasizes it. Eumenius remarked on the symbolism of the hero-poet relationship (*Pan. Lat.* 9.7.3: . . . *quia mutuis opibus et praemiis iuvari ornarique deberent: Musarum quies defensione Herculis et virtus Herculis voce Musarum*), as noted by Sauron 1994: 96.

59. Cicero's reference to Nobilior's temple at *Pro Archia* 27 appeals to his aristocratic judges on this basis.

60. Galinsky 1972: 101–25 on a cultured Hercules gaining prominence in the Hellenistic period.

61. Suet. *Aug.* 29.5; Degrassi 1963: 475. L. Marcius Philippus (trib. 49 BCE, cons. suff. 38BCE), *RE* no. 77 (not no. 76, the father of the same name, stepfather of Augustus). Newlands 1995a: 209–36 ("The Ending of Ovid's *Fasti*"); Richardson 1992: 187 (Hercules Musarum, Aedes), 318 (Porticus Philippi).

62. Ov. *F.* 6.803–4: *Marcia, sacrifico deductum nomen ab Anco, / in qua par facies nobilitate sua.* Newlands 1995a: 215.

63. Ancus Marcius, the grandson of Numa Pompilius (Liv. 1.32.1), who had selected Numa Marcius as the *pontifex* in charge of recording the religious rites and the calendar (Livy 1.20.5).

64. Macr. *Sat.* 1.13.21 attests Fulvius' reference to the law. As Michels wrote (1967: 102): "One must . . . accept that in 191 BCE something drastic needed to be done about the state of the calendar," due to priestly manipulation of intercalation. Livy records for 190 BCE an eclipse of the sun on July 11 (37.4.4), but the eclipse actually occurred on March 14 by modern reckoning.

65. For the history of Romans' increasing knowledge of sundials (beginning with the importation of dials from conquered Sicily to Rome, a latitude for which they were not constructed): Plin. *H.N.* 7.211–15; Gibbs 1976.

66. Politics of intercalation in the Republic: Taylor 1971: 78–79.

67. While Caesar had the new calendar inscribed on bronze and displayed in public (Macr. *Sat.* 1.14.13; Degrassi 1963: xxi), the exact process of the edict's dissemination is not known.

68. Macr. *Sat.* 1.14.13. Herbert-Brown 1994: 19–21 emphasizes the practical rather than symbolic effect of Caesar's calendar reform. Wallace-Hadrill 1997 couches such reform as part of the imperial displacement of control of knowledge from amateur elites to experts, often freedmen (e.g., freedman Verrius Flaccus, scholar and tutor of Augustus' grandchildren; see below).

69. Dio 40.62.1–4 implies that Caesar himself proposed inserting an entire inter-calary month, outside proper timing, to manipulate politics.

70. Plut. *Caes.* 59.3; trans. Perrin 1919: 581.

71. The *pontifices* were intercalating at the beginning, rather than at the end, of the third year (Macr. *Sat.* 1.14.13). Augustus' solution: twelve years without intercalation ordered in a bronze inscription (*Sat.* 1.14.14). During his rise, Octavian, too, manipulated calendar time away from Julius Caesar's calendar (Dio 48.33.4).

72. *Horologium Augusti,* Richardson 1992: 190–91; Buchner 1982; Plin. *H.N.* 36: 72–73. Date of obelisk's importation, 10 BCE, attested by inscription on its base (*ILS* 91 = *CIL* VI 702).

73. Proposed by Simpson 1992. The astronomer Facundius Novus probably helped (Plin. *H.N.* 36.72).

74. The gnomon's use echoes the contemporary rise of non-elite, professional, knowledge in the early empire, superseding elite Republican amateurism: see Wallace-Hadrill 1997 (in Habinek and Schiesaro 1997).

75. Beard 1987. Nicolet 1991 on the Augustan geographic project supporting imper-ial fiscal management. The obelisk's inscribed base: *CIL* 6.702 = *ILS* 91. On the symbol-ic placement of Augustus in time: Wallace-Hadrill 1987.

76. Clodius' use of *collegia,* local district and tradesmen societies: Cic. *Pis.* 4 (8); Asconius' commentary; Lintott 1968: 77–83; Accame 1942; Beard, North, and Price 1998, 1: 139, 184 (Julius Caesar's attempt to suppress them), 230; Taylor 1971: 43–44. Festivals at *compita, Ludi Compitalicii* or *Compitalia* continue: Cic. *Att.* 2.3.4. The Senate sup-pressed the *collegia* (referring to *sodalicia,* or brotherhoods, Cic. *Q. Fr.* 2.3.5); Julius Caesar completed it: Suet. *Jul.* 42 and Taylor 1931: 185.

77. Beard, North, and Price 1998, 1: 184–86. Taylor 1931: 181–203, esp. 181–93. Augustus' fourteen urban *regiones* and 265 *vici:* Plin. *H.N.* 3.66; Suet. *Aug.* 30.1; Cass. Dio 55.8.7; Ov. *Fast.* 5.128–48. For inscriptional record of *vici* (names, officers) during the Hadrianic period: the Capitoline Base, *CIL* VI 975 = *ILS* 6073. Seasonal cult at crossroad shrines: Suet. *Aug.* 31 (*Compitales Lares ornari bis anno instituit vernis floribus et aestivis*). To the traditional day (May 1, Ov. *F.* 5.128–48) was added August 1, the day when *mag-istri vicorum* took office each year, honoring the *Genius Augusti* (Suet. *Aug.* 31.4). See Richardson 1992: 329 ("Regio"), 413–14 ("Via").

78. On *compita,* local *vicomagistri,* and cult of *Genius Augusti,* see Frazer 1929, 2: 453–54 (on *F.* 2.615; cf. *F.* 2.634, 5.129–46). Crossroad altars of the *Lares et Genius Augusti* are collected and illustrated in Hano 1986. The social impact of freedman *magistri* and slave *ministri:* Zanker 1988: 129–35; Beard, North, and Price 1998, 1: 185–86, 347; also Holland 1937 and Waites 1920. On earlier worship of the patron's Genius, related to *pater* and Augustus' title *pater patriae* (*F.* 2.633–38): Taylor 1931: 47–51, esp. 48–49 (offer-ings to Marius after his victories over the Cimbri and Teutones, and Marius Gratidianus, praetor, 86 BCE).

79. Zanker 1988: 3 emphasizes "autonomous and mutual interactions" characteriz-ing the period's ideology of governance (this according to Galinsky 1998 who notes mis-translation of Zanker's *Wechselwirkungen* as "in varying ways").

80. New Year's *stips* or *strena:* see chapter 3 below. Augustus used the *stips* or offer-ing *pro Salute* (for his Health) to purchase statues which he dedicated *vicatim,* in the *vici.* For *stips* (*strena*) on Jan. 1: *CIL* VI 456 = *ILS* 99, *Laribus publicis sacrum. Imp. Caesar Augustus . . . ex stipe quam populus ei contulit. CIL* VI 457 = *ILS* 93, *ILS* 92, *CIL* VI 30974; cf. *CIL* VI 30770 and 30771. Dio 54.35.2 (statues of Salus Publica, Concordia, and Pax purchased with proceeds) emphasizes the reciprocity with Augustus, who gave larger

stipes in return. Suet. *Aug.* 57.1: *stips* used to buy statues of Apollo Sandaliarius and Jupiter Tragoedus for two *vici* (*vicus Sandaliarius* at *CIL* VI 448 = *ILS* 3614; *CIL* VI 761 = *ILS* 3308; and *BullCom* 5 [1877], 162–63 and *BullCom* 18 [1890], 132).

81. For the cult of the image of Augustus' Genius and Lares in Ovid's *Fasti*, see 5.129–46, on May 1, a day for the Lares also in the *Fasti Esquilini* (ca. 7 CE) and *Venusini* (between 16 BCE and 4 CE, Degrassi 1963: 56). Ovid *F.* 2.631–38 attests prayers to the *Lares Augusti* offered on many occasions, such as the family banquets (here, *Karistia*): incense and wine to the Lares and to the *Pater Patriae*.

82. Altar and statue of Vesta dedicated April 28, 12 BCE: Ov. *F.* 4.949–54, *Met.* 15.864–65, and Degrassi 1963: 452 for calendar record and other sources. Paternal honors and the worship of the father's Genius and Lares are a step removed from divinity: Taylor 1931: 181–204.

83. On the voted title *pater patriae:* Ov. *F.* 2.119–44 (Feb. 5), esp. 127–28. *Fasti Praenestini* (Degrassi 1963: 407): Aug. *RG* 35; Dio 55.10.10 (on 2 BCE); Suet. *Aug.* 58.1–2 (on the proposal before the Senate by Valerius Messala).

84. *Fasti Magistrorum Vici*, without doubt a collegial calendar (Degrassi 1963: 98). Other calendars that seem to refer to local persons (this list is not exhaustive): *Fasti Caeretani* (Degrassi 1963: 64–68: the list of officers—Roman consuls or municipal magistrates—appeared above); *Maffeiani.* (Degrassi 1963: 84: the *praescriptio* or heading mentions the *collegium*); *Esquilini* (Degrassi 1963: 89: it had a list of magistrates, probably of a local *collegium* appended; an inscription to the *Lares Augusti* for 203 CE was found with this calendar), *Tusculani* (Degrassi 1963: 102: found beside an altar dedicated in 147 CE by C. Prastina Pacatus Messalinus, consul; *CIL* XIV 2588); *Vallenses* (Degrassi 1963: 152: heading mentions *magistri* of the *collegium*); *Foronovani* (Degrassi 1963: 156: plural dedicators in heading implies *magistri* or local men honoring the emperor). Large size of some fragments indicates calendars for local display in monumental form: *Fasti Praenestini* (Degrassi 1963: 141; Suet. Gram. 17); *Verulani* (Degrassi 1963: 170); *Amiterni* (Degrassi 1963: 200: inscription of three local men and their other local public works may belong with this calendar; *CIL* IX 4201).

85. For such a calendar, see *Fasti Foronovani*, heading and Degrassi 1963: 156, who observes that the "Caesar" named could be Gaius or Lucius Caesar or Tiberius. Altars and ceremonies: Galinsky 1996: 300–12, esp. his fig. 146 (votive altar of carpenter guild; Augustus bestows them with a statue of Minerva; Zanker 1988: 135, fig. 111); Hano 1986: 2344–45: the Belvedere Altar, right lateral face, showing Augustus and two grandsons, Gaius and Lucius, bestowing statuettes of Genius and two Lares (Planche VII.13; Zanker 1988: 133, fig. 109).

86. Local Italian elites expressed their ambitions through public offices and benefaction: Dyson 1992, esp. ch. 7 ("The Life Cycle within the Community," 180–214).

87. See respective entries in Degrassi 1963 for fragments of *praescriptiones* and inscribed lists (*fasti*) of magistrates accompanying extant calendars (e.g., the *Fasti Fratrum Arvalium, Caeretani, Maffeiani, Magistratorum Vici, Vallenses, Foronovani, Antiates Minores*, and *Praenestini*, which has *praescriptiones* for each month comparable to Ovid's prefaces).

88. E.g., only a few include both the new hebdomadal and nundinal letters (7-day and 8-day weeks): *Fasti Sabini, Foronovani, Nolani*, and the late *Fasti Filocali* (354 CE).

89. Small sundials also merged calendar and hour-lines: examples in Gibbs 1976.

90. Degrassi 1963: 107 and 141–42 dates Verrius' *Fasti Praenestini*, based on internal references, between 6 and 9 CE. Ovid was exiled in 8 CE.

91. Suet. *De Grammaticis* 17: *decessit aetatis exactae sub Tiberio. Statuam habet Praeneste,*

in superiore fori parte circa hemicyclium, in quo fastos a se ordinatos et marmoreo parieti incisos publicarat.

92. Size: Degrassi 1963: 107.

93. The calendar-hemicycle (Coarelli 1984:133–34; Zevi 1976: 38–41) contained a fountain decorated with the two Grimani relief-sculptures (figs. 138a–c at Zanker 1988: 178–79). Buchner 1982 speculates that the Ara Pacis and the sundial were mathematically oriented so that the gnomon's shadow pointed to the door of the Ara Pacis on September 23, Augustus' birthday and the fall equinox; Schütz 1990 questions Buchner's calculations.

94. For the concepts of Imaginary, Symbolic and Real: J. Lacan 1977: 1–7 and 2002: 2–9 ("The Mirror Stage as Formative of the Function of the 'I,'"), tr. Alan Sheridan 1978; Myers 2003: 20–29; Kay 2003: 169–70. Applied to Catullus: Janan 1994: 1–36, esp. 16–21. Propertius: Janan 2001: 11–32.

95. Janan 1994: 22.

96. Bourdieu 1990: 200–70; Bourdieu 1977: 96–158. For Bourdieu's theory and the calendar of Rome, see Rüpke 1995: 12–36.

97. On this reading of the fantasy supports (ideologies) of the symbolic order versus the return of the repressed Real: Zizek 1989: 114–28; Zizek , "The Spectre of Ideology," 53–86, and "Fantasy as an Ideological Category," 87–101 in Wright and Wright 1999.

98. For Lacanian *capitonnage:* Janan 1994: 24–26; Zizek 1989: 87–105.

99. Ovid's exile as death: e.g., Nagle 1980: 22–32 and passim. Cf. memorial function of poetry: Ov. *Met.* 15.871–79; *Tr.* 3.3.69–78; 3.14.1–8. Psychic poise between symbolic and physical death: See Zizek 1989: 131–49 ("You Only Die Twice").

Chapter Two

1. Ovid's address to Germanicus: see Fantham 1985; Herbert-Brown 1994: 173–212 (politics of Germanicus as exilic addressee).

2. Erotic star notices: Newlands 1995a: 17–18. Cat. 66 explains the "astrification" of newlywed Berenike's lock of hair (cf. Callim. *Coma Berenices*), vowed for the safe return of her warring husband, Ptolemy Euergetes (reign, 247–222 BCE). Cf. Ov. *F.* 3.459–516 (March 8; Corona of Ariadne and Bacchus' return from East). Germanicus' *Phaenomena:* Santini 1975: 4–5; Newlands 1995a: 30; Fantham 1985: 244–56 (and Manilius' *Astronomica*) and 254 (with 275n11) specifically associates *Phaenomena* translations with young men (cf. Cicero, who was still an adolescent when he translated it, Cic. *ND* 2.104). Echoes between *Fasti* dedication and Germanicus' *Phaenomena:* Fantham 1985: 254–55

3. "Caesar" in *praescriptiones:* Degrassi 1963: 93, 96 (*Fasti Magistratuum Vici*) and 156 (*Foronovani*).

4. Germanicus, surrogate Muse or Apollo, Fantham 1985: 246, Newlands 1995a: 54; *F.* 1.6 (*numen*), 19–20 (Apollo).

5. Anxiety about literary presence: e.g., *Tr.* 3.14. Personified Book (*Liber*) rejected at libraries: Ov. *Tr.* 3.1.59–68 (Apollo Palatinus), 69–70 (Porticus Octaviae), 71–72 (Atrium Libertatis). Cf. *Tr.* 3.3.65–84 (esp. 77–78, books longer lasting *monumenta*). Yet, at *P.* 2.2.7–8, his verses are permitted in private ownership (cf. *Tr.* 3.1.79–82).

6. Imperial cult and social rituals evoked Ovid's fantasies of "seeing" Rome, friends: Nagle 1980: 91–99; *Tr.* 3.8, 3.13 (Ovid's birthday), 5.3 (Bacchic cult with poet-friends), 5.5 (wife's birthday); *P.* 1.8 (esp. 31), 1.9 (death of Celsus), 2.4 (travel with Atticus), 2.8 (faces of statuettes of the imperial family), 2.10, 3.3 (Amor appears), 4.9

(Graecinus' inauguration as consul). Cf. surrogate speech of *P.* 4.4 (winged Fama reports Sextus Pompeius' election as consul), 4.5 (personified *Elegi* celebrate Sextus Pompeius' inauguration), and *Tr.* 1.1 and 3.1 (the poet's personified *Libri*). Rituals often prompt these fantasies.

7. For these dates: Herbert-Brown 1994: 173–212 (15–16 CE); Syme (after May 26, 17 CE). I prefer some composition in 17: Germanicus compared to Apollo at Claros (*F.* 1.20). Germanicus' Eastern itinerary in 18, Tac. *Ann.* 2.54, was planned and known in advance.

8. Fantham 1985: 247: " . . . one implication of *devoveo* [*F.* 1.6: *devoto*] is surely that the offering is a *votum* in return for a blessing unspecified." Versnel 1980 demonstrates popular *devotio* to Germanicus upon his death.

9. "Leaf or slab," L-S, *Pagina*, IIB, citing Pall. 6.11, Juv.10.58; cf. Prop. 3.1.17–18, *sed, quod pace legas, opus hoc de monte Sororum/ detulit intacta Pagina nostra via. Intacta,* describing virgins (Hor. *C.* 1.7.5; Verg. *Aen.* 1.345; Cat. 62.45; Ovid on inauguration of consuls and the year: *F.* 1.79–82 (*vestibus intactis Tarpeias itur in arces*).

10. Zizek on fantasy's relation to desire (1991: 8). Support of desire: Zizek 1989: 44–49.

11. On gender and sexuality in inspiration: Fowler 2002 and Sharrock 2002 (Muse as goddess-whore).

12. E.g., *Am.* 2.18; *Tr.* 3.7.25; 4.10.45–46 (recitation as "right of comradeship [*iure sodalicii*] by which he [Propertius] was connected to me"); also 49, 113–14 (lack of audience in exile). *P.* 1.2.124–35; 1.5.55–62; 2.5.33–34, 41–56; 3.5.

13. Intimate male advisors in "care of the self": Foucault 1988: 51–54; Hadot 1981, 1990. Cf. Ovid's Atticus, *P.* 2.4, with Cicero's; intimacy of L. Lucceius and Dio of Alexandria (*Cael.* 24, 54).

14. Herbert-Brown 1994: 173–214; Fantham 1985; and Subias-Konofal 2003 cite themes repeated between *Fasti* 1.1–26 and Ovid's exilic poetry, particularly *Ex Ponto* 4.

15. Equality: e.g., Liv. 2.3.2: *erant in Romana iuventute adulescentes aliquot . . . equales sodalesque adulescentium Tarquiniorum. Sodalis* and *amicus:* Plaut. *Merc.* 475, *Casin.* 583, *Bacch.* 475; Cic. *De sen.* 13.45 (*sodalitas* and *sodales* near *coetu amicorum*).

16. See Nagle 1980: 44–46.

17. Syme 1978: 72–93 ("The Friends of Ovid"), index.

18. White 1982 on hierarchy of poets below the most independent; Zetzel 1982. Practically fluid, yet differentiated, categories *patrocinium* and *amicitia:* Quinn 1982; Saller 1982 and 1989: 49–62. Gradation of poets and poetry, the practical flexibility of *patrocinium-amicitia:* White 1982, stressing financial independence of famous poets. Dynamics of patronage in the early empire: Wallace-Hadrill 1996 and 1989 (manipulation of access to power centers); Bennett 1968; White 1978; Gold 1987: 111–72.

19. Johnson 2000; Dupont 1997; and Fitzgerald 1995: 5–10 (on Catullus) discuss recitation as social ritual, and also Quinn 1982.

20. Poetry at banquets of aristocratic *sodalitates:* Zorzetti 1990. On *sodalicium-collegium: Tr.* 5.3 (cult of Bacchus and wine held by poets) and *Tr.* 4.10, 39–56, esp. 45–46 (*iure sodalicii*); Gaius, *Dig.* 47.22.1 and 4 (*collegium* as *hetairia* and *sodalitas*). Guild-houses in Ostia as venues of male homosocial drinking: Balsdon 1969: 153. *Communia sacra* in the exile poetry as metaphor for poetic practices: see Nagle 1980: 145–47 and Ov. *P.* 3.4.67–70 to Rufinus (esp. 67, *sunt mihi vobiscum communia sacra, poetae*), 4.8.81–84 to Germanicus via Suillius (esp. 81, *prosit opemque ferat communia sacra tueri*), 4.13.43–50 to Carus (esp. 43, *per studii communia foedera sacri*); *P.* 3.4 (to Rufinus), esp. 67–68; 3.5 (Maximus Cotta), esp. 37–44 (oral recitation as surrogate intimacy; cf. the kiss commonly exchanged and

Dupont 1999); *P.* 2.5.71–72; 4.13.43–44; 4.8.43–44, 67–68, 81–82. King 1998 argues that *Tr.* 4.10 assimilates recitation of Ovid's poetry with funerary rituals and cult groups (*collegia;* cf. Prop. 3.1.1–4).

21. Germanicus as *augur* (by 7CE): Tac. *Ann.*1.62, 2.83; Dio 55.31; *ILS* 107 *addit,* 173, 174, 176, 177, 178, 222.1. As *flamen Augustalis:* Tac. *Ann.* 2.83; *ILS* 176 (after Germanicus' death), 177, 178, 222.1; Fishwick 1987, 1.1: 110, 161–62, 162nn 75–76. On Rome's *Flamen Augustalis* as model for provincial *flamines* and *sacerdotes divi Augusti:* Fishwick 1991a. Drusus, son of Tiberius, succeeded as *flamen Aug.: ILS* 169; after death of Germanicus (168 *sodalis Augustalis;* found with 176 indicates Drusus succeeded Germanicus as *Flamen Aug.*); then Nero (Germanicus' son) and Claudius (Kleiner 1971). Cf. Ovid's *cum Druso praemia fratre feres* (*F.* 1.12). Both were *fratres Arvales* (*CIL* VI 2023, p. 460) and *sodales Augustales* (Tac. *Ann.*1.54; *Tab. Heb.* 50–53, Oliver and Palmer 1954: 231; Ehrenberg and Jones 1955, no. 94a, 1. 50). "Germanicus Iulius Caesar," *RE* 19 Halbb. 444. Worship of *Gens Iulia* linked to *Augustales* (*sodales* and *flamen?*), Tac. *Hist.* 2.95 (rites to Nero, Vitellius 69 CE); *ara Gentis Iuliae, CIL* VI.2035.4 (*Acta Fratrum Arvalium*). Cf. *Ara Numinis Augusti* (ded. Jan. 17, before 6/9 CE): Degrassi 1963: 401, *Fasti Praen.* and *Verul.*).

22. Millar 2002: 351–52 and 1993: 15–16 (= 2002: 347): Ovid (*Ex P.* 4.9) reports to Pomponius Graecinus, consul designate of 16 CE, his worship of images of Divus Augustus and family (letter of 15 CE, same year as C. Norbanus Flaccus' consulship and dedication of status of Divus Augustus and *Domus Augusta* in the Circus Flaminius: e.g., Flory 1996, Tabula Siarensis).

23. Exiled Ovid as civilizer, reconstructing imperial subjectivity: Habinek 1998: 151–69. Domestic *cultores Augusti* (his *imago*) bridge provincial cults: Santero 1983; Fishwick 1991a, 2: 532–40. Ovid as *cultor* of Augustus: Fishwick 1991b; Millar 1993. Cf. Plin. *Ep.* 10.96.5 (Christians must supplicate emperor's *imago ture ac vino*) and Tac. *Ann.* 3.70 (L. Ennius melted silver imperial *effigies*). Other evidence: Fishwick 1991a, 2: 533–40, esp. 537–38 and Santero 1983. Emperor worship in Ovid: Scott 1932. Imperial cult at Tomis (unknown date): Ferguson 1970: 94–95; *sodalis Hadriani, CIL* III 6154. Self-promotion through worship of emperor: Turcan 1996.

24. E.g., *Tr.* 3.14.1 addressing *cultor et antistes doctorum sancte virorum.* Cf. cult of the Muses: e.g., *Tr.* 2.13–14 (Muses are *numina cultori perniciosa suo*). Cf. literary cult(ure) at an annual festival of Bacchus attended by poets (*Tr.* 5.3); cf. gods as *cultores Lyaei* (*F.* 1.395–402). The relation of cult and agriculture is extensive, such as in the cults of Ceres and Bacchus (first at *F.* 1.655–704); see key references below.

25. *Cultor-cultus* in patronage involves morning *salutatio* (e.g., Saller 1989 in Wallace-Hadrill 1989: 57–58, 63; Juv. *Sat.* 1 and 3 (in Wallace-Hadrill 1989: 209, 213, 214). At imperial court: Wallace-Hadrill 1996: 283 and 290. Ovid's exilic memory and absence from similar "services" (*officia*): *P.* 4.9.15–24; *Tr.* 3.1, Ovid's personified book attends. Literary patronage-*cultus* includes "rites": *P.* 1.2.145–50, 1.3.55–56, 1.7.15–16.

26 Ovid's exilic *cultus* includes agriculture or its lack and Ovid's desire of it: literal, *P.* 1.3.55–56, 1.8, 2.7.67–70; metaphor for poetry, *P.* 4.2.41–50 (cf. *F.* 5.225–26, 495, 515; *Met.* 7.653).

27. Sedgwick 1990: 15; Girard 1965.

28. Sedgwick adapted Gayle Rubin's "male traffic in women" (Sedgwick 1985: 25–26; Rubin 1975). Rubin in turn shaped her concept from Lévi-Strauss's observation of the role of women in barter and marriage used to form bonds between men in traditional patriarchal societies (Rubin 1975: 174 cites Lévi-Strauss 1969: 115; see Lévi-Strauss 1966: 109–33).

29. "Homosexual panic," legal defense for males charged with battery or murder of

gay males: Sedgwick 1985, 1990.

30. Similar gender dynamics in addresses to patrons in Tibullus, Propertius, and Horace: Oliensis 1997. See also Fowler 2002.

31. Bömer 1957, 2: 8 (*Fasti* 1.6); *TLL* 5.883.29–30 (*devotus*). Cf. Grat. 533 (*tibi [Diana] devotae Cirrhae*), but cf. *TLL* 5.881.18–55, listing Prop. 4.9.67; Prop. 2.32.9; *CIL* VIII.2670; cf. Juv. 9, 72: *ni tibi deditus essem devotusque cliens* (surrender to another person or activity, as in a devotee or "fanatic," cf. "fan").

32. P. Decimus Mus, Liv. 8.9.6–8; the son, 10.28–29; father, son and grandson, Cic. *Tusc.* 1.37.88. Seneca, *Ep.* 67.9: the Decii model Stoic endurance (not self-sacrifice for the state); Roller 2001: 103–4; Feldherr 1998: 82–92. Cf. Turnus, Verg. *Aen.* 11.442, 12.234 (Leigh 1993; Pascal 1990). Cf. Cic. *ND* 2, 3; *Fin.* 2, 19, 61; Suet. *Caes.* 67. Cf. *devotus* describing sacrificial victims in the meaning of *devoveo* (*s.v.* OLD, *devoveo*, 1 "to vow as an offering or sacrifice").

33. Suetonius describes Caesar's own troops as loving him so much that they were *devotissimos sibi* (*Jul.* 67.2–68.1).

34. On Iberian *devotio:* e.g., Galinsky 1996: 327–28; Curchin 1996; Fishwick 1987: 141–43; Étienne 1958.

35. Caes. *BG* 3.22. Bömer 1957–1958, 2: 8.

36. *Eros-philos* in Plato, *Symposium* and *Phaedrus*, with Cic. *Amic.* 48 (*passim*) on manly honor (*virtus*) attracting friendship [*amicitiam*], "yoking" men together, inspiring love (*amor*). Manly honor (*virtus; illud honestum*) has a "copulative" or "linking" function: Cicero *Off.* 1.55–56 ("But nothing is more conducive to loving and pairing [*amabilius ac copulatius*] than similarity of character between good men").

37. Cicero on male friendship as basis of the state: see, e.g., Konstan 1994–95; Leach 1993. Heroic pairs: Halperin 1990: 75–87.

38. Public *devotio* to Germanicus: Versnel 1980 (esp. 562–77). Tac. *Germ.* 14.1; Ammianus 16.12.60. Curchin 1996: 143 (*Germanoi*, subgroup of *Keltoi;* Dio 53.12.5–6). Germanicus' German campaigns 14–16 CE (his triumph in 17 CE), *F.* 1.285–86; natural father's (Drusus') successes, death in Germany, *F.* 1.597–98 (addressing Germanicus). Honoring Tiberius' German triumph and rebuilding temple of Concordia Augusta (12 CE), *F.* 1.645–46. Altar of the Three Gauls: Liv. *Epit.* 139 (12 BCE; census, altar's vow, says Taylor 1931: 208–9, fig. 45, coin), Suet. *Claud.* 2 (10 BCE, altar's dedication); see Fishwick 2004, III.3: 105–20, also III.1: 13–19; I.1, pls. I.XI–XIII. *Ara Ubiorum* (Two Germanies), by 9 CE, Tac. *Ann.* 1.57; altar of Augustus on the Elbe banks (2 BCE), Dio 55.10a; Benjamin and Raubitschek 1959.

39. Germanicus' address to the troops in mutiny in Germany echoes loyalty oaths (Wardle 1997): Tac. *Ann.* 1.42.1 (*non mihi uxor aut filius patre et re publica cariores sunt*) Cf. *CIL* II.172 (*ILS* 190), just after Caligula's accession in 37 CE, lines 10–11: *neq(ue) me <neque> liberos meos/ eius salute cariores habebo*, and *ILS* 8781.15–16 (3 BCE to Augustus and his descendants). Roller 2001: 59–62 examines the idiom in Lucan's retrojection of fractured loyalty onto the civil war (1.373–86, Laelius's oath, and 7.318–22, Caesar's appropriation), and notes (2001: 61n86) the possible origin of such oaths in the late republic (Diod. Sic. 37.11, M. Livius Drusus, 91 BCE).

40. Ov. *P.* 2.1 (to Germanicus), 2.5 (asking Salanus to address Germanicus), 4.8 (asking Suillius to address Germanicus), 4.13 (addressing Carus regarding Germanicus).

41. Roller 2001: 59–62 cites such loyalty oaths as *ILS* 8781, sworn (in Greek) by residents of Paphlagonia in 3 BCE to Augustus and his descendants, and *ILS* 190 of 37 CE on Tiberius' accession (*CIL* II.172), the same year of *devotio* to Caligula in Rome, Dio Cass. 59.8.3). Earlier loyalty oaths to generals: Diod. Sic. 37.11 (to M. Livius Drusus in

91 BCE). "Imperial" oaths (cf. Lucan, *BC* 1.357–86; Laelius to Caesar; 7.318–22) deconstructed devotion to all others: Roller 2001: 59–62.

42. Men devoted themselves as gladiators for Caligula's health (Suet. *Gaius* 12.2). Caligula compelled some to fulfill vows; one, driven out of town, killed as "scapegoat": Suet. *Calig.* 27.2. Dio Cassius 59.8.3 (year 37 CE) names "devotees," plebeian Publius Afranius Potitus and equestrian Atanius Secundus. Gladiatorial *devotio* connected with idealized elite male self-sacrifice: Barton 1993: 15, 40–45. Elites may have vowed pantomime performances: Slater 1994: 132n71. Suet. *Calig.* 30: Caligula criticized equestrians as "devotee of the stage and arena" (*ut scaenae harenaeque devotum*).

43. For *Tabula Larinas* (*TL*): Levick 1983: 105–8. For prior restrictions on public performance by members of the upper classes: Lebek 1990; McGinn 1992; Slater 1994:140–43. For decree of 11 CE, *TL* 17–21; Dio 56.25.7–8. While Dio does not say the equestrians fought as *devotio pro salute principis,* such dedication would provide cover for Augustus' grant of permission.

44. Rival poets as gladiators: Hor. *Epist.* 2.2.97–98. Ovid as gladiator: *P.* 1.5.37 (to Cotta Maximus), 2.8.51–56 (Cotta Maximus), 4.16.51–52; *Tr.* 2.17 (to Augustus) and 4.6.31–34. *Militia* among Getae, an exilic motif: e.g., *Tr.* 4.1.69–86. Willing gladiatorial combat and elite military *devotio:* Barton 1993: 40–45.

45. *Munera* as most popular entertainment on imperial cult days: Fishwick 1991 (II.1: 574–874). Cf. amphitheater near Federal altar at Ludgunum (Lyon, started 10–15 CE by C. Iulus Rufus and *nepos:* Fishwick 2004 (III.3): 307–36 (esp. 306).

46. *Tituli* of *devoti* for Caligula: Suet. *Calig.* 12.2; Beard 1992: 42; Veyne 1983: 288–89. Cf. *F.* 1.12, Germanicus gets *cum Druso praemia* [cf. *munera,* 2.17] *fratre* (1.12) with gladiators Drusus presented in 15 CE n his own and Germanicus' name (above).

47. Miller 1991: 143–47 (with bibliography) surveys rival theories that part of the preface of February had once introduced the whole *Fasti.*

48. *Parentatio:* Scullard 1981: 74–79, esp. 74–76. L-S, *munus,* II.B.2; Cat. 101.3; Verg. *Aen.* 11.25, 6.85.

49. Augustus' body carried by senators through the *Porta Carmentalis* to the Campus Martius: Suet. *Aug.* 100; Tac. *Ann.* 1.8; Dio 56.42.1 (senate, equestrian order, their wives, praetorian guard and all others in the city). *Decursio equitum* around the funeral pyre: Dio 56.42.2. Equestrian *decursio* for deceased Antoninus Pius on base of the column of Antoninus Pius: Richardson 1992: 94. *Equites* gathered Augustus' cremated remains: Suet. *Aug.* 100; Dio 56.42.4 (Livia oversaw *equites*). *Equites* in Augustus' political ideology: Yavetz 1984: 16–20.

50. Equestrian display at Anchises' funeral games: Verg. *Aen.* 5.545–603. Cf. *Equirria:* Feb. 27, *F.* 2,857–62; March 14, *F.* 3.515–22.

51. On Sacred Band of Thebes: Plut. *Pelopidas* 18–19. Sparta: e.g., Xen. *Lac. Pol.* 2.12–14; Arist. *Pol.* 2.10.1272a22–26; Plut. *Lyc.* 17.1, 18.4. Two views of Antinous' death: he "devoted" his life—died—in exchange for the health of Hadrian (*eum devotum pro Hadriano*); secondly, perhaps erotic despair: *Historia Augusta* (*de vita Hadriani*) 14.5–7, esp. 6. Surrendering one's life for another, ideal homosocial love: Xen. *Anab.* 7.4.7; Plut. *Dial.* 761c etc. cited at Dover 1989: 50–52. Nisus and Euryalus, *Aen.* 9; cf. *John* 15:13.

52. Mentioning no eroticism, Val. Max. 2.6.11 and Caesar, *BG* 3.22.1 emphasize daring *amicitia* (Plut. *Sert.* 14 and Serv. *G.* 4.218). Others attest sexuality (Arist. *Pol.* 2.9.7 and 2.6.6 [1269b], Athen. 13.603A). Addressing Romans, Posidonius (in Diodorus Siculus 5.32.7) and Strabo (*Geogr.* 4.4.6 [C119]) cite homosexuality in Celtic bands among predatory savageries (human sacrifice) or as violation of young nobles (cf., e.g., Marius' tri-

bune C. Lusius, Val. Max. 6.1.12; centurion C. Laetorius Mergus, Dion. Hal. 16.4; Val. Max. 6.1.11). Aristotle and Athenaeus offer famous Greek *comparanda:* Spartans and Sacred Band of Thebes. See Greenberg 1988: 111–12. Performers as sexually suspect and class-abasing *(infamis):* Edwards 1993.

53. Elite male anxiety over activity-passivity in sex, gender, and other fields: e.g., Gleason 1990, 1995, 1999; Gunderson 2000; Barton 1993, 2001, esp. 34–87; Richlin 1997a; Williams 1997, 1999. Anxiety about feminization (castration) in male subjectivity, its contemporary use in modern film: Silverman 1992, e.g., 52–121 ("Historical Trauma and Male Subjectivity"). See Skinner 1997 (Cat. 63), revising modern Freudian "castration" (feminization or male passivity). In Cat. 63 self-castration symbolizes Attis' ultimate devotion to Cybele.

54. *Devotio* to Germanicus: Versnel 1980; e.g., Tac. *Ann.* 2.82 (his death prompted mass *devotio*); Suet. *Calig.* 5 (exposure of newborns dramatizing betrayal by the gods). Cf. honors for Germanicus at Tac. *Ann.* 1.83. Family group sculptures were common; see esp. Ov. *P.* 2.8 (to Cotta Maximus); *P.* 4.9.105–10 (his house shrine of the Caesars). Germanicus' children with Agrippina: Lindsay 1995; significance for Germanicus' position: Suet. *Aug.* 34 (Germanicus' fertility as a model for equestrian men). Cf. posthumously erected *arcus* or *Ianus Germanici* (19 CE) with statues of Germanicus and family in the Circus Flaminius, near statues of Augustus and the *Domus Augusta* (by C. Norbanus Flaccus, consul, in 15 CE; Tac. *Ann.* 1.55.1): Richardson 1992: 25 ("Arcus Germanici"); *Tabula Siarensis* (*ZPE* 55 [1984]: 55–82 with Tac. *Ann.* 2.83); Flory 1996. Versnel 1970 on divine felicity and fertility attending the military *imperator* and *triumphator;* also Beard, North, and Price 1998, 1: 44–45, 142–43.

55. Prayer and hymn language in the dedication: e.g., Subias-Konofal 2003; Fantham 1985. On *F.* 1.20 (Germanicus compared to the "Clarian god" Apollo): e.g., Le Bonniec 1965: 26; Bömer 1957–1958, 2: 10. Ov. *Ars.* 2.80; *Met.* 1.516, 11.413; cf. Vergil, *Aen.* 3.360. Callim. *Hymn* 2.70; *Pal. Anth.* 9.525.11.

56. Jan. 1, the date when consuls traditionally offered *vota pro salute rei publicae* to Jupiter Optimus Maximus (upon entry into magistracy; Degrassi 1963: 389). Ovid notes these *vota: F.* 1.63–86, *P.* 4.4.29–34 (to Sextus Pompeius); see also Dio 21.63.7 (217 BC); Dio fr. 102.12. I, p. 347 ed. Boiss (86 BCE); Dio 45 17.9 (43 BCE); Tac. *Ann.* 4.70. In 44 BCE, *vota pro salute rei publicae* were joined with *vota pro Caesare* (Dio 44.6.1, 44.50.1); in 30 BCE, with *vota pro salute imperatoris* (Dio 51.19.7), perhaps with the family (Dio 59.3.4, 37 CE; 59.9.2, 38 CE). Suet. *Tib.* 54.1 (Germanicus' sons). In 38 CE vows for the emperor and *domus* were separated from those of the state and placed on Jan. 3, usual date for the *Compitalia,* a moveable feast (Degrassi 1963: 390–91).

57. Tiberius' letter to Senate at Suet. *Tib.* 67 (Tac. *Ann.* 6.6) manipulates language of prayer-*devotio* to the senate: *dii me deaeque peius perdant quam cotidie perire sentio, si scio* and *si quando autem, . . . de moribus meis devotoque vobis animo dubitaveritis* (a conditional clause addressing the senators).

58. The formula: Appel 1909:146. Examples: Appel 1909, no. 34 (= *ILS* 5032 = *CIL* VI. 2028) from the *Acta Fratrum Arvalium* (probably Tiberius' reign): *si . . . eventum bonum ita uti nos sentimus dicere dederis* (cf.Appel n. 36 [pp. 21–22], n. 37 [p. 22] and 39). Cf. Eumolpus' spoof at Petron. *Satyr.* 85: *domina Venus, si ego hunc puerum basiavero, ita ut ille non sentiat, cras illi par columbarum donabo;* again at Petron. *Satyr.* 86. On *scimus* (Ov. *F.* 1.23) in conditional clauses of *devotio* and *consecratio:* see phrases at Appel 1909, no. 21 (= Macrob. *Sat.* 3.9.10): *si haec ita faxitis, ut ego sciam sentiam intellegamque.* Likewise at Appel 1909, no. 22 (Macrob. *Sat.* 3.9.7–8). Ovid echoes *votum pro salute* offered each

New Year by consuls and others, Degrassi 1963: 389. Dio 51.19.17, 59.3.7 (37 CE, Caligula's reign) with *CIL* VI.2028 (=*ILS* 5032, Acta Arv. For 38 CE). Ovid's request for felicity of year (*F.* 1.26, 63–64).

59. Appel 1907: 19 (no. 34), dated to 38 at *CIL* VI. 2028. Due to lacunae, imperial names are not legible. Similar quadrennial vows to the emperor are attested by Augustus (*Res Gestae* 9) and by a denarius (16 BCE, minted by L. Mescinius Rufus) having an obverse legend reading in part: *votum susceptum pro salute Imperatore Caesaris* (*RIC* 358).

60. *F.* 1.63–86 celebrates inauguration of consuls, January 1, traditional date for *vota pro salute rei publicae.* Inaugural *vota pro salute: ex P.* 4.4.23–34 (imagined inaugural *vota* of Sextus Pompeius in 14 CE); *ex P.* 4.9.49–56 (of C. Pomponius Graecinus, *consul suffectus,* May, 16 CE). Cf. *F.* 1.587–616 with sources at Degrassi 1963: 396–97; Tertull. *Apol.* 35 (*augeat Iuppiter annos*), and devotions on anniversary of emperor's accession: Plin. *Epist.* 10.52 (Bithynia; honoring Trajan's accession, Jan. 28; oath of allegiance from soldiers; celebrated 110 CE); 10.53 (Trajan's acknowledgment); similar, 10.102–3. *Vota pro salute,* Jan. 3: Plin. *Epist.* 10. 35 (110 CE, Bithynia; 10.36: Trajan's recognition); sim. 10.100–101 (10.111; *commilitones* and *provinciales* vie to take up the *vota*). Börner 1957–1958: 2 compares *F.* 1.613 to protocols of *Arvales.* Versnel 1980: 568 and nn. 134–36 cites the formula as *devotio.* Cf. Henzen 1874: 197 and 207 (3rd cent. CE); *Der neue Pauly,* 3 (1996): 493–94. Augustus' prayer to the *Moerae* (Fates), *Acta Sacrorum Saeculaorum* (17 BCE); *ILS* 5050, 93–95, . . . *quaeso precorque uti imperium maiestatemque p. R.] | quiritium duelli domique au[xitis utique simper Latinum nomen tueamini, incolumitatem sempiter-] | nam victoriam valetudine[m.* On *augurium Salutis* at the *Ara Pacis Augustae:* Dio 51.19.2, 51.20.4; Suet. *Aug.* 31; Torelli 1982: 34–35.

61. Earlier near-personifications of *Pagina* include, e.g., Ov. *Am.* 1.1.17 (*cum bene surrexit versu nova pagina primo,/ attenuate nervos proximus ille meos. Tr.* 2.303–4: *et procul a scripta solis meretricibus arte / summovet ingenuas pagina prima manus*); Prop. 2.21.1–4, 2.34b.89–90 (*haec etiam docti confessa est pagina Calvi,/ cum caneret miserae funera Quintiliae*); 3.1.17–18, 3.3.21 (*cur tua praescriptos evectast pagina gyros?*); Prop. 3.25.17–18 (*has tibi fatalis cecinit mea pagina diras*).

62. Rhetorical φαντασία (*visio*), a type of *enargeia* (vividness), emotionally sways the speaker, then audience (Quint. *Inst.* 8.3.88, 6.2.29–31) or aids memory (10.7.15). In Hellenistic (Stoic) theory of imagination and aesthetics: see, e.g., Pollitt 1974: 58–63, 293–97; Imbert 1980; Goldhill 1994. As "imaginative ingenuity" it is related to *ingenium,* Pollitt 1974: 387; Bundy 1927.

63. Trafficking: Sedgwick 1990: 15. "Submission" of *Pagina* (*subitura* 19; cf. [*sub*]*missa* 20) recalls Ovid's personification of exilic Books (*libri*) as his freedmen-child surrogate (*libri* and *liberti*) between their father-patron and potential patrons: *Tr.* 1.1, 3.1. Nagle 1980: 83. Cf. Hor. *Epist.* 1.20 on Book as trafficked slave. Sexual passivity associated with slavery and femininity: e.g., Walters 1997; Williams 1999; Edwards 1993; Joshel 1992b: 30–31.

64. For this anxiety, see Rudich 1993, introduction.

65. Gender, sexuality, and external inspiration: Fowler 2002; Sharrock 2002. On performative gender identity, gender subversion, and "gender trouble": Butler 1990.

66. Cf. Catullus (Skinner 1997; Fitzgerald 1995: 34–58) and Tibullus, Propertius and Horace (Oliensis 1997).

67. See Oliensis 1997. For soldier's oath, *sacramentum,* Hor. *C.* 2.17.9–12 (Versnel 1980: 569–70 connects Horace's *sacramentum* with *devotio*). Cf. Prop. 3.9.47 to Maecenas: *te duce vel Iovis arma canam.*

68. Cf. *Her.* 9, Deianira uses gender shame against Hercules; *Ars.* 1.497–524, Ovid recognizes that some males (the *male vir,* 524) signal, via "feminine" grooming, their desire of a man. For "sexual identity: in urbane Rome (*pace* Foucault), see, e.g., Habinek's essay in Habinek 1997.

69. Less careful than Horace's patrons: cf. Suet. *Vit. Hor.* for Maecenas' poems; Augustus' letters vying for Horace, positioned as "woman" or as *phallus* (e.g., Augustus' calling H. "my penis"). Erotic vocabulary of *Am.* 1.1–2: Kennedy 1993: 58–63; Adams 1982: 179–80.

70. At *A.A.* 1.177–228, esp. 219–28, Ovid tells Gaius Caesar that his anticipated Triumph over the Parthians would offer erotic opportunities.

71. Germanicus' triumph on May 26, 17: Tacit. *Ann.* 2.41 (17 CE) with 1.55 and 2.26; Degrassi 1963: 462 (*Fasti Amiternini,* May 26); *Fasti Ostienses* (*Inscr. Italiae* XIII.1, n. 5 with supplement). Syme 1978: 46, 63 identifies *F.* 1.285–86 as referring to the triumph of 17 CE. If 17 CE, Ovid did not revise his May 26 entry to reflect the triumph (*F.* 5.731–32).

72. Desire and mantic divination: e.g., Plat. *Phaed.* 242b–c, 244b–d. Cf. reins of soul's horses: 237d–e. Muses and erotic inspiration: Prop. 2.30.25–30; 3.3.33–38 (Calliope's inspiring erotic touch). Cf. Cassandra's prophecy from Apollo (Aesch. *Ag.* 1202–12; Hyg. *Fab.* 93; Serv. *Aen.* 2.247; Apollod. *Bibl.* 3.12.5). Sibyl's quasi-sexual possession by Apollo: Verg. *Aen.* 6.77–80; Fowler 2002: 149 (cf. Lucan's Phemonoe: *BC* 5.184–97; Fowler 2002: 149–50). Cf. Ovid's Sibyl at *Met.* 14.101–53 remembers Apollo's love. Cranae (*F.* 6.100–130): Janus rapes, repays her with magical whitethorn (*virga Ianalis*), which she uses as witchdoctor: Frazer 1929, 4: 141–46. Ovid's Carmentis as *vates* penetrated by divine powers producing prophecy: *F.* 6.537–40 (she "becomes full of her god in all her chest," 6.538); a deepened male (Apollo's) voice transgenders her somewhat (6.539–40); cf. Tiresias' sex changes: Ov. *Met.* 3.316–38; Paus. 9.33.2; Hyg. *Fab.* 75; Apollod. *Bibl.* 3.6.7. Also *F.* 1.473–474, where Carmentis "had conceived" (*conceperat*) ethereal fires (1.475) and prophesies "full of god" (*carmina plena dei*).

73. Wariness of appearances, an Ovidian theme: e.g., *Ars* 1.459–86, 3.625–30, 671–746 (Cephalus and Procris as model); *Rem.* 357–60.

74. As a general, Germanicus undertook missions from the temple of Mars Ultor (cf. Dio 55.10.1–10); as *flamen Augustalis* he worshiped Divus Augustus' golden image in temple of Mars Ultor (Dio 56.46.4; until Claudius completed a temple of Divus Augustus). An arch honored Germanicus beside Mars Ultor (19 CE; Tac. *Ann.* 2.64; *CIL* VI.911). His *sellae* or *sedes curules,* posthumously honoring Germanicus as *flamen* or *sodalis Augustalis,* were stored inside and transported from Mars Ultor to theaters (Tac. *Ann.* 2.83; *Tab. Heb.* 50–54; Oliver and Palmer 1954: 231).

75. Hinds 1992: 87–105

76. Temple of Mars in Circus Flaminius (D. Iunius Brutus, 133 BCE) contained seated, naked (disarmed) Mars shield aside, sword in hand ("Ares Ludovisi"); nude Venus and Cupid under Mars' leg (Plin. *H.N.* 36.26); Richardson 1992: 245. "Ares Ludovisi" (by Scopas; copy Mus. Naz. Rom. 8602): *LIMC* II.1.514 (no. 23), II.1.481 (no. 24 Simon); II.2.360 (fig. 24). Sacrifice to Mars, 23 Sept., Augustus' birthday, commemorates Augustan restoration (Degrassi 1963: 512). Cult images in Temple of Mars Ultor (Algiers relief): Armed Mars Ultor, Venus with Cupid holding sword, Divus Julius: Richardson 1992: 162; Ov. *Tr.* 2.295–96; Galinsky 1996: 208, fig. 120; Zanker 1988: 195–201, fig. 151. Kellum 1996: 177–78, 1997: 176; *CIL* XI 3805, 5165; Galinsky 1996: 233–34.

77. Lucr. 1.1–61 seeks Venus' help to seduce Mars and stop civil wars from distracting men from philosophy (24–30).

78. Dupont 1999: 101–70: "kisses" as metaphors of eroticized literary exchange.

79. Laws of 18 BCE and 9 CE, collectively called *Lex Julia et Papia*, punished unmarried men and women with heavier taxes and rewarded marriage and childbirth (Dio 54.16.1–2). In proposing the legislation, Augustus read aloud a speech by Q. Caecilius Metellus Macedonicus (from 131 BCE), who had previously advocated a law requiring men to marry and produce children (Liv. Per. 59). State purview over adultery was claimed by the Augustan laws. On the legislation's promotion of marriage and fertility among the elite classes, see Suet. *Aug.* 34 and Treggiari 1991 and 1996. Romulus and Remus in the Lupercal were depicted (now in fragments) on the Ara Pacis Augustae (Zanker 1988: 205–6; Torelli 1982: 27–61, esp. 37–39), in other contemporary relief sculpture (e.g., the terracota revetment in Zanker 1988: 205, fig. 158), as well as in wall paintings (e.g., the "foundation frieze" depicting the origins of Rome: Ling 1991: 111; Nash 1961–1962, 2: 359–63, figs. 1139–48). Silvia's tale and Lucretius' Venus invite immorality in women: Ovid, *Tr.* 2.259–60 and 261–62, quoting Lucr. 1.1. Again: *Tr.* 2.421–30. Cf. Silvia's (Ilia's) dream narrative at Enn. *Ann.* fr. 32–48 (Warmington) = 35–51 (Vahlen³).

80. Competition between Poseidon and Athena: Herodotus 8.55 (competition); Eur., *Troj.* 45–94; Apollod. *Bibl.* 3.14.1; cf. Hom. *Il.* 1.399–400, 15.213–17, 20.32–37. Represented on western front of the Parthenon in Athens (*LIMC* II.1.978–79, no. 234; Athena Promachos strikes the ground with her lance). Also no. 453 in *LIMC* II.1.996 and II.2.753 (photo: vase depicting Athena planting the *cuspis*; Poseidon with trident).

81. Mars and agriculture: Scullard 1981: 86. Dumézil 1996 (1970), 1: 205–45 prioritized Mars' warrior functions. But see Beard, North, and Price 1993, 1: 15–16 and n. 41, and sources cited (esp. Cato, *Agri.* 141). *Semina* (*F.* 1.10),"slips," "cuttings," in propagation: L-S, *semen* II.A; *OLD, semen* 3, citing Cato, *Agri.* 46.2; Var. *RR* 1.40.4; Vitruv. 8.3.12.

82. "Minerva" meaning "mind": e.g., Hor. *S.* 2.2.3, *Ars P.* 385; Cic. *Off.* 1.31.301, *Amicit.* 5.19; Paul. Ex Fest. 109: "Minerva." Actors, scribes met in the Aventine Temple of Minerva: Cf. Festus 446–48L; Liv. 27.37.7 (207 BCE); *collegium poetarum* met in the temple of Minerva Capta. See Richardson 1992: 254–55 ("Minerva, Aedes [1]").

83. *Cuspis* of the phallus in literary farce, Pomponius 69 *coleatam cuspidem* ("the betesticled lance"; Adams 1982: 20, 219). The usage belongs to standard metaphors for the penis as "weapon"; cf. Adams 1982: 14–19, 19–22.

84. Ovid earlier (3.1–166) manipulates Mars' competitiveness with Greeks to seek his help (see chapter 4; cf. Mars' competition with Minerva, 3.5, 175–76). Verbal similarities between persuasion at *F.* 3.101–4 (*artes* 101, *facundum* 102, *artem* 103, *disertus*, 104) and in dedication (*facundia* 1.21, *nostras artes* 1.23), emphasize weaponry skills as metaphorical eloquence (*Caesaris arma* 1.13; *civica arma*, oratory, 22).

85. Stephen Hinds 1992: 89–180 discussing Ovid's introduction to "March," Book 3.

86. Adams 1982: 19–22 and weaponry metaphor for the penis (e.g., *hasta*-phallus, *Priap.* 45.1).

87. Cf. Prop. 3.5.1 (cf. 3.4.1, *arma deus Caesar . . . meditatur*).

88. Cf. *castrensibus utilis armis*, and *semina* at Prop. 3.9.19–20. *Utilis* and *castra* at *F.* 3.173–74 appeared in Horos' warning to Propertius (4.1.135–40): "But fashion elegies, deceptive work: *this is your camp!*" (*at tu finge elegos, fallax opus: haec tua castra!* 135), where "you will endure military service under Venus' seductive weapons, and you will be an enemy *fit for Venus' boys*" (*militiam Veneris blandis patiere sub armis,/ et Veneris pueris utilis hostis eris*, 137–38). Cf. Prop. 4.8.27–28; Ov. *Am.* 3.8.9–28, *F.* 4.377–86. At *Am.* 3.15.15–20, Ovid withdraws Venus and Cupid's "military standards" (*aurea signa*) for heroic poetry. At *F.* 4.1–14, he returns to Venus' *signa*. Amatory *castra*: e.g., Tib. 2.3.34; Prop. 4.1.135–40; Ov. *Am.* 1.2.29–32, *Ars* 2.236, *Her.* 7.32 (Dido).

89. Erotic libido and didacticism in the *Ars am.*, Kennedy 2000: 159–76, esp. 170, quoting Plato, *Phaedrus* 276E–277A, on Ovid's Platonic use of carnal *amor* to structure *didaxis*. Kennedy 1993: 60. The *Remedia amoris* as resituating elegiac love in a broader discursive "horizon"enabling "healing" of desire: Conte 1994a: 35–65.

90. Ov. *H.* 11.48 (Canace writes of her pregnancy and birth pangs): "I was a raw recruit and new soldier for childbirth" (*et rudis ad partus et nova miles eram*).

91. On *morari*, Adams 1982: 178, "to spend the night," euphemistic for sex: Verg. *Aen.* 5.766; *CIL* IV.2060, *Romula hic cum Staphylo moratur* (prostitution?). On *pars* for sexual body parts: Adams 1982, index, esp. 45, "special class" where a demonstrative (cf. *hac parte*) modifies *pars*, common in Ovid; e.g., *Am.* 3.7.73, *A. A.* 2.584, 3.804 (*pars ista*); with added relative clauses, Petron. 129.1, 132.12; Ov. *A. A.* 2.707–8; *Priap.* 37.8–9, 48.1–2. Cf. *pars obscena* at *Ars* 2.584, *Priap.* 9.1; *pars pudenda, A. A.* 2.618.

92. Mars' male or female objects: cf. Polypyrgonices, braggart soldier in Plaut. *Miles* 1102–1114. Male homosocial *castra* imply "castration": Serv. *Aen.* 3.519, *dicta autem "castra" quasi casta, vel quod illic castretur libido: nam numquam his intererat mulier* (Isid. *Orig.* 9.3.44; 15.2.6). Ov. *Ars* 3.559–60, woman offers sex to virgin recruit (*hic rudis et castris nunc primum notus Amoris, / qui tetigit thalamos praeda novella tuos*). Cf. Mars' *nunc primum* and *nova castra, F.* 3.173–74. Cf. Mars' desire of Minerva (*F.* 3.675–696): *armifer armiferae correptus amore Minervae* (381); *armifer* and *armiferae* emphasize sameness, "homosociality," between a god and a masculinized goddess.

93. Cupid's arrow penetrates Ovid, *Am.* 1.1.21–30; "stick" or "weapon" prods, like the *thyrsus* of Tragoidia at *Am.* 3.1.23–24; cf. *thyrsus* of Bacchus at *Am.* 3.15.17–20. Cf. Lucr. 1.921–27, esp. 922–23, *acri / percussit thyrso laudis spes magna meum cor.* Cf. Venus' myrtle at *Fasti* 4.15–18 (Venus touches Ovid's temples), and *A. A.* 3.53–56 (Venus gives Ovid myrtle leaves, berries).

94. Ov. *H.* 18.175–78 (Leander to Hero) uses *calescere* and *flamma* for passion. Ter. *Eun.* 1.2.5, *calescere* for erotic inflammation. *Agitare*, "to masturbate": Adams 1982: 144–45, citing "the obscene interpretation" of *incipiunt agitata tumescere* (Verg. *Georg.* 1.357) attributed to Celsus (Quint. *Inst.* 8.3.47). With *clunes* as object, *agitare* suggests *cevere* of the passive partner in anal intercourse: see Adams 1982: 194, citing Juvenal 2.21.

95. Plato's discourse as (re)productive love between men (*Symposium, Phaedrus*): e.g., DuBois 1988: 169–83; Halperin 1990: 257–308. Cf. Quint. *Inst.* 2.9.3 (mixed anatomical-agricultural metaphor for education), *Inst.* 3.6.60 (*semina*, elements of rhetoric).

96. Cf. scattering *semina* of doctrine at Cic. *Div.* 1, 3, 6, *Fin.* 5, 7, 18 (Stoic context). Quint. *Inst.* 2. 20. 6 ("germs" of virtues, divine reason, native to a person); Prop. 3.9.19–20 (*naturae semina suae*). Tac. *Or.* 33 (*initia et semina veteris eloquentiae*).

97. *Semen*, meaning *causa, origo*, via biological etiology: *OLD*, "semen," 7A; L-S, *semen*, II. Sowing *semina* (*spermata*), metaphor of discourse: Plato's dialectic, *Phaedrus* 276E–277A; DuBois 1988: 177–78. Cf. Varr. *LL* 6.7, on *disertus*, "eloquent" from *sero*, to "sow."

98. Like his student Ovid, Aurelius (or Arelius) Fuscus received official disapproval: he was degraded from equestrian rank because of sme scandal (Plin. *H.N.* 33.12.152); Ovid was exiled.

99. Tacitus (*Ann.* 2.54.3–4) reports Germanicus' consultation of Apollo Clarius in 18 CE; Ovid died 17–18 CE. Would Ovid have known of Germanicus' relations with Claros? Ovid also makes reference to Claros prior to Germanicus' visit: *A. A.* 2.79; *Met.*1.514, 11.410. Moreover, preparations for and perhaps news of Germanicus' eastern itinerary probably preceded his arrival.

100. Slight sexual innuendo of *subitura* (*subire*): *Priap.* 33.12; Adams 1982: 191.

Chapter Three

1. Taylor and Holland 1952: possible association of Janus with *Fasti consulares*. Janus' "bifocal" implication of ambiguity in the poem: Hardie 1991; also Barchiesi 1991 (Janus supplements inadequacy of the Muses, constructing program for Ovid's ambiguous poetry); Barchiesi 1997a: 230–35. Boyle 1997 treats Ovid's *Fasti* as a major work of exile thwarting Augustus' control of discourse by producing a Janus-like text.

2. Gunning 1994 outlines how preliminary remarks by showmen guided expectations of early film "marvels" (e.g., trains racing into the viewer). Thaumaturgic showmanship in antiquity (cf. *agyrtai, circulatores,* street magicians of sorts): Dickie 2001; MacMullen 1981: 14–34 (mime dancing mixed with displays of divine images); Plecket 1965 (imperial "mysteries" orchestrating sudden revelation of *imagines* using theatrical lighting). Ovid's Janus compares not only with Callim. *H.* 2 (to Apollo), but also to Herm. *Corp. Herm.* (*Poem.*1–2). Luck 1985 passim, e.g., 135–59 (*thaumatourgoi,* miracle workers; often healing), 149 (epiphany reported in Aelius Aristides, *Sacred Orations* 2), 163–225 (epiphanies of *daemones* and ghosts). Ovid's narrating marvels of metamorphosis: Wheeler 1999. Cf. quakery of *vates* in pre-Augustan sense of street preachers and seers: Enn. *Trag. Fr.* 332–36 (*supertitiosi vates impudentesque harioli*). Naev. 231–34; Lucr. 1.102–5; Newman 1967: 13–18.

3. The shift from "things" in the calendar (*haec,* 61) to Janus as "present" (*ecce . . . Ianus adest,* 63–64) implies that Ovid has presented the code as a "chain" or series of events whose explication should not be broken up because they belong to one symbolic system (the *seriem rerum* at 62 is the calendar code, not Ovid's imaginative elaboration of it). Ovid's "gathering" of calendar definitions into one unit (1.27–62) contrasts with Verrius' distribution of definitions into distinct days within his inscribed calendar.

4. *Nuncupatio,* the utterance of inaugural vows (*OLD nuncupatio* 1). See Degrassi 1963: 389 and *RE* Suppl. Bd. 14 (1974) *votum* p. 969 (Werner Eisenhut). Liv. 21.63.7–12 and 22.1.4–5 using the verb *nuncupare* and the noun *nuncupatio.*

5. *RE* Suppl. XIV.1974.969 (*votum*) connects *F.* 1.75ff indirectly with the *nuncupatio votorum publicorum;* cf. parallels between the *vota publica* and Ovid's own prayer in *F.* 1.63–74—especially the three levels of Roman hierarchy secured by *vota publica:* see Degrassi, *Insr. It.* 13.2.389 and Ov. *Ex P.* 4.4.29ff. Julius Caesar in *vota pro salute* in 44 BCE: Dio 44.6.1, 44.50.1. Prayer *pro salute imperatoris* in 30 BCE: Dio 51.19.7. For imperial family in 37 CE, Dio 59.3.4; in 38, Dio 59.9.2.; Suet. *Tib.* 54.1

6. Ovid, master of ceremonies, influenced by Callimachus: Miller 1980.

7. Following Zizek 1993: 203 (also Zizek 1997: 32). Kay 2003: 136 provides this succinct description of the theft of Enjoyment in fantasy's retroactive narratives of how some "others" have plundered our supposedly original complete enjoyment.

8. Turner 1969: 133–96: *communitas,* ritualized at seasonal rites of passage, is "an unstructured or rudimentarily structured and relatively undifferentiated comitatus, community, or even communion of equal individuals." Turner 1974: 24, 48–49; 274: "The bonds of communitas are anti-structural in the sense that they are undifferentiated, equalitarian, direct, . . . communitas is spontaneous, . . . not shaped by norms, . . . not institutionalized."

9. The calendar of the Decemvirs (450 BCE) aligned consular and festival years, addressing concerns about stable transmission of power after creation of the consulship: Michels 1967: 98, 119–30.

10. Ovid identifies as an equestrian, imagining his presence at Graecinus' inauguration day (*P.* 4.9.15–24).

11. Frazer 1929, 2: 83 interprets *duces* as "the emperor Tiberius, his son Drusus and his adoptive son Germanicus." Ovid at *F.* 4.408 uses the term *dux* to refer to the emperor. Ovid militarizes these leaders because it is by their "work" (*labore*, 67) that land and sea have "peace with security" (*secura otia*).

12. "Jupiter, when he looks from his own citadel upon the whole world, has nothing to watch over, except what is Rome's" (*Iuppiter arce sua totum cum spectet in orbem,/ nil nisi Romanum quod tueatur habet, F.* 1.85–86).

13. Problems with the debated number of Augustan closures of Janus: Syme 1979.

14. Peace, restraint of *Bella* (hostilities): 1.121–24, 277–88. Janus denies participation in warfare at 1.253–54, 265–72. For war-peace at tension, cf. Germanicus, *Aratea* 5–10; cf. Verg. *Aen.* 1.293–96 for imprisoned Furor of war in a Janus-like structure, which Servius (*ad Aen.* 1.294) associates with Apelles' painting at the entry of the Forum Augustum showing War (*Bellum*), hands tied behind his back (cf. Plin. *H.N.* 35.93: *restrictis ad terga manibus*) along with personified Triumph, (Plin. *H.N.* 35: 27).

15. *Iane biceps, . . . / solus de superisque tua terga vides* (*F.* 1.65–66). The description of Janus as "the origin of the silently gliding year" (65) suits Ovid's prayer to Janus while beginning his account of the Roman year and the gods' month, January. However, other epithets Ovid uses are not the honorific ones of pragmatic, non-literary prayers to Janus (e.g., Janus as *sancte pater* [Mart. 10.28.7], *sator omnium rerum* [Lact. 1.23.4], and *annorum nitidique mundi* [Mart. 10.28.1] or "god of gods" in the Salian hymn at Varr. *LL* 7.27). Instead, the poet focuses not just upon Janus' biformity or deformity—his two heads (*biceps*)—but also upon the fact that he is the only god who watches his rear (*solus de superis qui tua terga vides,* 66).

16. Vergil describes a Janus as *bifrons* or two-faced, in *Aen.* 7.180, but Vergil is a literary source. Vergil does not refer to Janus' back(side)-watching (*tergum*). *Janus Geminus* in inscriptions (*ILS* 3319) seems to be more rare than *Ianus Pater* (*ILS* 3321, 5047, 5048, 3322, 3324) or even than *Ianus Augustus* (*ILS* 3327) or *Ianus Pater Augustus* (*ILS* 3320, 3323, 3325, 4473a). Repeating Ovidian phrasing, the fourth/fifth-century scholar Macrobius (*Sat.* 7.20) writes: *Ianum . . . qui creditur geminam faciem praetulisse ut quae ante quae post tergum essent intueretur.*

17. Bramble 1974: 115–17. *OLD*, s.v. *postica,* says the word means "backdoor," ignoring related terms, such as *posticum* (neuter) as the buttocks or anus: see *non peperit, verum postica parte profudit* ("did not give birth, but poured forth from the rear"), Lucil. ap. Non. 217, 17; and *retrimenta cibi, quae exierunt per posticum* ("the holdback of food, which exited through the rear"), Varr. ap. Non. 217, 24. The word also appears in the plural at Arn. 2. 54 cited at L-S, *posticus* II.B (*posticum, -i*), definition 4. See also Adams 1982: 115

18. On the stork as derisive gesture behind one's back: Persius 1.58 schol; *Schol. Cod. Bern.*: *ciconia dixit quia manus solent formare derisiones digitis in modum ciconi<ni> rostri plicatis, latenter derident recitantes.* Jerome, *Epist.* 125.18 (*si subito respexeris aut ciconiarum deprehendes post te colla curvari aut manu auriculas agitari asini aut aestuantem canis protenti linguam*); Jer. *in Soph. Praef. P.* 671–72 (*numquam post tergum meum manum curvarent in ciconiam*). Bramble 1974: 116 cites Call. *Iamb.* fr. 192.5–13 (Pf.) for dog (with wagging tongue) and ass. More relevant (*pace* Bramble 1974.116n3) Call. *Iamb.* 191.82–83 (Pf.): "the Corycaean from behind grins (greedily) wagging his tongue like a dog, when it drinks, and says. . . ." An agricultural implement, *ciconia,* dug trenches (*sulcos*); "trench" is a euphemism for anus (Adams 1982: 24) and vagina (Adams 1982: 28, 83–84; Columella 3.13.11–12; *RE* III.2542; Daremberg-Saglio II.1171). Poles, stakes, and agricultural instruments as phallic metaphors: Adams 1982: 14–25.

19. A painting from an ancient columbarium of the Villa Doria Pamphili in Rome (25–20 BCE) shows a large bird, crane or stork, using its long beak to "tweak" the *tergum* of a naked pygmy bent over, headfirst: Bendinelli 1941, Tav. agg. 2, parete B, XIX, a (photo) and a' (Ruspi's watercolor, 1850): "combattimento di pigmei con una gru [crane]." Pygmies as objects of laughter in art: Clarke 1998: 42–46. Cranes (*grues*) linked with storks (*ciconiae*): Plin. *H.N.* 10.30.60, 54.111. War between Pygmies and cranes: *Pygmaioi*, in *LIMC* VII, 1 and 2, citing other sources, e.g., a Boeotian cantharus (Berlin Staatl. Mus. V I 3159), number 17 (v. 1, 595–96; v. 2, p. 471): four armed pygmies, one of whom is bent over, while a crane sits atop, poking his rear end.

20. Hats: Dieterich 1897. Their clacking linked *ciconiae* to entertainers, *crotalistae* and *crotalistria* (*crotalum*, castanet; see Prop. 4.8.39 and Petr. 55.6): esp. Publilius Syrus, *com. 7*; Suet., frag. 161, *ciconiarum (est) crotalare*; Plaut. *Truc.* 691. Cf. Ov. *Met.* 6.97: *sumptis quin candida pennis/ ipsa sibi plaudat crepitante ciconia rostro.*

21. Cf. the proverb, not cited by Bramble: *frons occipitio prior est* (Cat. *R.R.* 4), implying that a master derives more benefit from his slaves and workers by showing his face (watching them) than letting them see the back of his head. Also Plin. *H.N.* 18.5.6.31.

22. Aug. *CD* 7.2: *nam ipse primum Ianus, cum puerperium concipitur, unde illa cuncta opera sumunt exordium minutatim minutis distributa numinibus, aditum aperit recipiendo semini. ibi est et Saturnus propter ipsum semen; ibi Liber, qui marem effuso semine liberat; ibi Libera, quam et Venerem uolunt, quae hoc idem beneficium conferat feminae, ut etiam ipsa emisso semine liberetur.*

23. Adams 1982: 89 notes that the metaphor of door/anus is more common in Latin than door/vagina (e.g., Cat. 15.18 and 12; Pers. *Sat.* 4.36; *Priap.* 52.5). But cf. Isid., *Etym.* 8.11.69: *Iunonem dicunt quasi ianonem, id est ianuam, pro purgationibus feminarum eo quod quasi portas matrum natorum pandat et nubentum maritis;* 11.1.137: "*vulva vocata quasi valva, id est ianua ventris, vel quod semen recipiat, vel quod ex ea foetus procedat.* Henderson 1975: 137–39 (Aristoph. *Vesp.* 768, *Lys.* 250); Antiphilus, *AP* 9.415.6; and Eratosthenes, *AP* 5.242.3ff.).

24. *CD* 7.3: *confert enim selectus Ianus aditum et quasi ianuam semini; confert selectus Saturnus semen ipsum.*

25. See, for instance, duBois 1988, esp. ch. 3 ("field," 39–64) and ch. 4 ("Furrow," 65–85).

26. *Posticum* (neuter) as outhouse, bathroom: Lucil. ap. Non. 217, 20. *Posticum* = anus: *retrimenta cibi, quae exierunt per posticum,* Varr. ap. Non. 217, 24; also in plur., Arn. 2.54. See Lewis and Short, *posticus* and, e.g., *non peperit, verum postica parte profudit,* "did not give birth, but poured forth from the anus," Lucil. ap. Non. 217, 17

27. On *Ianus Consivius,* Macr. *Sat.* 1.9.16 says, "*consivium*" a *conserendo, id est a propagine generis humani, quae Iano auctore conseritur.* Human and agricultural reproduction are parallel. Thus, Janus can open a "door" for grain seed too. Cf. Ovid's *Sementiva,* or seed-sowing festival, *F.* 1.657–704 (ch. 5).

28. Aug. *CD* 7.4:

de Iano quidem non mihi facile quicquam occurrit, quod ad probrum pertineat. et fortasse talis fuerit, innocentius vixerit et a facinoribus flagitiisque remotius. Saturnum fugientem benignus excepit; cum hospite partitus est regnum, ut etiam civitates singulas conderent, iste Ianiculum, ille Saturniam. sed isti in cultu deorum omnis dedecoris adpetitores, cuius vitam minus turpem invenerunt, eum simulacri monstrosa deformitate turparunt, nunc eum bifrontem, nunc etiam quadrifrontem, tamquam geminum, facientes. an forte voluerunt, ut, quoniam plurimi dii selecti erubescenda perpetrando amiserant frontem, quanto iste innocentior esset, tanto frontosior appareret?

29. In Plato's *Symposium* (189–193d), Aristophanes tells of the origin of sexual desire in the splitting of the original two-sided human beings composed of female-female, male-male, and male-female doubles.

30. *Deformitas* applied metaphorically to character: L-S s.v. *deformitas* II and *OLD* s.v. *deformitas* 3 (morality) and 4 (taste). Cf. Ps. Aug. *serm* 129.1 PL 39, 2001 and Otto von Vercelli (10th c. CE) in Migne *PL* 134, 836 who links Janus to both sacrilege and perversity: Bömer 1957–1958, 2: 18.

31. "Cruisers of every vice" (for *omnis dedecoris appetitores*) ascribe to Janus' two heads qualities suited to their own cruising for sex: cf. Ovid's tale at *Fasti* 6.101–30, where Janus' double-face aids his rape of Carna ("flesh"). Juv. *Sat.* 2 cites bearded philosopher-types; although they seem manly in public, they perform the passive role behind closed doors.

32. *F.* 1.97–98: *extimui sensique metu riguisse capillos,/ et gelidum subito frigore pectus erat.*

33. Mental medium: cf. *percipe* at *F.* 1.165–66 answering Ovid's mere contemplation. Aural sensation marks divine realization at 1.181–82 (*templa patent auresque deum, nec lingua caducas/ concipit ulla preces, dictaque pondus habent*) and is nearly tangible at 1.183–84 (*desierat Ianus. nec longa silentia feci,/ sed tetigi verbis ultima verba meis*). Ovid's inaugural ecphrasis (1.73–86) engages readers in synthesis of sight, sound, and even smell, evoking imagination of an absent ceremony (1.73–86).

34. Statues of Peace, Salus, and Concordia, possibly at the Forum Shrine of Janus: cf *F.* 3.881–82 (March 30): *Ianus adorandus cumque hoc Concordia mitis et Romana Salus Araque Pacis erit.* Also Dio 54.35.2 on 11 BCE.

35. In exile Ovid lacks home and country (*P.* 4.4.7): *ecce domo patriaque carens oculisque meorum.* Imagined to be at Sextus Pompeius' home prior to inauguration, *P.* 4.4.23–28; after the inauguration, *P.* 4.4.41–42. Imagined present at Graecinus' home prior to inauguration, *P.* 4.9.9–22.

36. On "fantasy" as answer to the question *"Che vuoi?"*: Zizek 1989: 87–129, esp. 110–14. Myers 2003: 89 summarizes: *"Che vuoi?"* as shorthand for "What does the big Other [the anomaly of the symbolic order] want from me?" The question's very articulation distances the questioner from the symbolic order, and it indicates the failure of the Symbolic Order. Crucially it marks the "moment of subjectivity." Cf. Kay 2003: 13–14, 89–90, of relation of the *"Che vuoi?"* to hysterical symptoms of incessant doubt, on which see fear of attack, penetration *a tergo* as symptom of internal doubt in Edelman 1991.

37. Zizek, "Fantasy as a Political Category," in Wright and Wright 1999: 87–101; 93.

38. "Primal fantasies": Laplanche and Pontalis 1973: 331–32; Laplanche and Pontalis 1968: 18; Farmer 2000: 54. In psychoanalytic theory, these include primal scene (viewing one's own conception, cf. Janus), seduction (depicting the origin of one's sexual awakening), and castration (depicting the origin of one's gender).

39. Barchiesi 1997a: 232–33, citing *F.* 1.103 (*me Chaos antique . . . vocabant*); Call. *Ait.* fr. 2.3 Pf. (Χάεος γένεσιν); and Hes. *Theog.* 116 ("The beginning was Chaos . . ."); cf. *F.* 1.101 (Janus calls Ovid *vates operose dierum*) with Hesiod's *Works and Days*.

40. A distinct *deus* fashions raw material (*Met.* 1.5–20) at the beginning of time in the *Met.* 1.21–31. In the *Fasti* Janus professes to be Chaos, the consciousness behind cosmos, and also cosmos.

41. Retroactivity or deferred action, *Nachträglichkeit* (Freud), *Après-coup* (Lacan): Kay 2003: 18–19. Retroactivity, triggered by contemporary events, (re-) activates previously unrecognized meanings of prior (cf. primal) events.

42. Freud associated ambivalence with anal fixation. For this theory associated with "sodomitical" fantasy in Freud: Edelman 1991. Livy claims (Liv. 1.19.2) that Numa created the double-gated Janus shrine to impose, by closing and opening, control over the male impulse for violent war.

43. *F.* 1.145–48: *dixerat: et voltu, si plura requirere vellem,/ difficilem mihi se non fore pactus erat./ sumpsi animum, gratesque deo non territus egi,/ verbaque sum spectans plura locutus humum.*

44. Buds sprout, 152; trees grow leaves, 153; shoots grow from seed [*seminis*], 154, etc.

45. *F.* 1.161–64: *quaesieram multis; non multis ille moratus/ contulit in versus sic sua verba duos: / "bruma novi prima est veterisque novissima solis: / principium capiunt Phoebus et annus idem."*

46. *F.* 1.159–60: *tum patitur cultus ager et renovatur aratro. / haec anni novitas iure vocanda fuit.* The passage recalls Mars' calendar beginning with March; 1.39–40, 3.135–50, 4.25–26

47. *Bruma*, derived from an old Latin superlative *brevima* (< *brevis*), is the Latin for the "briefest" day of the year (Romans marked it on Dec. 25). Phoebus (the Sun) tracks human maturation: he is "born" at the solstice. At this time, he is his "shortest" (*brevima* > *bruma*) and therefore youngest (*novissimus*). As the months progress, the sun matures and grows "longer" ("taller").

48. *F.* 3.235–42, 4.85–114; cf. 4.1–18, esp. 7–8 to Venus: "Wounded or not, did I ever abandon your 'signs'? You are always my theme always my work."

49. *F.* 1.139–40: *sic ego perspicio caelestis ianitor aulae / Eoas partes Hesperiasque simul. Aula* traditionally referred to the palaces of Hellentistic or other kings. At *F.* 1.139 Janus' use of *caelestis aula* anticipates the subsequent reference to the Palatine residence of the emperor. Cf. Ov. *Met.* 1.176, *Palatia caeli.*

50. Power "graded" according to proximity to the emperor. Brokering access to imperial court: Wallace-Hadrill 1996 (*CAH²* X): 296–306 and 1989: 63–85, esp. 81–84.

51. The New Year's *strenae-stipes* are a ritual gift exchange linked to customs of salutation on New Year's. Roller 2001: 131–212 discusses how a gift-economy (debt-reciprocity) contributed to the formation of the emperor's authority. On *strenae*: Suet. *Aug.* 57, *Tib.* 34.2; Dio 57.8.6 and 57.17.1; Suet. *Calig.* 42. *Strenuae* (*sic*) are mentioned in the bylaws of clubs (*collegia*) making gift-distributions to members on New Year's day: *ILS* 7213.12–13; 7214.8–9, which mentions figs and dates, as does Mart. 8.33.11. *CIL* VI. 456 = *ILS* 99 (3 BCE): dedication to Lares Publici *ex stipe, quam populus ei | contuli k. Ianuar.* Similar: *CIL* VI. 457 = 93 (for Vulcan). Cf. Gatti, *BullCom.* 1888, p. 228 for altar, statue to Mercury. *Strenae* and goddess *Strenia* were important to the monthly calendar rituals: Fest., "Sacram Viam," 372L.

52. *F.* 1.195–96: *tempore crevit amor, qui nunc est summus, habendi: / vix ultra quo iam progrediatur habet.*

53. *F.* 1.211–12: *creverunt et opes et opum furiosa cupido, / et, cum possideant plurima, plura petunt.*

54. Cf. Hor. *Ep.* 1.1.52–61, etc.; Livy 1, pref.

55. Verg. *Aen.* 8.319–27; see Ovid's own *Met.* 1.131 and *Am.* 3.8.

56. *F.* 1.193–94: *vix ego Saturno quemquam regnante videbam, / cuius non animo dulcia lucra forent.*

57. Turner 1969 identifies poverty or simplicity as symbolic of *communitas*.

58. Janus' puns weave different registers—greed and idealized agriculture—into one verbal fabric. *Frondibus* (boughs) and *gemmis* (gemstones) at either end of line 203 contrast archaic and modern décor of the Capitoline Hill and temporalize the growth of

wealth. Subsequent puns derive from money lending and profit making. In the old days "it was no shame to have taken quiet rest *in stipula*"—"upon straw," alluding to one's *stipe*, or "cash" (205) and *stipulatio*, "financial agreement." Hay (*faenum*) beneath their "head" or *caput* (206) recalls *fenus*, interest accrued from *caput* (*capiti*, 206), principal.

59. Moneylenders, merchants, etc., at several *iani* from the Forum Boarium into the Forum Romanum: see Richardson 1992: 205–6 ("Janus"). Hor. *Epist.* 1.1.53–54 demonstrates Ianus' association with moneymaking: "*o cives cives quaerenda pecunia primum est; virtus post nummos*"; *haec ianus summus ab imo* (tagging the whole Forum marketplace). Hor. *Epist.* 1.20.1 addresses his book going on sale near Vortumnus and Ianus; cf. Cic. *Off.* 2.87; Hor. *Sat.* 2.3.18; Ov. *Rem. Am.* 561–62 on *Ianus Medius*. The temple of Saturn, whom Janus himself received in hospitality (*F.* 1. 193, 235–40), served as the state treasury (Paul. *ex Fest.* 2L, Macrob. *Sat.* 1.8.3; Solin. 1.12; cf. Varr. *LL* 5.183. Richardson 1992: 343, "Saturnus, aedes") and quartered the state financial officers, quaestors (Plut. *Ti. Gracch.*10.6, App. *BC* 1.31).

60. *F.* 1. 209–18:

at postquam fortuna loci caput extulit huius
  et tetigit summo vertice Roma deos,
creverunt et opes et opum furiosa cupido,
  et, cum possideant plurima, plura petunt.
quaerere ut absumant, absumpta requirere certant,
  atque ipsae vitiis sunt alimenta vices:
sic quibus intumuit suffusa venter ab unda,
  quo plus sunt potae, plus sitiuntur aquae.
in pretio pretium nunc est: dat census honores,
  census amicitias; pauper ubique iacet.

61. Janus represents the competition—the *opum furiosa cupido,* the raging desire of wealth—as comparable to drinking salt water: the more one consumes, the more one desires.

62. On contradictions (dilemmas) of values (eroticism, poverty, agricultural simplicity among the wealthy elite) in contemporary landscape painting and poetry: Silberberg-Peirce 1980; Leach 1980 and 1988: 286–87, 304–5 (landscape paintings, Horace and Tibullus).

63. *F.* 1.219–20: *tu tamen auspicium si sit stipis utile quaeris, / curque iuvent nostras aera vetusta manu.*

64. *F.* 1.221–26:

aera dabant olim: melius nunc omen in auro est,
  victaque concessit prisca moneta novae.
nos quoque templa iuvant, quamvis antiqua probemus,
  aurea: maiestas convenit ipsa deo.
laudamus veteres, sed nostris utimur annis:
  tamen est aeque dignus uterque coli.

65. Janus' new temple (1.223) was that of the Forum Holitorium, begun by Augustus and finished by Tiberius in 17 CE. It contained a gold-plated image of Janus that Augustus imported from Egypt (Plin. *H.N.* 36.28). See Bömer 1957, 2: 29–30 and Le Bonniec 1965: 55.

66. For *maiestas*, see ch. 4. *Maiestas* names the inflated "grandiosity" epitomizing elite male social presence (see Bourdieu 2001).

67. Macr. *Sat.* 1.7.20–21 provides the story: cf. Euhemerus' account and Ennius' translation influencing Vergil (*Aen.* 8, also *Georgics*): Johnston 1977.

68. See Daremberg-Saglio s.v. *hospitium*, 3.1: 296–302. In some ways, *xenium*, Greek for the guest-gift, refers to *strena* (though *xenium* is not restricted to New Year's): LS, "strena," II. Vitr. 6.7.4; Plin. *Ep.* 6.31.13 (Emperor's gifts to guests). Martial's Book 13, entitled *Xenia*, includes descriptions of foodstuffs: cf. *F.* 1.185–88 (New Year's dates, figs, and honey).

69. LSJ, σύμβολον; L-S, *tessera* III, *tessera hospitalis*. Halved coins as σύμβολα: Pollux, *Onomasticon* 9.70–71 ἡμίτονον νόμισμα; Babelon 1901, 1.1: 716–17. See Buttrey 1972 on the halving of Roman coins, usually for change: cf. Hor. *C.* 1.3.5–8.

70. Material abstraction as an unconscious symptom in market behavior: Zizek 1989: 11–53 ("How Did Marx Invent the Symptom?"), esp. 16–21, citing Alfred Sohn-Rethel's *Intellectual and Manual Labor* (London: Macmillan, 1978).

71. Suet. *Aug.* 57; Suet. *Tib.* 34; Dio 57.8.4–6, esp. 6.

72. Aug. *CD* 7.8 develops the notion that Janus is a "mouth."

73. *F.* 1.213–14: "People compete to ask how they may consume, and how to get it again once it's consumed, and these spirals are food [*alimenta*, 214] for vices."

74. *Ianual*-cake contained grain seeds; Ovid calls it *libum Ceriale*. Paulus-Fest. "Ianual" 93L; Lyd. *Mens.*, 4.2, pp. 64–65 (Wünsch). "Alternating" language, cf. Ov. *Ex P.* 4.2.6: *cessavit epistula numquam ire per alternas officiosa vices*. Prop. 4.4.58 (Tarpeia to Tatius): *me rape et alterna lege repende vices*.

75. *Mola salsa*, typical of sacrifice (Le Bonniec 1965: 44, on 1.128), Festus 124L. Besides the seeds, the salt is suggestive: cf. *salax*, "eager for sexual intercourse" (*OLD*), though derived from *salio*, "to leap" as in ejaculation (*OLD salio* 2, 3 and 4 [= to mount]), is similar in sound to *sal*, "salt." *Sal*, "salt" (*OLD* 6) refers to a witticism in language or "character" or "life" in a person. Thus, salty wit can attain a connotation of prurience: E.g. Mart. 12.95.3, *tinctas sale pruriente charta*.

76. Frazer 1929, 2: 113 on *F.* 1.179 (citing Bouché-Leclercq 1882, 1: 154). Definition, LSJ, κλήδων, I; Festus, "Lacus Lucrinus," 108 L; Cic. *Div.* 1.102–4; Plin. *H.N.* 28.22.

77. L-S, *concipio* I. B. 1; also *OLD* 3a, b, c, d. and e (figurative uses).

78. *Pondus* and *onus* can refer to a fetus. *Pondus*: Ov. *Met.* 9.684, *Am.* 2.14.14; Prop. 4.1.96; Mart. 14.151. *Onus*: *F.* 1.624 and 2.452. Adams 1982: 51, 71, and 243n.3, adding that *pondus* and *onus* can refer to male sexual/ reproductive organs.

79. *F.* 1.183–84: *desierat Ianus. nec longa silentia feci, /sed tetigi verbis ultima verba meis.*

80. Cf. *F.* 4.15–16, 19, 35–40 exploiting "touch" linked to Venus; *A.A.* 2.292 (sexual intercourse) and 2.719–20 (manual stimulation). Prop. 3.3.37–38: *e quarum numero me contigit una dearum [Musarum] / (ut reor a facie, Calliopea fuit)*. (Calliope then instructs the poet to continue singing erotic elegy). Adams 1982: 185–87.

81. Kissing as elite male social ritual showing degree of rank, then, perhaps friendship: Wallace-Hadrill 1996: 291, citing Cic. *Att.* 16.5.2 and Suet. *Ner.* 37 (Nero withholds the kiss from all senators on his return from Greece). Cf. mouth disease among the elite during Tiberius' reign spread through kissing: see Plin. *H.N.* 26.3; Suet. *Tib.* 34.4, 68.2; Val. Max. 11.6.17.

82. Tiberius' distaste for public levity and expense of *ludi*: Tac. *Ann.* 1.54.3–4, 1.75.5–7, 1.77; 1.84.3; Dio 57.14.1–2 and 10; Suet. *Tib.* 34.1, 47.1 (cf. Augustus' behavior: Suet. *Aug.* 44.2). Pantomime riots in reaction to reduced funding: Slater 1994 with sources.

83. Cf. Venus' *loquellas* (language/tongues) with Mars at Lucr. 1.38–40. Cf. Dupont 1992: 285–86 and 1999: 101–69. *Presserat ora* may have erotic meaning: *premo* and its compounds for sexual pursuit and, perhaps, for insertion (*OLD premo* 2); see Adams 1982: 182–83. Cf. *Prema* as divine patroness of deflowering brides (Aug. *Civ.* 6.9).

84. Kiss at banqueting and literature as cultural symbol, see Dupont 1999, esp. Part
II, 101–69. Briefly, at Dupont 1992: 285–86: "This *basium*, or erotic form of kissing, may
have been just a slight brushing of the lips, a tiny gesture towards a wider sensuality
that took a mainly verbal form and never really materialized."

85. The follow-up question (1.185–90) confirms somatizated exchange. The dates
and figs are both "seeds" in their way; together with the honey, they all evoke a sensuous sweet taste evocative of enjoyment, sexual or otherwise. On figs as sexual objects,
see Adams 1982: 113–14 (Latin) and Henderson 1975: 134 (no. 122), 117–19 (Greek).

86. See Holland 1961; Richardson 1992: 206 ("Janus").

87. According to Barchiesi 1997: 236, Janus is unaware of the Myth of the Return
(under the Golden Age of Augustus) and laments the loss of Saturn.

88. The *exclusus amator* and *paraclausithyron:* Copley 1956. Tarpeia's name references
"shame" (*turpis*, Prop. 4.4.1) linked to the Capitoline Hill and punishment of criminals.
Cf. Prop. 1.16.1–2. Alternatively, Tarpeia is daughter of Tarpeius, the watchman of the
citadel, e.g., Liv. 1.11–5–9; sometimes, a Vestal Virgin: Prop. 4.4. For Capitoline as *Mons
Tarpeius* (Varro, *Ling.* 5.41; Prop. 4.4.93–94; *ILS* 4438) or *Arx Tarpeia* (Verg. *Aen.* 8.652;
Prop. 4.4.29; F. 1.79: *vestibus intactis Tarpeias itur in arces*): Richardson 1992: 378 (*Tarpieus,
Mons*). *Rupes Tarpeia* (also called *Saxum Tarpeium*) designated cliffs where executed
criminals were thrown (Richardson 1992: 377–78).

89. There are eroticizing implications, too: readers might interpret the *arma* (254,
260) as phallic: Adams 1982: 17 (*ventris arma, Priap.* 31.3), 19–22 (weapons generally), 21
(*arma* specifically), 224 (Ov. *Am.* 1.9.26). For popular justice, violence, and doorway scenarios: Lintott 1963.

90. *Porta Ianualis*, a pomerial gate of Romulus' city: Varr. *LL* 6.165; Richardson 1992:
303–4; cf. Macr. *Sat.* 1.9.17–18. The gate/mouth analogy was Varronian (prob. source for
Aug. *CD* 7.8, on the puns on Janus' double mouth, Greek οὐρανὸν (palate/heaven) and
Latin *palatum* (palate), and Janus as figure for the heavens and its rising and setting
(astronomical) "gates."

91. City as body: see Gowers 1995.

92. Door or gate in Latin referring more often to anus than vagina: Adams 1982: 89.

93. Wallace-Hadrill 1990; Barchiesi 1997: 132n43 (end).

94. Cic. *ND* 1.15.38, 2.23.60, 2.28.71.

95. Adams 1982: 110–11 cites compounds of *culus*, including *culibonia* (Pompeian
graffito *CIL* IV.8473), Perusine sling-shots at *CIL* XI.6721.7, 14, and *Sesquiculus*, a nickname that Marius Victorinus (*Grammatici Latini* 6.8.9) reports for Julius Caesar Strabo,
"ample-assed" (cf. *sesquicyathus*, a *cyath*, "ladle" and a half). On the Perusine "shots":
Hallett 1977; Kellum 1996: 174 and 1997: 173. Cf. verbs *culare* (Petr. 38.2) and *apoculare*
(Petron. 62.3, 67.3) to shove someone or thing in the ass (away) toward a particular
direction: Adams 1982: 111–12.

96. Lookout point where a red flag was raised upon attack during *Comitia Centuriata*
(in the Campus Martius): Dio Cass 37.27.3–28.1.

97. *Contingo:* Adams 1982: 186 and 227.

98. *Oebalius* may have erotic associations: when Ovid uses *Oebalius*, it typically identifies characters in erotic tales. Cf. *Oebalius* of Hyacinthus (*Met.* 10.196, 13.396); *Oebalidae*
of Castor and Pollux pursuing the daughters of Leucippus (F. 5.705); and the *Oebaliae
matres*, the Sabine women (F. 3.230). Ovid so uses *Oebalius* again of Sabines at F. 3.230
(Mars calls Sabine women *Oebaliae matres*, who were raped) and 5.705 (of Castor and
Pollux; they are fighting for love).

99. Uses of sulfur for purification: Frazer 1929, 3: 346–47 on F. 4.739; Hom. *Od.*

22.481–94; Theoc. 24.96–98; Tib. 1.5.9–12; and Plin. *H.N.* 25.177.

100. Macr. *Sat.* 1.9.18 (*per hanc portam magnam vim torrentium undis scatentibus erupisse*), Serv. *Aen.* 1.291, 8.361. Possible hot springs of Janus Geminus: Festus ex Paul. *Lautolae*, 105L, and Serv. *Aen.* 8.361, with Varr. *LL* 5.156, on Forum flooding.

101. See Richardson 1992: 207–8 (*Ianus Geminus*), who accepts the view of Holland 1961 that *Ianus* was originally associated with covering or bridging old water courses (Holland 1961: 108–37 on Ianus Geminus). One such "covering" was the Cloaca Maxima, the great sewer and drain of the Roman Forum. It has terminological alignment with the intestinal tract (*cloaca*). As Richardson says (1992: 206), "Probably, there were *iani* at frequent intervals along the *cloaca* from its mouth on the Tiber in the Forum Boarium to high on its course along the Clivus Suburanus."

102. Other associations of Janus with Tiberius: Tiberius' completion of Augustus' restoration of the Temple of Janus (with Fors Fortuna; Flora; Ceres, Liber, and Libera; and Spes, Tac. *Ann.* 2.41.1, 49, 17 CE). For January 1, 28 CE, Tac. *Ann.* 4.70.1–2 records Sabinus was charged via Tiberius' New Year's letter and became a "victim" to Se-Janus.

103. Where Janus shot out his water is near where Ovid reportedly met a barefooted old woman (*anus*) returning from the *Vestalia*, June 9, who told him about Forum flooding (6.395–416). Cf. the seedy associations: near where stood a *Ianus Medius*, Plautus identifies an open sewer (*canalem*) and *ostentatores meri* (*Curc.* 476), street prostitutes, the shrine of Venus Cloacina, and the fish-salesmen (*Curc.* 470–83). Bankers: Cic. *Off.* 2.87; Hor. *S.* 2.3.18; Ov. *Rem.* 561–62. Forum flooding: Prop. 4.2.5–10 (Vortumnus speaks of Tiber flooding).

104. Plin. *H.N.* 15.119–20 identifies Cloacina, goddess of the brook, with Venus and links her to purification of the Sabines and Romans in founding peace between them. Janus Geminus and peace: Serv. *Aen.* 12.198. See esp. Holland 1961: 108–37; Coarelli 1986: 84–97. The treaty in the *Comitium*: Plut. *Rom.* 19.7; Cass. Dio fr. 5.7. See also Richardson 1992: 92 (*Cloacina, Sacrum*); Plaut. *Curc.* 471, Liv. 3.48.5.

105. Coarelli 1986: 98–97, esp. 97. Cf. concord between them in handshake: *F.* 6.94.

106. As Barchiesi 1991: 14–17 suggested, Janus makes up for Ovid's displacement of failed Muses, who appear finally in the preface of May (Book 5). Cf. Ovid's Janus with Propertius 3.3, who attempts to mouth the big epic fountain (thereupon follow Apollo's redirection, and Calliope's instruction and trickling of Philetan aqueduct into his mouth).

107. For digressivity as a mode of social commentary, see Chambers 1999, Worton 1998.

108. Germanicus' triumph declared on Jan. 1, 15 CE: Tac. *Ann.* 1.55. May 26, 17 CE, date for Germanicus' triumph *ex Germania: Fasti Ostien., Inscr. Ital.* XIII.1.5 (under 17 CE). Also *Fasti Amit.* May 26 (Degrassi 1963: 462), and Tac. *Ann.* 2.41. On Janus and Germanicus, Herbert-Brown 1994: 185–96, esp. 186.

109. See Herbert-Brown 1994: 187–96, who surveys the evidence for the number of closures and a widespread ancient confusion about the meaning of closing Janus' doors. Ovid's confusion is not unusual (195).

110. Frazer 1929, 3: 158–59. *ILS* 92, 93. 99 record individual statues and altars at crossroad shrines for which Augustus used the *stips*.

111. On the doorkeeper scenario as model, Hardie 1991: 60–62; Barchiesi 1997a: 231. No one has noted similarities between Ovid's Janus episode and Aristophanes' *Peace;* cf. the *Lysistrata*, where a beautiful feminine personification, Armistice, is shared between Spartans and Athenians as remedy for their sexual deprivation. Cf. Newiger 1980.

112. *Strena* as *omen*: Plaut. *St.* 461, 672.

113. For split *symbolon* as model of love relation: Pl. *Smp.* 191d4 and Janan 2001: 41 on its psychoanalytic implication.

Chapter Four

1. Cf. critical moralizing audiences at *Am.* 1.15, 3.1.15–22; *Rem.* 357–96; after exile, e.g., *Tr.* 2. Cf. Ovid's dilatory life as poet with Bourdieu 1987. Lifestyle polemics in Ovid's prefaces: Korzeniewski 1964.

2. Cf. Lacan's distinction between "goal" and "aim" used by Zizek 1991: 5.

3. Consonant with the views of Wyke in essays (1987, 1990) republished in Wyke 2002, esp. 11–45 ("Mistress and Metaphor in Augustan Elegy") and 115–54 ("Reading Female Flesh: Ovid *Amores* 3.1"), namely, that in elegy women are markers for the identities of the male speaker in relation to men.

4. For "nodal points" ("suture points" or Lacanian "points de capiton") in ideological fantasy, see Zizek 1989: 87–129, esp. 87–89, 100–105.

5. Augustus' policy promoting imitation of heroic models: e.g., heroic statues and *tituli* of the Forum Augustum: Yavetz 1984. See Merli 2000 and Hinds 1992 on *arma* as symbolic of the epic genre. Underestimating eroticism, Merli views *arma* in the *Fasti* as altering elegy. Pedagogic use of epic to inculcate *virtus:* Keith 2000. Rudich 1993: xvii–xxxiv on the tension between traditional values and attitudes of "withdrawal" from public service among early imperial elite

6. Cf. Epicurus' heroism with Hercules: Lucr. 1.62–79, 5.1–54, esp. 23–54.

7. Since equestrians might exceed the senatorial minimum, wealth was not definitive (*mores,* holding senatorial office, and birth were important): Nicolet 1984: 91–93 (Augustus raised senatorial census amount from 400,000 to 1 million), 98–99 (equestrian census at 400,000); Treggiari 1996: 875–82. Aspects of morality under review, see Edwards 1993, Barton 2001, Greenidge 1894.

8. *Recognitio equitum:* Ov. *Tr.* 2 89–90, 541–42. Greenidge 1894: 88–105, esp. 93–94; Nicolet 1974: 47–102. *Probatio* (testing) also at the *transvectio equitum,* a parade of knights on July 15 (but, cf. Suet. *Aug.* 38: *equitum turmas frequenter recognovit, post longam intercapedinem reducto more transvectionis;* Val. Max. 2.2.9. Different origins of *recognitio:* Dion. Hal. 6.13, after Lake Regillus battle, and Liv. 9.46, 304 BCE). Various phrasing: *equitatum recognoscere, equitum turmas recognoscere, centurias [equitum] recognoscere.* Liv. 39.44; Val. Max. 2.9.6–7, 4.1.10. Adjutant commissions: Suet. *Aug.* 37–39 (*triumviratum recognoscendi turmas equitum,* 37); *ILS* 9483 (*III vir centur. equit. recosnosc. cens. pot.*). Cf. Suet. *Aug.* 39: board of ten managing *recognitio equitum* at five-year census (not annual *transvectio;* Nicolet 1984: 97). Also Suet. *Tib.* 61, *Claud.* 16; Plut. *Pomp.* 22. Val. Max. 2.2.9 lists the *transvectio* with the Lupercalia as spectacles displaying young equestrians. Mounted exhibitions of armed youths (*equites*) in the Forum Augustum (temple of Mars Ultor), where youths assumed *toga virilis:* Taylor 1924 on *seviri equitum.* Forum Augustum: Dio 55.10.2–5 (activities there); Richardson 1992: 162.

9. *A.A.* 1.3.7–8, 3.8.9–10, 3.15.5–6 with *Tr.* 4.10.7–8 and *P.* 4.8.17–18.

10. Ovid's early public career: *F.* 4.383–84 (*decimvir stlitibus iudicandis*); *Tr.* 4.10.33–34 (*tresvir capitalis*); *P.* 3.5.23–26 (*iudex* in centumviral court). De Mirmont 1905: 199–200. Nicolet 1974: 255 on prosopography of Ovid's father.

11. On *Tr.* 2.7, 89–90, 541–42: G. Luck 1977, 2: 96. Ovid characterized moralizing criticism of his erotic poetry as *censura* (*Rem. Am.* 357–96, esp. 361–62). *Tr.* 2.275–78 suggests malevolent readers; cf. Bartsch 1994. Cf. Davis 1999.

12. "Censorial" views in Roman literary criticism and Horace particularly: Hor. *Epist.* 2.1.1–4, 34–49, 63–75, etc.; Too 1998: 151–86, esp. 160–62. Also Ahl 1984b: 58. Cf. *recognoscere* meaning "to scrutinize," especially records (cf. calendars) prior to publication: Cic. *Verr.* 2.2.18 and 190, *Balb.* 5.11; *Dig.* 10.2.5 (*ceteri descriptum et recognitum faciant* [of a will]); Plin. *Epist.* 4.26.1 (*libellos recognoscere et emendare*). Sen. *De ira* 3.36, borrows *recognitio sui* and *censor sui* from the equestrian censorial events and applies them to the self (cited by Foucault 1988 without reference to censorial *recognitio*).

13. *Nota* and *infamia*: Greenidge 1894: 93–100. Ov. *Tr.* 2.541–42 (*te delicta notantem/ praeterii . . . eques*). Suet. *Tib.* 35 refers to this act: *et ex iuventute utriusque ordinis profligatissimus quisque, . . . , famosi iudicii notam sponte subibant* (rebellious sons of senators and equestrians provoking stigmatization at *recognitio*, demoting them to plebeian rank to allow performance on stage and in the amphitheater, simultaneously avoiding exile. Cass. Dio 56.25.7–8 dates the ruse from 11 CE. A subsequent senatorial decree (*Tabula Larinas*) addressing this mode of evading the senate's will (19 CE): Lebek 1991 and 1990, McGinn 1992, and Levick 1983. Slater 1994 and Jory 1984 on the growing participation of young elites in pantomime and ensuing theater riots (early years of Tiberius' reign, starting just after Augustus' death.)

14. Cf. *Tr.* 2.167, *tui, sidus iuvenale, nepotes* (of Germanicus and Drusus); *Pont.* 4.8.23: *di tibi sunt Caesar iuvenis* (Germanicus), 4.13.31: *esse duos iuvenes, firma adiumenta parentis*.

15. The youth (*iuvenes*) in question: male elites between 17 and 35 years of age, sons of *equites* and senators who, due to their youth, were classed as *equites*, although some might later pursue senatorial careers (minimally, the quaestorship). The term *iuvenis*, "youth," mixes class and age distinctions: *OCD³ iuvenes* (or *iuventus*), 791–92 (Balsdon and B. Levick). Elite *iuvenes* (equestrian performances) as ceremonial representing the wider elite: e.g., Taylor 1924.

16. When Augustus died in 14 CE, Germanicus was conducting a census in Gaul. Tac. *Ann.* 1.31.2 (14 CE): *summae rei penes Germanicum agendo Galliarum censui tum intentum*. Cf. Suet. *Aug.* 97 on the omens when Augustus and Tiberius conducted the final census in 14. Augustus' census of Gaul (27 BCE): Dio Cass. 53.22.5, "he conducted a census and ordered their life and government" (ἀπογραφὰς ἐποιήσατο καὶ τὸν βίον τήν τε πολιτείαν διεκόσμησε). He then went to Spain, and "set it in order too" (κατεστήσατο καὶ ἐκείνην). Even at his death (19 CE), Germanicus was honored by the *iuvenes/equites*: e.g., the seats reserved for the equestrian order in the theater, the section called *cuneus iuniorum*, the "wedge of the younger elites," became officially called *cuneus Germanici* (Tac. *Ann.* 2.83).

17. *Ratio* as "policy," *OLD* 10; as "guiding principle," *OLD* 11; "ruling principle," *OLD* 12; a "pattern," *OLD* 13.

18. F. 1.39–40: *Martis erat primus mensis, Venerisque secundus;/ haec generis princeps, ipsius ille pater. Genus*, "offspring," *OLD* 2; "family line," *OLD* 1; "nationality," *OLD* 3.

19. Marcus Fulvius Nobilior (calendar in the temple of Hercules Musarum) promoted this view (Macr. *Sat.* 1.12.16; cf. Varro, *Ling.* 6.33; Fest. 120L; Placidus, *Corpus glossar. Lat.* 5.82–83). For *Maius* named after Maia mother of Mercury: Censor. *De die nat.* 22.12; Fest. 120L; cf. F. 5.79–104, 6.35–6. For *Maiores*/May: also F. 5.55–78 (Urania's speech arguing that May honors *maiores*). For *Iuvenes* (*Iuniores*)/June, see F. 6.65–88 and below.

20. Herakles Protector (*Alexikakos*) of *ephêboi* or *neoi*, young men, in Athenian cult: Harrison 1962 [1912]: 376–381, figs. 101–4 (relief showing Hercules before two- or four-pillar shrine, approached by young men). The *ephêboi* offered libations to Hercules

before cutting hair in rite of passage: Eup. 135; Photius, οἰνιστήρια (Eust. 907.18) and Hesychius, οἰνιστήρια (as cited in LSJ s.v.). Picard (1951, 1952, 1953) recognizes the shrine-building, a quasi-portal, in depictions of Prodicus' "Hercules at the Crossroad," in which Hercules is expressly entering manhood: Xen. *Mem.* 2.1.21; Cic. *Off.* 1.118. For rites of passage in early Rome: Torelli 1984.

21. Ovid's tales of Hercules in Latium not discussed here: Hercules' killing of Cacus (1.543–86), Hercules cross-dressing with Omphale (2.303–58; while the event takes place in Lydia not Latium, Pan imports required nudity at the Lupercalia, a Roman cult), the origin of the Argei (straw men tossed into the Tiber) with some of Hercules' Argive men left in Latium (5.621–62).

22. Janus' "work of art" (*artis opus* 1.268), substituting a sulfuric flood for fighting with weapons, offers a surrogate military *labor* (*F.* 1.67, *Pont.* 1.6.10, generalship; Tib. 1.1.3, war; Caes. *BG* 7.41.2, fighting; Liv. 44.3.9, marching). At the *Quinquatrus Minores* (June 13), *tibia*-players, cross-dressing and wearing masks while playing the pipes, offered another *artis opus* serving the public (6.661–62). Cf. Mamurius' fashioning ritual shields of the Salii: *Mamurius, morum fabraene exactior artis / difficile est, illud, dicere, clausit opus* (3.383–84); cf. exile as rupture of Ovid's *Fasti*: *Tr.* 2.552, *rupit opus*.

23. Poetic composition is *labor* in Ovid's exilic works: e.g., *Tr.* 2.322 (*est patriae facta referre labor*); *Ponto* 3.4.35, 3.5.34, 3.9.20 (*corrigere et longi ferre laboris onus*), 3.9.21–22 (*scribentem iuvat ipse labor minuitque laborem . . .*), 4.14.25. Cf. *Am.* 3.9.29 (Homer: *vatis opus, Troiani fama laboris*). Cf. Horace's metaphorical comparison (*Epist.* 2.1) between the rewards recognizing Hercules' and Augustus' feats, but the absence of rewards for poetic labor (see Galinsky 1996:126). Cf. *F.* 2.125–26: *quid volui demens elegis imponere tantum / ponderis? heroi res erat ista pedis* (contemplating celebrating Augustus as *pater patriae*).

24. *Nonis* ("Nones"), singular at *F.*1.311, names one of the *Parcae*, or Fates (Nona, Decuma, Morta): Gell. 3, 16, 11; Varr. ap. Gell. 3, 16, 10; *Parcae* are mentioned at *F.* 6.795 (Book 1 "predicts" the premature ending). On *Parcae* limiting gods: *Met.* 15.780–81: "Venus persuades the gods, who although they can't break the iron decrees of the old sister [*Parcae*], still give doubtless signs of coming woe [for Aeneas]." *Tr.* 5.3.17–18: the *Parcae* (14) govern even the gods so that (19–24) Bacchus too had to earn a place in heaven; "by no slight labor was the path made" (20).

25. Hercules in heavenly banquet with muses, an Athenian relief: Cumont 1942: 291–94, esp. pl. xxv, 1. Cf. Ov. *Tr.* 4.10.117–22 (Muse leads Ovid into heaven). In the Porticus Octaviae, adjacent to Porticus Philippi around Hercules Musarum, a painting by Artemon depicted Hercules ascending to heaven with his mortality burned away (Plin. *H.N.* 35.139). Statue of *Hercules tunicatus* beside the *rostra* in the Forum Romanum; in agony, he wore a long robe from his wife Deianira tainted with Hydra-blood leading eventually to his apotheosis (Plin. *H.N.* 34.93).

26. Poetry rewards heroic leaders: *Pont.* 4.8.43–92 (to Germanicus via Suillius).

27. Aeneas as Herculean, see Galinsky 1972: 131–38, tracking uses of *labor* in the *Aeneid*. Augustus and Hercules: Hor. *C.* 1.2.41; 1.12.25–27, 49–52; 3.3.9–12; *Epist.* 2.1.1–17; *C.* 3.14 (24 BCE, Augustus returns from Spain where, Dio Cass. 53.22.5 implies, he set in order imperial governance). Wyke 2002: 135–37, citing Galinsky 1972: 126–66, esp. 153. Ovid compares deceased Augustus with Hercules, also Liber Bacchus: *P.* 4.8.61–24. Tiberius compares Augustus to Hercules in Augustus' funeral speech: Dio 56.36 (esp. 4). Augustus' triple triumph commences August 13 (13, 14, 15 Aug.), the anniversary of the Ara Maxima of Hercules. Several marble sculptures of Hercules' club in the Porticus Octaviae advertise Augustus' world mastery through a comparison

between Augustus' return from Spain (24 BCE; Hor. C. 14.1–4, 3.3.9–12) and Hercules' path from Spain to Latium herding the cattle of Geryon: Lauter 1980–1981, plates X; X,1; and XI, 1 and 2.

28. Ovid's other friends' heroic epics: Pedo's *Theseis* on Theseus' heroic feats (*Pont.* 4.10.71, 75); Pedo also composed epic verses on Germanicus' sailing the North Sea (Sen. *Suas.* 14). Cf. Tuticanus' *Phaeacis* on Odysseus' stay with the Phaeacians [*Pont.* 4.12.25–30]); Macer's *Iliad* prequel (*Pont.* 2.10.13–14, *Am.* 2.18.1–2).

29. This choice between Virtue and Vice was, by Ovid's day, common in popular ethics, since Hesiod (*Op.* 285–92), reiterated variously in multiple authors (cf. Callim. *Aet.* fr. 1, with Snell 1953: 268; cf. Prop. 3.3). Prodicus's tale is outlined by Xen. *Mem.* 2.1.21–34. Cic. *De off.* 1.118, cites it, labeling the personifications *Virtus* and *Voluptas*. Prodicus' tale appeared probably in his *Horai*, "Seasons" (schol. Aristoph. *Clouds* 361; Nestle 1936). As a prominent pedagogic tool of Pythagoreans, who gave it the emblem Y, figuring the bifurcating paths: cf. Pers. *Sat.* 3.52–57 and 5.30–40. See Kuntz 1994; Wyke 2002: 115–54; Nestle 1936; Panofsky 1930; Alpers 1912.

30. Fundamental still, Wyke 1990 in Wyke 2002: 115–54, revised edition in Cameron 1989, and Wyke 1987 in Wyke 2002: 46–77 and "Mistress and Metaphor in Augustan Elegy" (Wyke 2002: 11–45).

31. *Militia amoris:* see, e.g., Lyne 1980: 71–8, 251–52, esp. Cahoon 1988 ("Bed as Battle Field") and Fredrick 1997 ("Reading Broken Skin").

32. On "irresponsibility" in the erotic elegist's persona, Wyke 2002: 44.

33. Propertius (3.5) had proposed such a shift, too, for his maturity, but to philosophical poetry. Elegy 4.1a projects patriotic poetry thwarted by an astrologer's warning, 4.1b.

34. *Militia equestris:* Nicolet 1984: 99–101; Vell. 2.111 (*militiae equestres*), ILS 2682 (*castrenses honores*). The *tres militiae* included *praefectus cohortis, tribunus cohortis, praefectus alae* (often called *militia prima, secunda,* and *tertia*). Le Bohec 2000: 42. Watson 1969: 164n45, citing Birley 1953: 133ff: the sequencing of the offices was less stable prior to Nero. In the Republic, "the *equites equo publico* [like Ovid] owed a certain number of *stipendia*, i.e., [probably 10] years on military campaign" (Nicolet 1974: 73–74): Liv. 37.11.8; Plut. *Pomp.* 22.7 (70 BCE: Censors ask Pompey if he had performed all the campaigns required by law); Plut. *Gaius Gracch.* 29.19 (similar); Polyb. 6.19.4 (attesting requirement of ten years of campaigns before seeking magistracies).

35. Nicolet 1974: 74 citing P. Aebutius (186 BCE), who denounced the Bacchanals in Rome, for whom the senatus consultum granted *vacatio* (Liv. 29.19). *Vacatio* granted to equestrians in exchange for supplies in Spain (215 BCE). A 5-year portion of *vacatio* was granted to soldiers who showed exceptional courage (Liv. 23.20). Cic. *Phil.* 5.19.53 to Caesar's veterans and their children. Liv. 42.33.4: abrogation of all *vacationes* for persons under fifty (also Liv. 42.34).

36. *Vacatio*, RE ser. 2, v. 7, pt. 1–2, 2028–32. *Der neue Pauly* 5.952, *immunitas*; 12.1.1074–75, *vacatio*. *OCD³*, *immunitas*, 749–50; *munus*, 1001. On *vacatio militiae munerisque*. *Dig.* 50.5.13.1, 50.16.18 (Paulus 9 ad ed.).

37. See Liv. 7.2 and Val. Max. 2.4.4; Kleijwegt 1994: 88–90 cites evidence from Rome's past, as well as imperial evidence for pantomimes as honorary members of *collegia iuvenum*. See Morel 1969 for origins of the association of *iuvenes* with theater; Jaczynowska 1970 stresses how *iuvenes* gave performances (cf. *Lusus Troiae*) in local towns that displayed/trained the next elite generation. See Taylor 1924. Education: Mohler 1937.

38. *Nudus* as "unarmed, defenseless, stripped of cover" or "weapons": Sall. *J.* 107.1; Liv. 5.45.3; Hom. *Il.* 21.50; Jos. *Ant. Jud.* 6.2.2; Gell. 9.13; Xen. *De rep. Lac.* xi.9. It also

applied to all without a wrap (*amictus* or *toga*), and wearing only a *tunicus* (James Yates, "Nudus," 808 in Smith 1875, citing Hes. *Op.* 391; Verg. *G.* 1.299; Serv. *G.* 1.299; Ael. *VH* 6.11, xiii.27). Cincinnatus was found *nudus* and plowing when summoned to be dictator; he asked for his *toga* to travel to speak to the senate: Liv. 3.26; Plin. *H.N.* 18.4; Aur. Vict. *Vir. Ill.* 17. Isid. *Orig.* 19.22.5: "The most ancient male clothing was the loincloth [*perizomatum id est subcinctorium*] by which just the genitals are covered [*quo tantum genitalia conteguntur*]. . . . These loincloths are also called *campestria*, due to the fact that youths, who are being trained 'naked' in the campus, cover their genitals with these." *Orig.* 19.33.1 (*cinctu autem iuvenes in exercitatione campestri verecunda velabant; unde et campestris dicebatur;* cf. Isid. *Or.* 18.17.2 on *gymnasium*). See Wiseman 1995a: 77–88 ("The Lupercalia")

39. Valerius Maximus (2.2.9) describes the origin of the Lupercalia as an extemporaneous posse of Romulus and Remus, roused during Pan's festival, to pursue cattle rustlers with strips of hide; cf. Ov. *F.* 2.359–80; Serv. *Aen.* 8.343; Put. *Rom.* 21.7 (citing Gaius Acilius). Especially, the Greek elegiac couplet of Butas from his poem on Roman ways, at Plut. *Rom.* 21.6 (esp. ἐμφοδίους τύπτοντας, οπως τότε φασγαν᾽ ἔχον— τας); Butas (freedman of Cato Minor; Plut. *Cat. Min.* 70).

40. *Velis . . . maioribus* (*F.* 2.3) suggests "longer" clothing. Besides prohibiting prepubescent boys from attending the *Lupercalia* (Suet. *Aug.* 31.4), Augustus may have lengthened coverings worn by *Luperci*: Wiseman 1995a: 82–83, citing Pomp. Trogus in Justin 43.1.7 on god of the Lupercal as *ipsum dei simulacrum nudum caprina pelle amictum,* implying less clothing (just a cape) than subsequent images (long aprons: Veyne 1960; Wiseman 1995a: 83, fig. 10; Zanker 1988: fig. 105; Wrede 1983). Ovid (*F.* 5.101: *cinctuti;* cf. Val. Max. 2.2.9) and Plutarch (*perizômata,* Plut. *Rom.* 21.5) imply the loincloth called *campestre* by Isid. *Orig.* 19.22.5, 33.1, above.

41. Lupercalia and male rites of passage: Sabbatucci 1988: 56–59.

42. Wiseman 1995b: 81–82, 194.

43. Serv. *ad Aen.* 8.343 (*februis caedere*); see Wiseman 1995a: 81. Alternatively, Caesar was derived from *caedere,* to cut from the womb (Wiseman 1995a: 194n31, citing Plin. *H.N.* 7.47 and Festus [Paul] 50L), and associated with *caesaries,* "head of hair," and the comet (*komêtês*) portending Julius Caesar's astrification (Paul. Fest. 50.7L; Vergil, *Aen.* 8.678–81. O'Hara 1996: 134, 173, 216).

44. Suet. *Jul.* 76.1–2; Cass. Dio 44.6.2, 45.30; Cic. *Phil.* 3.5.12, 13.15.31; Plut. *Caes.* 61, Anton. 12. Frazer 1929, 2: 332–33.

45. Lashes from their goat-hide whips substituted for sexual penetration by Faunus/Pan, the fertility deity honored by the *Lupercalia*: *F.* 2.441–44. The interpretation depends upon identifying Pan, Faunus, and Inuus (god of penetration, from *ineo,* "to go in") as at Liv. 1.5.2.

46. Ovid reasserts Minerva's role in arts at *F.* 3.809–48, the *Quinquatrus* (March 19, temple foundation 835–38); her military interests shown by gladiatorial contests (3.811–14), also by tale told about Mars' love of Minerva (3.675–96, esp. 681: *armifer armiferae correptus amore Minervae*). Ovid was born on March 20, during the festival: *Tr.* 4.10.11–14. Frazer 1929, 3: 144–55.

47. Cf. *Tr.* 2.215–16 (*non vacat exiguis rebus adesse Iovi*) and *Tr.* 2.237–40 (of Augustus' time, *si . . . vacuum tibi forte fuisset,* 239). *Tr.* 2.557–60 (wishing that Augustus, when "free," *vacuo,* would have someone read to him parts of the *Metamorphoses*).

48. *Ingenuae artes* are a civilizing source of bonds between men. Ovid's poetry civilizes barbarians in exile: e.g., *P.* 2.9.27–50 (to King Cotys in Tomis, who, Ovid says, has learned faithfully *ingenuas artes,* which *emollit mores nec sinit esse feros,* 48). *P.* 2.5.65–66:

Salanus and Ovid are each a cultivator of *artes ingenuae* (culture shared between them). *P.* 1.6.5–10 (Ovid shares civilizing, cultured, *artibus ingenuis* with Graecinus, whose spirit is far from "unlovable savagery," *feritas inamabilis*. Cf. *Tr.* 1.571–76 (Ovid compares himself in exile to Odysseus; Odysseus has a *corpus . . . durum patiensque laborum*, Ovid has *invalidae vires ingenuaeque;* Odysseus was constantly in *saevis armis*, but Ovid was accustomed to *studiis mollibus*).

49. Especially their growth into manhood (signs of first beard): *F.* 3.59–60. While still Octavian, "Augustus" held temporary games to celebrate his first beard-shaving: Dio 48.34.3. In 59 CE, Nero created the *Iuvenalia*, annual theatrical games to commemorate his first beard-trimming: Dio 61.19.

50. Sons promoting their fathers as a means of self-aggrandizement: cf. *F.* 2.144: "Your father [Mars] made you divine [Romulus was divinized, *F.* 2.481–90]; that man [Augustus] made his father a god." At *F.* 5.545–98 Augustus, Mars' descendant, honors Mars with a grand temple, that of Mars Ultor.

51. Cf. *F.* 1.29–30 (Romulus' ignorance of astronomy); 3.155–66 (Julius Caesar's use of Greco-Egyptian astronomers to reform the Roman calendar).

52. Hor. *Epist.* 2.1.156: *Graecia capta ferum victorem cepit et artis / intulit agresti Latio*. Cf. Verg. *Aen.* 6.581–83; Ov. *F.* 3.103, 2.508 (Roman arts as military).

53. 3.157–58: *non haec ille deus tantaeque propaginis auctor/ credidit officiis esse minora suis.*

54. *F.* 3.5–8 (above) with 3.175–76 (Mars agrees to contribute saying he's doing it "so that Minerva does not think that she alone has mastery over this").

55. See, e.g., Cohen 1991; Treggiari 1996, esp. 886–93. *F.* 2.139–42 refers to Augustus' moral-social legislation in the same sentence in which he refers to Romulus' rape of the Sabine women: see commentary in Frazer 1929: 311–12 and notes.

56. See Leon 1951; also Dio 55.10.12; Suet. *Aug.* 63 (marriages of Augustus' daughter Julia), 64 (Augustus' grandsons from his daughter; granddaughter Julia), 101 (prohibition on burial of the banished Julias, daughter and granddaughter, in the Mausoleum Augusti); Sen. *De brev. vitae* 4.6 (Augustus' weariness with these *ulcera*). For rumors of night carousing: Plin. *H.N.* 21.6.9.

57. *F.* 3.615–16 (Aeneas to Anna, Dido's sister, on the beach at Lavinium): "and [I swear] by my companion deities, located recently in this abode, that they often criticized my delay" (*saepe meas illos increpuisse moras*). "To entertain": L-S, *moror*, II.2. Hor. *Epist.* 1.13.116–18, *Ars* 319–20: "Sometimes, a play, though it lacks sexiness, and is without art and importance, because it's attractive in spots and suitably suspenseful [*morata recte*], *delights people more and draws lingering attention more* [*valdius oblectat populum meliusque moratur*] than verses empty of substance, mere sing-song."

58. More common are *bruma, cardo, solstitium, aequinoctium,* or constellation names (e.g., *Cancer, Capricornus*) where solstices and equinoxes reside. See these words in L-S.

59. Here are some of the reasons: *F.* 3.233–34, Mars made Rhea Silvia pregnant with Romulus and Remus; 235–44, the start of spring suits mothers bearing children to supply new soldiers; 245–48, a temple was built for Juno Lucina on March 1 (see above).

60. On the grander burdens and sizes of more heroic words, see, e.g., Ov. *Tr.* 2.457–62; Hor. *Epist.* 2.1.257–59; cf. Verg. *Aen.* 7.45, *maius opus moveo*. On *onus* referring to an embryo or fetus: *F.* 1.624, 2.452. On onus referring to male genitalia: Adams 1982: 21.

61. *F.* 3.1–2: *bellice, depositis clipeo paulisper et hasta,/ Mars, ades et nitidas casside solve comas;* 3.7–8, *Palladis exemplo ponendae tempora sume/ cuspidis: invenies et quod inermis agas;* 3.172: *sed tamen in dextra missilis hasta fuit.* Adams 1982: 17, 19–20, 74 for *hasta* as metaphor for penis/*mentula*. The *hasta* was used to comb the hair of the bride before the

wedding, in part, as symbol of *her* sexual and gender submission. Cf. *hasta caelibaris*, Paul. exc. Fest. 55.

62. Mars' spear in hand: *F.* 3.1–2, 3.172. Minerva's spear as symbol: 3.7–8. *Hasta Martis* in Mars' shrine in the Regia (with *ancilia*) symbolized the god's potency in war and fertility: Serv. *Aen.* 7.603, Gell. 4.6.12, Cass. Dio 44.17.2; Obseq. 6, 44, 44a, 47, 50; Serv. *Aen.* 8.3. *Hasta* could stand as a metaphor for penis/*mentula*: Adams 1982: 17, 19–20, 74. The eroticism and fertility of a *hasta* from a gladiator's body is indicated by the *hasta caelibaris*, used to part the hair of the bride before her wedding; but it is perhaps a symbol of *her* submission. Paul. exc. Fest. 55: *caelibari hasta caput nubentis comebatur, quae in corpore gladiatoris stetisset abiecti occisique, ut, quemadmodum illa coniuncta fuerit cum corpore gladiatoris, sic ipsa cum viro sit, . . . vel quod nuptiali iure imperio viri subicitur nubens, quia hasta summar armorum et imperii est.*

63. Cf. *A.A.* 1.405–6, March and April conjoined; *Met.* 4.170–89, retelling Homer's Ares-Aphrodite tale; *Tr.* 2.295–96, their statues in Forum of Augustus; *Tr.* 2.261–62, alluding to Lucretius' proem; *Tr.* 2.377–78, referring to Homer's tale of Ares and Aphrodite. For prominent public art: Plin. *H.N.* 36.26 on the famous Ares and Aphrodite by Skopas in the Temple of Mars Decimus Junius Brutus Callaecus erected in the Circus Flaminius (cos. 138 BCE, triumph over Callaeci 132 BCE). See also Kellum 1997 and 1996 for sexual symbolism of the physical conjunction of the temples of Venus Genetrix and Mars Ultor at the Forum of Julius Caesar and the Forum of Augustus and the statues of Venus and Mars at the temple of Mars Ultor itself (cf. Ov. *Tr.* 2.295–96).

64. Zizek 1989: 5: "All 'culture' is in a way a reaction formation, an attempt to limit, canalize—to *cultivate* the imbalance, this traumatic kernel, this radical antagonism through which man cuts his umbilical cord with nature, with animal homeostasis." On the fundamental "mismatch" or incommensurability of sexual relations: Zizek, "There Is No Sexual Relation," in Salecl and Zizek 1996: 208–49.

65. Cf. Ovid with *eques* at *F.* 4.9–10 with the funerary monument of T. Flavius Verus, *eques Romanus* (end of second cent. CE), showing him, having passed the *transvectio equitum*, posing before his mother's admiration: Veyne 1960: 99–101, pl. VII.

66. Myrtle, associated with shrines of Venus: *Fasti* 4.139–44; Bömer 1957–1958, 2: 207; Frazer 1929, 3:164–65 on *F.* 4.15. Also Coarelli 1986: 82–86, esp. 85 applying the text of Plin. *H.N.* 15.119–120 on myrtle purifying Sabines and Romans entering reconciliation and peace. See also "Cloacina, sacrum" in Richardson 1992: 92. South Italian vases sometimes show satyrs or pans frolicking in ecstasy to the birth from the earth (an agricultural Aphrodite in Italy); she sometimes holds myrtle or it is nearby: *LIMC* 2. 1:113–14; 2.2: 115–16, esp. figs. 1158, 1159, 1160, 1163, 1165, 1166: these scenes with Pan's and Satyrs at Venus' *anodos* may derive from a parody scene or satyr play of the birth of Aphrodite (*LIMC* 2. 1: 113; cf. Hes. *Theog.* 173–206).

67. On *tangere* and compounds: Adams 1982: 185–87. Erotic "touch" occurs at a programmatic place in Propertian elegy, poem 3.3 precisely, where Propertius dreams of actually meeting the Muse Calliope. Calliope touches him and communicates to him his erotic poetic theme. *F.* 4.19 (*pars te . . . tangere debet*) recalls Mars' eroticization of poetic engagement with Ovid: *nec piget incepti: iuvat hac quoque parte morari* (3.175, "delay" connoting erotic lingering). For euphemistic erotic meaning of *pars*: Adams 1982: 57–61. On the erotic meaning of "delay," *mora* and *morari*: Verg. *Aen.* 5.766: *complexi inter se noctemque diemque morantur. CIL* IV. 2060: *Romula hic cum Staphylo moratur* (cited from Adams 1982: 178).

68. Interpretation depends on how well one thinks Ovid has integrated revised address to Germanicus into the whole of the preface. At *F.* 4.81–82 Ovid addresses

Germanicus: *Sulmonis gelidi, patriae, Germanice, nostrae. / me miserum, Scythico quam procul illa solo est!*

69. Cf. statues of the goddess at the Temple Venus Genetrix in the Forum of Julius Caesar (Richardson 1992: 165–67, Forum Iulium) and statues of her at the Temple of Mars Ultor in the Forum Augustum (interior, Richardson 1992: 162, "Forum Augustum"; pediment, Richardson 1992: 161–62). She stood as dynastic mother in Julius Caesar's Forum at its Temple of Venus Genetrix and at the Temple of Mars Ultor inside the Forum of Augustus. Cf. Ov. *Tr.* 2.295–96 (Venus beside Mars in the Temple of Mars Ultor, Forum Augustum).

70. These challenges appeared in the scholarship of Lucius Cincius and Marcus Terentius Varro (Macr. *Sat.* 1.12:12–13), Republican commentators on the calendar. Degrassi 1963: xxv. Varro, *Ling.* 6.33 specifies that Junius Gracchanus and M. Fulvius Nobilior (in his calendar in the temple of Hercules Musarum) argued that Venus was the honoree of April, but Varro derived April from *aperire*, the spring "opening."

71. Frazer 1929, 3: 180 on 4.61. Bömer 1957–1958, 2: 211 notes the *aphros*-etymology. Ovid's phrasing *a spumis est dea dicta maris* (62) alludes to derivation of April from "Aphrodite" (the Greek name for Venus), interpreted as "given from the sea-foam" in Hes. *Th.* 190–93, where Aphrodite is born from foam (ἄφρος) around the castrated genitals of Uranos (Heaven) cast by his son Cronos (Saturn) into the sea. Cf. Macr. *Sat.* 1.8.6 on Ἀφροδίτη *nomen* and genitalia (in discussing Saturn and Saturnalia). Latin homonyms of *maris* (genitive), "male" and "sea," imply "from the foam of a male [*maris*]" (*semen*) and allude to migrations of Greek heroes to "father" their towns and lineages in Italy (4.63–80). *F.* 4.63–80.

72. *Venus* and Ἀφροδίτη as "sexual intercourse": Adams 1982: 188–89.

73. The *Solymoi*, a tribe in Asia Minor: Hom. *Il.* 5.184, cf. 6.190. Ovid specifically says (*F.* 4.79) that Solimus was from Phrygian Ida, where the Magna Mater (Cybele) was worshiped by *galli*, eunuch priests. Might this allude to Ovid's "regression" to mother in this preface? Ida is mentioned two other times in this book, and both in Ovid's celebration of the cult of Magna Mater (4.182, 264).

74. *F.* 4.85–6: *quo non livor abit? sunt qui tibi mensis honorem/ eripuisse velint invideantque, Venus.* Cf. "censorship" (*censura*) over Ovid's sexual themes: *Rem. Am.* 357–98, *Livor* attacking poets, but esp. Ovid. Note in particular the use of *censura* at 3. 61–62: *nuper enim nostros quidam carpsere libellos,/ quorum censura Musa proterva mea est.* Then, *Rem.* 389–90, Ovid's response to carping at his poetry as *proterva*, "shameless": "Destructive Envy, go get screwed . . ." (*rumpere, Livor edax*).

75. Ovid sums up the situation, as if it were a competition over "ownership" (*F.* 4.89–90).

76. The hymn to Venus at *F.* 4.91–114 echoes Lucretius' hymn to Venus 1.1–49: Bömer 1957–1958, 2.214.

77. Venus' power of fertility: cf. Ov. *A.A.* 2.467–92, and Lucr. 1.1–20. Cf. Ov. *F.* 1.147–60 (year should begin in spring). Cf. Prop. 3.5.23–26, esp. "[when he ages and loses interest in Venus] it would be pleasing to learn the morals of nature, what god tempers this house of the world with art" (3.5.26: *tum mihi naturae libeat perdiscere mores, quis deus hanc mundi temperet arte domum*).

78. See Frederick 1997.

79. In regard to gender in the art of male grooming, I am reminded of *A.A.* 1.505–24, where Ovid instructs young men how to groom themselves to be attractive to a woman who would watch admiringly the effeminate pantomime artist. The key is to absorb enough refinement to separate one's masculine self from connotations of dirty brutality

but not so much as to appear to others as a *male vir*, "hardly a man who wants a man" (*A.A.* 1.523–24).

80. See, e.g., Treggiari in *CAH²* (1996) X: 873–904; Cohen 1991; Cantarella 1991; Della Corte 1982.

81. *F.* 4.113–14: *studioque placendi,/ quae latuere prius, multa reperta ferunt*. Freud developed a close association between culture and repressing of the pleasure principle in *Civilization and Its Discontents*. But in this work Freud identifies civilization with overcoming the perilous aggression of the individual, with weakening and disarming him or robbing him of pleasure. Here in the *Fasti* and in the *Ars amatoria* Ovid proposes the opposite: culture is a mechanizing of the attainment or even the prolongation of pleasure.

82. Cf. *F.* 3.104: *mittere qui poterat pila, disertus erat*. In regard to the thematics of "opening," *F.* 4.125–32 evokes Ovid's address to Janus at *F.* 1.149–60, esp. *patitur cultus ager* at 159: *tum patitur cultus ager et renovatur aratro*.

83. See Habinek 1997: 23–43, esp. 30–38, in Habinek and Schiesaro 1997 on this possible emergence of a sense of "sexuality" within the urban setting of Augustan Rome.

84. One important model for Ovid's treatment of the bath of Venus is Callimachus, *Hymn* 5 (Bath of Pallas Athena). Another would be the paintings of Venus (Aphrodite) Anadyomene (rising from the sea); one such painting was brought from Cos (Apelles the painter was from there) to Rome by Augustus: Str. 14.2.19, p. 657 and Plin. *H.N.* 35.91. Ovid refers to such paintings elsewhere (*Am.* 1.14.33–34, *A.A.* 3.401, and *P.* 4.1.30, perhaps *Met.* 5.634–35). See Frederick 1995 and 1997.

85. *LIMC* 2.1:113–14; 2.2:115–16, see above (Venus-Aphrodite's anados with Satyrs; use of myrtle).

86. *Tueor* also means to "observe," "maintain," "take care of" (L-S II). Venus here might figure a principle of calendar structure to be maintained, even if "mistaken." Cf. *F.* 1.32: [Romulus] *errroremque suum quo tueatur habet* (" . . . [Romulus] has a way to see/ defend [*tuearis*] his own error"). But *tueor* refers to cleaning and maintenance (L-S. II: Cic. Verr. 2.1.50.130, temple of Castor; cf. Cic. *Rab. Post.* 15.41, *simulacrum pristinae dignitatis*); implicitly, Caesar is to keep Venus' *imago*, image/statue (21) in good order.

87. At *F.* 1.397, satyrs are called "young manhood prone to Venus [sex] (*in Venerem Satyrorum prona iuventus*, 1.397). *Iuventus* could also denote elite young males of the equestrian order whom Germanicus patronized.

88. Degrassi 1963: 434: *frequenter mulieres supplicant | Fortunae Virili, humiliores etiam in balineis, quod in iis ea parte corpor[is] | utique viri nudantur, qua feminarum | gratia desideratur*. Mommsen offered a supplement, *CIL* 1.2 p. 314 (*honestiores Veneri Verticordiae*): Ovid permits mingling of prostitutes and matrons. Lydus (*Mens.* 4.65, p. 119, ed. Wuensch) does not mention Fortuna Virilis, only Aphrodite-Venus, but seems aware of a class distinction, which Mommsen proposed was omitted by the inscriber of Verrius' calendar: " . . . women of rank [αἱ σεμναὶ γυναικῶν] worshiped Aphrodite (Venus) for the sake of concord [μονοίας] and a chaste life [βίου σώφρονος]. Women of the masses [αἱ δὲ τοῦ πλήθους γυναῖκες] bathe themselves in the baths wearing crowns of myrtle as a service of the goddess."

89. One can imagine that a festival of prostitutes in men's baths was good for business and, from some male perspectives, good for men, perhaps explaining the name "Men's Fortune," "Fortune from Men."

90. Val. Max. 7.1.7 extols deference between spouses as entirely consistent with modesty shown even between male family relations such as father and son and father-in-law and son-in-law; they would not bathe together. Ovid's celebration of bathing on

April 1 plays upon the prurience beneath such a façade.

91. *F.* 4.155–56: *sub illa [Venere]/ et forma, et mores et bona fama manet.* Note the competition among women over *castitas* in the cult of Venus Verticordia (estab. in 216 BCE); especially Sulpicia, wife of Q. Fulvius Flaccus, specially selected by matrons for her exemplary modesty to consecrate the statue of Venus Verticordia. Cf. Val. Max. 8.15.12 and Plin. *H.N.* 7.120. Cf. the conflict between plebeian and patrician women over cult for Pudicitia, sexual integrity: the shrine of Pudicitia Plebeia was created in 295 by Verginia, a patrician who had married a plebeian, L. Volumnius, to match the shrine of Pudicitia Patricia, from which she was excluded: Liv. 10.23.3–10, Festus 282L (Patricia), 270–1L (Plebeia).

92. Three calendars (in Degrassi 1963: 452) attest the commencement of the *Ludi Florae* (*Floralia*) on the 28th of April: *Fasti Caeretani, Fasti Maffeiani,* and *Fasti Praenestini.* The *Fasti Caeretani* and *Praenestini* both attest the installation of Vesta in the *domus* of Augustus. See below. The *Fasti Maffeiani,* inscribed after 8 BCE (the month *Sextilis* is called Augustus), does not mention the installation of Vesta in the House of Augustus, an event of 12 BCE. Tac. *Ann.* 2.49 (17 CE) speaks of Augustus' start of restoration on Flora's temple, but Tiberius' completion of it.

93. An addition to the *Fasti Caeretani* refers to the *signum Vestae in domo Palatina,* while the *Fasti Praenestini* reads: *feriae ex s(enatus) c(onsulto), quo eo di[e signu]m et [ara] | Vestae in domu Imp. Caesaris Augu[sti po]ntif(icis) max(imi) | dedicata est Quirinio et Valgio co(n)s(ulibus)* [Degrassi 1963]. Augustus became Pontifex Maximus (March 6, 12 BCE): Ov. *F.* 3. 415–28; *Fasti Praenestini* and *Feriale Cumanum* under March 6. August. *RG* 10 dates his becoming Pontifex Maximus to 12 BCE. On the priesthood and the house of Augustus: Dio 54.27.2 (13 BCE). See also *Fasti Praenestini* (entry into office to March 6, 12 BCE): Degrassi 1963: 420.

94. *F.* 4.943–54:

> cum Phrygis Assaraci Tithonia fratre relicto
> sustulit immenso ter iubar orbe suum,
> mille venit variis florum dea nexa coronis;
> scaena ioci morem liberioris habet.
> exit et in Maias sacrum Florale Kalendas:
> tunc repetam, nunc me grandius urget opus.
> aufer, Vesta, diem: cognati Vesta recepta est
> limine; sic iusti constituere patres.
> Phoebus habet partem: Vestae pars altera cessit:
> quod superest illis, tertius ipse tenet.
> state Palatinae laurus, praetextaque quercu
> stet domus: aeternos tres habet una deos.

95. Prostitutes performed from the Vinalia on April 23, a cult of wine associated with Venus and Jupiter, to the end of the Floralia on May 3. For an interpretation linking Ovid's Floralia with Ceres, Liber, and Georgic/anti-Georgic themes, see Fantham 1992a. On prostitutes and lascivious shows at the *Floralia:* Ov. *F.* 4.945–46 (*ioci morem liberioris*), *F.* 5.183, 331–34, 367–68. Val. Max. 2.10.8 *Schol. ad Juv.* 6.249 and 250. Arnobius, *Adv. nat.* 7.33 and Lact. *Div. inst.* 1.20.10. The *Vinalia* seems linked to the *Floralia.* Ovid, *F.* 4.863–900 associates the *Vinalia,* a festival of the opening of the new wine vats, with both Venus and Jupiter. The *Vinalia Rustica* (Aug. 19), also associated with Venus and Jupiter (Degrassi 1963: 444–47 and sources). For the *Vinalia,* Ovid, *F.* 4.865–68 mentions the *volgares puellae:* "Girls of the crowd, celebrate the deity of Venus, abundant Venus good for the revenue of girls who admit 'it.'"

96. Richardson 1992: 151–52 ("Flora, Aedes" not "Flora, Templum," which was on the Quirinal). The aediles Lucius and Marcus Publicius Malleolus built Flora's temple (*aedes*) in 241 BCE (Vell. Pat. 1.14.8) or in 238 (Pliny, *H.N.* 18.286) according to a Sibylline oracle. The Floralia extended from April 28 to May 3. Augustus did show interest in Flora's temple: he started rebuilding it, but Tiberius completed it in 17 CE (Tac. *Ann.* 2.49). Degrassi (1963: 497) thinks the celebration for Flora on Aug. 13 refers to Tiberius' rededication of the temple.

97. *Am.* 3.1.67–70: *"exiguum vati concede, Tragoedia, tempus!/ tu labor aeternus; quod petit illa, breve est."/ mota dedit veniam—teneri properentur Amores,/ dum vacat; a tergo grandius urget opus!*

98. Ov. *Am.* 3.15: *corniger increpuit thyrso graviore Lyaeus.*

99. In *Am.* 3.1, Tragedy's staff (*thyrsus*) threatens phallic penetration of (and generic mixing with) the poet from behind (cf. *Am.* 1.1 for Amor's arrow). As Kennedy 1993: 58–63 has observed, *opus* in the *Amores* could allude to love's penetration of the male author. The erotic ménage of Ovid, Elegy, and Tragedy occurs at a generic "intersection" or crossroad. Crossroads as loci for sexual encounters or at least "cruising," loitering, and gossip about sex: Ovid's own *Am.* 3.1 (Tragedy says people are talking at crossroads); Prop. 1.16, 2.17, 3.14 (on Spartan custom). *Compita*: Prop. 2.20 (people talking). Prop. 2.22a (girls dancing pantomime at crossroads).

100. Vesta can approach from behind (*a tergo*): consider how earlier, *F.* 3.697–98, Ovid was about to fail to mention Julius Caesar's murder, but Vesta intervenes in his thematic choices: *praeteriturus eram gladios in principe fixos, / cum sic a castis Vesta locuta focis. Maius opus* at Verg. *Aen.* 7.44–45 (*maior rerum mihi nascitur ordo, / maius opus moveo*), heralds treatment of Aeneas' arrival in Latium, ruled by king Latinus, and the wars that ensue.

101. See especially Foucault (1990 [1985], 1988 [1986]). Augustus, too, was subject to elite male evaluation; Suetonius (*Aug.* 64) records Augustus' strict observation of affairs within his household, particularly the behavior of daughter Julia.

102. Dio 54.27.2 (13 BCE). Richardson 1992, "Vesta, Ara," 413.

103. Cf. also Ov. *Met.* 15.864–65: *Vestaque Caesareos inter sacrata penates,/ et cum Caesarea tu, Phoebe domestice, Vesta.* On the concept of the *domus Caesaris* as composed of multiple households and houses: Wallace-Hadrill, *CAH²* X (1996): 288–89. Janus' comparison of his two-faced head at a house gate or door (1.128–40) with Diana Trivia's three faces and her tripartite gaze at crossroads (1.140–44) anticipates the juxtaposition of the "crossroad motif" with the motif of "family values" and the *domus* in the May and June prefaces.

104. 5.951–52: *Phoebus habet partem; Vestae pars altera cessit: / quod superest illis, tertius ipse tenet.*

105. *F.* 4.954: *aeternos tres habet una deos.*

106. *F.* 5.110: *turbae pars habet omnis idem;* 6.97: *dicta triplex causa est;* 6.100: *plus laedunt, quam iuvat una, duae.*

107. Foucault 1988 (1986): 39–68 (quote from 51), also Hadot 1981 and 1990. On male anxiety and homosocial consultation about domestic management: cf. Xenophon's *Oeconomicus.*

108. Waites 1912 observes the similarities between various allegorical debates in antiquity. Comparing Judgment of Paris and Choice of Hercules: Athenaeus, *Deip.* 11.510c; Panofsky 1930: 60 and n. 3; cf. the *Krisis* of Sophocles (*Deip.* 15.687, Aphrodite debates Athena as *Hedone*, pleasure, and *Arete*, manly honor). Pythagorean model: Pers. *Sat.* 3.55; Panofsky 1930: 44.

109. Cf. Var. *LL* 6.33; Fest. 120L (with rival etymology); Censor. *De die nat.* 22.9.

110. *Maiestas,* May preface: Mackie 1992; Feeney 1992. On the divine or sacred aspects of *maiestas:* Wagenvoort 1980: 39–58. Republican treason (*crimen maiestatis*), i.e., *laesa maiestas,* was against the majesty of the Roman people and (or) the senate: Cic. *Verr.* 2.4.42.88, *Clu.* 36.97. But in the empire, the insulted divine greatness was that of the emperor or a divinized (deceased) emperor, linked to the identity of the state itself: *CAH²* 1996: 110–11, 143–44 (widening scope of *maiestas* in the last years of Augustus); 212–13 and 219 (esp. under Tiberius), 893 (adultery and *maiestas*). *Maiestas* labeled the emperor's demeanor or divine being, Phaedr. 2.5.23 (*tum sic iocata est tanta maiestas ducis*), cf. Ov. *Tr.* 2.511–12 (*haec tu spectasti spectandaque saepe dedisti / (maiestas adeo comis ubique tua est*). But in the empire, *maiestas* was also ascribed to the senate (referring to due respect and awe for the senate's position): *S.C. Tab. Lar.* line 6: *adhibita fraude qua maiestatem senat[us minuerent]* (Levick 1983: 98) and Vell. 2.89.

111. Newlands 1995a: 74–86, 225

112. Livia's special (propagandistic) favor for the goddess Juno: Taylor 1931: 232. Inscriptions to Livia/Juno (or Hera): *ILS* 120 (3 CE): *Iuno Liviae Augustae sacrum*. Others cited at Barrett 2002: 104, 193–94, 209. For the complex ideological significance of Juno: Mueller 1998. See also Herbert-Brown 1994: 159; Ov. *F.* 1.649–50. See the same comparison of Juno and Livia at *Tr.* 2.161–62, *P.* 2.8.29, 3.1.117–18, and 145–46. At *Tr.* 2.161–62, where the context compares Augustus with Jupiter, Ovid compares Livia and Juno. *P.* 3.1.117–18 describes Livia as possessing the form of Venus and the stern demeanor of Juno. At *P.* 3.1.145 Ovid says, "When you [Ovid's wife] get the opportunity to approach the face of Juno, you mind the persona [Ovid's and her own] that you're defending" (*cum tibi contigerit vultum Iunonis adire, / fac sis personae quam tueare memor*). I wonder whether having a stern face like Juno's was exactly flattering, given Ovid's potentially ambiguous comment at *Tr.* 2.161–62. Cf. Ov. *P.* 4.13.30 and *F.* 6.28.

113. When censor in 204, Livia's ancestor M. Livius Salinator began the temple, which he vowed at the battle of the Metaurus river in 207, but C. Licinius Lucullus dedicated it in 191: Liv. 36.36.5–6. It burned completely in a fire in 16 BCE (Cass. Dio 54.19.7) and Augustus restored it (*Res Gestae* 19). See Richardson 1992: 228 (Iuventas, Aedes).

114. Another possible link between Livia and *Iuventas* is an altar belonging to a crossroad shrine (Vicus Sandaliarius), dating to 2 BCE (according to the consuls inscribed), depicting three figures, two males (left and center) and one female (right). According to Erika Simon, this crossroad altar depicts the day of Lucius' assumption of the *toga virilis* in 2 BCE, and the two young males are Lucius and Gaius, as *principes iuventutis,* while the *Iuventas/Iuventus* figure bears traces of Livia's portraiture. This was also the year they were named *principes iuventutis* and Augustus was called *pater patriae,* but Julia, their mother and Augustus' daughter, was caught in an alleged adulterous conspiracy. For the altar: see E. Simon, "Iuventus" *LIMC* 4.1: 465 and 4.2: 277, no. 3 (photo), with 4.2: 467; Hano 1986: 2338–39 and Planche VII.14. Why represent such a scene on an altar dedicated to the Lares and Genius of Augustus at a local crossroad? Crossroad shrines were a suitable public site for a young man to dedicate his *bulla,* or necklace of boyhood, before entering manhood and taking up the *toga virilis:* cf. Pers. 5.30–36; Hild s.v. "Lares" in Dar.-Sag. 3.2.943 (limits the hanging of bullae to the *Lares familiares,* inside the house). But cf. the crossroad Altar of the *Lares Augusti* (Rome, Palazzo dei Conservatori, decorated with two carved *bullae:* Hano 1986: 2342–43, Pl. X, 21).

115. In late first- and second-century CE art, Concordia stands as *pronuba* (matron of honor) centered behind the altar and *iunctio dextrarum* (handshake) between newlywed wife and husband. *LIMC* s.v. "Homonoia/Concordia," 5.1: 479–98 and 5.2: 333–340. For Concordia figured on coins under the image of "shaking hands," see *LIMC* 5.1.490–91;

for Concordia as *pronuba* on second-century sarcophagi, nos. 44, 74, 81, 83, 86, 89; Concordia between men on coins: see nos. 91 (Titus and Domitian), 93 (Hadrian and Aelius Verus), but also between the emperor and wives as at nos. 92 and 95. Cf *Aen.* 4.166, where Juno seems to perform her conventional role of *pronuba* for Dido in "marriage" with Aeneas, but in a "questionable" cave-wedding performed in isolation from other mortal eyes.

116. Livia's *aedes/ara* to Concordia and the Porticus Liviae: Ov. *F.* 1.649–50; 6.637–38 says *aedes* (639–48 concerns the Porticus Liviae). Richardson 1992: 99–100 states, "Evidently the *porticus* and the *aedes* were substantially identical," and compares Livia's porticus to that of Eumachia at Pompeii, which is also dedicated to Concordia, probably in imitation of Livia's. Flory 1984. Also Richardson 1992: 314 (Porticus Liviae). Tiberius' refurbishment of the temple of Concord: *F.* 1.637–50; work commenced in 7 BCE with Tiberius' spoils from triumph over Germany (Cass. Dio 55.8.2). Dedication was Jan. 16, 10 CE (Cass. Dio 56.25; Suet. *Tib.* 20 [date of 12 CE]).

117. Zizek, "Fantasy as a Political Category: A Lacanian Approach," in Wright and Wright 1999: 93. Castration, because the "Choice of Hercules" is the scene in which the male subject (here Ovid) foregoes immediate enjoyment, for endurance of labor. For castration fantasy as a "primal fantasy" (Freudian term), Farmer 2000: 54–55; primal castration fantasy figures the origin of sex-gender difference; Laplanche and Pontalis 1973: 331–33 ("Primal Phantasies").

118. Cf. Newlands 1995a: 51–86 on Ovid as a narrator of lessening confidence and growing uncertainty.

119. Kay 2003: 61–62. Zizek 1991: 88–106, esp. 91–93 on "Blot" in Hitchcock's cinema.

120. The simplistic nature of the "Choice of Hercules": Cic. *Off.* 1.118.

Chapter Five

1. For example, months were renamed: the "Fifth" (*Quintilis*) became *Julius* (Dio 55.7.2, 44 BCE; Macr. *Sat.* 1.12.34); the "Sixth" (*Sextilis*) became *Augustus* (Liv. *Per.* 124, *Fasti Praenestini*, "August" pref., Dio 55.6.6; Suet. *Aug.* 31.2; Macr. *Sat.* 1.12.34). Festivals in the calendar for Divus Augustus (after his death): Degrassi 1963: 369. Augustan festival lists, *Feriale Cumanum* and *Amerinum:* Degrassi 1963: 279–28, 281. Tac. *Ann.*1.15.3: *ludos qui de nomine Augusti fastis addidit Augustales vocarentur* (also 1.54). Anniversaries advertising the life-narrative of imperial family members and creating a symbolic center for the Julio-Claudian calendars: Beard 1987, Wallace and Hadrill 1987.

2. On Tiberius' hesitancy to use the title in Rome: Barrett 2002: 151–53; Scott 1932.

3. Nicolet 1991. On *gnomon* in sundials: Gibbs 1976. In Roman land surveying: Stone 1928; Dilke 1971: 66–81. Sundial-*gnomon* in mapping latitude: Nicolet 1991: 110. *Gnomon* orienting streets of a town: Vitr. 1.6.5–6, 12. *Gnomonike* as part of the architect's knowledge-base: Vitr. 1.1.17, 1.3.1 (along with *aedificatio* and *machinatio*). A gnomon's shadow oriented centuriated land: Blume, Lachmann, and Rudorff 1848, 1: 184.1, 188.14–191.11.

4. Lacan 2002: 145–46 (1966: 503), 281–312 (1961: 793–827); Lacan 1993: 267–270 (1981: 303–305). Clear explanation of *points de capiton* applied to Catullus: Janan 1994: 24–24. Important discussion of "quilting points" and Lacan's graphs of desire: Zizek 1989: 87–129

5. Catullus' sound-effects communicating outside syntax: Fredrick 1999. Lacan's notions of voice and gaze are, like libidinal objects in Freudian psychoanalysis (phallus,

anus, mouth), conditioned by the self-division occurring when individuals enter into subjectivity through speech and language. This division of prior self—separation from voice and gaze of mother—causes desire's repression from the construction of the subject. See Janan 1994: 29. Lacan 2002: 138–69 (1966: 493–528); 281–312 (1966: 793–827). Cf. Zizek 1991: 88–106, esp. 89–91, who distinguishes oral, anal, and phallic stages of cinematic composition; the phallic (typical of Hitchcock) constructs fear, panic, from some place within, usually under the symbolic world of representation (see discussion of Cacus below).

6. Ovid's other associations of Augustus with Jupiter: Herbert-Brown 1994: 201–202; e.g. *Met.* 15.353–60; *Tr.* 3.1.47–8.

7. Historical sources on these and the following names: Frazer 1929, 2: 226, Bömer 1957–1958, 2: 67.

8. Agreeing: Festus, "Augustus" 2L. Suet. *Aug.* 7.2 cites Ennius on augury at Rome's foundation: *Augusto augurio postquam incluta condita Roma est* (*Ann.* 502 Vahlen). Cass. Dio 53.16.8 says *augustus* meant "more than human" or "sacred."

9. Augural significance of the name *Augustus:* Beard, North, and Price 1998, 1: 181–84; Taylor 1931: 158–60. Major civic officers or military commanders conducted augury (Taylor 1931: 76–97; Botsford 1909: 100–18). Commander-in-chief, Augustus wielded greater augural status, the better to guide the state in war and peace (Scott 1932).

10. Types of *templa* (heaven, earth): Varr. *LL* 7.6–10. Universe as *templum* observed by Jupiter: Cic. *Re pub.* 6.16. Augurs watching for signs in *templa:* Cic. *Leg.* 2.20–21. Exemplary is Livy's account of Numa's inauguration as king: Liv. 1.18.7. Also Romulus' creation of the first earthly *templum* (Jupiter Feretrius) in Rome: Liv. 1.10.5–6. See Müller 1961; Rykwert 1988: 44–50. *Templa* for astrological zones in heaven: Manil. *Astron.* 1.13–24, 46–50, 420–21, 448; 2.354, 668, 857–967.

11. Atrium as setting inspiring elite male honor: Sall. *Jug.* 4.5, Val. Max. 5.8.3, Plb. 6.53, Juv. 8.19–20, [Tib.] 3.7.28–36; also, Frazer 1929, 2: 223, Bömer 1957–1958, 2: 66–67 (on *F.* 1.591). Wax masks: Ov. *Am.* 1.8.65, Plin. *H.N.* 35.6; Juv. 8.19–20. Plaques: Liv. 10.7.11, Tib. 3.7.28–36, and Val. Max. 5.8.3. Cf. portraits and plaques of *summi viri* displayed in the Forum Augustum; *F.* 5.545–598, esp. 563–66, statues of Aeneas and Romulus; Richardson 1992: 161; Coarelli 1995: 127; Anderson 1984: 93–97. On the pedagogy of masculinity at the Forum Augustum, where youths donned the *toga* of manhood (*toga virilis*): Dio 55.10.1–5. See Yavetz 1984, Kellum 1996 and 1997.

12. Tiberius' initial strategic hesitancy: Suet. *Tib.* 24; Tac. *Ann.* 1.11–13, esp. 11.1–3. Vell. 2.124 treats Tiberius' hesitancy as genuine. Cf. *F.* 1.615–616 (*auspicibus deis tanti cognominis heres/ omine suscipiat, quo pater, orbis onus.*) with *CIL* X. 3747 = *ILS* (Dessau) 137.1–2 (dedication of a temple to Gaius and Lucius Caesares at Acerrae): *templum hoc sacratum her[edibus qui] quod gerunt/ Augusti nomen felix [illis] remaneat/* . . . (text at Taylor 1931: 224).

13. The title *Germanicus* for Nero Claudius Drusus, Tiberius' brother: Frazer 1929, 2: 226; Suet. *Claud.* 1.3; Livy, *Per.* 139, 140; Vell. 2. 97; and Val. Max. 5.5.3; also Bömer 1957–1958, 2: 67, with Ov. *Tr.* 4.2.399ff.; Flor. 2. 30. 28; Dio 55.2.3. Frazer 1929, 2: 226 cites other causes of death than combat (poisoning, sickness, or fall from horse). Military disaster in Germany under command of P. Quinctilius Varus (9 CE): Vell. Pat. 2.117.2–119; Dio 56.18–22.2; Suet. *Aug.* 23; Oros. 6.21.27. *CAH*² X.110, 185, 187, 527. The *Gemma Augustea* (ca. 10 CE; Galinsky 1996: 120–21 and fig. 57) portrays both Tiberius and Germanicus conducting military campaigns (expressing *virtus*) under Augustus' *auspicium.*

14. Cult of Aeneas as Jupiter Indiges at Lavinium: Holloway 1994: 128–141, esp. 138. Wethers (*verveces*, castrated rams) sacrificed to family Lar, deceased ancestor: Cic. *De leg.* 2.55. Lares as spirits of departed ancestors: Taylor 1931: 49; Varr. *LL* 5.19. Cf. Plaut. *Bacch.* 1120–48: two Bacchides call the older fathers "ewes" (female *oves*); cf. Juv. 10.47–50 (50 *vervecum*). Castration in the sacrificial act: Mart. 3.24.1–5; Burkert 1983: 68 and 283, 44, citing Clement of Alexandria, *Pr.* 2.15.2 (myth on castration of ram), Arnob. 5.20, and Hermes' phallic image and association with sacrificial rams.

15. The *Flamen Dialis* (a priest of Jupiter) offered the sacrifice to Jupiter on all the Ides (Macrob. *Sat.* 1.15.16). "Rather big ewe lamb" (*F.* 1.56) may euphemistically name the castrated ram of 1.588. Ewe-lamb as victim is implied by *quae* at Festus 93L: *Idulis ovis dicebatur, quae omnibus idibus Iovi mactabatur*. Bömer 1957–1958, 2: 13 and 66 (on *F.* 1.56, 588: *semimaris*). Frazer 1929, 2: 74 (1.56), 218–19 is disconcerted by the gender change; Le Bonniec 1965: 33 (on *F.* 1.56), 96 (on *F.* 1.588) comments, "Cette divergence est inexpliquée," concluding, "La question mériterait une étude d'ensemble." Augustus is Lar (see above).

16. *Omnis provincia*, "every province," includes resubjugated Egypt. The "error" of dating bestowal of the title Augustus to 13th, not 16th: Degrassi 1963: 400 citing January 16 as the correct date: *Fasti Praen.* and *Feriale Cumanum;* Censor. 21.8. Ovid correctly ascribes to Jan. 13 the senate's vote of *corona civica* (1.614, *protegat et vestras querna corona fores*); Aug. *RG* 34 (28–27 BCE); *Fasti Praen.* on Jan. 13 (Degrassi 1963: 112–13); Dio 53.4 (27 BCE).

17. Hardie 1991: 62–64 on two-faced Janus as emblematic of dichotomous meaning; Barchiesi 1997a: 231–32 describes Janus as having "two voices," but does not develop the idea.

18. Ovid's Callimachean etymologizing about the *Agonium-Agonalia:* Miller 1992, Newlands 1995a: 58–59.

19. The Chorus in Aristophanes' *Birds* explain that various events, including other animal sounds, are called "bird" (ὄρνις and οἰωνός: *Birds* 717–22, esp. 721: ὄνον ὄρνιν, "an ass is a bird [omen]."

20. Agriculture-plant metaphors for oratory: Connors 1997. Oral reading in tension with silent reading: Svenbro 1993: 160–86. Note Janus' shift in symbolic register from sweet verbal exchanges as omens (1.175–84), to sweet consumable goods (honey and figs, 185–88) and even money (189–225).

21. Cf. Io's "mooing" at *Met.* 1.635–50 turned into her hoof-written *nomen*.

22. Svenbro 1993: 160–86 discusses silent reading. *Verbenae*, generally grasses or herbs, usually had in poetry a specifically ritual meaning, such as that given by Servius (commenting on Verg. *Aen.* 12, 120: *verbenas vocamus omnes frondes sacratas, ut est laurus, oliva vel myrtus*, or on *E.* 8, 65. Such plants were worn by various priests and signaled those suing for peace (such as the Fetiales) or supplicants (see examples cited by L-S, *verbena*).

23. As Newlands 1995a: 35 observes, Ovid's sympathy with sacrificial animals alludes to Pythagorean belief in reincarnation and his language echoes that of Ov. *Met.* 15.453–78.

24. Ovid here imitates Callimachus' handling of *aetia*. For this intertext here and in the subsequent paragraphs: Miller 1992: 14–22, esp. 20.

25. Water as symbol of poetry: Prop. 3.3, 4.6.7–8; Commager 1962: 11–16, 322–24; cf. Hor. *C.* 3.13 (goat's blood in water of fountain).

26. Lacan's notion of "voice" among the libidinal objects: Lacan 1993: 117–29. Salecl-Zizek 1996: 2–3; Miller 1989: 182; and Dolar 1996: 7–31 also offer concise discussions.

Chion 1999 (1982) and 1994 (1990); Silverman 1988; and Zizek 1991: 125–40 apply Lacanian notions of voice to cinema. This serendipitous wordplay was also theorized by Lacan as *Lalangue* (*llangue*), Lacan 1998 (*Sem. XX*). *Lalangue* and *voix* refer to the acoustic level of language in which homonymy develops polysemy. Jacques-Alain Miller commenting at Lacan 1998: 44n15: "[*llangue*] is the level at which an infant (or songwriter) may endlessly repeat one syllable of a word (for example, "la la la"), the level at which language may 'stutter.'" From such speech events come unexpected discoveries of meanings answering off-screen desire.

27. Mis-hearing (*le malentendu*) and auditory tropes are fundamental to a Lacanian *lalangue:* Miller 1975: 32. Quint. *Inst.* 9.2.64–99 discusses *emphasis* in figured covert communication enabling adumbration of hidden desire that exceed decorum; see also [Longinus] *On the Sublime* 17 and Demetr. *Eloc.* (*On Style*) 287–298. *Kakemphaton:* Quint. *Inst.* 8.3.42–45. For a synthesis of ancient discussions of figured speech (*schema*), see Ahl 1984a, 1984b. Tacitus' *interpretatio prava* provides a more political form of *kakemphaton:* see Bartsch 1994.

28. For ἐσχηματισμένη λέξις, see Quint. *Inst.* 9.1.11–14; [Longin.] *On the Sublime* 16–17; Demetr. 287–94 (λόγος ἐσχηματισμένος). Lausberg 1960, 1: 308–9 offers other sources. Miller 1989: 182–83 explains how Lacanian "voice" concerns the "fantasy of a dispatch" ("le fantasme de dépeçage") that "entend résonner le mot de son être." Similar is the notion of *lalange:* Miller 1975. As for deliberate (mis)construal, Roof 1996 and Farmer 2000 analyze how lesbian and gay male groups perceive and interpret differently what are ostensibly heteronormative tales in novels or films, maintaining views counter to the tales' so-called objective surfaces as acknowledged by others. Likewise, I suggest, Roman readership was not monolithic.

29. Juncture of syllables across words or disjuncture within a word causing ambiguity and inviting repressed desire and meaning: Quint. *Inst.* 7.9.1–6 (2 for homonyms; 5–6, *iunctura* and *divisio*). *Kakemphaton* can involve ambiguity in division of syllables: *kakemphaton*, Quint. *Inst.* 8.3.44–47; Richlin 1983: 13–26. Cf. *amphibolia . . . obscena*, Quint. *Inst.* 6.3.47. Grammatical ambiguity: Quint. *Inst.* 7.9.7–9. "Acousmatic" sound and voice: Chion 1999 (esp. 17–29), 1994: 71–73.

30. Metaplasm-*transformatio* of words: Lausberg 1960, 1: 259–65. Plays upon names (*paronomasia:* Lausberg 1960, 1: 322–35) in Ovid offer tropes of transformation (cf. *metamorphoses*) via polyvalence: Hardie 2002: 227–57, esp. 239–57; cf. "Aias" on Narcissus' flower of "woe" (*Met.* 10.207–8, 13.397–98: *AIAS, AIAI*); Io, as cow failing to vocalize her name (she "moos"), writes *IO* with her hoof (1.635–50). In the *Fasti:* Boyd 2000 on F. 4.507–8 and Boyd 2001 for F. 5.379–414 (Chiron); play upon Ovid's own name is not discussed. Cf. Vergil's use of names in etymological wordplay: O'Hara 1996. Paronomastic puns were a technique of Callimachean poetry: cf. Cairns 2002; Peraki-Kyriakidou 2002.

31. Problems of sound and name extend to Ovid's exilic works: P. 4.12.5–16 (Tuticanus' name will not fit properly into elegiac verse); 2.6.1–4, esp. 3 (Graecinus); 2.10.4; 2.4.24. Cf. *Rem.* 476.

32. As Barchiesi describes this *sphragis* (1997a: 134), "The narrator's relationship with Flora is marked by a fellow feeling that has few parallels in the poem." On this wordplay, Naso-nose: Barchiesi 1997a: 134; Newlands 1995a: 123. Augustus' sphinx as *signum*, seal-sign: Suet. *Aug.* 50.

33. Macr. *Sat.* 1.15.14 and 17.

34. Cf. Ovid's *semibovemque virum semivirumque bovem*, describing the Minotaur (*A.A.* 2.24) and the anecdote at Sen. *Contr.* 2.2.12, where this line (among two others) is

subject to criticism from friends for its sound, if not its allusion to castration (*Am.* 2.11.10, similarly criticized). Cf. *Met.* 12.499–509, where the centaur Monychus, a *semivir,* describes centaurs as being defeated by the *semimas* Caeneus, formerly and still (he argues) the female Caenis; castration is literalized in the combat scene. Phallic dominance over gender differences is at the "quilting point."

35. At a temple to Apollo at Actium, Augustus erected bronze statues of both: Kellum 1996: 174 and fig. 72. Kellum 1997: 163–64 and fig. 4 discusses a satyrical Pompeian wall painting showing an ithyphallic ass driven by a man crowned by Victory; the ass sexually mounts the lion (Antony).

36. Shifting accent and word division enhances puns of uncertain meaning in *llangue:* Lacan 1998: 136–46, Miller 1975. Rhetorical *ambiguitas (amphibolia)* as *vitium* producing *obscuritas* (obscurity) versus the verbal *virtus* of *perspicuitas* (clarity): Quint. *Inst.* 8.2.12–13. Yet, this *vitium* can render ornament (8.2.11). Language of virtue and vice of language is abundant (ἀρεταί, κακία λέξεως); cf. Galen, *De capt.* 2 (Edlow 1977). Accent, division and juncture causing *amphibolia:* Galen, *De Capt.* 4 (Edlow). Homonymy causing ambiguity in single words: Quint. *Inst.* 7.9.2–3, 8.2.13. Also division of one word into two: Quint. *Inst.* 7.9.4; Arist. *Soph. El.* 4.166a33–36; cf. Edlow 1977: 25–26. Ambiguous accent is part of the figure: Arist. *Soph. El.* 21.177b37–178a2 (cited at Edlow 1977: 27–28).

37. Cf. the "eyes" with which Augustus both watched staged adultery mimes and *totus orbis* at *Tr.* 2.513–14 (*luminibusque tuis, tutus quibus utitur orbis, scaenica vidisti lentus adulteria*).

38. Jupiter's nod troubling Atlas' support of the world: *F.* 2.487–90; similar, Luc. *BC* 1.57 (Nero's apotheosis, *sentiet axis onus*), 6.464, 6.483; Man. 2.896; Petr. 139.2 (verse 3). Atlas as cosmic support: Gee 2000: 39–40. Atlas was allegorized as *axis mundi* (Hardie 1986: 280 n132, 374), astronomer-philosopher (Hardie 1986: 58n62), "guarantor of cosmic order" (Hardie 1986: 278, 374–75). For the Farnese Atlas, see, e.g., Nicolet 1991: fig. 22. *Orbis* as starry heaven: Gee 2000: 38–39; Hardie 1986: 267 (sphere as earth or spherical universe), 336–76 (shield of Aeneas in *Aeneid* as *orbis,* cosmic icon).

39. Ὄνος as turning post, capstan: Arist. *Mech. quaest.* 853b12; Hippocr. *Fract.* 31; Hdt. 7.36. Upper-millstone: e.g. Xen. *Anab.* 1.5.5; Poll. 7.4.119; cf. Var. *RR* 10.4, 11.4. Spindle or distaff: Poll. 7.32, 10.125.

40. Latin equivalents in *TGL,* ὄνος (5.2038). Vitr. 10.1 4 associates practical instruments with the functioning mechanism of the cosmos.

41. At Tac. *Ann.* 4.70, we find the association of Tiberius with Janus uncannily reactivated by ill-omened timing and antagonism with Sejanus: one of Sejanus' victims jests about "Se-janus" and murderous anxiety on a New Year's Day lacking proper joy and a proper Janus: see Morgan 1998.

42. Marking celestial-solar events, sundials served as astronomical calendars: Gibbs 1976: 5, 17, 69; 88 (dials with names of months). Sundial atop *Menologium Rusticum Vallense,* Degrassi 1963: 291–98, Tab. LXXXIII–VI. Aveni 1989: 92 cites Price 1975: 53 for the idea that Greco-Roman water-clocks and sundials are "'simulacra' or simulations of how things work," noting the ancient builders' "aesthetic satisfaction derived from making a device that imitated the heavens." Mechanical astronomical calendar-clocks in antiquity: King 1978: 3–14.

43. Augustus imported two obelisks in 10 BCE; the first arriving (in the Circus Maximus), Pliny calls an *onus,* burden (Plin. *H.N.* 36.70). Augustus memorialized its transport ship at Puteoli. Similar fascination with erection of obelisks: Amm. 17.4.15.

44. On this obelisk at Heliopolis: Str. 17.1.27. As *gnomon* in *horologium,* Plin. *H.N.* 37.71–72. On the erection of the obelisk: Amm. 17.4.12. On the *Horologium* as a version

of the calendar: Wallace-Hadrill 1987: 228; Salzman 1990: 9 n19; Barton 1995: 45–46. Basic descriptions of the *Horologium* can be found, e.g., at Buchner 1982; Richardson 1992: 272–73 ("Obeliscus Augusti [Gnomon]") and 190–91, fig. 42 ("Horologium Solare Augusti"); Sauron 1994: 511–19; Galinsky 1996: 146. Ideological import of calendars: Herbert-Brown 2002: 101–28 (esp. 114–15); Feeney 1998: 127; Barchiesi 1997a: 9–10; Wallace-Hadrill 1987; Newlands 1995a: 23–26. Critique of Buchner's mathematical model: Schütz 1990. Caution interpreting astrological significance: Gee 2000: 7n19,

45. The obelisk and base: Zanker 1988: 144–45 (figs. 116, 117); *Kaiser Augustus und die verlorene Republik*, 240–45 (Buchner); Buchner 1982: 81–82 (plates 108–109).

46. *CIL* 6.702: *Imp. Caesar Divi F./ Augustus/ Pontifex Maximus/ Imp. XII Cos XI Trib. Pot. XIV/ Aegypto in potestatem/ Populi Romani Redacta/ Soli Donum dedit.*

47. *Augustales* worshiping emperor: Taylor 1931: 219–23; Galinsky 1996: 310–12. As status-group: Beard-North-Price 1998, 1: 358.

48. Trimalchio's anxiety about time: Toohey 1997. The *gnomon-nomen* shadows the grid of the sundial: cf. Luc. 1.135–36: "the shadow of the name 'Magnus' [Pompey's cognomen] stands, just as a lofty oak on a grain-bearing field . . ." (*stat magni nominis umbra,/ qualis frugifero quercus sublimis in agro . . .*). Cf. *CIL* VI. 25063.9–10: *dunc annos titulo, nomine ut ipse legas.*

49. "Unexpected" references to *horologium Augusti* (*A.A.* 1.68 and 3.388): Simpson 1992.

50. Amm. 17.4.7 defines *obeliscus: est autem obeliscus asperrimus lapis in figuram metae cuiusdam sensim ad proceritatem consurgens excelsam* (Plin. *H.N.* 36.64 calls it a *trabes*). Cf. Gloss. ὀβελίσκος. *Lapis nimiae altitudinis;* Gloss. V Aa o 42: *meta finis.* Surveyors refer to obelisk-like boundary markers: *terminus in summo acutus* (*Agrim.* 250.14 [*Liber Coloniarum I*], 19; 405.11); *Circulatus pyramis [per ramos] metae [mitae] acutae similis* (*Agrim.* 250.15); cf. *terminus in summo acutus./ circulatus pyramis [peramus] item acuto similis/ item perramus metae [uittae] praecisae similis* (*Agrim.* 405.11–13). Cf. Gell. 1.20.3: *metae triangulae, quas "pyramidas" appellant.* Philo, *De sept. mirac.* 7 applies the term *pyramis* to a gnomon-like shape (τὸ πᾶν ἔργον εἰς πυραμίδα καὶ γνώμονος σχῆμα).

51. At *Metam.* 1.135–36, surveying portends greedy ownership-values of the Iron Age. Cf. celebration of the *Terminalia*, festival of boundary stones or *termini: F.* 2.639–684. Cf. Coma Berenikes: Cat. 56.1–9 and Call. *Aet.* 110.1, "Having examined the entire *boundary in writing* [i.e., charted heavens] where [the stars?] are born along . . ." (πάντα τὸν ἐν γραμμαῖσι ἰδὼν ὅρον ᾗ τε φέρονται).

52. See Cic. *Tusc.* 1.25.63, *N.D.* 2.35.88. Lactantius said it was bronze (*Inst.* 2.5); Claudian, of glass (*Carm. min.* 51 [68]). Frazer 1929, 4: 204 (*F.* 6.277) summarizes. King 1978: 3–14 places these globes among other ancient astronomical mechanisms.

53. Paul. exc. Fest. 123.13: *metari castra dicuntur, quod metis deriguntur.* Metaphorical application to agriculture: Varr. *R.R.* 1.4.1, *hinc profecti agricolae ad duas metas derigere debent, ad utilitatem et volutem;* 1.18.1, *de familia Cato derigit ad duas metas, ad certum modum agri et genus sationis.* Cf. *F.* 1.4, *timidae derige navis iter.*

54. *Metae:* Blume, Lachman, and Rudorff 1848, 1: 32, line 1 (*moeta*); 33, line 2, 11 (*moeta*); (*meta*) 33, 2, 20; (*moeta*) p. 34, 4, 10; (*meta*) 192, 8; 193, 7; 287, 6; 401, 21; (*signa*) p. 2, 6, 24; p. 6, 27; p. 11, 6; p. 13, 41; etc.

55. See L-S, *pilum* I and *OLD pilum¹. Pila* (feminine) has similar ambiguity at Prop. 4.1.75–6 and 4.1.91 (fictional astrologer Horos). The meaning of *polus* (πόλος) varies. Vault of heaven: Aesch. *Prom.* 427 (Atlas supporting the πόλος, sphere surrounding earth). A sundial's concave surface into which the *gnomon* casts a shadow (Hdt 2.109; Poll. 9.46, πόλον as ὡρολόγιον; Luc. *Lex.* 4; Ar. *Fr.* 163); Smith's *Dictionary of Greek and*

Roman Antiquities, pp. 929–30; LSJ πόλος IV. A post, pivot in Greek (LSJ) or Latin (L-S). Ovid's uses of *polus: F.* 1.653, 3.106, 4.576, 834, 5.180, 6.718; *Met.* 2.75, 131, 173; *Pont.* 2.7.64; *Tr.* 4.3.15.

56. A *Pertica* of ten feet was called *decempeda* (L-S II.B) and was used in surveying: Cic. *Mil.* 27.74; *Philip.* 14.4.10, 13.18.37, *Acad. Quaest.* 2.41.126; Hor. *C.* 2.15.14. Metal ends of a *pertica* among remains of a surveyor's office in Pompeii: Dilke 1971: 73; general description: Stone 1928: 218.

57. Design of the *groma* (from *gnoma, gnomon* via Etruscan; Dilke 1962: 176, cf. Paul. ex Fest. 68L): *Brill's New Pauly* 5 (2004) col. 1033–34; *OCD³* 658, *gromatici. Stella,* mechanical horizontal cross-shaped device (also termed *machina,* Blume-Lachman-Rudorff 1848.1.295.11; *machinula,* Paul. ex Fest. 86L, *groma*): Stone 1928: 223; Rudorff in Blume, Lachmann, and Rudorff 1852, 2: 336. *Asteriskos* in Greek: Hero, *Dioptr.* 33. Meton's *kanones* and star-pattern of roads (*asteros*) at *Birds* (1007–8) and Hyg. *Mun. Castr.* 12.

58. On *metas dictare:* Blume, Lachman, and Rudorff 1848.1, p. 33, 2 (Front. Grom.), *tunc dictare metas et easdem transposito interim extrema meta ferramento reprehendere . . .* ; p. 34.9–11 (Front. Grom.); *dictare rigorem* (Front. Grom. 33.10–11, 14. Nipsius 285.9, 11; 286.1–2), *cannas* (Nips. 286.21; cf. Meton's *kanones*), *limitem* (32.10; 287.7). Cf. Hyg. *mun. castr.* 12 *in dictatione metarum* (cf. 15; 21). Lewis 2001: 328 (no. 56) translates *dictare metas* (*cannas, rigorem*) as "to sight poles," "line" etc. (e.g., Nipsius Blume-Lachman-Rudorff 1848.286.1, 21). But *TLL, dictare* (vol. 5, col. 1013, lines 44–50) reports that the verb means to dictate the markers to be positioned by slaves.

59. Other inter-texts: Gee 2000; Barchiesi 1997a: 177–80; Newlands 1995a: 32–44 (e.g., Verg. *G.* 2.490: *felix qui poterit rerum cognoscere causas; F.* 1.397). Newlands (1995a: 33) views this passage as praising astronomers for virtuous attainments, but that virtue may be ironic. Astronomy aids sailing and demarcation of land, the stock features of arrogant desire in the Iron Age (*Met.*1.125–50); cf. Giants' attack upon heaven (*Met.* 1.151–62).

60. *Kanones* of Meton may be the *gnomon;* cf. *Etym. Magn.,* s.v. *gnomon,* identifies it as *kanonion,* part of a dioptrical instrument. Meton's observation of summer solstice with Euctemon, in 432 BCE using the ἡλιοτρόπιον: Sch. Ar. *Av.* 998, Ptol. *Alm.* 3.1; Philochorus, *FGrH* (Jacoby) 328 F 122 (defined as sundial in LSJ, citing Moschion ap. Ath.5.207f, *IG* 11[2].287 A117 [Delos, 3rd cent. BCE], Plu. *Dio* 29); Diod. 12.36.2–3. See *OCD³, Meton* (969–70); on Meton: Toomer 1974.

61. Such representations appeared rather commonly on ancient sundials: Gibbs 1976; "Clocks," *Brill's New Pauly* 3 (2002), coll. 457–64, ill. 459. On *parapegmata,* a type of calendar often fitted with moveable pegs and often emphasizing meteorological and astronomical data: Hannah 2005, esp. chs. 3 and 5; Rehm 1949; and Diehls and Rehm 1904.

62. For the animate, personified quality of stars as gods, one might cite Balbus' Stoic proof, Cic. *ND* 2.39–44, but the animate quality of stars is evident in love poetry as well, such as Cat. 7.7–8: *aut quam sidera multa, cum tacet nox, / furtivos hominum vident amores.* Addresses to astral or weather phenomena are common in "door-way" love scenes in ancient literature (*paraclausithyra*): see Copley 1956 and Tarán 1979.

63. Carmentis' sacred names, *Porrima* and *Postverta,* label prophecy about "what has been" and "what was to come afterwards" (631–36); cf. *antica* and *postica,* terms designating direction of orientation in the land surveyor's texts: Blume, Lachmann, and Rudorf 1848: 28.3–4, 166.17–167.1, 249.29 (*limites per antica et postica dividuntur*), etc.

64. At *F.* 2.676–68 (February 15), Dawn again watches (*aspicit*) a festival, running of naked youths, Luperci.

65. Sol was considered *oculus Iovis,* "Eye of Jupiter" (Macr. *Sat.* 1.21.12); he is "eye of heaven" (*mundi oculus*) at Ov. *Met.* 4.228. Noting the designation *ad Titan* for San

Lorenzo in Lucina in eighth-century liturgies (traceable perhaps to the fifth century), Platner 366 (and n. 1) suggests an allusion to the obelisk dedicated to Sol (citing *Atti dell'Accademia Pontificia, Rendiconti* 4.261–77). Note as well that an Augustan inscription (*CIL* VI. 30975) dedicated to Sol and Luna (line 4), among other gods, was found some 500 meters to the west of the obelisk dedicated to Sol. Palmer 1990: 18–28 provides an accessible copy of the inscription, a commentary, and a description of its context.

66. Cf. Ov. *Metam.* 4.226–28, the Sun describing himself: *"ille ego sum," dixit, "qui longum metior annum,/ omnia qui video, per quem videt omnia tellus,/ mundi oculus."* Plin. *H.N.* 2.5.4.10, cf. Vitr. 3.5 technical term, *oculus* in a vault. Cf. Vell. 2.52.3 (*Romani imperii lumen*), 299.1 (*reipublicae lumen et caput*). Cf. distanced aerial viewpoint of the Epicurean sage: Lucr. 2.1–12 (cf. 1.62–79; 3.14–30). World or cosmos as stage: Curtius 1953: 138–44. *Scaenae frons* as symbol of *mimus vitae* (terrestrial life on show for gods): Sauron 1994: 434–39 (atrium 5 of Villa Oplontis), 537–40 (different types and interpretation).

67. Also the view of Santini 1975.

68. Svenbro 1993: 160–86 discusses silent and vocal reading. Ancient elemental or atomistic models of wordplay: Malamud 1989: 27–36 (on explicit comparisons at Lucr. 1.814–829 and 1.907–913); Svenbro 1993: 175–76, Steiner 1994: 116–22. *TGL* and LSJ, στοιχεῖον. Arist. *Poet.* 20 (1456b22) defines *stoicheion* as "indivisible sound" (φωνὴ ἀδιαίρετος) "from which intelligible sound can come into existence" (ἐξ ἧς πέφυκε συνετὴ γίγνεσθαι φωνή); Arist. *Metaph.* 998a23; Plat. *Cratyl.* 424d, 426d., *Theaet.* 202e; Latin: Maur. 1168 (Gramm. Lat.).

69. *Stoicheion* as Cosmic element: LSJ II.2; Lucil. 786; Vitr. 1.4.5. Celestial bodies: LSJ II.5 and *TGL* 7.790; Diog. Laert. 6.102 of Zodiac signs; Justin Martyr, *Apol.* 2.11, *ourania stoicheia*; Paul, *Ep. Gal.* 4.3, *Ep. Col.* 2.8.

70. *Palatum*, "palate," yet heaven's "vault": LS I, *palatum*. Palate as organ of voice, not taste: Ov. *Am.* 2.6.47–48; Cat. 55.21–22; Hor. *S.* 2.3.274.

71. *Stoicheion* as shadow of a *gnomon* or person to tell time: LSJ I and Pollux 6.8 (44); Aristoph. *Eccl.* 652, Eubulus ap. Athen. 1.8c; Menander ap. Athen. 6.243a, Philemon ap. Photius, στοιχεῖον. Tables showing hour equivalents of men's shadow lengths: Pattenden 1978: 338; Pallad. *Op. agr.* (4th cent.) 2.23, 3.34; 4.15, 5.8, 6.18, 7.13, 8.10, 9.14. 10.19, 11.23, 12.23, 13.7; *ILS* 8644 (*CIL* XIII. 11173; shadow lengths by locations in empire); Bede, "Libellus de Mensura Horologii" in J.-P. Migne, ed., 1862. *Venerabilis Bedae Opera Omnia.* Paris: J.-P. Migne. Pl. XC, coll. 953–55.

72. Functioning horizontally, the *groma* aided land surveys (cf. *libella*); the *dioptra* aided astronomical and terrestrial observations (perfected by Hero of Alexandria, 1st cent.). The *dioptra* (from the Greek for "sight-through," *diopteuein*; cf. Janus' *perspicere, F.* 1.139–40), consisted of a (horizontally-vertically) moveable plate mounted with a straight bar that pivoted around it; the bar had two "sights" at each end (*augeia*, small plates with holes), for fore-sighting and back-sighting astronomical signs, landmarks or *metae*. Fore- and back-sighting: e.g., Lewis 2001: 42 (on earlier Hipparchan *dioptra*), but passim. *Dioptra*: Lewis 2001: 51–108; types of sights (73–74). Untrained readers confused terms: *dioptra* or *optra* as *groma, gnoma, gnomon: Corpus Gloss. Lat.* II.278.25; *Etym. Magn. gnomon* as part of a diaoptrical instrument. See Heron, *Peri dioptras;* Vitr. 8.5; Plin. *H.N.* 2.69.69; Stone 1928: 226–33. Other references: LSJ, *dioptra. Dioptra* as a sighting-tube used to view military signals: Plb. 10.46.1; Lewis 2001: 37.

73. Altar of imperial cult in Germany among Ubii at Cologne: Tac. *Ann.* 1.39, 57. Cf. on the Elbe river in eastern Germany: Dio 55.10a. At Lugdunum in Gaul: Suet. *Claud.* 2; Liv. *epit.* 139. Taylor 1931: 209–11, 213.

74. Calculations and discussion: Büchner 1982. Schütz 1990 disputes them. Sept. 23,

Augustus' birthday: *Fasti Arvales, Fasti Pinc., Maff., Vall., Pigh., Filocali,* and *Feriale Cumanum;* Suet. *Aug.* 5; see Degrassi 1963: 512. Jan. 30, Livia's birthday: *CIL* VI. 2028 (*Acta Arvalium* of 38 CE). Jan. 30, dedication day of *Ara Pacis Augustae:* Ov. *F.* 1.709–12, *Fasti Caer., Praen., Verul.,* and the *Feriale Cumanum;* Degrassi 1963: 404–5.

75. Γνώμων in an obscene sense: Diog. *Ep.*35, γνώμων ἀνίσταται, cited at LSJ, s.v. γνώμων, II.8. Cf. Tert. *Spect.* 8.5 on the circus obelisk: *obelisci enormitas, ut Hermateles affirmat, Soli prostituta.*

76. July 4 in *Fasti Amiternini* and *Antiates Minores: ara constituta* (Degrassi, 1963). January 30: Fasti Caer., Praen., and Verul. *ara dedicata.* Jan. 31: no public feast (however, the birthday of Antonia Maior: Crinag. *Pal. Anth.* 6.345; *CIL* VI. 2028 c, *Acta Arvalium,* 38 CE).

77. Cic. *Arch.* 30: *vero omnia quae gerebam, iam tum in gerendo spargere me ac disseminare arbitrabar in orbis terrae memoriam sempiternam; Fin.* 5, 7, 18, *in animis, quasi virtutum igniculi atque semina; Div.* 1, 3, 6 *quod et Zeno in suis commentariis quasi semina quaedam sparsisset, id.*

78. De Grummond 1990, identified the *mater* as *Pax.* Galinsky 1992: 45 and n2 supports the polysemy of the "Tellus" panel. Galinsky 1996: 141–55. On Pax, Ceres, and Tellus in the *Sementiva,* January 24, see *F.* 1.704 (*Pax Cererem nutrit, Pacis alumna Ceres*) and *F.* 1.671–74 (*placentur frugum matres, Tellusque Ceresque,/ farre suo gravidae visceribusque suis:/ officium commune Ceres et Terra tuentur;/ haec praebet causam frugibus, illa locum*).

79. Cf. the references to birds (*F.* 1.683–84), ants (685–86), plant disease and overly rich growth (687–90) and various "weeds" (691–92).

80. Cf. the *Sementiva* with devotion of desire to agricultural activities advised at Ov. *Rem.* 169–224 (sublimation of elegy's theme within the screen of other activities).

81. This language recalls *pictos signantia fastos . . . praemia* (1.11–12), the rewards that Ovid promises Germanicus will get in reading his text (*praemia feres,* 12).

82. These agricultural signs recall that Ovid reads similar signs as suggesting that the New Year should begin in spring (1.147–66). Cf. the "augural" metaphor of tablets (*tabellae* and ill omens of love) at *Am.* 1.12.1–6.

83. To help Camillus pay off the vow to Apollo at Delphi in 396 BCE, women donated jewelry and won the privilege of riding in *carpenta* on all occasions; then in 215 BCE the Oppian Law on luxury restricted use to going to religious festivals. Frazer 1929, 2: 236–37 on *F.* 1.619, citing Liv. 5.25 (Camillus; the vow, 5.21), Festus, "Pilentis" 282 (Lindsay) and "Pilentum," 225 (Lindsay). On the *Lex Oppia,* Liv. 34.1–8. Plut. *Quaest. Rom.* 56: women refused to have sex with men. At some time, Livia received the privilege of riding in the *carpentum* at public games, perhaps 22–23 CE, but perhaps earlier. Coins of 22–23 CE show the *carpentum* (covered wagon). Barrett 2002: 95, fig. 5, and n58. Dio 60.22 2 (43 CE): Messalina granted same privileges.

84. Corbier 1995 demonstrates how conferral of legitimacy through women gave coherence to the Julio-Claudian *domus* as a dynasty (through marriage and adoption as much as birth). This dynamic depends on scarcity of male heirs. King 1995 (esp. 141–44) traces some male anxiety over female homosocial gynecological knowledge (versus that of male physicians); Richlin 1997b.

85. A speech that Dio ascribed to Augustus (chastising unmarried, childless men, mostly equestrians) illustrates ideology of male potency, fertility in "masculinity": Dio 56.2.2, 4.2, 9.1. *Dig.* 47.11.4 describes women as defrauding husbands of children; *Dig.* 48.8.8 and 48.19.39. Yan 1986: 226–28. But, as Hopkins notes (1965: 73), "In the Roman law of the *Digest* there is no prohibition of abortion as such," and in a law of Septimius

Severus, "which penalized a wife who aborted in deceit of her husband, it was the deceit, not the abortion, which was unlawful."

86. Ovid refers to use of such objects; Corinna uses one at *Am.* 2.14.47, cf. 2.14.3 (also Ov. *Nux* 23); this recalls the bronze needle or spit that Tertullian mentions at Tert. *An.* 25.5 (*est etiam aeneum spiculum, quo iugulatio ipsa dirigitur caeco latrocinio*); cf. Vitr. 1.6.6: *conlocetur aeneus gnomon, indagator umbrae qui graece* σκιοθήρης *dicitur*. On mechanical methods of abortion: Rousselle 1983: 51, Yan 1986: 211–36, esp. 234n88, where Yan interprets *ictus* at *F.* 1.623 as referring to "fers plongués dans la cavité uterine," noting *ictus* in the *Digest* in categorizing two kinds of abortion, violent and pharmacological, citing the expression *visceribus suis . . . vim . . . inferre* in Roman law (*Dig.* 48.8.8 and 48.19.39). Abortion and body politics: Rousselle 1992. Gourevitch 1984: 195–216 includes discussion of ancient mechanical means of abortion, 206–7 (citing Soranus, *Gynecology* 1.64), and surgical means, 209 (Soran. *Gyn.* 1.65; Tert. *An.* 25.5). Women's knowledge of pharmacological abortifacients: Ov. *Her.* 11.37–44 (cf. *F.* 5.229–60); Richlin 1997b: 208–10; Riddle 1997; Kapparis 2002.

87. M. Furius Camillus vowed the first temple of Concord in the Forum (367 BCE), during a secession of the armed plebs from senators, a civil discord leading to passage of the Licinian Laws, giving plebeians the right to hold consulships (Liv. 6.42.9–14; *F.* 1.643–44). Camillus' vow: Plut. *Cam.* 42.3–4 (cf. Livy 39.56.6, 40.19.2). Flavius' *aedicula Concordiae* in the Forum (304 BCE): Richardson 1992: 100, "Concordia, Aedicula." But the main Forum temple was perhaps not built (Richardson 1992: 99, "Concordia Aedes [2]") until the Senate bolstered conservative patrician associations (Herbert-Brown 1994: 165–66n 72) by ordering its construction (vowed by L. Opimius) in 121 BCE following assassination of Gaius Gracchus (22 July, Degrassi 1963: 486; Plut. *C. Gracchus* 17.6 and Appian, *Bell. civ.* 1.3.26.). Gracchi as dangerous demagogues (*populares*): Cic. *Off.* 2.80.

88. As part of triumph (7 BCE), refurbishment began: Dio 55.8.2. Dedication in 10 CE: Dio 56.25.1; Suet. *Tib.* 20 claims 12 CE (a mistake according to Herbert-Brown 1994: 164n70). Richardson 1992: 99, "Concordia, Aedes (2)." Programmatic iconography of the *Aedes Concordiae Augustae:* Kellum 1990: 276–307.

89. Political symbolism of "brother" myths (e.g., Romulus-Remus, Castor and Pollux): Bannon 1997: 174–88. Concordia and brotherly love: Bannon 1997: 126. Valerius Maximus 5.5.3 records the idealized fraternal bond (*fraternum iugum*, fraternal yoke) between Drusus and Tiberius, symbolized in Castor and Pollux (*specimen consanguineae caritatis*), and the co-naming of the refurbished temple of the Castors in the Forum Romanum (6 CE: Suet. *Tib.* 20; Cass. Dio 55.27.4; *F.* 1.705–8; and Degrassi 1963: 117). Ovid's ironic depiction of Romulus-Remus as harmonious brothers: *F.* 4.807–862 (Romulus' only guilt in killing Remus is bad instructions to a third party, Celer, watching the walls) and *F.* 5.449–84 (Romulus at Remus' burial). Castor and Pollux (brothers) fighting against Lyceus and Idas (brothers): *F.* 5. 693–720.

90. Germanicus and Claudius joined celebrating games in memory of Drusus, their father (Tiberius' brother), in the same year (6 CE) that Tiberius dedicated the refurbished Temple of the Castors: Dio 55.27.3.

91. Triumph over Germany 7 BCE: Vell. Pat. 2.97.4. Tiberius used spoils from German campaign to renovate Concord's temple: Dio 66.8.2, *F.* 1.645–48.

92. Tiberius held a "collegiate" position like that which Agrippa had held and from which he could not become heir: J. A. Crook in *CAH²* (1996) X.100–101; Herbert-Brown 1994: 162–71.

93. Vell. Pat. 2.100.1; Dio 55.9, esp. 5–8. On Tiberius' departure from Rome to Rhodes as background to interpreting these lines, see Herbert-Brown 1994: 163–64, who

is following Levick 1978: 224. After return from Rhodes (4 CE), Tiberius received *tribunicia potestas* for ten years and command of Germany (*CAH²* X.105, 187). Velleius 2.105–7 records Tiberius' military successes in Germany in 4–6 CE. For subsequent background, 6–9 BCE, see *CAH²* X.176, 184.

94. The quote: Herbert-Brown 1994: 165. Flory 1984. At *F.* 6.637 Ovid says that it is an *aedes Concordiae* in a porticus. *F.*1.649–50 mentions "altar" (*ara*). On the *Porticus Liviae*: Cass. Dio 54.23.6, 55.8.2; Suet. *Aug.* 29. See "Porticus Liviae" (Richardson 1992: 314).

95. Ovid's poetry as important evidence of emergence of *domus Augusta* as dynasty, including family statuary groups: Flory 1996 (esp. 292–97) and Millar 1993. Ovid refers to this "family" function of Concordia at *F.* 2.631 in a passage on the Karistia, a family tomb festival on February 22 (*F.* 2.217–38), followed by a prayer (633–38) to the Lares and *Pater Patriae* (Augustus). *Domus Augusta* in Valerius Maximus: Wardle 2000. The language tracks insertion of civic ideology into family cult; Severy 2003: 96–139.

96. Herbert-Brown 1994: 169–71.

97. Ovid says Livia blends traits of Venus and Juno at *P.* 3.1.117–18, echoing the *F.* 1.649–50.

98. Herbert-Brown 1994: 167–71, cf. 169:

> But in his celebration of Tiberius' temple [Concordia], the language selected by the poet not only accords the "dux venerandus" an inferior status to the divine rank of his mother, but also uses Livia's divine image to bring to its climax a passage ostensibly in honour of Tiberius. The overall effect is that the mother is now a political partner in power—and more. She is the dominant partner in the Concordia of partnership evoked in the verse.

99. Livia's adoption into Julian family as Julia Augusta: Tac. *Ann.* 1.8.2; Suet. *Aug.* 101.2. Tiberius' not using the *nomen Augustum*: Dio 57.2.1, 57.8.1; Suet. *Tib.* 26.2. Tiberius' hesitancy before undertaking the *regendi omnia onus* (Tac. *Ann.* 1.11–13; quote, 11) Livia with *Augustus*, with *Maiestas* beside Jupiter, *F.* 5.27–46, esp. 45–46: *assidet inde Iovi, Iovis est fidissima custos,/ et praestat sine vi sceptra timenda Iovi.*

100. Inscriptions associating Livia and other imperial women with Juno/Hera and Ceres/Demeter: Fischler 1998, esp. 174–75; Severy 2003: 115; Spaeth 1996: 119–20 (Livia-Ceres); Barrett 2002: 209 (Ceres and Juno), 161 (Cybele in iconography), 143–44 (Vesta). Ov. *P.* 3.1.117, 145 (Livia has Venus' form, Juno's face), *Pont.* 4.13.29 (Livia as Vesta of matrons).

101. Fischler 1998: 171, 179. Initially queens represent felicitous, fertile rule of Hellenistic kings, then a transition to queens in masculine guise suggests queenly mastery (Cleopatra): Roy 1998.

102. See Fantham 1992b.

103. Cf. the *Matralia* and Mater Matuta and Portunus (Portunus is young), *F.* 6.473–550.

104. Tullia and Tarquin: Cf. Ov. *F.* 6.594: *si vir es, i, dictas exige dotis opes;* Liv. 1.42.1–2, 46–48, esp. 46.6–7, 47.3–5. Dion. Hal. 4.28.

105. Claudius gave Livia divine honors: Suet. *Claud.* 11.2.

106. Le Bonniec 1965 on *F.* 1.531 (commentary) and Frazer 1929, 2: 205. Bömer 1957–1958, 2: 60, observes that *F.* 1.531 assumes Augustus' death.

107. Cf. *F.* 1.532, "to control empire's reins" (*imperii frena tenere*), language Ovid applied to Augustus (*Tr.* 2.41–42, *P.* 2.9.33–4; cf. Germanicus, *P.* 2.5.75–76, *F.* 1.25). Celsus, the Augustan-Tiberian physician (perhaps born 25 BCE) offers the first use of *frenum*, foreskin ("bridles"): Adams 1982: 74; Cels. 7.25.2.

108. Cf. Verg. *Aen.* 8. 280–305, esp. 285, and 663–66 (on the warrior cult dancers, Salii); Torelli 1990; Zorzetti 1990 on Roman poetry for this and other cults.

109. Carmentis rejected an invitation to the first sacrifice or came late: Aur. Vict. *Orig.* 6.7; Plut. *Q.R.* 60. Frazer 1929, 2: 215–17 (on *F.* 1.581) cites prohibitions on female participation elsewhere: e.g., Lanuvium and Phocis (Paus. 3.22.6–7), where Hercules was called the *Misogynos,* or "woman-hater," because his priest during his one-year term could not have sex with a woman.

110. *Obex* as door-bolt: Fest. Paul. Exc. 201L: *obices pessuli, serae.*

111. *Onus* as male genitalia: Adams 1982: 71, 243n.3 *Opus* as penis: Adams 1982: 57; Maxim. *Eleg.* 5.84; add Ov. *Am.* 1.1.24 (Kennedy 1993: 58–63).

112. *Furtum:* Adams 1982: 167–68. "Cave" signifies the orifice of penetration, usually the vagina in Latin sexual vocabulary (Adams 1982: 85 with sources), but can be applied to both (Auson. *Epigr.* 79.7, p. 341 P. *deglubit, fellat, molitur per utramque cavernam* (Adams interprets *cavernam* as referring to *cunnus* and *culus,* but in the context of *deglubit* and *fellat,* one "cavern" might be the mouth).

113. Victors castrating the defeated (also offerings of ram's genitals first at sacrifices): Burkert 1983: 68. Egyptian paintings, written records of Libyan penises heaped to display subjection of Libya: Trexler 1995: 14–20 (esp. 16, 18). Latreus, a centaur, attempts to castrate Caenus, returning him to his formerly female sex: Ov. *Met.* 12.485–88.

114. Club as phallic instrument of sacrifice, associated with masculinity and hunting: Burkert 1983: 59. Cf. Cacus and his anal-phallic cave with grotesque emerging from below in Zizek's "The Undergrowth of Enjoyment," in Wright and Wright 1999, 28–33 (applying the real to two stories by Patricia Highsmith); gaze and voice as heralding the kernel of the real: Zizek 1991: 125–40; Salecl-Zizek 1996.

115. Cattle as Hercules' tithe: Festus, "Potitium," 270L *(decimam bovum);* Dion. Hal. 1.40.3.

116. Cf. Apollo's contest with Hercules over the Delphic tripod on a terracotta plaque from the temple of Apollo Palatinus: *Kaiser Augustus,* p. 269 (Kat. 121).

117. Fabii and the title *Maximus* (first, Q. Fabius Maximus): *F.* 1.605–6, 2.239–42; Frazer 1929, 2: 325. Hercules as progenitor of the Fabii, *F.* 2.235–38, *P.* 3.3.99–100 (letter to Paullus Fabius Maximus; also *P.* 1.2, 3.8, and 4.6 on his death). On Fabii and Hercules in the poem's last vignette (June 30, 6.797–312): Newlands 1995a: 209–36. Ovid's third wife was a Fabia, close to Marcia, Paullus' wife (*Tr.* 4.10.73, *P.* 1.2.136).

Chapter Six

1. On father-son relation reconstructing (screening) the master-slave relationship: Roller 2001: 213–87, esp. 233–47.

2. Rudich 1993: *dissimulatio* as response of elite males to the anxiety before the emperor's domination; cf. Concordia's dissimulation, 6.89–92. "Deferred action" structures temporality in fantasy, a concept inspired by Freudian *Nachträglichkeit* ("experiences, impressions and memory-traces may be revised at a later date to fit in with fresh experience"): Laplanche and Pontalis 1973: 111–14; Farmer 2000: 55–56, 65–66. Zizek 1989: 100–105 on "retroactivity" in meaning formation. Lacan's notion of *après-coup* and retroactivity broadens the scope of Freud's idea:

3. Father-son tensions: Plescia 1976, Bertman 1976. Cf. Barton 2001: 88–130 for strategies of recuperating honor, esp. acquiescence. "Feminine manhood" borrows from the notion of masochism, particularly "feminine masochism," answering to

sadism (cf. the "sadistic" rule of Tarquinius Priscus). Laplanche and Pontalis 1973: 244–45: "feminine masochism," in which a subjects places himself (typically male in the case studies) "in a characteristically female situation" (245). For application to narrative and male subjectivities, see, e.g., Mulvey 1992: 29 (1975: 14); De Lauretis 1984: 103–57. esp. 103–4; Silverman 1992: esp. 185–213; Farmer 2000: 241–46; and Savran 1998: esp. 3–38.

4. *Fasti Praen.* at Degrassi 1963: 407 (Feb. 5): *a senatu populoque Romano Pater Patriae appellatus* (only the Senate and People of Rome); Ovid adds the *equites,* identifying himself with them (2.128), as does Augustus himself (*RG* 35: *equester ordo*).

5. Degrassi 1963: 400 cites the calendar inscriptions.

6. Dolphin's rescue of Arion, inventor of dithyrambic hymns to Dionysus: Herod. *Hist.* 1.23–24 (Hooker 1989) and Lonsdale 1993: 93–97. Cf. Hyg. *Astron.* 2.17. Statue of Arion at Taenarum: Paus. 3.25.7, 9.30.2. Cf. *h. Hom. Bacch.* (no. 7), in which pirates kidnap Dionysus, who turns them into dolphins. Prop. 3.17.25–26, and Ov. *F.* 3.713–90 (March 17, Liberalia), esp. 723–24; Ovid, *Met.* 3.597–691, esp. 670–86. Apollo *Delphinios* in dolphin form commandeered a ship, *h. Hom. Ap.* 397–403. Frazer 1929, 2: 304–5 cites other dolphin-riding stories: Melicertes (Paus. 1.44.8), Phalanthus (Paus. 10.13.10), sometimes with homoerotic element: Paus. 3.25.7; Aelian, *De nat. animalium* 2.6; Aulus Gellius 6 (7).8; Pliny, *H.N.* 9.24–32, esp. 26, perhaps source for Plin. *Epist.* 9.33.

7. Cf. Arachne's portrayal of Poseidon mating with Melantho as a dolphin: Ov. *Met.* 6.120 (*sensit delphina Melantho*). In the *Fasti,* Ovid says that the dolphin "was a felicitous 'index' in hidden loves" (*seu fuit occultis felix in amoribus index, F.* 2.81). *Index* can mean a "pointer,"—apparently, an indicator in secret lovemaking (*amores*). Note the semi-erotic exchange of boy and dolphin at Pliny the Younger, *Epist.* 9.33: *agnosci se amari putat, amat ipse.* Cf. *lascivaque corpora* of the pirates whom Dionysus turned into dolphins at Ov. *Met.* 3. 685–86. Cf. other references to the Dolphin constellation in the *Fasti:* Ovid. *F.* 1.457, 6.720, 6.471; cf. Aratus 316, Eratosth. *Cat.*31.

8. This part of Ovid's tale recalls Verg. *Ecl.* 8.51–56, where reversals of animal aggressor and victim lead to praise of Orpheus and *inter delphinas Arion* (56). Ovid's Arion also recalls Propertius' *vates,* such as Orpheus (Prop. 3.2.3–4) and Amphion (Prop. 3.25–26)

9. Perhaps *pauca* (2.104), "little," in this translation, is an allusion to elegiac style: Newlands 1995a: 188n42.

10. *F.* 2.105–10:

dant veniam ridentque moram: capit ille coronam,
    quae possit crines, Phoebe, decere tuos;
induerat Tyrio bis tinctam murice pallam:
    reddidit icta suos pollice chorda sonos,
flebilibus numeris veluti canentia dura
    traiectus penna tempora cantat olor.

11. On the feminine appearance of *Apollo Kitharoidos: LIMC* II.1. nos. 82–238 (Wassilis Lambrinudakis, Philippe Bruneau, Olga Palagia et al.), esp. 200: he wears the *peplos,* female dress, from the Hellenistic period. Hercules wears the *peplos:* Loraux 1990: 33–40.

12. The reference to a "crown" that "could adorn Apollo's hair" (104–5) suggests that, wearing it, Arion's long hair has the appearance of Apollo. Apollo's hair-care: Hor. *C.* 4.6.25–26 (*doctor argutae fidicen Thaliae, Phoebe, quo Xantho lavis amne crinis.*

13. The *palla* is perhaps an improper Roman borrowing of the Greek term for the garment of the *citharoedus,* says Bömer 1957–1958, 2:89. But the *palla* ("gown," above) was

a garment of Greek women. Compare the feminine garb of musicians at *F.* 6.654 (*longa stola*) and 6.678 (*in longis vestibus*), of tibia players representing females (*tibicina,* 6.687). Double-dyed purple suggests luxury, associated with an effeminate lifestyle.

14. Cf. so-called Anacreontic vases, showing "transvestite" musicians, often barbiton-players (a type of lyre), discussed by Frontisi-Ducroux and Lissarrague 1990.

15. Castrated transvestite *galli* and their music at the Megalensia of Cybele: *F.* 4.181–90, 211–14 (April 4). *Quinquatrus Minores* and "transvestic" *tibia* players (June 12–13): *F.* 6.651–91, esp. 653–54 and 685–90.

16. Newlands 1995a: 22, 178–79,188–90: Ovid's language situates Arion as an elegiac artist by appealing to hard epic (cf. the *dura penna* piercing the temples of the swan, 109–10) and lamentation, a style linked to elegy at its origin.

17. Ship of state: Alcaeus (frg. 6 in 326 LP). Ambiguities of his sex, poetry and state metaphor: Anderson 1966 on Hor. *C.* 1.14. Quint. *Inst.* 8.6.44 (metaphor for the state). Ship as "woman," erotic metaphor (Alcaeus 306.14.ii LP) continues in Hellenistic epigram (e.g., Diosc. *AP* 5.54; Meleager *AP* 5.204). Hor. *C.* 1.5.6–7, 13–16 describes "sea of love." Cf. Ov. *A.A.* 1.3, 6 (Love as controllable like a ship). Poet's ship in *Fasti*: 1.4 (*timidae derige navis iter*), 2.3, 863–64; 4.17–18,131–32, etc.

18. E.g., Newlands 1995a: 178–88, who balances poetics and politics in the Arion tale.

19. Stebbins 1929: 83 notes the Greek tales of dolphin-riding and their persistent male homoerotic element. But here lament and desire of salvific love between men (*amicitia*) probably displaces the erotic *amor* of Neptune (*F.* 2.81). *Amor* is a quality that Ovid emphasizes in men who try to help him in exile (cf. Brutus in *P.* 4.6.23–24: *nam cum praestiteris verum mihi semper amorem, hic tamen adverso tempore crevit amor.*).

20. Interpreting the imperial imagery of Hercules and Omphale, especially on sarcophagi, Kampen 1996: esp. 237–44 describes how the transvestism of Hercules and Omphale in the transition to the second century assumes spiritual allegorical meaning. Erotic significance (Kampen 236; e.g., in the painting of Hercules in a dress between club-wielding Omphale and Priapus from the House of M. Lucretius, Kampen fig. 99). Transvestism was an ingredient in ancient puberty rites, where young males or females assumed markings of the opposite sex (Vidal-Naquet 1986: 114–17 and 140; Loraux 1990: 34–35). For Callisto's tale and female puberty rites at Brauron honoring Artemis (Diana): e.g. Vidal-Naquet 1986: 145–46.

21. *F.* 2.155–62:
> inter hamadryadas iaculatricemque Dianam
> Callisto sacri pars fuit una chori.
> illa, deae tangens arcus, "quos tangimus arcus,
> este meae testes virginitatis" ait.
> Cynthia laudavit, "promissa" que "foedera serva,
> et comitum princeps tu mihi" dixit "eris."
> foedera servasset, si non formosa fuisset:
> cavit mortales, de Iove crimen habet.

22. Cf. the gender-sex contract between Attis and Cybele at *F.* 4.225–44. The *Metamorphoses* contains many stories of gender transformation. Cf. *Met.* 3.316–38 of Teiresias. The story of Hermaphroditus is relevant to Ovid's interest in transgenderism and transvestism (*Met.* 4.288–388), as is that of Caenis-Caeneus, whose female-to-male sex change is precipitated by her rape by Neptune (*Met.* 12.189–535; cf. Keith 2000: 82–85).

23. On *testis,* cf. the double-entendres at Plaut. *Curc.* 30–31, *Mil.* 1415–26, and Adams

1982: 67, 70n1, and 212 (citing Mart. 2.72.3 and 8). *Arcus* as metaphor for *mentula*-penis: see Adams 1982: 21. Cic. *Fam.* 9.22.4 refers to the risqué sense of the word *testis*.

24. For Roman *arcus*, "bow," see the passages cited by Adams 1982: 21–22. Many (*Priap.* 68.33; Ov. *Am.* 1.8.47–48) recall Penelope's testing the suitors to find a husband.

25. See Ross 1969: 80–95 on Catullus' vocabulary of political alliance applied to love, in which Ross classifies *foedus*, 84–85.

26. Callisto's oath to Diana "transgenders" Callisto; parallel to that of Attis devoting himself to Magna Mater, although Callisto is masculinized, while Attis is feminized (castrated ultimately of his false *testes*) Again, Catullus (*Carm.* 63, on Attis) is a model for Ov. *F.* 4.223–44 (castration at 4.237–44). Skinner 1997.

27. As for the rape of Callisto, Ovid does not describe actual violence at *F.* 2.161–62 (*foedera servasset, si non formosa fuisset: / cavit mortalis, de Iove crimen habet*), although it may be implied by *crimen* (*stuprum*).

28. E.g., there are the matching ass brays in Priapus' failed rapes of Lotis, *F.* 1.433–34, and Vesta, 6.341–42, *intempestivo sono*. Similar sounds occur in *F.* 2. 351; a sound (*fit sonus*) calls attention to Faunus' fall to the ground after attempting the rape of Hercules (see below). At 442 the populace at grove of Juno Lucina is frightened by *dubio . . . sono* (her oracular voice demanding he-goats penetrate Roman women). At 840, Brutus "issued fearless sounds with a threatening mouth" over Lucretia's body (*edidit impavidos ore minante sonos*).

29. This recalls, of course, the weight of the womb aborted by Roman women at *F.* 1.623–24 in a strategy "not to renew ungrateful men" (1.622). See the previous chapter.

30. Ovid uses a similar meaning at *F.* 2.121–26, a passage describing the weakness of elegiac couplets and his talent for the "weightiness" of celebrating another title of the emperor, "Father of the Fatherland" (*Pater Patriae*). See discussion below.

31. Erotic meaning associated with Arion's ride on the dolphin could be retroactively constructed from the position of *F.* 2.453–72, where Aphrodite and Cupid are rescued during Jupiter's war with the giants by the two pisces, the Constellation Pisces; cf. Dolphin.

32. In each star myths (Arion-Dolphin, Callisto) *Lesbida . . . lyram* (*F.* 2.82) and the use of *foedus* (2.159) recall Catullus. The phrasing *Lesbida . . . lyram* at *F.* 2.82 recalls Sappho, signaled in Catullus 51.

33. Concepts of rites of passage (puberty rites) inform the Callisto myth, particularly that of girls becoming women at Brauron in Attica. See *LIMC*, "Callisto" V.1.940–44; V.2.604–5 (Jean Baltry), esp. nos. 5 (Apulian vase frg. head of Kallisto with pointed ears; 380–70 BCE), 6 (Apulian oenochoe, Kallisto seated on hillock hands are paws, skin is hairy, pointed ears) and 15 (Pompeii VI 12.12 ca. 70 CE, wall painting).

34. Cf. Juno's anxiety at *F.* 6.35–40: "Or was the concubine [Maia] able to bestow her name on the month of May? Will this honor be denied me?" (*an potuit Maio paelex dare numina mensi, / hic honor in nobis invidiosus erit?*). Cf. Juno to Flora, seeking a way to reproduce without the help of Jupiter, at *F.* 5.239–42.

35. The bear-appearance imposed by Juno, the wife, makes Callisto the hussy (*paelex*, 2.179) who is dirty (*squalida*) on *incultos montes* (181)—unappealing for Jupiter the husband. Cf. the Bath of Venus at *F.* 4.133–62 in which bathing with Venus is a mechanism for Venus to bestow beauty upon Roman wives to keep their husbands (fear of *paelices?*); also *F.* 4.107–8 (from Venus come *cultus mundaque cura sui*).

36. *F.* 2.177–78: "Insulted, Juno goes mad, and she changes the beauty of the girl:/ what are you doing? She endured Jupiter with an unwilling heart" (*laesa furit Iuno, formam mutatque puellae: / quid facis? invito est pectore passa Iovem*).

37. E.g., *Tr.* 2.189–90; 3.2.1–2, 3.4b.47–8, 3.11.7–8 (*barbara me tellus et inhospita litora Ponti/ cumque suo Borea Maenalis Ursa videt*). Ovid addresses *Tristia* 4.3 to his wife via the intermediary of the *magna minorque ferae* (1), the Great and Small Bears. Perhaps the Bear symbolizes the exile's use of female intermediaries (Ovid's wife, Marcia; cf. *F.* 6.801–6).

38. Cf. Cic., *Planc.* 72 *onus beneficii* owed to one's social *parens: at id etiam gregarii milites faciunt inviti ut coronam dent civicam et se ab aliquo servatos esse fateantur, non quo turpe sit protectum in acie ex hostium manibus eripi—nam id accidere nisi forti viro et pugnanti comminus non potest—, sed onus benefici reformidant, quod permagnum est alieno debere idem quod parenti.*

On Fabius Cunctator, Ovid follows Ennius (*Ann.* 370), quoted by Cic. *Off.* 1.24.84 and *Sen.* 4.10 (*unus homo nobis cunctando restituit rem*), reshaped by Verg. *Aen.* 6.846 (see Servius *ad loc.*)

39. Weinstock 1971: 149–50. *ILS* 56: *Q. Fabius Q. f. Maximus . . . exercitui profligato subvenit et eo nomine ab exercitu Minuciano pater appellatus est.* For Minucius hailing Fabius Maximus as *parens* or *pater:* Liv. 22.29–30 (the actual proclamation and surrender of Minucius' army to Fabius's *imperium* and *auspicium*). See also Val. Max. 5.2.4; Plut. *Fab.* 11–13; Plb. 3. 102.10–105.11; Diod. 26.3.23; Cass. Dio 56.12–20; Corn. Nep. *Hann.* 5.3. In fact, in one version, Fabius received the *corona obsidionalis* (a wreath of grass) from the state because he had liberated Rome from a siege (Weinstock 1971: 150 and Plin. *H.N.* 22.10, Gell. 5.6.10). Such a crown marks a man worthy of being called *pater* (cf. the *corona civilis* for saving citizens). Cf. Augustus' *corona civica.*

40. Weinstock 1971: 200–27, 202: while Livy and others ascribe the title *parens patriae* or *Pater Patriae* to Romulus (Liv. 5.49.7) and Camillus (Liv. 7.1.10; Plut. *Cam.* 1.1, 31.2), evidence is not earlier than Cicero. The title "new founder" or "new Romulus" was created earlier: Weinstock 1971: 177–78.

41. The dolphin is honored in a constellation for his *facta pia* (*F.* 2.117–80). Augustus obligates not merely men, but also gods, by rescuing temples from collapse (2.61–62).

42. At *F.* 2.121–22, "there is heaped up honor" (*accumulatur honor*); *honor* is connected with *onos*, the "burden" carried to achieve honor. Carrying a burden earns an honorary title (*F.* 1.615–16). As the dedication implies (*F.* 1.9–12), the title *Pater Patriae* is one of the *praemia* (12) "marking the painted calendar" that Ovid says Germanicus' grandfather and father (10) "carry" (*ferunt*, 11), and he will carry along with Drusus (*feres*, 12). At 2.123, "greater things crush" (*urgent* = put weight upon) Ovid's elegiac strength (*viribus*). *Urgeo*, meaning "to put weight upon": L-S I.B.1.b. Plaut. *Poen.* 4.235: *at onus urget* (cf. the effect of aging, Cic. *Sen.* 1.2; of death and disease at Hor. *C.* 1.22.20, 1.24.5). Proclaiming his nature deficient (*deficit ingenium*, 123), Ovid echoes Propertius' *recusatio*, or refusal of epic themes, in elegy 3.9.5–6, where he describes how he would be unable to carry the burden (*pondus*) of the epic themes of Augustus' military exploits.

43. *Tr.* 2.573–74: *his precor, atque aliis possint tua numina flecti, / a pater, o patriae cura salusque tuae!* (four lines from the end). *Tr.* 2.39–40, 2.179–82. Cf. the reference to Achilles and Priam's pleas for Hector's body: *Tr.* 5.1.55–56.

44. He fears his elegiac verse (*alterno carmine*) is too weak (*deficit*, 123) for the weight of the *Pater Patriae*, which crushes Ovid's *vires* (123). Ovid is using the "alternating verse" of elegy instead of epic hexameters. Cf. Ov. *Tr.* 3.1.11, 3.1.56, and 3.7.10.

45. In Petronius' *Satyricon*, Trimalchio's rise from slave status to that of rich freedman comes through sexual favors. .

46. Here, the *puer* Ganymede-Aquarius is not called "Trojan," but "Idean" (*puer Ideaeus*, 145), from mount Ida, the home of Cybele and her castrated priests (cf. Cybele, the *Magna Mater*, called the *Idaea parens* at 4.182). *Parens* was used in titles such as *parens*

patriae, a title that senators tried to extend to Tiberius' mother, Livia, in 14 CE, after the death of Augustus (*pater patriae*, Tac. Ann. 1.14.1–2), among other honors Tiberius repudiated for Livia. Tiberius' attitude toward the public role of women: Tac. *Ann.* 1.6.3, 1.13.6, 1.14.3; Suet. *Tib.* 50.1–2, 50.3; Dio 57.3.3 (on Tiberius and Livia: Barrett 2002: 146–73, esp. 147).

47. For the metaphor of water or wine for religious elegy, see Propertius 4.6.7–8: *spargite me lymphis, carmenque recentibus aris / tibi Mygdoniis libet eburna cadis.* Cf. *F.* 2.247–50 (Apollo orders the raven, interpretable as the poet, to fetch water for a ritual; instead he brings back cryptic words and a symbol; see below). Cf. *F.* 3.39–40 (Silvia has filled her urn with holy water while she has been ravished by Mars. She now feels the growth of divine pregnancy, and has delivered a visionary dream narrative; see ch. 4).

48. On *mollitia* and *mollis*, see, e.g., Williams 1999: 125–59, 160–64, and passim.

49. Such atmospheric effects of divine reception (here the *Pater Patriae*, akin to Jupiter, 2.131–32) are not unusual in ancient literature. Cf. Venus in the opening of Lucretius' *De rerum natura;* Juno influencing Aeolus to release the winds and a storm in Verg. *Aen.* 1. Also, Venus' sign of favorable response in the atmosphere answering to Ovid's persuasion at *F.* 4.5–6, 15–18.

50. Cf. Iarbas' description of effeminate Aeneas at Verg. *Aen.* 4.215–17: *et nunc ille Paris cum semiviro comitatu,/ Maeonia mentum mitra crinemque madentem/ subnexus, rapto potitur. . . .*

51. Evidence in Frazer 1929, 2: 328–29.

52. Dionys. Hal. *AR* 9.18–21: the same story as Livy for the setting out of the Fabii against Veii, but two different accounts of their demise. In the first (9.18–19), the Fabii are returning to Rome to make a clan sacrifice (perhaps at the Lupercalia, as they formed a college of Luperci), when they were slaughtered. The second version (9.20–21) recalls Ovid and Livy—lured by the Veientines into an ambush. See Frazer 1929, 2: 321–26.

53. *F.* 2.197–98: *una domus vires et onus susceperat urbis:/ sumunt gentiles arma professa manus.* Liv. 2.49.1: *manat tota urbe rumor; Fabios ad caelum laudibus ferunt: familiam unam subisse civitatis onus.* Cf. *F.* 1.531–32: *et penes Augustos patriae tutela manebit: / hanc fas imperii frena tenere domum.*

54. Of two days (Feb. 13, July 18), Ovid chose the Ides of February. See Harries 1991: 151–56, who argues that Ovid, faced with two different traditions on the date, selected Feb. 13 to give slanted treatment together with the Fabian interest in the Lupercalia (that formed one of two traditional colleges of Luperci-priests). Liv. 6.1.11 explicitly dates the battle of Cremera to July 18; the battle's story, Liv. 2.49–50, is fairly consonant with that date. Harries 1991: 153 suggests rival traditions.

55. Harries 1991 ("Ovid and the Fabii"): 156–57 discusses these similes and Vergilian models (*Aeneid*): Fabii as lion at 2.209–12, *Aen.* 9.339–42, Euryalus' killing; the torrential river of *F.* 2.219–22; *Aen.* 2.3–4, 8 (of the Greeks rushing Troy); the Fabii as a boar at 2.231–34; *Aen.* 10.707–18 (Mezentius as a boar).

56. *Simplex* at 2.226, describing Fabian *nobilitas*, alludes to simple open speech with meaning on the surface, without dissembling with rhetorical figures. Key references to rhetorical openness-dissimulation include *aperte* and *tecta arma* at *F.* 2.213–14 (*ubi vincere aperte / non datur, insidias armaque tecta parant*); *latet* at 218, and *apertos* at 227–28. Cf. the possible pun on the trapped *aper* at 231. As for *arma tecta*, compare Quint. *Inst.* 9.2.75. Cf. Germanicus' speech at *F.* 1.22, *civica pro trepidis cum tulit arma reis.* At *F.* 3.101–4 Ovid elaborates on an analogy between skill in war and language. Cf. *P.* 4.6.35–36 (on Brutus, Ovid's editor-friend): *hostibus eveniat quam sis violentus in armis /*

sentire et linguae tela subire tuae. Weapons, metaphor for arts of love in *A.A.*, e.g. 3.1–2 (*arma dedi Danais in Amazonas; arma supersunt, / quae tibi dem et turmae, Penthesilea, tuae*). For similar language—particularly about the notion of *dicere aperte* in rhetorical treatises (about surprise and ironic attack in oratory): Ahl 1984a: 192–96 ("Art of Safe Criticism") and 1984b: 80–85 ("Rider and the Horse"). Also panegyric or flattery is a possible mode of dissimulation (lack of *simplicitas*): cf. Cicero, *De amicitia* 99.

57. Q. Fabius Maximus Cunctator developed his strategy after the slaughter of the Romans at Cannae by the forces of Hannibal in 216 BCE. See Plut. *Fab. Max.* 19. Ovid imitates Verg. *Aen.* 6.845–46: *. . . tu Maximus ille es,/ unus qui nobis cunctando restituis rem.* Vergil imitates Ennius; at Cicero, *Off.* 1.24.84, *Sen.* 4.10, *unus homo nobis cunctando restituit rem* (Enn. *Ann.* 370). See Serv. *Ad Aen.* 6.846.

58. Letters to Paullus Fabius Maximus: *P.* 1.2, 3.3; cf. 4.6.7–14, to Brutus, lamenting Paullus' death.

59. Barchiesi 1997a: 148.

60. Harries 1991: 158 and Barchiesi 1997a: 152 and n18, who note that in a letter complimenting Tiberius, Augustus had applied to Tiberius the pattern found in lines of Ennius and Vergil about Q. Fabius Maximus Cunctator (Enn. *Ann.* 363 [Skutsch]; Verg. *Aen.* 6.845–48) about his "delaying" tactics; the language of Ennius and Vergil is parallel to *F.* 2.241–42.

61. Harries 1991: 160.

62. Marcia was his maternal aunt's (*matertera*) daughter; *F.* 6.801–10, the end of the *Fasti* and Bömer 1957–1958: 2. *F.* 6.801 and Frazer 1929, 4: 348–53 on the passage. Also *P.* 1.2.137–40.

63. Syme 1978: 144–45. See Sedgwick 1990: 182–212 theorizing the bachelor as inspiring homosexual panic in the observer.

64. Barchiesi 1997a: 148–49 notes what I would call the "triangular desire" (after Sedgwick and Girard) of the Faunus-Omphale-Hercules scene.

65. On the delay to reproduce in the *gens Fabia:* Harries 1991: 158–61. On the congenital transfer of dilatory character, cf. Prop. 3.9.19–20; *F.* 2.237–40 on the *Herculeae semina gentis.* Ovid's ambiguous language (*impubes* can also mean "chaste," i.e., not having sex with women, or even "hairless"). Cf. Liv. 2.50.11: *unum prope puberem aetate relictum stirpem gentis Fabiae.* Ovid's "left behind" Fabius may have been boyish in manner.

66. For *impubes*, "celibate, virgin, chaste," see L-S, *impubes*, II. In discussing German warrior society, Caesar notes the high praise for male virginity. Caesar, *BG* 6.21.4: "In fact, they consider it among the most disgraceful things to pay attention to a woman before the age of twenty. There is no hiding this matter, because they bathe in rivers with genders mixed and they use skins or little swaths of fur, with most of the body naked." Cf. male warrior bonds of Germans to the Luperci in Rome, whose nakedness evokes earlier rustic warrior groups. The Fabii both formed one of the cult groups of the Lupercalia and went out as a group of around three hundred men (cf. the Theban Band and the Spartan warrior unit, the *mora*).

67. For *impubes* as beardless or youthful, see L-S, *impubes*, I. *Pueri delicati:* Lyne 1980: 170–74, 200. For ancient anxiety over desire for boys and adolescents and the emergence of facial and body hair: Williams 1999: 26. Castration was an extreme step in transgendering: Lucan 10.133–34; Statius *Silv.* 4.4.68–71; Cat. 63. Depilation: Scipio ap. Gell. 6.12.5; Williams 1999: 129–32. For *galli* and the *male vir* see *A.A.* 1.505–24, a passage where Ovid advises *neglecta forma* for real men and hair plucking for non-men (505).

68. In 2.9–14 Ovid seems, like the Fabian *puer*, "still not useful in arms"; thus the disclaimer in 14. Cf. Mars at *Fasti* 3.173–74: *nunc primum studiis pacis deus utilis armis / advo-*

cor, et gressus in nova castra fero (part of the authorial subject's dilatory management of Mars' manhood, ch. 4).

69. For Ganymede at 2.145–46, see below. Among Roman males, *impubes* were more attractive sexual objects than a bearded male. Cloelia selected *impuberes* to return with her to spare their being used sexually and to protect her own virginity: Liv. 2.13.10. *Puer Idaeus* recalls Attis and Cybele of Mt. Ida, who wants Attis to remain a *puer* (F. 4.226); he promises to remain celibate or devoted to her (227–28), but fails (229–30), and so castrates himself (237–44), making him permanently "not a man" (therefore, boy or woman). Cf. the *puer Ampelon intonsum* ("unshaven Ampelon," implying beardlessness, F. 3.409–20) beloved by Bacchus,.

70. Festus 245.13–17: *pullus Iovis dicebatur Q. Fabius, cui Eburno cognomen erat propter candorem, quod eius fulmine icta erat. Antiqui autem puerum, quem quis amabat, pullum eius dicebant.* See Williams 1999: 26–27.

71. Harries 1991: 162–63 (and 151n8): Ovid's inaccurate placement of the Raven-Bowl-Snake etiology on Feb. 14 indicates a thematic shaping focusing on Ovid's ironic claim that the story will not create a *tarda mora*, yet the raven delays. Newlands 1991 observes how Ovid's language refers to elegy as a genre. For word play in the *Fasti* similar to what I observe: Boyd 2000a (on *Celeus Rusticus* at F. 4.507–8) and 2001 (catasterism of Chiron at F. 5.379–414).

72. Water is a symbol of poetry (cf. Prop. 4.6). Commager 1962 discusses the symbolism of water and wine as poetry, especially the mixing of the two, which was done in a *crater*. The urn is the poetic form or the poet, a vessel in symbolic metonymy with the ritual servant, the priest(ess) or *vates; F.* 3.9–40, esp. 39–40, where Silvia's weakness is like Ovid's in the *Pater Patriae* passage: *deficit ingenium, maioraque viribus urgent, F.* 2.123; cf. Prop. 4.4.15–16, 21–22.

73. F. 2.258: *ad dominumque redit, fictaque verba refert.*

74. Archilochus states in an elegiac verse about the sexual availability of Pasiphile (331): "Just as a fig tree on its rock feeds many crows, / this plain girl sleeps with strangers" (Henderson 1975: 23). The *korōne* or *corvus* as phallic: Henderson 1975: 20. "Fig," an "important metaphor" in Latin, refers to the *anus* (*culus*): see Adams 1982: 15n1 (Mart. 1.65.4, 4.52.2, 7.71, 12.33.2; *Priap.* 41.2, 50.2), 113–14, where Adams notes the Roman use of *ficus* for "anal sore." The graphic image may derive from the portrayal of adolescent boys as ripening figs; e.g., *AP* 12.185 (boys are figs ripe on tree) and *AP* 12.9 (boys are good-looking, *kalos,* and ripe for lovers' picking). Theoc. *AP* 7.120: a boy "riper than a pear."

75. The opening makes clear that "delay" is a theme (*F.* 2.247–50): *forte Iovi Phoebus festum sollemne parabat/ (non faciet longas fabula nostra moras): / "i, mea" dixit "avis, ne quid pia sacra moretur,/ et tenuem vivis fontis adfer aquam."*

76. Nudity: *F.* 2.274, 283, 285–86, 297–98, 379, where it is joined with running. The Fabii traditionally had provided one of two primary Luperci cult groups (375–78); in 44 BCE a third college, called the *Iulii,* started to honor Julius Caesar (Dio Cass. 44.6.2, 45.20.2; Suet. *Jul.* 76.1; soon it ended, Cic. *Philipp.* 13.15.31). Lupercalian "running" recalls how on the Ides the Fabian family nearly perished because they rashly ran into an ambush lured by false signals.

77. Fertility is also an important issue (2.425–52, perhaps 381–422). Pan-Faunus is here the *numen* who receives *munera* for protecting flocks and herds of people and animals and helping produce offspring (277–78, 425–52), much as do the *genii* of the deceased ancestors during the *Parentatio.* For the crowd of people at the *Lupercalia* as a "flock": Varr. *LL* 6.34: *ego magis arbitror Februarium a die februato, quod tum februatur populus, id est*

Lupercis nudis lustratur antiquum oppidum Palatinum gregibus humanis cinctum.
78. Wiseman 1995a: esp. 77–88; 1995b tracks these changes; those of Augustus are most relevant (below).

79. *F.* 2.169–70 (Callisto disrobes). Cf. Ovid's self-description at 2.9–14: he seems to wear no armor in his military service (*militia*); he is *nudus* (undefended). *F.* 2.693–98: the Gabii soldiers "bare" their swords when they see Sextus Tarquinius (*nudarant gladios,* 693), but Sextus "bares" his backside (*terga*) to show lash-marks from his father—a ruse (*tergaque deducta veste notata vident,* 698).

80. Evidence for Luperci as ritual evocations of wild men (cf. cave people): Wiseman 1995a: 77–88, esp. 85, 87, 100–101. *F.* 2.301–2: *nunc quoque detecti referunt monimenta vetusti / moris et antiquas testificantur opes. F.* 2.299–30: *sub Iove durabant et corpora nuda gerebant, / docta graves imbres et tolerare Notos.*

81. Plutarch (*Rom.* 21.7) cites Gaius Acilius, the senator writing in the 140s BCE (identified at Liv. *Per.* 53); see also Frazer 1929, 2: 365, commenting on *F.* 2.359. In 155 BCE, Acilius served as interpreter between the senate and the philosophers Carneades of the Academy, Diogenes the Cynic, and Critolaus the Peripatetic, whom Athens sent as envoys to Rome (Plb. 33.2, supplied from Gell. 6 [7].14.9–10).

82. Only Ovid mentions the gymnastic exercises. Plutarch *QR* 40 shows awareness of traditionalist Roman anxiety about *gymnasia* and wrestling, and suspicion of oil in these practices. Serv. *Aen.* 8.343 offers a tale similar to Plutarch's.

83. On *campus* as a contemporary term for *palaestra,* see Gros 1996, 1: 377–79. On the possible involvement of equestrian *iuvenes* trained the *campus-palaestra* involved at theatrical pantomime-riots: Slater 1994.

84. The effect is rather like Verg. *G.* 2.531–34. Barchiesi 1997a: 155–59 cited this passage, and noted parallels of Ovid's *Romulus et frater* (2.365) with Vergil's *Remus et frater* at *G.* 2.2533, as well as the theme of nudity at *G.* 2.531 (*corpora . . . nudant*) and *F.* 2.366 (*solibus et campo corpora nuda dabant*), but he did not make the point that both Vergil and Ovid "Grecize" and perhaps eroticize the athleticism of Romulus and Remus.

85. On Hellenization and Roman moralizing anxiety about it, see Edwards 1993: 22–24, 80, 92–97, 102–3, 203–4. Cf. Polyb. 31.25.2–5 and Cic. *Tusc.* 4.70.

86. See Edwards 1993. Tacitus (*Ann.* 14.14–15, 20–21) connects degeneracy of Rome's *iuventus* to foreign ways (*gymnasia et otia et turpis amores*) introduced by Nero. According to Cato and Cicero, Greek athletic nakedness and rhythmical, dance-like movements (apart from practical horsemanship or combat) led to sex between elite males: Slater 1994: 132–36, citing Plut. *QR* 40; Vitr. 9, pref. 1ff.; Cic. *Resp.* 4.4.4. On Plin. *Ep.* 4.22.7, Sherwin-White commented, "It was the homosexual tendency that was feared" (citing Plin. *Pan.* 13.6; Pliny the Elder, *H.N.* 15.19, 22, 26). Cf. Martial 7.32; Lucan 7.270. See also Hor. *C.* 3.24.51, *S.* 2.2.10; and Suet. *Dom.* 4. Slater 1994: 132–36 judiciously observes the hypocrisy of ancient authors who sometimes grant virtues to Greek training and sometimes criticize them (Cic. *De or.* 3.83, 3.200 etc., at Slater 1994: 135; Quint. 1.11.15). Cicero criticized Marc Antony's nude performance as a *Lupercus* in 44 BCE, because naked and oiled (enticing sexual views) he offered a crown, symbolizing kingship, to Julius Caesar in the *Forum Romanum:* Cicero implies Antony's sexual "service" of Julius Caesar as well (*Philipp.* 2.34.85–87; 3.4.8–5.12; *Pro Cael.* 26 implies a current view of Luperci as questionable).

87. Burkert 1983: 61 observes how abstinence prepares for sex. Cf. *improbus amor: Aen.* 4.412; Hor. *S.* 1.3.24.

88. See reproductions and discussion at Clarke 1998: 49–55. Ov. *Met.* 4.285–388 reports the event that transgendered Hermaphroditus. In some versions Priapus, not

Faunus, could play the part of the "third," such as in the wall painting from Pompeii (House of Marcus Lucretius): Pompeii, House of M. Lucretius (IX.3.5), 1st cent. CE, Naples, Museo Nazionale Archeologico, Inv. 8992; cited by Kampen 1996: 238, fig. 99.

89. Cf. Juv. 2, where Juvenal remarks scathingly about the confusing hairy Stoic philosopher types who are really sexually passive, which seems rather similar to the modern notions of "passing." Also in Juv. 2 is the use of women's clothes by effeminate males in the adapted rites of Bona Dea.

90. Cf. Prop. 3.14.27–28: *nec Tyriae vestes errantia lumina fallunt, / est neque odoratae cura molesta comae.*

91. Serv. *E.* 5.20, 8.68, 10.26; cf. Verg. *E.* 2.25–30. Ancient representations of Pan show him embracing Daphnis, who practices the pipes: Hubbard 2003: fig. 25 (copy of marble sculpture by Heliodorus, ca. 100 BCE). In the Saepta Julia in the Campus Martius in Rome were two statue groups similar to that of Pan-Daphnis above: Pan with Olympos and Cheiron (the centaur) with Achilles (Plin. *H.N.* 36.29): see Zanker 1988: 142–43, citing Bieber 1961: 135, fig. 628. Both homoerotic sculptures represented a mythologized Greek education or pedagogy, so probably also alluded to Hellenic pederasty as well. Ovid used the Achilles-Cheiron pairing at *F.* 5.379–414 to explain the constellation Sagittarius and used that same pairing at *A.A.* 1.9–18 to stage his own role as "teacher of Love [personified as a high-spirited youth]." Suetonius (*Tib.* 43) reports that, at the imperial villa on Capri, Tiberius staged fantasy scenarios of sexual desire that sometimes involved prostitutes of both sexes dressed as little Pans and Nymphs. This staging of desire or fantasy caused people to nickname the island "Goat-Horns," *Capricorni* (cf. Ov. *F.* 2.346: *et tumidum cornu durius inguen erat.*)

92. Aurora's abduction of Cephalus is famous: Pl. *Phdr.* 229b–d; Ov. *A.A.* 3.686–746, *Met.* 7.700–58; Apollod. 3.14.3

93. Ov. *F.* 2.267–68: *tertia post Idus nudos aurora Lupercos / aspicit, et Fauni sacra bicornis eunt.* Cf. Ov. *F.* 1. 461–62: *proxima prospiciet Tithono nupta relicto / Arcadiae sacrum pontificale deae,* and *F.* 4.713–14. Aurora is often a spectator. Cf. Aurora's abductions of Cephalus, Orion, Cleitus (descended from Melampus), and most famously Tithonus: Hom. *Od.* 5.121–24, 15.249–51; Hes. *Theog.* 371–82, 984–991; *h. Hom. Aphr.* (no. 5) 218–38; *h. Hom. Hel.* (no. 31) 1–7; Ov. *Met.* 9.421–22, 13.576–622; Apollod. 1.4.5, 3.12.4, 3.14.3.

94. Nakedness became a concern; Augustus may have banned it. Lupercci wear loincloths of considerable size in images in imperial sculpture: see Wrede 1983; Wiseman 1995a; 1995b: 77–88 (quote, 82–83), where he observes that, in the equestrian funerary relief sculpture of the second century CE, Luperci wear long aprons, not small *perizomata* (Wiseman 1995a: 83, fig. 10; *CIL* XIV. 3624, *Tibur, Ti. Claudius Liberalis*); this may show Augustan alteration of the *perizoma* attested by Q. Aelius Tubero (fl. 30s BCE), ap. Dion. Hal. 1.180.1 (cf. Plut. *Rom.* 21.5; Val. Max. 2.2.9 [*cincti*]; and Ov. *F.* 4.101 [*cinctuti*]). But, between the fourth century BCE and Pompeius Trogus (Augustan writer, ap. Justin 43.1.7), the *perizoma* probably had displaced the still earlier nudity reflected in the god's *simulacrum nudum,* except for a goat-hide cape.

95. See Corbeill 1997, 2002 for discussion of general signals of male gender deviance in deportment and oratory. Ovid's emphasis on the antiquity of Lupercalian nudity may counterbalance Augustus' regulation of cult. Suet. *Aug.* 31.4 on prohibition on *imberbes,* boys or gender nonconforming males as at Lucil. 1058 Marx (994 Krenkel): *inberbi androgyni, barbati moechocinaedi* ("beardless ones of indeterminate sex, bearded catamite-adulterers").

96. Ovid's interpretation of the *Regifugium* aligns with that of other ancient writers, who more explicitly link exile of the Tarquinii with a ritual performed in the Forum:

Festus, "Regifugium" p. 346L and the epitome at 347L; Aus. *Ecl.* 23, *de feriis Romanis*, 13–14. Cf. *Fasti Polemii Silvii* (449 CE): *cum Tarquinius Superbus fertur ab urbe expulsus* (Degrassi 1963: 265, 415). Plut. *QR* 63 describes the ceremonial: the *rex sacrorum* (a ceremonial king of rituals) along with the Salii perform a sacrifice in the *Comitium* and then flee the Forum. Cf. the similar designation of days as *QRCF*—i.e., *Quando Rex Comitiavit, Fas*, which labeled March 24 and May 24 (one month and three months later; Scullard 1981: 95, 123). But scholars doubt the connection of the *Regifugium* ritual with the flight of Tarquinius Superbus: Degrassi 1963: 416: Scullard 1981: 81–82.

97. For historiographers: e.g., Livy 1.56–58; Val. Max. 7.3.2; Dion. Hal. *Ant. Rom.* 4.64–69; Zonaras 7.10–11.

98. Joplin 1990: 54, passim, on Ovid's "Lucretia," applies Lévi-Strauss' notion of the exchange of women between men and Girard's theory of the scapegoat to argue that Lucretia is a surrogate victim; cf. Sedgwick's use of Girard; ch. 2.

99. As Newlands 1995a: 147–48 observes, Ovid might follow Livy's version, but "he downplays the political significance of the legend, according only two concluding couplets to the revolution and establishment of the Republic (2.849–52)." She sees Ovid as going beyond mere generic requirements to expose the sexual violence at the heart of Roman history. The difference between Livy and Ovid has been interpreted in terms of genre; Ovid eroticizes the material: cf. Newlands 1995a: 147 citing Heinze 1919: 53.

100. This emergence of libido in Ovid's narrative of Sextus Tarquinius recalls Lacan's "Real" in which enjoyment (*jouissance*), which exceeds representation in available discourses, grows or creeps in upon those discourses. Containment requires endless, eventually futile, social and psychological labor. See Zizek, "The Undergrowth of Enjoyment," in Wright and Wright 1999: 11–36. Cf. the creeping of Faunus' libido in *F.* 2, above; that of Priapus (upon Lotis) at 1.391–440 and 6.311–48 (upon Vesta).

101. The word order effects surprise and emotional undertones. Hyperbaton in the two pentameters, both alluding to shame—the shame of an elite male of having endured lashes (696) and to the immodest Sextus revealing his backside (698)—contrasts with the orderly arrangement of the hexameters that introduce the facts or circumstances advancing the narrative (695, 697).

102. *Nota* and the verb *notare* refer to written notes, often erotic (*Am.* 1.4.20, 1.11.14; *A.A.* 2.595–6); female writers of the *Heroides*-letters use such references (1.62, 2.1, 5.24, 11.2). Some uses in the *Fasti* refer to calendar notations: *F.* 1.8 (*quaeque notata dies*) or notations Ovid takes from divine informants (Mars: *F.* 3.178: *et memori pectore dicta nota*). But Sextus' *terga notata* (*F.* 2.698) recalls not only the written notes (above), but also the notion of the censorial mark, *nota* (Ov. *Tr.* 2.7–8, 541–42 (*carminaque edideram, cum te delicta notantem/ praeterii*), concerning the *recognitio equitum* (above; ch. 4)

103. A stream of gently sounding water divides the garden (2.703–4). The setting recalls the grotto where Hercules and Omphale cross-dress ("a garrulous river was at the entry" [*garrulus in primo limine rivus erat*], 2.316).

104. This *anguis* (711) echoes Ovid's epic simile comparing Faunus (touching the bristly lion hide) to a traveler who steps back *viso angue* ("when a snake is seen," (339–42). The snake signifies the Herculean phallus. Cf. Faunus' own *inguen* at 346; Barchiesi 1997a: 149 observes the assonance of *angue/inguen* in the Faunus-Hercules-Omphale episode and the "farcical register" in which it "degrades an elevated rhetorical figure" from *Aeneid* 2.

105. At Liv. 1.56.4–13 the sons of Tarquin go to consult the Delphic oracle along with Brutus their cousin (son of Tarquin's sister); while there, they also ask who will succeed their father or will assume rule next. Apollo's prediction about kissing the mother

responds to this question. This is not in Ovid's version.

106. Cic. *Sen.* 11.36 associates *stultitia* with mentally weak old men. Cic. *Am.* 26.100 quotes the lines of Caecilius at greater length in a passage discussing the shame of being duped by flatterers. Ov. *F.* 2.513–32, *festa Stultorum,* "Feast of Fools" on the *Fornacalia,* and the failure of some citizens to know the districts where they could perform the *Fornacalia* (oven) rites. Festus "Quirinalia" and "Stultorum feriae," 304, 305, 418, 419L.

107. Brutus' "offensive," "offended," or "offending foot" also marks his persona. The word *pes* can also mean "poetry" or "metrical speech."

108. Cf. Ariadne vexed over whether Bacchus has been faithful; Liber-Bacchus' reassuring response (Ov. *F.* 3.511–12) promises eternal juncture between them in the heavens, in name as well as in bed. Cf. *P.* 3.3.47–52; *Amor lascivus* (47) can swear with a clear conscience that Ovid did not disturb the legal (marriage) couches (*non me legitimos sollicitasse toros*).

109. Nussbaum 2002: 298 notes that by Cicero's time marriage based on complete male domination had already become muted and ideals of life-long friendship and affection were ascendant. See also Treggiari 1991. Foucault 1988: 151–52 on mutual care or mutual solicitude found in the discussions of marriage by Musonius Rufus (b. 40 CE), *Reliquiae* XIII A, "On the Purpose of Marriage," tr. Cora Lutz, 67–68.

110. Cf. Livy's *De uxoribus mentio* (1.57.6), *suam quisque laudare miris modis* (1.57.6), *quantum ceteris praestet Lucretia sua* and *invisimusque praesentes nostrarum ingenia* (1.57.7).

111. Liv. 1.57.6–7 does not portray Sextus as instigating the topic; Ovid emphasizes Sextus', not Collatinus' discourse. Instead, Livy gives greater impetus to Collatinus' careless boasting (longer direct speech in Livy) challenging other men to go to catch women at home unawares.

112. A metaphor of "publishing" related to a public-private binary may be present in Livy's prose version and more certainly appears in Shakespeare's "Rape of Lucrece." See Breitenberg 1996: 97–127 on Shakespeare. See Feldherr 1998: 194–203 for Livy on public/private binary.

113. This is a kind of "undergrowth" of the Lacanian "Real"; as Zizek in Wright and Wright 1999: 15–36 calls it, "the undergrowth of enjoyment" (*jouissance*).

114. On the verb *sollicito:* Adams 1982: 184–85, 200, 208.

115. *Arma,* another possible innuendo for the penis: Adams 1982: 17, 21.

116. At 2.729 (*ecquid in officio torus est socialis?*), the expression *torus socialis* does bear the special meaning that Ovid gives it, the marital bed, as L-S, *socialis,* recognizes. Here Ovid places the adjective *socialis* after the verb *est,* which separates *socialis* from *torus,* implying the function of *socialis* as predicate and its other main meaning, "common to associates," "companionable."

117. On *mutuus* as "lent, borrowed"—based on "sharing"—usually of money, see L-S, *mutuus* I. It applies metaphorically to love, such as at Plaut. *Amph.* 819, *Curc.* 47–49.

118. The men, Ovid says, "suffer long delay" or deferral in attaining this desired goal (*et patitur longas obsidione moras,* 722). Cf. Cynthia's complaint to Propertius of his long absence—delay—in lovemaking outside the house, leaving her alone to weave and play the lyre (Prop. 1.3.43–44): *interdum leviter mecum deserta querebar/ externo longas saepe in amore moras.*

119. *ante torum calathi lanaque mollis erat, F.* 2.742.

120. See Tib. 1.3.83–94 for Tibullus wishing to return home suddenly from *militia* to find Delia weaving beside an old lady, the guardian of her chastity, telling her *fabellae.*

121. Such figures are numerous: Penelope in the *Odyssey* waiting for return of Odysseus; Horatia weaving a *lacerna* for her betrothed (Liv. 1.26.2), which she now sees

as her brother's war booty. See also Propertius' Cynthia (1.3.41–44) and Arethusa (4.3.17–18, 33–34), who are concerned about male monogamy.

122. Lucretia also requests information from maids who have mobility and contact with the public; she is chastely confined for her husband, whom she calls "master" (*domino*, 745–48).

123. Newlands 1995a: 170–71 shows how Ovid uses such language to associate Lucretia, qua woman, with elegiac poetics and, generally, with women as voices of protest and subversion.

124. Upon seeing Hercules and Omphale, Faunus declares, *hic meus ardor erit* (308), and from there unfolds the daring of "shameless desire" (*quid non amor improbus audet?* 331). By sound, the name *Ardea* in Lucretia's speech (2.751) recalls its use in Sextus' speech (727). The name *Ardea* recalls the adjective *arduus,*"steep," "difficult to reach or attain." Yet, *Ardea* recalls the noun *ardor* (flame, fire, or a burning) and the verb *ardeo,* both describing passions of various types, specifically erotic desire (cf. *ardor* of the passions: Ov. *Met.* 14.683).

125. For the "weaving" in the imperial palace as proper behavior for Augustus' daughter and grandaughters: Suet. *Aug.* 64. For the adultery, see Suet. *Aug.* 65 and Vell. Pat. 2.100.2 (conspiracy involving Iulus Antonius). Also, see Plin. *H.N.* 21.6.9 (Iulia's drunken night revels); Plin. *H.N.* 7.149 (suggestions of parricide); Sen. *brev. Vit.* 4.6. Sources are neatly gathered in Leon 1951. For Iulia's (un)chastity (*im-pudicitia*) as a social model, cf. Valerius Maximus' prayer to *Pudicitia*, sexual integrity, at the beginning of Book 6 and the first example (6.1.1) of Lucretia.

126. On *phantasiai* in relation to sexuality, see Foucault 1988: 132–44 ("Work of the Soul"), esp. 134–39 on the dangers of images for the erotic impulse and examples in Roman elegists (particularly in women's viewing of artworks and reading erotic literature, Prop. 2.6, 2.15; Ov. *A.A.* 3.808, 3.209; *Rem.* 399 and 345–48). For Ovid, Hardie 2002: 1–22, esp. 12 on the Lucretia narrative in *Fasti* 2 (esp. 769–70, 777–78). This psychology, primarily Stoic cognitive-emotion theory: Nussbaum 1994: 316–401. For historical presentation of ancient *phantasia:* Bundy 1927. For *phantasia* in the late Hellenistic theory of creative (artistic) imagination, see Pollitt 1974: 52–58 (late Hellenistic and imperial philosophy). On *ecphrasis* and *enargeia*, see Pollitt 1974: 58–63. Ancient sources on *phantasia* in art history, see Pollitt 1974: 293–97. Imbert 1980; Goldhill 1994.

127. *F.* 2.761–62 recalls the prophetic inspiration of Carmentis (1.473–74, *aetherios animo conceperat ignes*), except different adjectives qualify the flames (*aetherios* and *furiales*).

128. Liv. 1.58.3 states the womanishness of Sextus in the attempted seduction: *tum Tarquinius fateri amorem, orare, miscere precibus minas, versare in omnes partes muliebrem animum.* Translators sometimes take the last clause to mean that Sextus tries to turn Lucretia's "womanish mind"(*muliebrem animum*). Instead, his womanish mind turns in every direction. By contrast, it is Lucretia who is inflexible (*obstinatam,* 1.58.4), having inflexible sexual integrity (*obstinatam pudicitiam,* 1.58.5); she has the qualities of manly firmness. Cf. Lucretia as a "matron of manly spirit" (*animi matrona virilis, F.* 2.847).

129. For the ancient idea that women's bodies are more liquid and leaky than a man's: Carson 1990. This imagery recalls Cat. 64.60–62: abandoned Ariadne stands in Naxian waves looking longingly over the sea for Theseus: *quem procul ex alga maestis Minois ocellis, / saxea ut effigies bacchantis, prospicit, eheu, / prospicit et magnis curarum fluctuat undis.*

130. For the rhetoric of *fictio personarum*, an imitation (*mimesis*) of the ethos of another character (*ethopoeia*), see Quint. *Inst.* 9.2.29–31, 9.2.58.

131. I suspect that Ovid is manipulating a gender stereotype that women are better

at concealing their desire than men. Cf. *A.A.* 1. 274–75: *utque viro furtiva venus, sic grata puellae:/ vir male dissimulat: tectius illa cupit.*

132. Laplanche and Pontalis 1968: 17 portray "phantasy" in terms of a metaphor of "drama": "Fantasy . . . is not the object of desire, but its setting," or by extension, "phantasies are still scripts (scenarios) of organized scenes" (318). Farmer 2000 applies fantasy theory to film interpretation.

133. Richlin 1992b surveys various analytical methods for analyzing Ovid's rape narratives (as pornography) including feminist approaches (pro- and con-pornography), fantasy theory ("Fantasy and Representation"), and political models.

134. Sextus plays a *hostis-hospes*, not unlike Paris visiting the home of Menelaus (cf. absent Collatinus): Apoll. 3.12.5–6, "Epitome" 3.1–5, 5.8.

135. See Cohen 1991 for Roman traditionalist ideas that a mere approach to a woman posed questions about her chastity.

136. *F.* 2.793–94: *surgit et aurata vagina liberat ensem / et venit in thalamos, nupta pudica, tuos.*

137. On "phantasy" as *mise-en-scène*, see Laplanche andPontalis 1973: 318: the staging of desire, i.e., its lack of fulfillment (Zizek 1991: 6). Ovid's dramatic monologues appeal to the reader's voyeuristic fantasy in a way recalling modern film, perhaps ancient theater (mime, pantomime; see Richlin 1992 on these influences).

138. Boyle and Woodward, tr. 2000: 51.

139. For *agere* meaning "to act," see L-S, *ago*, II.D.10, "to represent by external action, to perform, pronounce, deliver, etc."

140. *F.* 2.807–10: *"nil agis: eripiam," dixit "per crimina vitam: / falsus adulterii testis adulter ero: / interimam famulum, cum quo deprensa fereris." / succubuit famae victa puella metu.*

141. At *Tr.* 2. 497–516, Ovid defends his poetry's erotic content by comparing it to adultery scenes in Roman theatrical mime. See Fantham 1983 on Ovid's use of mime as a source for "sexual comedy" in the *Fasti*. Fantham's prime examples are the Hercules-Omphale tale in *Fasti* 2, and the two attempted, but frustrated, rapes by Priapus, one in *Fasti* 1 (of Lotis) and one in *Fasti* 6 (of Vesta).

142. *Eloquar* specifically refers to oratorical speech, not gender-appropriate for Roman matrons, although there are remarkable exceptions. See *eloquor*, L-S, esp. II. Cf. Tanaquil speaking to the public at Liv. 1.41.4–5, smoothing the transition of Servius to power.

143. For rape as an insult to a father's or husband's dignity and honor killings in traditional Rome versus regulation of killing in Augustan legislation (*lex Iulia de adulteries*), see Cohen 1991 and Cantarella 1991. Subsequent imperial law returned to rights to killing (Cantarella). See Treggiari 1996: 890; Cantarella 1991.

144. As Sen. *Contr.* 3.5 suggests, Romans expected a girl to attempt suicide in such circumstances; her value to men as a badge of honor had been depleted. See Cohen 1991: 113.

145. Cf. Ovid on Achilles cross-dressed and hidden among girls by his mother to help save him from the Trojan War: "Shamefully . . . Achilles had dissimulated his manhood with a long gown" (*A.A.* 1.689–90: *turpe, nisi hoc matris precibus tribuisset, Achilles / veste virum longa dissimulatus erat*). In Hor. *C.* 1.8: Leach 1994.

146. Brutus' voice publicizing the sexual violations is both similar to, yet different from, the braying of asses in two passages: when Priapus tried to rape Lotis and Vesta, the ass "produced untimely noises" (*intempestivos edidit ore sonos*, 1.434) or "bellows with an untimely sound" (*intempestivo cum rudit ille sono*, 6.342).

147. Garber 1992: 1–17, esp. 9–13, 16–17.

148. This "gendering" that exceeds the bounds of gender and the sourcing of such love-bonds in Plato's text may have suggested the "spiritualization" of Hercules and Omphale that Kampen (1996) has observed in first- and second-century representations.

149. Sospita wore a goatskin cape, like Hercules in his lion skin, so that the goat's head formed a horned helmet; her shoes were upturned; she was armed with a spear and shield. Sospita's clothing and arms: Frazer 1929, 2: 295–97. Douglas 1913 gathers artistic and literary evidence on Italic Juno Sospita with Hercules (male fertility deity): she is his new virginal bride worshiped with him (cf. Bayet 1926: 115–16). Juno Sospita's symbolism of young male prowess, young women's chastity, and civic integrity: Douglas 1913. Cult at Lanuvium (a cave inhabited by an oracular serpent, where annually local girls, blindfolded, brought barley cakes as offerings): Prop. 4.8; Beard, North, and Price 1998, 1: 82–83, 89 and Fig. 2.1. If the serpent devoured the cakes, the girls were considered virgins and the crops would prosper: Prop. 4.8.3–14; Ael. NA 11.16.

150. Wyke 1987, 1990, 1995, essays gathered in Wyke 2002. See Fredrick 1997 reasserting the reality of violence.

151. Lucretia's body as symbol in male politics: Joshel 1992a. Quint. Inst. 5.11.10: "Cato and Scipio will not carry so much momentum for facing death as will Lucretia." Cf. Val. Max. 6.1.1 on the sexual integrity of Lucretia, "whose masculine soul by a cruel mistake of fortune obtained the lot of a woman's body" (cuius virilis animus maligno errore fortunae muliebre corpus sortitus). Cf. Tullia's rhetoric of male shame to motivate her husband Tarquinius Superbus to kill her father, Servius Tullius (Liv. 1.47.3–7; Ov. F. 6.587–96).

152. Roller 2001: esp. 233–47, articulates key aspects of the double father. For the psychosocial dynamics: cf. Zizek 2001: 149–93 ("Why Are There Always Two Fathers?").

153. Tiberius' repudiation of the title Pater Patriae: Suet. Tib. 67; Tac. Ann. 1.72.

154. At F. 2.131–32, the sound play on tu-pi/pa-ter stresses the root of Iu-piter from pater: hoc tu per terras, quod in aethere Iuppiter alto, nomen habes: hominum tu pater, ille deum.

155. In Tr. 2, Ovid's self-defense from exile, he offers an elaborate comparison of Augustus and Jupiter (33–40, 69; cf. 143–44, etc.) and appeals to Augustus' mercy as pater patriae several times (39, 147, 181–88, 574; cf. 208, 321–22).

156. See Rudich 1993, Roller 2001. Cf. Brutus' dissimulation in Livy 1.56.8. For covert communication, Ahl 1984a, 1984b, 1985 (wordplay generally). Ancient theory of covert (figured) speech before despots (where one emphasizes or shows meaning while hinting at another "beneath"): Quint. Inst. 9.2.64–80, esp. 67–69; "Longinus," On the Sublime 17–18; Demetr. Eloc. 287–98, esp. 289–96.

Epilogue

1. Nagle 1980: 22–32.

2. For uncanny effects of objects "between two deaths," Zizek 1989: 131–49; 1991: 21–29.

3. Fasti as a dimidium: cf. Hor. C. 1.35–8, crediting Vergil, a dimidium of his soul, to a departing ship, warning half should be returned (Buttrey 1972: 47–48). Pollux, Onomasticon 9.70–71 of ἡμίτομον νόμισμα as a σύμβολον.

4. Non finito works and "involvement of the beholder, who is invited to complete the forms in his mind": Rosand 1981 (esp. 21).

5. Compare Pliny's earlier account of the ultimate skill in painting (*H.N.* 35.67–68): Pliny describes how the edge between the seen and hidden in painting a three-dimensional dfigure is defined by the panel's two-dimensional surface. The supreme artist can so render the borders of figures to suggest to viewers the unseen parts of an ojbect that lie behind it (*post se*). The notion of front and behind of the painting's vidual surface is analogous to exile, which imposed a broken edge on Ovid and the *Fasti:* The unseen other half of Ovid and the *Fasti* lie behind or beyond his exile at the edge of Rome's empire.

6. Cf. Plin. *H.N.* 35.91–92: two paintings of Aphrodite by Apelles left incomplete, because no artist dared challenge Apelles' genius, fearing the contrast. Competition-complementation between poets: Ovid wrote letters from heroines to hero-lovers (*Heroides*); Sabinus wrote heroes' epistolary answers (*P.* 4.16.13; cf. *Am.* 2.18.27). Cf. Sabinus' calendar work left *imperfectum* by death with incompletion of Ovid's *Fasti* (*Tr.* 4.16.15–16).

BIBLIOGRAPHY

Accame, S. 1942. "La legislazione romana intorno ai collegi nel 1 secolo a.C." *BMusImp* 13: 13–48.

Adams, J. N. 1982. *Latin Sexual Vocabulary.* Baltimore: Johns Hopkins University Press.

Ahl, F. 1984a. "The Art of Safe Criticism in Greece and Rome." *AJPh* 105: 174–208.

———. 1984b. "The Rider and the Horse: Politics and Power in Roman Poetry from Horace to Statius." *ANRW* 2.32.1: 40–124.

———. 1985. *Metaformations: Soundplay and Wordplay in Ovid and Other Classical Poets.* Ithaca: Cornell University Press

Alpers, Johannes. 1912. *Hercules in Bivio.* Göttingen: Dieterich.

Alton, E. H., D. E. W. Wormell, and E. Courtney. 1988. *Ovidius, Fasti.* Leipzig: Teubner.

Anderson, James. 1984. *The Historical Topography of the Imperial.* Brussels: Latomus.

Anderson, William. 1966. "Horace *Carm.* 1.14: What Kind of Ship?" *CPh* 61: 84–98.

Appel, Georg. 1909. *De Romanorum Precationibus.* Giessen: Alfred Toepelmann

Austin, J. L. 1962. *How to Do Things with Words.* Cambridge, Mass: Harvard University Press.

Aveni, Anthony. 1989. *Empires of Time: Calendars, Clocks, and Cultures.* New York: Basic Books.

Babelon, Ernest. 1901. *Traité des monnaies grecques et romaines.* Paris: E. Leroux.

Balsdon, J. P. V. D. 1969. *Life and Leisure in Ancient Rome.* London: Phoenix.

Bannon, C. 1997. *The Brothers of Romulus: Fraternal Pietas in Roman Law, Literature and Society.* Princeton: Princeton University Press.

Barchiesi, Alessandro. 1991. "Discordant Muses." *PCPhS* 37: 1–21.

———. 1997a. *The Poet and the Prince: Ovid and Augustan Discourse.* Berkeley: University of California Press.

———. 1997b. "Endgames: Ovid's *Metamorphoses* 15 and *Fasti* 6." In Roberts, Dunn, and Fowler 1997, 181–208.

Barrett, Anthony A. 2002. *Livia: First Lady of Imperial Rome.* New Haven: Yale University Press.

Barsby, John. 1978. *Ovid.* Oxford: Clarendon Press.

Bartsch, Shadi. 1994. *Actors in the Audience: Theatricality and Doublespeak from Nero to Hadrian.* Cambridge, Mass: Harvard University Press.

Barthes, Roland. 1986 (1975). *The Pleasure of the Text.* New York: Hill and Wang.

Barton, Carlin. 1993. *Sorrows of the Ancient Romans: The Gladiator and the Monster.* Princeton: Princeton University Press.

———. 2001. *Roman Honor: The Fire in the Bones.* Berkeley: University of California Press.

Barton, Tasmyn. 1995. "Augustus and Capricorn: Astrology, Polyvalence, and Imperial Rhetoric." *JRS* 85: 33–51.

Bayet, J. 1926. *Les origines de l'Hercule Romain.* Paris: E. de Boccard.

Beard, Mary. 1987. "A Complex of Times: No More Sheep on Romulus' Birthday." *PCPhS* 33: 1–15.

———. 1991. "Writing and Religion: Ancient Literacy and the Function of the Written Word in Roman Religion." In Mary Beard, John North, and Simon Price. *Literacy in the Roman World,* 35–58. Ann Arbor: University of Michigan Press.

Beard, Mary, John North, and Simon Price. 1998. *Religions of Rome.* 2 vols. Cambridge: Cambridge University Press.

Bendinelli, Goffredo. 1941. *Le pitture del columbario di Villa Pamphili.* Sect 3, vol. 2, fasc. 5 in *Monumenti della pittura antica scoperti in Italia.* Rome: La Libreria dello Stato.

Benjamin, A. S., and A. E. Raubitschek, 1959. "Arae Augusti." *Hesperia* 28: 65–85.

Bennett, Alva Walter. 1968. "The Patron and Poetical Inspiration: Propertius 3.9." *Hermes* 96: 318–40.

Bertman, Stephen, ed. 1976. *The Conflict of Generations in Ancient Greece and Rome.* Amsterdam: B. R. Grüner.

Benton, C. 2002. "Split Vision: The Politics of the Gaze in Seneca's *Troades.*" In Fredrick 2002, 31–56.

Birley, Eric. 1953. *Roman Britain and the Roman Army: Collected Papers.* Kendal, England: T. Wilson.

Blume, F., K. Lachmann, and A. Rudorff, eds. 1848, 1852. *Die Schriften der römischen Feldmesser.* 2 vols. Berlin: G. Reimer.

Bömer, Franz. 1957–1958. *Ovid, Die Fasten.* 2 vols. Heidelberg: C. Winter.

Botsford, George Willis. 1909. *The Roman Assemblies.* New York: Macmillan Co.

Bouché-Leclercq, A. 1882. *Divination italique.* Vol. 4 of *Histoire de la divination dans l'antiquité.* Paris: E. Leroux, 1879–82.

Bourdieu, P. 1977. *Outline of a Theory of Practice.* Tr. Richard Nice. Cambridge: Cambridge University Press.

———. 1987 (1975). "The Invention of the Artist's Life." *Yale French Studies* 73: 75–103.

———. 1990. *The Logic of Practice.* Tr. Richard Nice. Stanford: Stanford University Press.

———. 2001. *Masculine Domination.* Tr. Richard Nice. Stanford: Stanford University Press.

Boyd, Barbara Weiden. 2001. "Arms and the Man: Wordplay and the Catasterism of Chiron in Ovid's *Fasti* 5." *AJPh* 122: 67–80.

———. 2000a. "*Celeus Rusticus:* A Note on Ovidian Wordplay in *Fasti* 4." *CPh* 95.2: 190–93.

———. 2000b. *Brill's Companion to Ovid.* Leiden: Brill.

Boyle, A. J., ed. 1995. *Roman Literature and Ideology: Ramus Essays for J. P. Sullivan.* Bendigo, Victoria, Australia: Aureal Publications.

———. 1997. "Postscripts from the Edge: Exilic *Fasti* and Imperialised Rome." *Ramus* 26.1: 7–28.

Boyle, A. J., and R. D. Woodard, tr., ed. 2000. *Ovid: Fasti.* New York: Penguin.

Bramble, J. C. 1974. *Persius and the Programmatic Satire: A Study in Form and Imagery.* Cambridge: Cambridge University Press.

Breitenberg, Mark. 1996. *Anxious Masculinity in Early Modern England*. Cambridge: Cambridge University Press.

Brill's New Pauly: Encyclopaedia of the Ancient World. Hubert Cancik, Helmuth Schneider, et al. Leiden Brill, 2002–.

Brunner, Theodore F. 1971. "*Deinon* vs. *eleeinon*: Heinze Revisited." *AJPh* 92: 275–84.

Buchner, E. 1982. *Die Sonnenuhr des Augustus*. Mainz: von Zabern.

Bundy, Murray Wright. 1927. "The Theory of Imagination in Classical and Mediaeval Thought." *University of Illinois Studies in Language and Literature* 12: 183–472.

Burkert, W. 1983. *Homo Necans*. Berkeley: University of California Press.

Butler, Judith. 1990. *Gender Trouble: Feminism and the Subversion of Identity*. New York: Routledge.

Buttrey, T. V. 1972. "Halved Coins, the Augustan Reform, and Horace, *Odes* 1.3." *AJA* 76.1: 31–48.

Cahoon, Leslie, 1988. "Bed as Battlefield: Erotic Conquest and Military Metaphor in Ovid's *Amores*." *TAPA* 118: 293–307.

Cairns, F. 2002. "Acontius and his οὔνομα κουρίδιον: Callimachus *Aetia* fr. 67.1–4 Pf." *CQ* 52.2: 471–77.

Cameron, Averil, ed. 1990. *History as Text: The Writing of Ancient History*. Chapel Hill: University of North Carolina Press.

Cantarella, Eva. 1991. "Homicides of Honor: The Development of Italian Adultery Law over Two Millennia." In Kertzer and Saller 1991, 229–44

Carson, Anne. 1990. "Putting Her in Her Place: Woman, Dirt, and Desire." In Halperin, Winkler, and Zeitlin 1990, 135–69.

Chambers, Ross. 1999. *Loiterature*. Lincoln: University of Nebraska Press.

Chion, Michel. 1994 (1992). *Audio-Vision: Sound on Screen*. Ed., Tr. Claudia Gorbman. New York: Columbia University Press.

———. 1999 (1982). *The Voice in Cinema*. Tr. Claudia Gorbman. New York: Columbia University Press.

Clarke, John R. 1998. *Looking at Lovemaking: Constructions of Sexuality in Roman Art: 100 B.C.–A.D. 240*. Berkeley: University of California Press.

Coarelli, F. 1984. *Lazio*. Rome: Laterza.

———. 1986. Il Foro Romano: Periodo Arcaico. Rome: Quasar.

———. 1995. *Roma*. Guide Archeologiche Laterza, 6. Rome: Laterza.

Cohen, David. 1991. "The Augustan Law on Adultery: The Social and Cultural Context." In Kertzer and Saller 1991, 109–26.

Commager, S. 1962. *The Odes of Horace: A Critical Study*. New Haven: Yale University Press.

Connors, Catherine. 1997. "Field and Forum: Culture and Agriculture in Roman Rhetoric." In Dominik 1997, 71–89

Conte, Gian Baggio. 1994a. *Genres and Readers: Lucretius, Love Elegy, Pliny's Encyclopedia*. Tr. Glenn W. Most. Baltimore: Johns Hopkins University Press.

———. 1994b. *Latin Literature: A History*. Baltimore: Johns Hopkins University Press.

Cook, A. B. 1914–40. *Zeus: A Study in Ancient Religion*. Cambridge: Cambridge University Press.

Copley, F. O. 1956. *Exclusus Amator: A Study in Latin Love Poetry*. Madison, Wisc.: University of Wisconsin Press.

Corbeill, Anthony. 1997. "Dining Deviants in Roman Political Invective" In Hallett and Skinner 1997, 99–128.

———. 2002. "Political Movement." In Fredrick 2002, 182–216.

Corbier, M. 1995. "Male Power and Legitimacy through Women: The *Domus Augustua* under the Julio-Claudians." In Hawley and Levick 1995, 178–93.

Crawford, Michael. 1974–. Roman Republican Coinage. New York: Cambridge University Press.

Cumont, Franz. 1942. *Recherches sur le symbolisme funéraire des Romains*. Paris: P. Geuthner.

———. 1959 (1929). *After-Life in Roman Paganism*. New York: Dover; originally published New Haven: Yale University Press.

Curchin, Leonard. 1996. "Cult and Celt: Indigenous Participation in Emperor Worship." In Small 1996, 143–52.

Curtius, Ernst. 1973 (1953). *European Literature and the Latin Middle Ages*. Tr. Willard Trask. Bollingen Series XXXVI. Princeton: Princeton University Press.

Daremberg, Charles, Edmond Saglio, et al., eds. 1877–1919. *Dictionnaire des antiquités grecques et romains d'après les textes et les monuments*. Paris: Hachette.

Davis, Peter. 1999. "Instructing the Emperor: Ovid, *Tristia* 2." *Latomus* 58: 799–809.

Degrassi, A. 1963. *Inscriptiones Italiae*. Vol. 13 (*Fasti et Elogia*), Fasc. 2 (*Fasti Anni Numani et Iuliani*). Rome: La Libreria dello Stato.

De Grummond, N. 1990. "*Pax Augusta* and the *Horae* on the *Ara Pacis Augustae*." *AJA* 94: 663–77.

De Lauretis, Teresa. 1984. *Alice Doesn't: Feminism Semiotics Cinema*. Bloomington: Indiana University Press.

Della Corte, Francesco. 1982. "Le *Leges Iuliae* et l'elegia Romana." *ANRW* II.30.1: 539–58.

De Mirmont, H. 1905. *La jeunesse d'Ovide*. Paris. A. Fontemoing.

Dickie, M. W. 2001. "Mimes, Thaumaturgy, and the Theatre." *CQ* 51.2: 599–603.

Diehls, H., and A. Rehm. 1904. "Parapegmenfragmente aus Milet." *Sitzungsberichte der königlich preussischen Akademie der Wissenschaften, philos.-hist. Kl.* 23: 92–111.

Dieterich, Albrecht. 1897 (1982). *Pulcinella: pompejanische Wandbilder und römische Satyrspiele, 1866–1908*. Leipzig: Teubner. Rpt. 1982 Aalen: Scientia Verlag.

Dilke, R. O. A. M. 1962. "The Roman Surveyors." *Greece and Rome*, 2nd ser., 9: 170–80.

———. *Roman Land Surveyors*. New York: Barnes and Noble.

Dolar, Mladen. 1996. "The Object Voice." In Salecl- i ek 1996, 7–31.

Dominik, William J., ed. 1997. *Roman Eloquence: Rhetoric in Society and Literature*. New York: Routledge

Douglas, E. M. 1913. "Iuno Sospita of Lanuvium." *JRS* 3: 60–72.

Dover, J. K. 1989. *Greek Homosexuality: Updated and with a New Postscript*. Cambridge, Mass.: Harvard University Press.

DuBois, Page. 1988. *Sowing the Body: Psychoanalysis and Ancient Reprpresentation of Women*. Chicago: University of Chicago.

Dumézil, G. 1996 (1970). *Archaic Roman Religion*. 2 vols. Tr. P. Krapp. Baltimore: Johns Hopkins University Press.

Dupont, Florence. 1992. *Daily Life in Ancient Rome*. Tr. Christopher Woodall. Cambridge, Mass: Harvard University Press

———. 1997. "*Recitatio* and the Organization of the Space of Public Discourse." In Habinek and Schiesaro 1997, 44–59.

———. 1999. *The Invention of Literature: From Greek Intoxication to the Latin Book*. Tr. Janet Lloyd. Baltimore: Johns Hopkins University Press.

Dyson, Stephen. 1992. *Community and Society in Roman Italy*. Baltimore: Johns Hopkins University Press.

Edelman, Lee. 1991. "Seeing Things: Representation, the Scene of Surveillance, and the

Spectacle of Gay Male Sex." In Fuss 1991, 93–116.

Edlow, R. B. 1977. *Galen on Language and Ambiguity.* Leiden: Brill.

Edwards, Catherine. 1993. *The Politics of Immorality.* Cambridge: Cambridge University Press.

———. 1996. *Writing Rome: Textual Approaches to the City.* Cambridge: Cambridge University Press.

Ehrenberg, Victor, and A. H. M. Jones, eds. 1955. *Documents Illustrating the Reigns of Augustus & Tiberius.* 2nd ed. Oxford: Clarendon Press.

Étienne, R. 1958. *Le culte impérial dans la péninsule ibérique d'Auguste à Dioclétien.* Paris: E. de Boccard

Fantham, Elaine. 1983. "Sexual Comedy in Ovid's *Fasti:* Sources and Motivation." *HSCP* 87: 185–216.

———. 1985. "Ovid, Germanicus, and the Composition of the *Fasti.*" *Proceedings of the Liverpool Latin Seminar* 5: 243–81.

———. 1992a. "Ceres, Liber and Flora: Georgic and Anti-Georgic Elements in Ovid's *Fasti.*" *PCPhS* 38: 39–56.

———. 1992b. "The Role of Evander in Ovid's *Fasti.*" *Arethusa* 25.1: 155–71.

Farmer, Brett. 2000. *Spectacular Passions: Cinema, Fantasy, Gay Male Spectatorships.* Durham: Duke University Press.

Fear, Trevor, ed. 2000. *Fallax Opus: Approaches to Reading Roman Elegy. Arethusa* 33.2 (Spring 2000).

Feeney, Denis. 1992. "*Si licet et fas est:* Ovid's *Fasti* and the Problem of Free Speech under the Principate." In Anton Powell, ed. *Roman Poetry and Propaganda in the Age of Augustus,* 1–25. London: Bristol Classical Press.

———. 1998. *Literature and Religion at Rome: Cultures, Contexts, and Beliefs.* Cambridge: Cambridge University Press.

Feldherr, Andrew. 1998. *Spectacle and Society in Livy's History.* Berkeley: University of California Press.

Ferguson, J. 1970. *The Religions of the Roman Empire.* Ithaca: Cornell University Press.

Fischler, S. 1998. "Imperial Cult: Engendering the Cosmos." In Foxhall and Salmon 1998, 165–83.

Fishwick, Duncan. 1978. "The Development of Provincial Ruler Worship in the Western Roman Empire." *ANRW* 2.16.2: 1201–53.

———. 1987. *The Imperial Cult in the Latin West.* I.1. Leiden: Brill.

———. 1991a. *The Imperial Cult in the Latin West.* II.1. Leiden: Brill.

———. 1991b. "Ovid and Divus Augustus." *CPh* 86: 36–41.

———. 2002. *The Imperial Cult in the Latin West.* III.2. Leiden: Brill

———. 2004. *The Imperial Cult in the Latin West.* III.3. Leiden: Brill.

Fitzgerald, W. 1995. *Catullan Provocations: Lyric Poetry and the Drama of Position.* Berkeley: University of California Press.

Flory, Marleen B. 1984. "*Sic exempla parantur:* Livia's Shrine to *Concordia* and the *Porticus Liviae.*" *Historia* 33: 309–33.

———. 1996. "Dynastic Ideology, the *Domus Augusta,* and Imperial Women: A Lost Statuary Group in the Circus Flaminius." *TAPA* 126: 287–306.

Foucault, M. 1990 [1985]. *The Use of Pleasure.* Vol. 2 of Foucault's *The History of Sexuality.* Tr. Robert Hurley. New York.

———. 1988 [1986]. *The Care of the Self.* Vol. 3 of Foucault's *The History of Sexuality.* Tr. Robert Hurley. New York.

Fowler, Don. 2002. "Masculinity under Threat? The Poetics and Politics of Inspiration in Latin Poetry." In Spentzou and Fowler 2002, 141–60.

Foxhall, Lin, and John Salmon, eds. 1998. *When Men Were Men: Masculinity, Power and Identity in Classical Antiquity*. New York: Routledge.

Fränkel, H. 1915. *De Simia Rodio*. Diss. Göttingen.

——.1945. *Ovid: A Poet between Two Worlds*. Berkeley: University of California Press.

Frazer, J. G. 1929. *Publii Ovidii Nasonis fastorum libri sex; The Fasti of Ovid*. 5 vols. London: Macmillan.

Fredrick, David. 1995. "Beyond the Atrium to Ariadne: Erotic Painting and Visual Pleasure in the Roman House." *ClAnt* 14: 255–87.

——. 1997. "Reading Broken Skin: Violence in Roman Elegy." In Hallett and Skinner 1997, 172–93.

——. 1999. "Haptic Poetics." *Arethusa* 32: 49–83.

——, ed. 2002. *The Roman Gaze: Vision, Power, and the Body*. Baltimore: Johns Hopkins University Press.

Frier, Bruce. 1979. *Libri Annales Pontificum Maximorum: The Origins of the Annalistic Tradition*. American Academy in Rome Monographs. Vol. 27. Rome: American Academy in Rome.

Frontisi-Ducroux, F., and F. Lissarrague. 1990. "From Ambiguity to Ambivalence: A Dionysiac Excursion through the 'Anakreontic' Vases." In Halperin, Winkler, and Zeitlin 1990, 211–56.

Fuss, Diana, ed. 1991. *Inside/Out: Lesbian Theories, Gay Theories*. New York: Routledge.

——. 1995. *Identification Papers*. New York: Routledge.

Galinsky, G. Karl. 1972. *The Herakles Theme: Adaptations of the Hero in Literature from Homer to the Twentieth Century*. Totowa, N.J.: Rowan and Littlefield.

——. 1992. "Venus, Polysemy, and the Ara Pacis Augustuae." *AJA* 96: 457–75.

——. 1996. *Augustan Culture: An Interpretive Introduction*. Princeton: Princeton University Press.

——. 1998. Review of Barchiesi, *The Poet and the Prince*. *BMCR* 98. 26 (online): http://ccat.sas.upenn.edu/bmcr.

Garber, Marjorie. 1992. *Vested Interests: Cross-Dressing and Cultural Anxiety*. New York: Routledge.

Gee, Emma. 2000. *Ovid, Aratus and Augustus: Astronomy in Ovid's* Fasti. Cambridge: Cambridge University Press.

Gibbs, Sharon. 1976. *Greek and Roman Sundials*. New Haven: Yale University Press

Girard, René. 1965. *Deceit, Desire, and the Novel: Self and Other in Literary Structure*. Tr. Yvonne Freccero. Baltimore: Johns Hopkins University Press.

——. 1977. *Violence and the Sacred*. Tr. Patrick Gregory. Baltimore: Johns Hopkins University Press.

Gleason, M. 1990. "The Semiotics of Gender: Physiognomy and Self-Fashioning in the Second Century C.E." In Halperin,Winkler, and Zeitlin 1990, 389–416.

——. 1995. *Making Men: Sophists and Self-Presentation in Ancient Rome*. Princeton: Princeton University Press.

——. 1999. "Elite Male Identity in the Roman Empire." In Potter and Mattingly 1990, 67–84.

Gold, Barbara K., ed. 1982. *Literary and Artistic Patronage in Ancient Rome*. Austin: University of Texas Press.

——. 1987. *Literary Patronage in Greece and Rome*. Chapel Hill: University of North Carolina Press.

Goldhill, Simon. 1994. "The Naïve and Knowing Eye: Ecphrasis and the Culture of

Viewing in the Hellenistic World." In *Art and Text in Ancient Greek Culture*, ed. Simon Goldhill and Robin Osborne, 197–223. Cambridge: Cambridge University Press.

Gourevitch, Danielle. 1984. *Le mal d'être femme: La femme et la médicine dans la Rome antique*. Paris: "Les Belle Lettres."

Gowers, Emily. 1995. "The Anatomy of Rome from Capitol to Cloaca." *JRS* 85: 23–32.

Greenberg, David. 1988. *The Construction of Homosexuality*. Chicago: University of Chicago Press.

Greene, Ellen. 1998. *The Erotics of Male Desire and the Mistress in Latin Love Poetry*. Baltimore: Johns Hopkins University Press.

Greenidge, A. H. J. 1894. *Infamia: Its Place in Roman Public and Private Law*. Oxford: Clarendon Press.

Griffin, Jasper. 1985. *Latin Poets and Roman Life*. Chapel Hill: University of North Carolina Press.

Gros, P. 1996. *L'architecture romaine: Du début du IIIe siècle av. J.-C. à la fin du Haut-Empire*. Vol. 1. Paris: Picard.

Gunderson, Erik. 2000. *Staging Masculinity: The Rhetoric of Performance in the Roman World*. Ann Arbor: University of Michigan Press.

Gunning, Tom. 1994. "An Aesthetics of Astonishment: Early Film and the (In)Credulus Spectator." In Williams 1994, 114–33.

Habinek, Thomas. 1997. "The Invention of Sexuality in the World-City of Rome." In Habinek and Schiesaro 1997, 23–43.

———. 1998. *The Politics of Latin Literature*. Princeton: Princeton University Press.

——— and Alessandro Schiesaro, eds. 1997. *The Roman Cultural Revolution*. Cambridge: Cambridge University Press.

Hadot, P. 1981. *Exercices spirituels et philosophie antique*. Paris: Études augustiniennes.

———. 1990. "Forms of Life and Forms of Discourse in Ancient Philosophy." *Critical Inquiry* 16: 483–505.

Hallett, Judith. 1977. "*Perusinae Glandes* and the Changing Image of Octavian." *AJAH* 2: 151–71.

Hallett, Judith, and Marilyn Skinner, eds. 1997. *Roman Sexualities*. Princeton: Princeton University Press.

Halperin, David. 1986. "Plato and Erotic Reciprocity." *ClAnt* 5: 60–80.

———. 1990. *One Hundred Years of Homosexuality*. London: Routledge.

Halperin, David, John Winkler, and Froma Zeitlin, eds. 1990. *Before Sexuality: The Construction of Erotic Experience in the Ancient Greek World*. Princeton: Princeton University Press.

Hannah, Robert. 2005. *Greek and Roman Calendars: Constructions of Time in the Classical World*. London: Duckworth.

Hano, M., 1986. "À l'origine du culte impérial: les autels des *Lares Augusti*. Recherches sur les thèmes iconographiques et leur signification." *ANRW* II.16.3: 2333–81.

Hardie, P. 1986. *Virgil's* Aeneid*: Cosmos and* Imperium. Oxford: Clarendon Press.

———. 1991. "The Janus Episode in Ovid's *Fasti*." *MD* 26: 47–64.

———. 2002. *Ovid's Poetics of Illusion*. Cambridge: Cambridge University Press.

———, ed. 2002. *The Cambridge Companion to Ovid*. Cambridge: Cambridge University Press.

Harries, B. 1991. "Ovid and the Fabii." *CQ*, n.s. 41: 150–68.

Harrison, Jane. 1962 (1912). *Themis: A Study of the Social Origins of Greek Religion*. Cleveland: World Publishing Co; originally published London: Merlin Press.

Hawley, Richard, and Barbara Levick, eds. 1995. *Women in Antiquity: New Assessments*.

New York: Routledge.

Heathcote, Owen, Alex Hughes, and James S. Williams, eds. 1998. *Gay Signatures: Gay and Lesbian Theory, Fiction and Film in France, 1945–1995.* New York: Berg.

Heinze, Richard. 1919. *Ovids elegische Erzählung.* Leipzig: Teubner.

Henderson, Jeffrey. 1975. *The Maculate Muse: Obscene Language in Attic Comedy.* New Haven: Yale University Press.

Henzen, W. 1874. *Acta Fratrum Arvalium.* Berlin: G. Reimer.

Herbert-Brown, Geraldine. 1994. *Ovid and the* Fasti: *An Historical Study.* Oxford: Clarendon Press.

———. 1997. Review of Newlands 1995a. *BMCR* 97. 10.11.

———, ed. 2002. *Ovid's* Fasti: *Historical Readings at Its Bimillennium.* New York: Oxford University Press.

Hinds, Stephen. 1987. *The Metamorphosis of Persephone: Ovid and the Self-Conscious Muse.* Cambridge: Cambridge University Press.

———. 1992. "*Arma* in Ovid's *Fasti* Part 1"; "*Arma* in Ovid's *Fasti* Part 2." *Arethusa* 25: 81–112, 113–54.

Holland, Louise. 1937. "The Shrine of the Lares Compitales." *TAPA* 68: 428–41.

———. 1961. *Janus and the Bridge.* Rome: American Academy in Rome.

Holloway, Ross. 1994. *The Archaeology of Early Rome and Latium.* New York: Routledge.

Hooker, J. T. 1989. "Arion and the Dolphin." *Greece & Rome,* 2nd ser. 36.2: 141–46.

Hopkins, Keith. 1965. "A Textual Emendation in a Fragment of Musonius Rufus: A Note on Contraception." *CQ* 15.1: 72–74.

Hubbard, Thomas K., ed. 2003. *Homosexuality in Greece and Rome: A Sourcebook of Basic Documents.* Berkeley: University of California Press.

Imbert, C. 1980. "Stoic Logic and Alexandrian Poetics." In M. Schofield, M. Burnyeat, and J. Barnes, eds., *Doubt and Dogmatism: Studies in Hellenistic Epistemology,* 182–216. Oxford: Oxford University Press.

Innis, Robert E., ed. 1985. *Semiotics: An Introductory Anthology.* Bloomington: Indiana University Press.

Jaczynowska, M. 1970. "Les organisations de *Iuvenes* et l'aristocratie municipale au temps de l'Empire Romain." In *Recherches sur les structures sociales dans l'antiquité classique* (Colloques Nationaux du Centre National de la Recherche Scientifique; Caen, 25–26 (April 1969), 265–74. Paris: Éditions du Centre national de la recherché scientifique.

Janan, Micaela. 1994. *"When the Lamp Is Shattered": Desire and Narrative in Catullus.* Carbondale, Ill.: Southern Illinois University Press.

———. 2001. *The Politics of Desire: Propertius IV.* Berkeley: University of California Press.

Johnson, William A. 2000. "Toward a Sociology of Reading in Classical Antiquity." *CPh* 121.4: 593–627.

Johnston, Patricia. 1977. "Vergil's Conception of Saturnus." *CSCA* 10: 57–70.

Joplin, P. K. 1990. "Ritual Work on Human Flesh: Livy's Lucretia and the Rape of the Body Politic." *Helios* 17 (1990): 51–70.

Jory, E. J. 1984. "The Early Pantomime Riots." In *Maistor: Classical, Byzantine and Renaissance Studies for Robert Browning,* ed. Ann Moffatt, 57–66. Canberra: Australian Association for Byzantine Studies.

Joshel, Sandra. 1992a. "The Body Female and the Body Politic: Livy's Lucretia and Verginia." In Richlin 1992a, 112–30.

———. 1992b. *Work, Identity, and Legal Status at Rome: A Study of the Occupational Inscriptions.* Norman: University of Oklahoma Press.

Kaiser Augustus und die verlorene Republik: Eine Ausstellung im Martin-Gropius-Bau, Berlin, 7.Juni–14.August 1988. Mainz: P. von Zabern, 1988.

Kampen, Natalie, ed. 1996. *Sexuality in Ancient Art.* Cambridge: Cambridge University Press.

Kapparis, Konstantinos. 2002. *Abortion in the Ancient World.* London: Duckworth.

Keith, A. M. 2000. *Engendering Rome: Women in Latin Epic.* Cambridge: Cambridge University Press.

Kay, Sarah. 2003. *i ek: A Critical Introduction.* Cambridge: Polity.

Keil, H. 1961. *Grammatici Latini.* Vol. 7. Hildesheim: G. Olms Verlagsbuchhandlung; originally published Leipzig: Teubner, 1885–1928.

Keith, A. M. 2000. *Engendering Rome: Women in Latin Epic.* Cambridge: Cambridge University Press.

Kellum, Barbara. 1996. "The Phallus as Signifier: The Forum of Augustus and Rituals of Masculinity." In Kampen 1996, 170–83.

———. 1997. "Concealing/ Revealing: Gender and the Play of Meaning in the Monuments of Augustan Rome." In Habinek and Schiesaro 1997, 158–181.

Kennedy, Duncan. F. 1993. *The Arts of Love: Five Studies in the Discourse of Roman Love Elegy.* Cambridge: Cambridge University Press.

———. 2000. "Bluff Your Way in Didactic: Ovid's *Ars Amatoria* and *Remedia Amoris.*" *Arethusa* 33: 159–76.

Kenney, E. J., and W. V. Clausen, eds. 1982. *The Cambridge History of Classical Literature: II, Latin Literature.* New York: Cambridge University Press.

Kertzer, David I., and Richard P. Saller, eds., 1991. *The Family in Italy from Antiquity to the Present.* New Haven: Yale University Press.

King, Helen. 1995. "Self Help, Self Knowledge: In Search of the Patient in Hippocratic Gynecology." In Hawley and Levick 1995, 135–48.

King, Henry C. 1978. *Geared to the Stars: The Evolution of Planetariums, Orreries, and Astronomical Clocks.* Toronto: University of Toronto Press.

King, Richard. 1998. "Ritual and Autobiography: The Cult of Reading in Ovid's *Tristia* 4.10." *Helios* 25: 99–120.

Kleijwegt, M. 1994. "*Iuvenes* and Roman Imperial Society." *Acta Classica* 37: 79–102.

Kleiner, Fred. 1971. "*Flamen* of the *Ara Pietatis.*" *AJA* 75: 391–94.

Koloski-Ostrow, A. O. 1997. "Violent Stages in Two Pompeian Houses: Imperial Taste, Aristocratic Response, and Messages of Male Control." In Ann Koloski-Ostrow and C. L. Lyons, eds. *Naked Truths: Women, Sexuality and Gender in Classical Art and Archaeology,* 243–66. London: Routledge.

Konstan, David. 1994–95. "Friendship and the State." *Hyperboreus.*1.2: 1–16.

Korzeniewski, Dietmar. 1964. "Ovid's elegisches Proömium." *Hermes* 92: 182–213.

Kritzman, Lawrence D., ed. 1981. *Fragments: Incompletion and Discontinuity.* New York: New York Literary Forum.

Kuntz, Mary. 1994. "The Prodikean Choice of Herakles: A Reshaping of Myth." *CJ* 89.2: 163–81.

Lacan, Jacques. 1966. *Écrits.* Paris: Éditions du Seuil.

———. 1977 (1966). *Écrits: A Selection.* Tr. Alan Sheridan. New York: Norton.

———. 1978 (1981). *The Four Fundamental Concepts of Psychoanalysis: The Seminar of Jacques Lacan, Book XI.* Ed. Jacques-Alain Miller, tr. Alan Sheridan. New York: Norton.

———. 1993 (1981). *The Psychoses, 1955–1956. The Seminar of Jacques Lacan, Book III.* Tr. Russell Grigg. London: Norton; previously published as *Les psychoses, 1955–1956*

(Séminaire III). Paris: Éditions du Seuil
———. 1998 (1975). *On Feminine Sexuality, the Limits of Love and Knowledge. Book XX: Encore 1972–1973.* Tr. Bruce Fink. New York: Norton.
———. 2002. *Écrits: A Selection.* Tr. Bruce Fink. New York: Norton.
Langer, Susanne. 1979. *Philosophy in a New Key: A Study in the Symbolism of Reason, Rite, and Art.* Cambridge, Mass: Harvard University Press
Laplanche, Jean, and J.-B. Pontalis. 1968. "Fantasy and the Origins of Sexuality." *International Journal of Psycho-Analysis* 49.1: 1–18.
———. 1973. *The Language of Psycho-Analysis.* Tr. Donald Nicholson-Smith. New York. W.W. Norton.
Lausberg, Heinrich. 1960. *Handbuch der literarischen Rhetorik.* 2 vols. Munich: M. Hueber.
Lauter, Hans. 1980–1981. "Ein frühaugusteinsches Emblem in den Porticus Octaviae." *BullCom* 87: 47–54.
Leach, E. W. 1980. "Sacral-Idyllic Painting and the Poems of Tibullus' First Book." *Latomus* 39: 47–79.
———. 1988. *The Rhetoric of Space.* Princeton: Princeton University Press.
———. 1993. "Absence and Desire in Cicero's *De Amicitia.*" *CW* 87.2: 3–20.
———. 1994. "Horace *Carmen* 1.8: Achilles, the Campus Martius and the Articulation of Gender Roles in Augustan Rome." *CPh* 89.4: 334–43
Lebek, W. D. 1990. "Standeswürde und Berufsverbot unter Tiberius: Das SC der *Tabula Larinas.*" *ZPE* 81: 37–58.
———. 1991. "Das SC der *Tabula Larinas:* Rittermusterung und andere Probleme." *ZPE* 85: 41–70.
Le Bohec, Yann. 2000. *The Imperial Roman Army.* New York: Routledge
Le Bonniec, Henri, ed. 1965. *P. Ovidius Naso: Fastorum Liber Primus.* Paris: Presses Universitaires de France.
Lee-Stecum, Parshia. 2000. "Poet/Reader, Authority Deferred: Re-Reading Tibullan Elegy." *Arethusa* 33.2: 177–216.
Leigh, Matthew. 1993. "Hopelessly Devoted to You." *PVS* 21: 89–110.
Leon, Ernestine. 1951. "Scribonia and Her Daughters." *TAPA* 82: 168–75.
Lesky, A. 1966 (1963). *History of Greek Literature.* 2nd ed. New York: Thomas Crowell; originally published Berne: Francke Verlag.
Levick, Barbara. 1978. "Concordia at Rome." *Scripta Nummaria Romana: Essays Presented to Humphrey Sutherland.* Ed. C. H. V. Sutherland R. A. G. Carson, and Colin M. Kraay, 217–233. London: Spink and Sons.
———. 1983. "The *Senatus Consultum* from Larinum." *JRS* 73: 97–115.
Lévi-Strauss, Claude. 1966. *The Savage Mind.* Chicago: University of Chicago Press.
———. 1969. *The Elementary Structures of Kinship.* Boston: Beacon.
Lewis, M. J. T. 2001. *Surveying Instruments of Greece and Rome.* Cambridge: Cambridge University Press.
Liebeschuetz, J. H. W. G. 1979. *Continuity and Change in Roman Religion.* Oxford: Oxford University Press. .
Lindsay, H. 1995."A Fertile Marriage: Agrippina and the Chronology of Her Children by Germanicus." *Latomus* 54: 3–17.
Ling, Roger. 1991. *Roman Painting.* Cambridge: Cambridge University Press.
Lintott, Andrew. 1968. *Violence in Republican Rome.* Oxford: Clarendon Press.
Little, Douglas. 1970. "Richard Heinze: Ovids elegische Erzählung." In *Ovids* Ars amatoria *und* Remedia amoris: *Untersuchungen zum Aufbau.* Ed. Ernst Zinn. Stuttgart: Klett, 64–105.

Lonsdale, Steven H. 1993. *Dance and Ritual Play in Greek Religion*. Baltimore: Johns Hopkins University Press.

Loraux, Nicole. 1990. "Herakles: The Super-Male and the Feminine." In Halperin, Winkler, and Zeitlin 1990, 21–53.

Luck, Georg. 1977. *P. Ovidius Naso: Tristia I-II*. 2 vols. Heidelberg: C. Winter.

———. 1985. *Arcana Mundi: Magic and the Occult in the Greek and Roman Worlds*. Baltimore: Johns Hopkins University Press.

Lutz, Cora. 1947. "Musonius Rufus, the Roman Socrates." *Yale Classical Studies* 10: 3–147.

Lyne, R. O. A. M. 1980. *The Latin Love Poets from Catullus to Horace*. New York: Oxford University Press.

Mack, Sara. 1988. *Ovid*. New Haven: Yale University Press.

Mackie, Nicola. 1992. "Ovid and the Birth of *Maiestas*." In Anton Powell, *Roman Poetry and Propaganda in the Age of Augustus*, 83–97. London: Bristol Classical Press.

MacMullen, Ramsay. 1981. *Paganism in the Roman Empire*. New Haven: Yale University Press.

Magi, F. 1972. "Il calendario dipinto sotto Santa Maria Maggiore." *MemPontAcc* 11.1: 1–103.

Malamud, Martha. 1989. *A Poetics of Transformation: Prudentius and Classical Mythology*. Ithaca: Cornell University Press.

Martina, Mario. 1981. "Aedes Hercules Musarum." *DArch*, n.s., 3.1: 49–68.

McGinn, T. A. J. 1992. "The *SC* from Larinum and the Repression of Adultery at Rome." *ZPE* 93: 273–95.

Merli, Elena. 2000. Arma Canant Alii: *Materia epica e narrazione elegiaca nei Fasti di Ovidio*. Florence: Università degli studi di Fierenze, Dipartimento di scienze dell'antichità "Georgio Pasquali."

Michels, A. K. 1949. "The 'Calendar of Numa' and the Pre-Julian Calendar." *TAPA* 80: 320–46.

———. 1967. *The Calendar of the Roman Republic*. Princeton: Princeton University Press.

Mierse, W. 1999. *Temples and Towns in Roman Iberia*. Berkeley: University of California Press.

Millar, Fergus. 1993. "Ovid and the *Domus Augusta:* Rome seen from Tomoi." *JRS* 83: 1–17 (= Millar 2002: 321–49).

———. 2002. *The Roman Republic and the Augustan Revolution*. Ed. H. M. Cotton and Guy Rogers. Vol. 1: *Rome, the Greek World and the East*. Chapel Hill: University of North Carolina Press.

——— and Erich Segal, eds. 1984. *Caesar Augustus: Seven Aspects*. Oxford: Oxford University Press.

Miller, Jacques-Alain. 1975. "Theorie de lalangue (rudiment)." *Ornicar?* 1: 16–34.

———. 1989. "Jacques Lacan et la Voix." In *La Voix: Actes du colloque d'Ivry du janvier 1988*. 175–84. Paris: Lysimaque.

Miller, John F. 1980. "Ritual Directions in Ovid's *Fasti:* Dramatic Hymns and Didactic Poetry." *CJ* 75: 204–14.

———. 1982. "Callimachus and the Augustan Aetiological Elegy." *ANRW* 2.30.1: 371–417.

———. 1983. "Ovid and Divine Interlocutors in the *Fasti*." *Studies in Latin Literature and Roman History III:* 156–92. Brussels: Latomus.

———. 1991. *Ovid's Elegiac Festivals: Studies in the* Fasti. Frankfurt am Main: P. Lang.

———. 1992. "The *Fasti* and Hellenistic Didactic: Ovid's Variant Aetiologies." *Arethusa* 25.1: 11–32.

Miller, Paul Allen, and Charles Platter. 1999. "Crux as Symptom: Augustan Elegy and Beyond." *CW* 92.5: 445–54.

Moeus, Maria T. M. 1981. "Le Muse di Ambracia." *BA* 66.12: 1–58.

Mohler, S. L. 1937. "The *Iuvenes* and Roman Education." *TAPA* 68: 442–79.

Mommsen, Theodor. 1893. "Fasti Anni Iuliani." *CIL* I², 203–339.

Morales, H. 1996. "The Torturer's Apprentice." In J. Elsner, ed., *Art and Text in Roman Culture*, 182–209. Cambridge: Cambridge University Press.

Morel, J.-P. 1969. "Pantomimus allectus inter iuvenes." In Jacqueline Bibauw, ed., *Hommages à Marcel Renard II*, 525–35. Brussels: Latomus.

Morgan, Llewelyn. 1998. "Tacitus, *Annals* 4.70: An Unappreciated Pun." *CQ* (n. s.) 48: 585–87.

Mueller, Hans-Friedrich. 1998. "*Vita, Pudicitia, Libertas:* Juno, Gender, and Religious Politics in Valerius Maximus." *TAPA* 128: 221–63.

Müller, Werner. 1961. *Die heilige Stadt: Roma quadrata, himmlisches Jerusalem und die Mythe vom Weltnabel.* Stuttgart: W. Kohlhammer.

Mulvey, L. 1992. "Visual Pleasure and Narrative Cinema." In *The Sexual Subject: A Screen Reader in Sexuality*, 22–34. New York: Routledge. Originally published in *Screen* 16 (1975): 6–18.

Murray, O., ed. 1990. *Sympotica: A Symposium on the* Symposion. Oxford: Oxford University Press.

Myers, Tony. 2003. *Slavoj i ek.* London: Polity.

Nagle, Betty Rose. 1980. *The Poetics of Exile: Program and Polemic in the "Tristia" and "Epistulae ex Ponto" of Ovid.* Collection Latomus, 170. Brussels: Latomus.

———. Tr. 1995. *Ovid's Fasti: Roman Holidays.* Bloomington: Indiana University Press.

Nash, E. 1961–1962. *Pictorial Dictionary of Ancient Rome.* 2 vols. New York: Praeger.

Nestle, Wilhelm. 1936. "Die Horen des Prodikos." *Hermes* 71: 151–70

Newiger, Hans-Hoachim. 1980. "War and Peace in the Comedy of Aristophanes." *Yale Classical Studies* 26: 219–37.

Newlands, Carole E. 1991. "Ovid's Ravenous Raven." *CJ* 86: 244–55.

———. 1992. "Ovid's Narrator in the *Fasti.*" *Arethusa* 25.1: 33–54.

———. 1995a. *Playing with Time: Ovid and the* Fasti. Ithaca: Cornell University Press.

———. 1995b. "The Ending of Ovid's *Fasti.*" In Boyle, *Roman Literature and Ideology*, 129–43

Newman, J. K. 1967. *The Concept of* Vates *in Augustan Poetry.* Collection Latomus, 89. Brussels: Latomus.

Nicolet, C. 1974. *L'ordre équestre à l'époque républicaine (312–43 av. J.-C.).* Vol. 2 (*Prosographie des Chevaliers Romains*). Paris: E. de Boccard.

———. 1984. "Augustus, Government and the Propertied Classes." In Millar and Segal 1984, 89–128.

———. 1991. *Space Geography, and Politics in the Early Roman Empire.* Jerome Lectures, 19. Ann Arbor: University of Michigan Press.

Nussbaum, Martha. 1994. *Therapy of Desire: Theory and Practice in Hellenistic Ethics.* Princeton: Princeton University Press.

——— and Juha Sihvola, eds. 2002. *The Sleep of Reason: Erotic Experience and Sexual Ethics in Ancient Greece and Rome.* Chicago: University of Chicago Press.

O'Hara, James. 1996. *True Names: Vergil and the Alexandrian Tradition of Etymological Wordplay.* Ann Arbor: University of Michigan Press.

Oliensis, E. 1997. "The Erotics of *Amicitia:* Readings in Tibullus, Propertius and Horace." In Hallet and Skinner 1997, 151–71.

Oliver, J. H., and R.E.A. Palmer. 1954. "Text of the *Tabula Hebana*." *AJPh* 75: 225–49.

Otis, Brooks. 1966. *Ovid as an Epic Poet*. Cambridge: Cambridge University Press.

Palmer, Robert E. 1990. *Studies in the Northern Campus Martius in Ancient Rome*. Philadelphia: American Philosophical Society.

Panofsky, Erwin. 1930. *Hercules am Scheidewege*. (Warburg Inst. 18). Leipzig: Teubner.

Pantel, P. S., ed. 1992. *From Ancient Goddesses to Christian Saints*. Vol. 1 in *A History of Women in the West*. Georges Duby and Michelle Perrot, gen. eds. Cambridge, Mass.: Belknap Press of Harvard University Press.

Parke, H. W. 1985. *The Oracles of Apollo in Asia Minor*. London: Croom Helm.

Pascal, Bennett 1990. "The Dubious Devotion of Turnus." *TAPA* 120: 251–68.

Pattenden, Philip. 1978. "Sundials." *CR* (n.s.) 28: 336–39 (rev. of Gibbs 1976).

Peraki-Kyriakidou, H. 2002. "Aspects of Ancient Etymologizing." *CQ* 52.2: 478–93.

Perrin, Bernadotte, tr. 1919. *Plutarch; Plutarch's Lives*. Vol. 7. Cambridge, MA.: Harvard University Press.

Picard, Charles. 1951. "Représentations antiques de l'Apologue dit de Prodicus." *Comptes Rendus d l'Académie des Inscriptions*, 310–22

———. 1952. "Auteur de l'Apologue de Prodicos de Céos." *REG* 65: xiv–xv.

———. 1953. "Nouvelles remarques sur l'Apologue dit de Prodicos," *RE* 42: 10–41.

Platner, Samuel. 1929. *Topographical Dictionary of Ancient Rome*. Rev. T. Ashby. London: Oxford University Press; H. Milford

Plecket, H. W. 1965. "An Aspect of the Emperor Cult: Imperial Mysteries," *Harvard Theological Review* 58: 331–47.

Plescia, Joseph. 1976. "*Patria Potestas* and the Roman Revolution." In Bertman, *Conflict of Generations*, 143–70.

Pollitt, J. J. 1974. *The Ancient View of Greek Art: Criticism, History, and Terminology*. New Haven: Yale University Press.

Potter, D. S., and D. J. Mattingly, eds. 1999. *Life, Death and Entertainment in the Roman Empire*. Ann Arbor: University of Michigan Press.

Powell, D. J. U. 1925. *Collectanea Alexandrina*. Oxford: Clarendon Press.

Price, Derek. 1975. *Science since Babylon*. New Haven: Yale University Press.

Quinn, Kenneth. 1982. "The Poet and His Audience in the Augustan Period," *ANRW* II.30.1: 75–180.

Rawson, E. D. 1987. "*Discrimina Ordinum:* the *Lex Iulia Theatralis*," *PBSR* 55: 83–114.

Rehm, A. 1949. "Parapegma," *RE* XVIII, 4: 1295–1366.

Richardson, L., Jr. 1992. *A New Topographical Dictionary of Ancient Rome*. Baltimore: Johns Hopkins University Press.

Richlin, Amy, ed. 1983. *Garden of Priapus: Sexuality and Aggression in Roman Humor*. New Haven: Yale University Press.

———. 1992a. *Pornography and Representation in Greece and Rome*. New York: Oxford University Press.

———. 1992b. "Reading Ovid's Rapes," 158–79 in Richlin 1992a.

———. 1997a. "Gender and Rhetoric: Producing Manhood in the Schools," 90–110 in Dominik 1997.

———. 1997b. "Pliny's Brassiere," 197–220 in Hallett and Skinner 1997.

Riddle, John. 1997. *Eve's Herbs: A History of Contraception and Abortion in the West*. Cambridge, Mass.: Harvard University Press.

Roberts, Deborah H., Francis M. Dunn, and Don Fowler. 1997. *Classical Closure: Reading the End in Greek and Latin Literature*. Princeton: Princeton University Press.

Robin, D. 1993. "Film Theory and the Gendered Voice in Seneca." In N. S. Rabinowitz and A Richlin, eds., *Feminist Theory and the Classics*, 102–21. New York: Routledge.

Roller, Matthew B. 2001. *Constructing Autocracy: Aristocrats and Emperors in Julio-Claudian Rome*. Princeton: Princeton University Press.

Roof, Judith. 1996. *Come As You Are: Sexuality and Narrative*. New York: Columbia University Press.

Rosand, David. 1981. "Composition/ Decomposition/ Recomposition: Notes on the Fragmentary and Artistic Process." In Kritzman 1981, 17–30.

Ross, David O., Jr. 1969. *Style and Tradition in Catullus*. Cambridge, Mass.: Harvard University Press.

Rousselle, Aline. 1983. *Porneia*. Paris: Presses universitaires de France.

———. 1992. "Body Politics in Ancient Rome." In Pantel, ed., *A History of Women*, 296–336.

Roy, Jim. 1998. "The Masculinity of the Hellenistic King." In Foxhall and Salmon 1998, 112–35

Rubin, Gayle. 1975. "The Traffic in Women: Notes toward a Political Economy of Sex." In *Toward an Anthropology of Women*. Ed. Rayna Reiter, 157–210. New York: Monthly Review Press.

Rudich, V. 1993. *Political Dissidence under Nero: The Price of Dissimulation*. New York: Routledge.

Rüpke, J. 1994. "Ovids Kalenderkommentar: Zur Gattung der *libri fastorum*." *A&A* 40: 125–36.

———. 1995. *Kalender und Öffentlichkeit: Die Geschichte der Repräsentation und religiösen Qualifikation von Zeit in Rom*. New York: W. de Gruyter.

Rykwert, Joseph. 1988. *The Idea of a Town: The Anthropology of Urban Form in Rome, Italy and the Ancient World*. Cambridge, Mass.: MIT Press.

Sabbatuci, D. 1988. *La religione di Roma antica: dal calendario festivo all'ordine cosmico*. Milan: Il Saggiatore.

Salecl, Renata, and Slavoj Zizek, eds. 1996. *Gaze and Voice as Love Objects*. Durham: Duke University Press.

Saller, Richard. 1982. *Personal Patronage under the Early Empire*. Cambridge: Cambridge University Press.

———. 1989. "Patronage and Friendship in Early Imperial Rome: Drawing the Distinction." In Wallace-Hadrill 1987, 49–62.

Salzman, Michele. 1990. *On Roman Time: The Codex-Calendar of 354 and the Rhythms of Urban Life in Late Antiquity*. Berkeley: University of California Press.

———. 1981. "New Evidence for the Dating of the Calendar at Santa Maria Maggiore in Rome." *TAPA* 111: 215–27.

Samuel, Alan. 1972. *Greek and Roman Chronology: Calendars and the Years in Classical Antiquity*. Munich: Beck.

Santero, J. M. 1983. "The *Cultores Augusti* and the Private Worship of the Roman Emperor." *Athenaeum* 61: 111–25.

Santini, Carlo. 1975. "Motivi astronimci e moduli didattici nei *Fasti* di Ovidio." *GIF* 27: 1–26.

Sauron, Gilles. 1994. *Quis deum?: L'expression plastique des idéologies politiques et religieuses à Rome à la fin de la République et au début du principat*. Rome: École française de Rome.

Savran, David. 1998. *Taking It like a Man: White Masculinity, Masochism, and Contemporary American Culture*. Princeton: Princeton University Press.

Scheid, John. 1992. "Myth, Cult and Reality in Ovid's *Fasti*." *PCPhS* 38: 118–31.

Schütz, M. 1990. "Zur Sonnnenuhr des Augustus auf dem Marsfeld." *Gymnasium* 97: 432–58.

Schwabe, Ludwig, ed. 1891–1892. *Teuffel's History of Roman Literature.* Tr. George Warr. London: G. Bell & Sons.

Scott, K. 1932. "Tiberius' Refusal of the title 'Augustus.'" *CPh* 27: 43–50.

Scullard, H. H. 1981. *Festivals and Ceremonies of the Roman Republic.* Ithaca: Cornell University Press.

Sedgwick, Eve Kosofsky. 1985. *Between Men: English Literature and Male Homosocial Desire.* New York: Columbia University Press.

———. 1990. *Epistemology of the Closet.* Berkeley: University of California Press.

Seeck, O. 1885. *Die Kalendertafel der Pontifices.* Berlin: Weidmann.

Segal, C. 1994. "Philomela's Web and the Pleasures of the Text." In I. J. F. DeJong and J. P. Sullivan, eds., *Modern Critical Theory and Classical Literature.* Leiden: Brill. Originally published in *Mnemosyne* 1994: 257–279

Segal, Erich. 1987. *Roman Laughter: The Comedy of Plautus.* 2nd ed. New York: Oxford University Press.

Severy, Beth. 2003. *Augustus and the Family at the Birth of the Empire.* New York: Routledge.

Sharrock, Alison. 2002a. "An A-musing Tale: Gender, Genre, and Ovid's Battles with Inspiration in the *Metamorphoses.*" In Spentzou and Fowler 2002, 207–28.

———. 2002b. "Gender and Sexuality." In Hardie 2002, 95–107.

Sherwin-White, A. N. 1966. *The Letters of Pliny: A Historical and Social Commentary.* Oxford: Clarendon Press.

Silberberg-Peirce, Susan. 1980. "Politics and Private Imagery: The Sacral-Idyllic Landscapes." *Art History* 3: 1–24.

Silverman, Kaja. 1988. *The Acoustic Mirror: The Female Voice in Psychoanalysis and Cinema.* Bloomington: Indiana University Press.

———. 1992. *Male Subjectivity at the Margins.* New York: Routledge.

Simon, Erika. 1986. *Augustus: Kunst und Leben in Rome um die Zeitenwende.* Munich: Hirmer.

Simpson, C. J. 1992. "Unexpected References to the *Horologium Augusti* at Ovid *Ars Amatoria* 1,68 and 3,388." *Athenaeum* 80 [70].2: 478–84.

Skinner, M. 1997. "*Ego Mulier:* The Construction of Male Sexuality in Catullus." In Hallett and Skinner 1997, 129–50.

Slater, W. J. 1994. "Pantomime Riots." *ClAnt* 13.1: 120–44.

Small, Alastair, ed. 1996. *Subject and Ruler: The Cult of the Ruling Power in Classical Antiquity.* Ann Arbor: University of Michigan Press

Smith, W. 1875. *A Dictionary of Greek and Roman Antiquities.* London: J. Murray.

Snell, Bruno. 1953. *The Discovery of the Mind.* London: Blackwell.

Spaeth, Barbette. 1996. *The Roman Goddess Ceres.* Austin: University of Texas Press.

Spentzou, Efrossini, and Don Fowler, eds. 2002. *Cultivating the Muse: Struggles of Power and Inspiration in Classical Literature.* New York: Oxford University Press.

Stebbins, E. 1929. *The Dolphin in the Literature and Art of Greece and Rome.* Menasha, Wis: George Banta Pub. Co.

Steiner, Deborah T. 1994. *The Tyrant's Writ: Myths and Images of Writing in Ancient Greece.* Princeton: Princeton University Press.

Stone, Edward. 1928. "Roman Surveying Instruments." *University of Washington Publications in Language and Literature* 4.4: 215–42.

Subias-Konofal, Verginie. 2003. "Poésie, politique et rhétorique rituelle: L'hymne à Germanicus dans les *Fastes* d'Ovide (1.3–26)." *Bulletin de l'Association Guillaume Budé* 1: 107–29.

Svenbro, Jesper. 1993. *Phrasikleia: An Anthropology of Reading in Ancient Greece.* Ithaca: Cornell University Press.

Syme, R. 1978. *History in Ovid.* Oxford: Clarendon Press.

———. 1979. "Problems about Janus." *AJPh* 100.1: 188–212.

Tara´n, Sonya Lida. 1979. *The Art of Variation in the Hellenistic Epigram.* Leiden: Brill.

Taylor, Lily Ross. 1924. "*Seviri Equitum Romanorum* and Municipal *Seviri*: A Study in Pre-Military Training among the Romans." *JRS* 14: 158–71.

———. 1925. "The Mother of the Lares." *AJA* 29.3: 299–313.

———. 1931 (1975). *The Divinity of the Roman Emperor.* Middleton, Conn.: American Philological Association.

———. 1971. *Party Politics in the Age of Caesar.* Berkeley: University of California Press.

Taylor, L. R., and Louise Holland. 1952. "Janus and the *Fasti*." *CPh* 47: 137–42.

Too, Yun Lee. 1998. *The Idea of Ancient Literary Criticism.* New York: Oxford University Press.

Toohey, Peter. 1997. "Trimalchio's Constipation: Periodizing Madness, Eros, and Time." In M. Golden and P. Toohey, eds., *Inventing Ancient Culture,* 50–65. New York: Routledge.

Toomer, G. J. 1974 "Meton." In *Dictionary of Scientific Biography.* Vol. 9: 337–39. New York: Scribner.

Torelli, M. 1982 (1992). *Typology and Structure of Roman Historical Reliefs.* Ann Arbor: University of Michigan Press.

———. 1984. *Lavinio e Roma: Riti iniziatici e matrimonio tra archeologia e storia.* Rome: Quasar.

———. 1990. "Riti di passaggio maschili di Roma arcaica." *MEFRA* 102.1: 93–106.

Treggiari, S. 1991. *Roman Marriage.* Oxford: Clarendon Press.

———. 1996. "Social Status and Social Legislation." In *CAH*² X, 873–904.

Trexler, Richard C. 1995. *Sex and Conquest: Gendered Violence, Political Order, and the European Conquest of the Americas.* Ithaca: Cornell University Press.

Turcan, Robert. 1996. "La promotion du suject par le culte du souvrain." In Small 1996, 51–62

Turner, Victor. 1969 (1974 rpt.). *The Ritual Process: Structure and Anti-Structure.* Harmondsworth, Middlesex: Penguin Books.

———. 1974. *Dramas, Fields and Metaphors: Symbolic Action in Human Society.* Ithaca: Cornell University Press.

Versnel, H. S. 1970. *Triumphus: An Enquiry into the Origin, Development and Meaning of the Roman Triumph.* Leiden: Brill.

———. 1980. "Destruction, *Devotio,* and Despair in a Situation of Anomy: The Mourning for Germanicus in Triple Perspective." In *Perennitas: Studi in onore di Angelo Brelich,* 541–618. Rome: Edizione dell'Ateneo.

Veyne, Paul. 1960. "Iconographie de la *Transvectio Equitum* et des Lupercales." *REA* 62: 100–111.

———. 1983. "*Titulus Praelatus:* Offrande, solennisation et publicité dans les ex-voto gréco-romains." *RA* 2: 281–300.

———. 1988. *Roman Erotic Elegy.* Chicago: University of Chicago Press.

Vidal-Naquet, P. 1986. *The Black Hunter.* Baltimore: Johns Hopkins University Press.

Wagenvoort, H. 1980. *Pietas: Selected Studies in Roman Religion.* Leiden: Brill.

Waites, Margaret. 1912. "Some Features of the Allegorical Debates in Greek Literature." *HSCPh* 23: 1–46.

———. 1920. "Nature of the Lares and Their Representation in Roman Art." *AJA* 24: 41–61.

Wallace-Hadrill, Andrew. 1987. "Time for Augustus: Ovid, Augustus and the *Fasti.*" In *Homo Viator: Classical Essays for John Bramble,* eds. Michael Whitby, Philip Hardie, and Mary Whitby, 221–30. Bristol: Bristol Classical.

———, ed. 1989. *Patronage in Ancient Society.* New York: Routledge.

———. 1990. "Roman Arches and Greek Honours: The Language of Power at Rome." *PCPhS* 36: 143–81.

———. 1996. "The Imperial Court." In *CAH² X,* 283–308.

———. 1997. "*Mutatio Morum:* The Idea of a Cultural Revolution." in Habinek and Schiesaro 1997, 3–22.

Walters, Jonathan. 1997. "Invading the Roman Body: Manliness and Impenetrability in Roman Thought." In Hallett and Skinner 1997, 29–43.

Wardle, D. 1997. "An Allusion to the *Kaisereid* in Tacitus, *Annals* 1.42." *CQ* 47: 690–713.

———. 2000. "Valerius Maximus on the *Domus Augusta,* Augustus, and Tiberius." *CQ* 50.2: 479–93.

Watson, George R. 1969. *The Roman Soldier.* Ithaca: Cornell University Press.

Weinstock, Stephan. 1971. *Divus Julius.* Oxford: Clarendon Press.

Wheeler, Stephen. 1999. *A Discourse of Wonders: Audience and Performance in Ovid's Metamorphoses.* Philadelphia: University of Pennsylvania Press.

White, Peter. 1978. "*Amicitia* and the Profession of Poetry in Early Imperial Rome." *JRS* 68: 74–92.

———. 1982. "Positions for Poets in Early Imperial Rome." In Gold 1982, 50–66.

Wilkinson, L. P. 1955. *Ovid Recalled.* Cambridge: Cambridge University Press.

Williams, Craig. 1997. "*Pudicitia* and *Pueri:* Roman Concepts of Male Sexual Experience." In *Queer Representations: Reading Lives, Reading Cultures,* ed. Martin Duberman, 25–38. New York: New York University Press.

———. 1999. *Roman Homosexuality: Ideologies of Masculinity in Classical Antiquity.* New York: Oxford University Press.

Williams, Linda, ed., 1994. *Viewing Positions: Ways of Seeing Film.* New Brunswick, N.J.: Rutgers University Press.

Wiseman. T. P. 1995a. *Remus: A Roman Myth.* Cambridge: Cambridge University Press.

———. 1995b. "God of the Lupercal." *JRS* 85: 1–22.

Worton, Michael. 1998. "Cruising (Through) Encounters." In Owen Heathcote, Alex Hughes, and James S. Williams, eds., *Gay Signatures Gay and Lesbian Theory, Fiction and Film in France, 1945–1995,* 29–50. New York: Berg.

Wrede, H. 1983. "Statuae Lupercorum Habitu." *RhM* 90: 185–200.

Wright, Elizabeth, and Edmond Wright, eds. 1999. *The i ek Reader.* Oxford: Blackwell.

Wyke, Maria. 1987. "Written Women: Propertius' *Scripta Puella.*" *JRS* 77: 47–61.

———. 1990. "Reading Female Flesh: *Amores* 3.1." In Cameron 1990, 111–43.

———. 1995. "Taking the Woman's Part: Engendering Roman Elegy." In Boyle 1995, 110–28.

———. 2002. *The Roman Mistress: Ancient and Modern Representations.* New York: Oxford University Press.

Yan, Thomas. 1986. "Le 'ventre': corps maternel, droit paternel." *Le Genre Humain* 14: 211–36.

Yavetz, Zvi. 1984. "The *Res Gestae* and Augustus' Public Image." In Millar and Segal 1984, 1–36.

Zanker, Paul. 1988. *The Power of Images in the Augustan Age.* Ann Arbor: University of Michigan Press.

Zetzel, James E. G. 1982. "The Poetics of Patronage in the Late First Century B.C." In Gold 1982, 87–89.

Zevi, F. 1976. "Proposta per un'interpretazatione dei Rilievi Grimani." *Prospettiva* 8: 38–41.

Zizek, Slavoj. 1989. *The Sublime Object of Ideology.* New York: Verso.

———. 1991. *Looking Awry: An Introduction to Jacques Lacan through Popular Culture.* Cambridge, Mass.: MIT Press.

———. 1993. *Tarrying with the Negative: Kant, Hegel, and the Critique of Ideology.* Durham: Duke University.

———. 1997. *Plague of Fantasies.* New York: Verso.

———. 1999a. "The Undergrowth of Enjoyment: How Popular Culture Can Serve as an Introduction to Lacan." In Wright and Wright 1999, 11–37. Originally published in *New Formations* 9 (1989): 7–29.

———. 1999b. "The Spectre of Ideology." In Wright and Wright 1999, 53–86. Originally published in *Mapping Ideology,* ed. S. Zizek. 1–33. New York: Verso, 1994.

———. 2001. *Enjoy Your Symptom!* New York: Routledge.

Zorzetti, Nevio. 1990. "The *Carmina Convivalia.*" In Murray 1990, 289–307.

GENERAL INDEX

abortion, 171–72, 175, 277–78n85, 278n86
Achilles, as model for Augustus, 192
Adams, J. N., 250n23
adultery, 212, 217, 246n79, 293n141
Aeneas, as exile, 129–30
Agonalia, 145, 152, 153, 156
agriculture, as metaphor, 45, 170
Ahl, F., 285–86n56
amicitia. See friendship
anamorphosis, Lacanian, 10–11
Ancus Marcius, and the development of the calendar, 26, 235n63
animals, as sources of omens, 152–54, 156, 158, 166–67, 171, 176, 179–80, 294n146. *See also* sacrifice
Annales Maximi, 31
antagonism: among social classes, 80, 81–82; between Ovid and Janus, 83. *See also* anxiety; competition; envy
anxiety: among men, 12, 79; concerning castration, 7, 13, 151, 157–58, 175, 269n117; concerning fathers, 14; concerning Greek influence, 200; concerning homosexuality, 200–201, 203; concerning infertility, 172; concerning nudity, 199–200, 204–5, 289n94, 289–90n95; concerning penetration, 12, 74, 76; concerning *terga*, 67–68, 73

Apollo, Germanicus compared to, 55, 56, 65, 247n99; oracle of, 198–99, 207
Appius Claudius Caecus, 233n37, 233–34n40, 234n47
April: naming of, 128–29, 130; preface to, 120, 126–35
Ara Maxima Herculis, 179, 181–82
Ara Pacis Augustae, 37, 169–70, 172
Archimedes, 234n51
Ardea, siege of, 208–10
Arion, 186–88, 190, 193, 220; delay by, 198; transvestism of, 187–88, 194
Aristophanes, 251n29
arma. *See* militia; weapons
arts: and effeminacy, 121, 123; and social class, 121; as softening influence on Mars, 123. *See also* Hercules Musarum, Temple of
Arval Brethren, 53
astronomy: praised by Ovid, 163–65; as type of surveying, 163–65, 182
audience. *See* readers
Augustus: as addressee of the *Fasti*, 116, 118–19; administrative reforms of, 35; calendar reforms of, 4, 34; compared to Achilles, 192; funeral of, 50–51; house of, 78, 84, 137–38, 160; identified with Jupiter, 151; and male competition, 267n101; as

Ovid's Pagina, 55; as poet, 68, 99; as *princeps iuvenum*, 108; as recipient of prayer, 52–54; as rescuer, 182; as rival to Tiberius, 49; as trafficker in texts, 47; triumph of, 57–58; as *vates*, 44, 45, 52; and water symbolism, 99
Girard, R., 9, 46
gladiators, *devotio* of, 49–51, 242n42
Gnaeus Flavius, and the posting of *fasti*, 27–28
gnomon: as axis, 160; definition of, 34, 146; as metaphor, 146–47; *nomen Augusti* as, 146–47, 160–62, 167, 169, 171; phallicism of, 186; as quilting point, 162
Greece: as source of Roman culture, 129, 164, 200, 288n85, 288–89n86, 289n91
guidance. *See* criticism
Gunning, T., 248n2
Habinek, T., 265n83
Hardie, P., 273n38
Harries, B., 196, 197, 198, 285n54, n55, 286n60, 287n71
Hebe, 111–12
Heinze, R., 229n5
Herbert-Brown, G., 4, 174, 229n3, 232n16, 235–36n68, 256n109, 278n87, 279n98
Hercules: and Cacus, 179–81; Choice of, 13, 109–110, 112–14, 120, 124, 126, 135, 136–37, 138, 140–41, 143; identified with Germanicus, 111; as model for masculinity, 104, 109–113; and Omphale, 185, 200, 201–3, 212, 214, 220, 282n20, 292n124; onus of, 179–81; as quilting point, 181, 182; as rescuer, 182; transvestism of, 197, 202–5
Hercules Musarum, Temple of, 30, 32, 110–11, 139. *See also* arts
Hinds, S., 59, 61, 229n5
Holbein, Hans, 10
Homer, and transvestism, 194–95
homosexuality: anxiety concerning, 200–201, 203; and homosociality, 46, 62, 65

homosociality: female, 172, 189, 190–91; male, and cooperation, 98; male, and gift exchange, 87; male, and homosexuality, 46, 62, 65; male, of Ovid and his readers, 8–12, 42, 43–47, 55–56, 61, 65, 78, 101–2, 105; male, in Roman society, 8–11, 18, 46–47, 67, 209, 210. *See also* competition; femininity; masculinity
Hopkins, K., 277–78n85
Horace, *devotio* of, to Maecenas, 57
Horologium Augusti, 34, 37, 160–62, 165, 169. See also *gnomon;* sundials
hospitium, 88

Ides, determination of, 21, 23
imaginary order, calendars as representation of, 38. *See also* Real; symbolic order
inauguration, 68–72, 81; of consuls, 71, 78, 81; Janus' role in, 66, 67; of the month by priests, 23
incompleteness: and desire, 2, 64, 101, 226; of the *Fasti,* 1–2, 4, 10, 15, 39, 41, 53–54, 110, 182, 227–28
indecision, by Ovid, 140–43
inspiration: Janus as source of, 94, 98; of Ovid by gods, 63–65, 126; of Ovid by Mars, 126; and orality, 93
intercalation, in the pre-Julian calendar, 24, 27, 34, 35, 144. *See also* calendar; Caesar, G. Iulius
interpretive community, 44, 71. *See also* readers

Jaczynowska, M., 260n37
January, 12, 13–14, 144–83
Janus: addressed by Ovid, 69, 249n15; as axis, 168; birth of, 79–80; as broker of male exchange, 68, 86, 90; and the Cloaca Maxima, 97; on coins, 224; as cosmos, 8, 80, 81, 87, 159–60; deformity of, 75–76, 80; dicephaly of, 12, 66, 72–73, 76–77, 78–79, 80–82, 84, 87, 249n16; as doorkeeper, 82, 84, 90, 138; and fantasy, 8, 66–67, 78–82; gaze of, 12, 80, 150; as inspiration, 94, 98; *maiestas*